REGULATORY POLICY IN LATIN AMERICA:
POST-PRIVATIZATION REALITIES

REGULATORY POLICY IN LATIN AMERICA: POST-PRIVATIZATION REALITIES

Edited by Luigi Manzetti

North·South Center Press
UNIVERSITY OF MIAMI

REGULATORY POLICY IN LATIN AMERICA: POST-PRIVATIZATION REALITIES

The publisher of this book is the North-South Center Press at the University of Miami.

The mission of the North-South Center is to promote better relations and serve as a catalyst for change among the United States, Canada, and the nations of Latin America and the Caribbean by advancing knowledge and understanding of the major political, social, economic, and cultural issues affecting the nations and peoples of the Western Hemisphere.

Library of Congress Cataloging-in-Publication Data

Regulatory policy in Latin America: post-privatization realities/
edited by Luigi Manzetti
    p. cm.
Includes bibliographical references and index.
ISBN 1-57454-073-4 (hardcover: alk. paper)
1. Public utilities--Government policy--Latin America. 2. Financial services
industry--State supervision--Latin America. 3. Privatization--Latin America. I. Manzetti,
Luigi.

HD2768.L294 R44 2000
338.98'05--dc21   99-089250

Printed in the United States of America/EB

∞ The paper used in this publication meets the requirements of the American National Standards for Information Sciences — Permanence of Paper for Printed Library Materials, ANSI Z39.48.1984.

03 02 01 00   6 5 4 3 2 1

*This book is dedicated to Cindy
and to the memory of Ines.*

TABLE OF CONTENTS

Preface

As the various manifestations of privatization have spread across Latin America, it has become clear that the fundamental issue to resolve is what the economic role of the state should be next. Public utilities typically were controlled by state-owned enterprises that made their own rules. As governments started to auction public utilities, it was clear that Latin American countries would require new regulatory frameworks to oversee the incoming private companies. It was also clear that there was not much knowledge about what results varying regulatory frameworks would produce. In the financial sector, although governmental experience in regulation was plentiful, the challenge was almost as great, since regulatory policy had to change substantially as government banks were being sold off and foreign financial institutions were allowed, for the first time in many decades, to come into many Latin American countries with few restrictions. The way the governments were about to respond to such problems was of fundamental importance for the future of market reforms in the region. As the state was about to move from the interventionist pattern of import-substitution industrialization to a more subsidiary role, in which it would act more as a referee among economic agents, it needed to set up new rules and regulations to ensure that truly competitive markets would emerge. How would reforming governments in Latin America redefine the role of the regulatory state under the aegis of market reform?

To answer this question, the Tower Center at Southern Methodist University, the Center for Latin American Economics of the Federal Reserve Bank of Dallas, and the Law School of the Universidad de Palermo in Buenos Aires jointly organized a conference entitled *Regulation in Post-Privatization Environments: The Latin American Experience*. The conference was made possible thanks to the generous financial support of the Tinker Foundation and to the assistance of the United States Information Agency's (USIA) office in Buenos Aires, where the conference took place in May 1998 at the Bolsa de Comercio de Buenos Aires. The edited and updated papers contained in this volume are the results of the conference.

This project would not have been possible without the help and assistance of many individuals who I would like to acknowledge personally. I would like to thank Robert D. McTeer, President and Chief Executive Officer, Federal Reserve Bank of Dallas, and Harvey Rosenblum, Senior Vice President of the Federal Reserve Bank of Dallas, as well as William C. Gruben, Director, Carlos Zarazaga, Executive Director, David Gould, Senior Economist, and Sherry Kiser, Coordinator, of the Center for Latin American Economics at the Dallas Fed. Roberto Saba, of the Universidad de Palermo Law School, did a superb job of organizing the conference in Buenos Aires. Alexander Almasov and Mirta Detrizio of the USIA office in Buenos Aires gave us important logistical and technical support. The Editor of the London-based *Infrastructure Journal*, Marco dell'Aquila, was kind enough to

i

allow us to advertise the event ahead of time and provide a forum for the early findings of the conference.

Special thanks also go to former President Gonzalo Sanchez de Losada of Bolivia, who took time from his busy schedule to give the keynote address and participate at the final roundtable that closed the conference. At the Tower Center, I would like to express my gratitude to Cal Jillson, who endorsed the project from its start, and to Noelle McAlpine, who was terrific in taking care of all the administrative tasks.

I am much obliged to all the paper presenters, the paper discussants, and the North-South Center Press's reviewers for their useful comments. Lastly, I am grateful to Jeffrey Stark, the North-South Center's director of research and studies; and to the North-South Center Press's Kathleen Hamman, editorial director; Mary M. Mapes, publications director; Michelle Perez, editorial assistant; Martha Reiner, free-lance copy editor; and Shirley Kessel, free-lance indexer — all of whom made it possible for this collective effort to come to fruition most expeditiously.

Thanks to all,
Luigi Manzetti

INTRODUCTION

Latin American Regulatory Policies in the Post-Privatization Era

LUIGI MANZETTI

SUMMARY

The aim of this book is to study the challenges that Latin American countries are facing in creating regulatory institutions in vital sectors of the economy that have been recently privatized and/or deregulated. Despite the broad agreement between scholars and practitioners that the establishment of credible regulatory institutions is fundamental in consolidating market reforms in Latin America, as elsewhere, few comprehensive studies exist on this subject that are not sector specific. Therefore, the main idea of this project was to ask researchers prominent in their fields to address a common set of questions to evaluate not only progress made so far by trend-setting countries of Latin America to create regulatory institutions, but also the costs and benefits of different types of regulation. In this volume, researchers examine the issue of regulation vis-à-vis competition in natural and quasi-natural monopolies from both theoretical and empirical grounds. In crafting the project, we selected those sectors that are most vital for the functioning of a market economy: public utilities (electricity, telecommunications, and water) and financial services. Accordingly, based upon the evidence gathered in this volume, researchers provide policy-relevant suggestions on ways to pursue regulatory policies that strengthen the emerging market economies of Latin America while protecting consumers.

INTRODUCTION

In the 1980s and more so in the early 1990s, market reforms swept all the regions of the developing world, particularly Latin America, which by itself accounted for 58 percent of the total privatizations in developing countries between 1988 and 1996. In fact, privatization of state-owned enterprises (SOEs) and deregulation of a wide variety of economic activities were the pillars of the market reform agenda. However, what characterized these policies in developing countries was that they were often carried out with a zeal so strong that no room was left for a critical evaluation of their consequences. For instance, despite much rhetoric to the contrary, many governments paid relatively little attention to the importance of creating competition through privatization and deregulation.

In the aftermath of the sobering effects of the 1994 Mexican financial crisis, many began to question the ways in which these policies were implemented as well as the results they produced. In several instances, it appeared as if former state monopolies of public utilities had been transferred into private hands without appropriate mechanisms to prevent the abuse of market power by the new private owners. By the same token, on a few occasions, some governments subsequently changed the rules of the game affecting privatized public utilities, a fact that has alarmed private investors. As a result, regulation has come to the fore as a much-debated issue in countries where privatizations have been carried out.

REGULATION AS A POLICY ISSUE

Extensive literature exists on the role of regulation. In general, students of regulation from economics and public administration have examined the problem from a normative standpoint. The most scholarly research has gone into the cost-effectiveness of regulation and the pros and cons of government intervention.

This characteristic notwithstanding, we can distinguish four different approaches to the study of regulation. Those who emphasize the public interest perceive regulation as a means of protecting consumers from the abuse of private monopolies. Others focus on the fact that regulatory agencies often are captured by the very companies that they should control, resulting in the regulator protecting the private sector rather than the consumer. A third line of thought is more conciliatory and looks at regulation as the best method to enforce contracts that safeguard the interests both of customers and producers. A fourth approach stresses the role of regulation as a mechanism for reducing the inherent inefficiency that arises within natural monopolies.

Some regulation is relatively uncontroversial, like that concerning safety standards for passenger airlines or the approval of safe drugs. However, regulation often touches very sensitive interests and does, therefore, become enmeshed with politics. Indeed, regulation can be used to alter socioeconomic relations. Examples of this are President Franklin D. Roosevelt's New Deal policy to create a "positive" government and Prime Minister Margaret Thatcher and President Ronald Reagan's conservative "revolution" to minimize the role of government in the economy through deregulation and privatization. As a result, since the 1980s, students of regulation have increasingly focused on the importance of politics and ideology in shaping regulation.

Latin American countries have long been engaged in government regulation of the private sector economy. However, state-led development policies centered around the idea of import-substitution industrialization (ISI) came to be widely regarded as counter-productive to economic growth. As many countries in the region embraced market reforms, privatization and deregulation began to be seen as remedies for the distortions provoked by decades of state intervention in the economy. As a matter of fact, a substantial amount of regulation was clearly unnecessary.

The general rule of thumb is usually that highly competitive markets (or at least markets open to contestability) can in theory regulate themselves. When markets characterized by natural monopolies (such as water) or by restricted contestability are privatized, they require regulation to avoid rent-seeking behavior by the firms' new owners. A "rent" in this context is defined as the part of the payment to an owner of resources over and above what those resources could command in any alternative use. In other words, rent is receipt in excess of opportunity cost. In one sense, it is an unnecessary payment required to attract resources to that employment.

In this regard, some analysts underscore the importance of establishing good regulatory mechanisms — and strong institutions to enforce such mechanisms — as prerequisites that must be in place *prior* to the privatization of public utilities. The reason is that, through regulation, a government can formalize and institutionalize its commitments to protecting consumers and investors. Seen in this way, regulation works as a sort of insurance policy for all parties: it assures that consumers receive goods and services from the private provider at a reasonable price while it protects private investors from sudden changes in the rules of the game by obligating the government to respect the terms of the contract stipulated when the public utility was privatized. This is no small concern to private investors in Latin America, since many Latin American countries have a long history of reneging on contracts and expropriating private companies. Two corporate managers portrayed the private sector's concerns about regulation prior to privatization as follows:

> The investor's evaluation of the company's future performance depends almost entirely on the rules of the game, that is, the regulatory conditions under which the company will operate. These include the method for determining future rate increases, the rules for incorporating inflation and productivity effects on rates, and the regulatory scheme imposed upon the company. The regulatory scheme under which the new owners will operate is, in fact, shaped in part by the companies that are bidding. Before these companies present their qualifications to bid, and during the bidding process, company representatives usually meet with the government to discuss and negotiate the regulatory rules. Companies that find the rules unacceptable do not bid (Sonnenschein and Yokopenic 1996, 348-349).

What are the institutions enforcing regulations? Usually, they are government agencies, special commissions, and offices in the public administration depending upon specific ministries or departments. However, there are broader institutional factors affecting the credibility of regulation, including property rights, an independent judiciary, and a competitive political system. With regard to property rights, Latin America does not have a good track record of protecting them. The second issue, an independent judiciary, is closely related and is equally troublesome in the context of Latin America. Although commercial laws across the region are on average adequate, their enforcement is poor. Other hurdles include high litigation costs, long delays in handing down decisions, poor organization of personnel, and cumbersome procedural codes. Yet, one of the most disturbing issues is the lack of independence of the judiciary from the executive branch in many countries. This leads to erratic court decisions that smack of political manipulation. When the judiciary cannot exercise checks on the executive's discretionary power, what ensues is an unpredictable situation that undermines the credibility of even the best-intentioned policies. On the third issue, some have advanced the hypothesis that the greater the political competition among parties and the greater the checks and balances among the three branches of government, the smaller the possibility for unilateral decisionmaking. In other words, the more arbitrary a political regime, the greater the chance that regulatory frameworks may be changed overnight. Some cite Chile as the best example of this. Although the foundations for a healthy economy were laid down by the authoritarian regime of General Augusto Pinochet (1973-1989), it was not until democracy was restored that foreign investors came back, and then they returned in unprecedented numbers. In turn, Chilean political leaders displayed an uncanny ability to strengthen the rules of the democratic game in a way that had no parallels in the region. For some observers, these developments gave even greater encouragement to investors.

Summing up, privatization per se is only the beginning, not the end, of an economic reform that truly aims at creating competition in the marketplace. When privatization affects public utilities in natural monopolies, regulation is necessary to strike a balance between the need of the private companies to generate good profits and the public's expectation of benefiting from low-cost, high-quality service. Striking the right balance is both critical and challenging. Unfortunately, it seems to many that Latin American countries are ill equipped to enforce effective regulation in a post-privatization environment. The initial efforts toward state divestiture in Argentina, Brazil, Chile, and Mexico in the second half of the 1970s ended up with several cases of what William Glade called "rent-seeking privatizations" (1989). Although one decade later subsequent privatizations in all these countries were more comprehensive and professionally done, the question of increasing regulation to assure that the market would work its ways continued to be a troubling concern. One of the most challenging tasks facing Latin American countries — or any country engaged in a privatization process, for that matter — is to design modern and efficient legal and institutional regulatory frameworks that protect consumers and enhance efficiency without choking off private initiative.

In order to assess the role of regulation in post-privatization Latin America, I asked the authors who contributed to this volume to address the following questions, drawn largely from Bernard Tenenbaum (1995). While not all these questions are pertinent to every paper in the volume, they do provide a common framework of analysis that is utilized by each author, depending upon the characteristics of his/her own field. Following these thematic issues, the authors have made this volume particularly relevant in the current scholarly debate:

1. Did privatization of public utilities lead to greater competition and better quality of service?
2. Was regulatory policy and its enforcing institutions put in operation before or after privatization?
3. Should be there a single regulator or a commission?
4. Should the regulatory entity have jurisdiction over one sector or several?
5. What activities or parameters should be regulated?
6. What are the control mechanisms for price and quality?
7. How are regulatory rules created and enforced?
8. What are the regulatory entity's desired political and legal attributes?
9. Should the regulatory entity be "independent" from the government?

10. Should the regulatory process be transparent?

11. Who regulates the regulator?

12. How should responsibility be divided between the regulatory entity and other government authorities?

The book is divided into two parts. In the first part, the authors tackle broad theoretical themes dealing with economic issues (Arnold C. Harberger); legal issues (Peter Schuck); institutional issues (Antonio Estache and David Martimort); political issues (Luigi Manzetti); and financial issues (George G. Kaufman). In the second part, the authors' attention shifts to sector-specific analyses of water (Mary M. Shirley); electricity (Antonio Estache and Martín Rodríguez-Pardina); telecommunications (Björn Wellenius); finance (William C. Gruben); and law (Roberto Pablo Saba). The idea behind this two-pronged approach was first to assess the state-of-the-art theory behind regulatory policy in different disciplines and then, in the second set of papers, where theory meets reality, to examine how effectively the regulatory policies have been implemented.

In the first part, all authors agree that the best way to promote regulation is to introduce, prior to privatization, as much market-based competition as possible. True competition in itself is the best regulatory means because it is self-enforcing. It also diminishes the regulators' bureaucratic burden by giving them more time to focus on the most crucial problems. Yet, when competition is hard to introduce, regulation must be present to safeguard investors' as well as consumers' rights. The more transparent the process and the less politically vulnerable the regulators, the better. In this volume's sector-specific chapters, authors underscore that regulation remains weak in the region and highly prone to government manipulation and/or regulatory capture by the regulated companies. Besides the introduction of competition prior to full divestiture, they also suggest that the best way to proceed in the future is to set up regulatory institutions that are politically as independent as possible, well financed, and flexible enough to address changes in technology and market conditions.

As expected, the chapters present a composite picture with variations, depending on the sector analyzed. In the first chapter, Harberger's essay concisely outlines the macroeconomic advantages of privatization but also points out why things often went astray. Harberger underscores how, particularly in early privatizations, governments frequently used this policy reform as a means to garner more money for their own purposes. In fact, advances in terms of improvement in economic efficiency, reduction of government waste, better services for consumers, and more effective use of taxpayers' money often seemed to be low priorities for reforming governments whose main preoccupation was to use privatization revenues to bridge fiscal deficits. Not surprisingly, in many cases, Harberger argues, public utilities were sold without establishing the appropriate regulatory frameworks prior to the transfer. Instead of using privatization revenues to cover deficits, Harberger suggests that the proceeds should go to pay off debt, as Mexico did. Yet, the Mexican example remains more an exception than the rule. Through a series of examples, the author shows how faulty regulatory frameworks prior to privatization in Chile's banking and electricity sectors were, which invariably led to poor results. The Mexican highway privatization is another case in point of a misconceived privatization that should never have taken place. The basic lesson, according to Harberger, is that optimal decisions ensue when policymakers use, as their guiding principles, cost and benefit criteria. Such criteria, in the end, should be the crucial considerations in setting up regulatory institutions if policymakers want to obtain true competitive, efficient markets as a result of any privatization process.

Schuck's Chapter 2 points out that the U.S. regulatory approach plays three roles. It institutionalizes a strong pro-market presumption, maximizes the effectiveness of regulation when used, and establishes extra-regulatory institutions to monitor the regulatory process. His essay, although confined to the case of the United States, is particularly interesting because much of the policy advice from multilateral lending agencies to reforming governments in Latin America has come from the Anglo-Saxon legal experience in the matter. For the first role, Schuck points out that the pre-market presumption is not explicitly addressed in the original U.S. Constitution, but U.S. common law since its independence has firmly established property and contract rights. Contract rights were eventually sanctioned as constitutional rights, shielded from political interference through the Due Process Clause during the nineteenth century. The U.S. law regulates in two ways: it promotes markets through the definition of private entitlements and spells out the preconditions for government intervention in the markets. With regard to the latter, institutional effectiveness has been articulated through the creation of a number of means, such as private litigation, information disclosure, antitrust law, public advocates, regulatory information, and the enhancement of the credibility of regulatory commitments, among others. Additionally, institutional arrangements have played a pivotal role. Besides constitutional guarantees, complex institutional mechanisms of checks and balances, and a very competitive political system — which prevents sudden regulatory changes — the U.S. approach has given strong emphasis to extra-regulatory institutions. They consist of legislative oversight, an independent judiciary, administrative law, interest group competition, and an adversarial media. Thus, whatever regulatory modifications occur, they are usually incremental in nature and subject to a very high degree of public scrutiny. Schuck also notes that in the United States the pro-market presumption has not necessarily meant a linear movement toward greater deregulation and government retrenchment. Indeed, the pattern has been mixed during the past three decades. While traditional economic regulation was curtailed, new regulation was ushered in in the areas of consumer rights, safety standards, environmental protection, and antitrust law.

In terms of institutions, Estache and Martimort emphasize in Chapter 3 that there is widespread agreement in the field that it is necessary to build regulatory institutions that promote economic efficiency while safeguarding both consumers (from monopolistic providers) and operators (from political interference). However, they contend that the normative approaches, which have dominated the policy advice in the field, suffer from severe shortcomings. Estache and Martimort contend that transaction cost theory (that is, the costs associated with monitoring and enforcing agreements) can better guide practitioners. Such transaction costs include information problems, fully contingent contracts, regulatory capture by vested interests, and the competition among political and bureaucratic institutions that influences regulatory policy. The core thesis that Estache and Martimort propose is that in designing incentive-based regulation, structures and processes affecting regulatory outcomes must be recognized from the start. Thus, the way regulatory rights are distributed across governmental institutions, the goals ascribed to regulatory agencies, and the voting system used to elect the political principals are regarded as the structures that affect the final outcome. The processes involved in the regulatory outcome are, in turn, the timing of government intervention, the tenure of regulatory bodies, and the design of the communication channels within the regulatory hierarchy. According to Estache and Martimort, failure to address the transaction costs involved in structures and processes is bound to result in poor regulatory policy and poor institutional performance. They stress the importance of factors such as autonomy, accountability, and independence in creating regulatory institutions. Likewise, they also underscore that less rent and less incentive need to be built into the regulatory framework if transaction costs in general and collusion problems in particular are minimized.

In Chapter 4, Manzetti further develops some of the issues related to the importance of the internal organization of government raised by Estache and Martimort and explores the politics involved in regulatory outcomes. Consistent with Harberger, Schuck, and Estache and Martimort's chapters in this volume, Manzetti shows how privatization under monopolistic conditions leads to poor results when compared to divestiture policies that instead introduced competition prior to a sale. Likewise, he also shows empirically, by examining the Argentine and Chilean cases, that once new companies acquire such monopolistic rights, it is very difficult to eliminate rent-seeking behavior. Chapter 4 also shows in detail that whenever monopolistic situations ensue after privatization, their roots can be clearly ascribed to political arrangements rather than to economic exigencies.

Kaufman's Chapter 5 tackles the issue of financial regulation from a broad theoretical perspective. Quite pointedly, the author underscores the peculiarity of financial regulation. Due to the crucial role of regulation in any economy, governments around the world have tried different approaches to affect financial regulation's goals and performance. Kaufman underscores how "prudential regulation," that is, the attempt by many governments to enforce deposit insurance and other safety nets to reassure investors, has usually resulted in poor economic performance of the sector as a whole. For Kaufman, governments, no matter how well intentioned, cannot replace market discipline with widespread regulations. Instead, the answer to the dilemma may lie in mixing regulation with market-driven discipline, through enhanced competition among financial institutions, patterned after the U.S. model. Of course, countries facing differing circumstances, Kaufman argues, should promote regulatory reform while taking into consideration their own domestic realities. Yet, when most deposit insurance schemes are removed, empirical evidence shows that moral hazard problems are minimized since depositors will avoid banks with large nonperforming portfolios, which in turn forces banks to better manage their assets.

In the second part of the book, the sector-specific analyses bring support to many of the theoretical arguments of the first part, notwithstanding some important differences across economic activities. Shirley's Chapter 6, for instance, compares attempts at privatization in the water sector in four major Latin American cities:

Buenos Aires, Lima, Mexico City, and Santiago de Chile. Her results point to the fact that among the sectors surveyed in this book, water seems to be the most problematic for a variety of reasons. Because of externality problems, post-privatization government regulation is likely to be more extensive than in other sectors. Likewise, potential payoffs for the government and for private investors are usually smaller while information problems are comparatively greater than in other public utilities. For instance, a major problem arises from the fact that in many countries water is scarce, and under public control its cost is heavily subsidized. Thus, governments are susceptible to harsh criticism because prices, under private ownership, are likely to rise to make water companies profitable. Consequently, projects are often delayed, contracts are likely to be renegotiated, and government interference is more common than in other public utilities, thus creating higher risks for investors. Indeed, of the four cases that Shirley examined, only one resulted in a successful privatization, as political and institutional barriers posed serious problems to both privatization and the creation of optimal regulatory schemes that were tied to divestiture programs.

In the electricity sector, Estache and Rodríguez-Pardina conclude in Chapter 7 that distribution and transmission are likely to remain under monopoly conditions, thus making regulation necessary. This means that regulators must have the authority to set tariffs in order to ensure that consumers can share in efficiency gains. In addition, issues of pricing related to access and interconnection will likely remain and will need clear rules. In the countries that Estache and Rodríguez-Pardina survey, the present market structure favors integrated firms (vertically and horizontally), which does not facilitate competition. Provisions ensuring equal access, therefore, are essential to further competition and should be of paramount concern for the next wave of privatizations worldwide.

The telecommunications sector offers a drastically different picture. As Wellenius underscores in Chapter 8, this is the sector that has shown the greatest development and dynamism in the last decade. His findings are consistent with some of the theoretical discussions of preceding papers in the volume. In fact, the best results among the countries that Wellenius surveyed can be found in those cases where regulatory institutions were operational prior to, not after, privatization and where the basic tenets of the telecommunications business were framed into a law, rather than an executive order, as often happens. The author also points out that the widely held view in the early 1980s, according to which SOEs in telecommunications had to be transferred to the private sector under monopolistic conditions to lure investors, is obsolete today. This is due to the rapid development of new technologies that have made competition possible in both local and long-distance service (see, for instance, Brazil's privatization in this sector as a benchmark case). Unfortunately, in many countries, regulatory institutions in telecommunications remain closely tied to government bureaucracy and prone to political interference. Information asymmetry problems, common in other public utilities, remain a thorny issue in privately held telecommunications companies that have been able to affect (if not capture) government regulators on several occasions. Anti-trust legislation, where sufficiently developed, has provided alternative means toward promoting competition and effective regulation. Given the rapid technological development of telecommunications, the general conclusion is that countries bound to privatize in the future will need new reform strategies, but how to proceed is still unclear. Worldwide agreements are likely to play a greater role in the future to set international standards and a leveled playing field. Moreover, regulatory policy may well shift from sector-specific to a more general approach, given the increasing importance of the internet and cable services. Thus, chances are that new regulatory policies will be conceived in a flexible manner to tackle the ever-increasing challenges posed by new technology.

In Chapter 9, Gruben examines in detail many of the issues discussed in Kaufman's chapter by comparing Argentina and Mexico's experience in financial reform. More specifically, Gruben looks at the relationships among market discipline, deposit guarantee regulations, bank performance, and exchange rate stability. What he finds is that market-driven policies seem to produce much better results in the banking sector than traditional regulatory policies aimed at sheltering inefficient banks from bad business practices. Gruben's evidence shows that Argentina first restricted deposit guarantees and bank bailouts and then went on to privatize several government-owned banks. On the contrary, Mexico's generous deposit guarantee scheme was closely linked to highly risky lending policies at the time when bank privatization started in the early 1990s. As a consequence of its market-based regulation, Argentina saw depositors leaving poorly managed banks for well managed ones. Notwithstanding the financial repercussions associated with the tequila crisis of 1994-1995 and the Asian crisis of 1997-1998 that severely affected emerging market economies, the Argentine banking system was in much better shape to weather the storm than its Mexican counterpart. According to Gruben, the difference can be traced back, to a large degree, to Argentina's discipline-oriented policies. This is because after privatization the Argentines bankers, unlike their Mexican colleagues, did not run their institutions to the point that marginal costs exceeded marginal revenues. Equally important, Gruben contends that typical indicators that bank regulators use in advanced industrial societies may be misleading in emerging markets. A way to avoid surprises, he suggests, is to adopt policies that provide market-based signals that produce substantial discipline without resorting to too much government intervention.

In Chapter 10, Saba examines Schuck's legal analysis when applied to the case of Argentina. The comparison between the United States and Argentina per se is quite interesting for at least two reasons. Argentina, among Latin American countries, has a Constitution closely patterned after that of the United States and, in the 1990s, Argentina has privatized more economic activities than any other nation on the continent. Saba's paper points out the dramatic contrast between Argentina and the United States in terms of regulatory policy. In fact, Argentina, despite implementing far-reaching market reforms in the 1990s, fares poorly when examined accordingly to Schuck's regulatory roles of the modern state. First, in Saba's view, unlike the United States, the Argentine constitutional tradition since World War II has been characterized by radical downturns. From the 1940s until 1989, the Argentine Supreme Court espoused a presumption "against," rather than pro-market. Then, starting in 1989, the pendulum swung back but this time against the state rather than toward a pro-market approach. Second, the effectiveness of social regulation in Argentina has been severely hampered because, of the 12 strategies and techniques that Schuck suggests, the great majority are largely deficient or nonexistent. Third, the extra-regulatory institutions and processes that Shuck described are also too weak to play any meaningful role in supplying the market with alternative mechanisms. In fact, the government eroded the independence of the judiciary in the 1990s. Moreover, legislative oversight, administrative law, and interest groups have too often conformed to the government agenda, leaving the media as the only true watchdog that has exposed governmental abuses and unfair practices of the privatized companies. In all, Saba concludes that the against-the-state approach that the Carlos Menem administration (1989-1999) espoused from its inception has prevented Argentina from developing the kind of regulatory state envisioned by Schuck. Consequently, consumers find themselves in a weak position even after privatization (see Harberger's anecdote in this regard), as the uncertain legal framework of many new regulatory frameworks leaves windows of opportunity — inviting either collusion between regulator and regulated or opportunistic behavior on the part of government regulators. Moreover, the arbitrary legal ground upon which many reforms have been built makes one wonder whether a change of political regime may give ammunition to a market-unfriendly government to reverse the reforms of the 1990s. Indeed, Saba's article raises the question of whether true, competitive markets, based upon strong governmental institutions and the rule of law, will emerge not only in Argentina but throughout Latin America, as several governments in the region have adopted similar policies and the legal means to enforce them.

In this volume, all the issues briefly outlined above are fully explored. As the field of regulation is a fast evolving one, the hope is that this collection of essays will be useful to specialists and the general public alike in finding better ways to promote modern, competitive, consumer-friendly markets that can improve the welfare of the people of Latin America.

References

Glade, William. 1989. "Privatization in Rent-Seeking Societies." *World Development* 17:673-682.

Sonnenschein, Mabelle G., and Patricia A. Yokopenic. 1996. "Multinational Enterprises and Telecommunications Privatization." In *Privatizing Monopolies: Lessons from the Telecommunications and Transport Sectors in Latin America*, ed. Ravi Ramamurti. Baltimore: The Johns Hopkins University Press.

Tenenbaum, Bernard. 1995. *The Real World of Power Sector Regulation*. Washington, D.C.: World Bank.

PART I.

THEMES AND ISSUES IN REGULATORY POLICY AFTER PRIVATIZATION

CHAPTER 1

Reflections on Efficiency and Government Regulation

ARNOLD C. HARBERGER

An impressive change has taken place in the way international organizations, such as the World Bank, the International Development Bank, and the International Monetary Fund, have approached the question of privatization.

Not too long ago, these organizations practically reserved their financing for public sector enterprises and activities and studiously avoided recommending privatization. Any step in that direction would have been considered an invasion of a country's sovereignty. But somewhere between the mid-1970s and the early 1980s, the attitude of the international organizations changed drastically, and the organizations began to address privatization as a technical, economic matter rather than as a political, ideological issue.

In making this change, the international organizations were recognizing certain inherent handicaps under which public sector companies have typically operated. In a nutshell, these handicaps consist of politically imposed constraints that inhibit public sector companies from achieving efficiency levels similar to those of private sector operations. These constraints include the following:

- The limits that keep their executive pay levels far below those prevailing in the private sector;
- Strong political pressures against abandoning unprofitable product lines and against downsizing in general;
- Artificially high wages for the unskilled and the semi-skilled, as the government tries to cultivate a reputation as a "model employer"; and
- An ethos of "don't rock the boat" within public enterprises that discourages efforts to reduce real cost, particularly when these efforts involve cutting the number of jobs or restructuring the chain of command.

While we can certainly point to an occasional public enterprise that has somehow overcome these constraints, they are the common lot of public enterprises. Discovering them has represented just as serious a social-scientific inquiry as learning about the different saving habits of families or the different educational levels achieved by young people in different population groups. The changing attitude of the international organizations toward privatization stems from their appreciation of this fact by dint of repeated, bitter lessons.

Looking at the proliferating wave of privatization over the last two decades, one might be tempted to conclude that governments throughout most of Latin

America and much of the rest of the world had learned the same lesson that the international organizations had learned. Unfortunately, that would be the wrong inference, at least as I read the evidence. A much more plausible explanation for many of the privatizations is that selling off public enterprises suddenly became a legitimized way for governments to get their hands on more cash.

The evidence favoring this more somber interpretation is the haste with which most privatizations were carried out, once the idea was taken seriously. If the objectives are to reduce waste, to promote economic efficiency, and to advance the interests of both consumers and taxpayers at the same time, then a government should treat an act of privatization just as seriously as General Motors or General Electric would take the sale of a product line or a division of the company.

When private companies sell off a division, they worry about getting it into shape to get the best price for it. This is the approach governments should take when they are privatizing anything. Regrettably, governments have not done this, and their lack of due diligence has often come back to haunt them. For example, many public utilities have been sold before an adequate regulatory framework was put into place. Also, with some of the telephone companies, what often was being sold was the monopoly right to exploit the consumer for a substantial period of time. A $420 charge that I once paid for a half-hour telephone call from Buenos Aires, Argentina, to San José, Costa Rica, substantiates this kind of consumer exploitation.

The best rule in privatizations is never to use the proceeds of asset sales to cover current deficits; instead, the proceeds should be used to pay off debt. Mexico followed this rule fairly well, dedicating substantial amounts of its privatization proceeds to pay off its debt and using the rest to accumulate assets through a politically popular program called Solidaridad. However, in following the rule, Mexico is an exception. Some countries, such as Argentina, followed a second-best rule, using the proceeds of privatizations to lower fiscal deficits while implementing major fiscal reforms — reforms that in the long run will independently and permanently close the deficit, the hemorrhage. But a great many countries have simply used the proceeds of privatization to put a patch over a gaping hole in the fiscal budget.

Chile, in the post-Allende period, offers an interesting case and an opportunity to digress to banking and to bank regulation in particular. Chile's first wave of privatizations took place during a huge recession in 1975-1976. Credit was extremely scarce. Banks recently had been made competitive, and they were paying the depositors 2 percent to 3 percent real interest per month. They were also collecting high rates from the other side in order to pay 2 percent to 3 percent to their depositors. It was into this maelstrom that the newly privatized companies of the first wave were thrown. Most were not actually being privatized, in the strictest sense of the word. They had undergone "intervention," which meant that the government had taken over their operations while their owners remained the owners. "Intervention" had been the process by which the great bulk of Chilean private companies had been taken under government control during the Allende period. For them, privatization just meant returning the companies to their legal owners. But the unfortunate legal owners received ailing, hemorrhaging companies with indifferent management and huge financial woes. At the time they were "privatized," these firms were running enormous cash flow deficits. In effect, Chile had been printing money to cover these deficits. What the Chilean government essentially did was to shove these firms off on the private sector. Most owners somehow patched them together for a time. However, many of these companies never really gained solvency and ultimately failed.

The only reason these companies stayed around was that bankers kept renewing their credits. Now, why would a banker renew a credit when the banker knows or strongly suspects that the company in question does not have the wherewithal to pay back the loan? The answer lies in the regulation of the Chilean banks.

Regulations allowed banks to have loans up to 20 times their capital and surplus. In "recognizing" a bad loan in the amount of, say, US$1 million, a bank would simultaneously reduce its loans by $1 million and reduce its capital and surplus by the same amount. That reduction by $1 million of capital and surplus had the effect of preventing the bank from lending $20 million that it otherwise might have lent. So the bank's manager did not want to tell anyone that this was a bad loan; the bank wanted everyone to overlook it. Nor did these bankers need to conspire with other bankers, because every single banker independently came to the same conclusion. As a consequence, an overwhelmingly large number of bad loans developed in the banking system. They occupied a place on the consolidated balance sheet that could have been and should have been occupied by good credit. The bad loans' taking the place of what could have been good credit resulted in high interest rates on good loans. These huge interest rates on the good loans ultimately drove many good firms into bankruptcy and turned good loans into bad ones. There was a snowball effect.

Chart 1 illustrates the problem. In order to determine the real amount of money that people are holding or the real amount of credit available, the GDP deflator or the cost of living index is used to deflate the balance sheets. This is important because the ultimate pillar of monetary economics is the demand for real cash balances. Ultimately, it is the people who decide how much M2 there will be in real terms. (M2 is the combination of currency, demand deposits, and time and savings deposits.) The M2 is on the right-hand side of the balance sheet. (See Chart 1.) Although the central bank does not dictate M2, it influences M2 through the effect of its policies on inflation. It does not print real money; it prints nominal money. The people then react and create enough inflation so they end up with the amount of real balances they want. It is people's desired holding of real balances that determines the right-hand side of the balance sheet in real terms. Now, the left-hand side of the balance sheet is occupied by three main components: net foreign assets, credit to the government, and credit to the private sector. Chart 1 distinguishes between good and bad credit. If the bad credits did not exist, the good credit could occupy the entire private sector loans area. At the bottom of the chart is a demand curve for good credits by business firms. If these firms had access to the full supply, interest rates would be potential equilibrium real interest rates. However, the bad loans constrained the supply of credit available to the good firms and caused the actual equilibrium real interest rate to be much higher — and, thus, the problem.

Chart 1.
Consolidated Balance Sheet of the Banking System
(All items are expressed in real terms, i.e., deflated by the CPI or other general price index.)

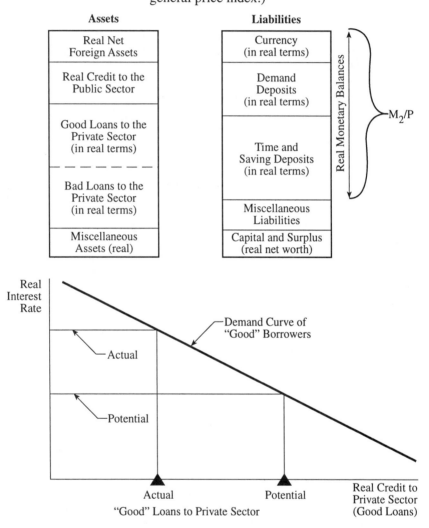

Source: Created by the author.

The flaw in the system was the Superintendency of Banks. The inspectors failed to blow the whistle on the unrecognized bad loans hidden in the portfolios of the banks. They failed to do so mainly because they lacked the needed resources. They were underpaid, understaffed, and underqualified. Good inspectors at that time, 1975-1976, tripled or quintupled their salaries by moving to the private banking sector. As these inspectors examined the books of the banks, they need not have been finding big flaws; they needed only to go to the manager of the bank with some intelligent question that showed they really had high qualifications. The bank manager would be elated and quite willing to offer the inspectors three or four times what they were earning because that was the going market price for people of their experience and capacity. These were offers that the inspectors were very pleased to accept. The result was like a vacuum cleaner sucking out all the best people from the Superintendency of Banks. Those who were left were mainly people who were simply incapable of doing the job.

The Superintendency's challenge is to find a way to pay an adequate salary scale — one that truly competes with the private sector. There is a solution: make the Bank Superintendency a joint enterprise between the government and the commercial banks, have it managed by a technical authority, and finance it by the banks themselves under the rule that the salary scale of the Superintendency must at least match that of the commercial banks. Inspectors would then earn at least as much as comparable employees of private banks. This is the only solution that has a good chance of maintaining a Bank Superintendency of sufficiently high quality.

Now, it is important to address a new topic, regulation, which is often needed to set the stage properly for privatization. The appropriate system for regulation of electricity is dictated by good economics — in contrast to regulation based on rates of return, simple price caps, and other traditional criteria. The key element in the system is marginal cost pricing. The spot price of energy at any given time is set equal to the marginal running cost of the least efficient plant functioning at the moment. So the least efficient plant gets paid just its running cost, while all the more efficient plants gain an economic rent or profit because they are getting that same price even though their running costs are lower. That economic rent or profit, accumulated over the whole year, may eventually cover all their capital costs.

If this were an ongoing system in a growing economy, the least efficient plants would never recover their capital costs. All they would gain is their running costs. A peak-time surcharge is necessary to cover the capital cost of the *marginal peaking capacity*. Gas turbines, which have a high running cost per kilowatt-hour but a low capital cost, are typically used for these peaking purposes. They are kept in storage much of the time, which trades off a low capital cost for a high running cost of capacity that is likely to be operating only a small fraction of the time. When some plants are operating and some are not, all operating plants collect the marginal running cost of the least efficient plant operating at each given moment. When all plants are in use, a peak-time surcharge is applied. That peak-time surcharge, applied over the number of hours when the plants hypothetically are all in use, is what covers the capital cost of the peaking capacity. The peak-time surcharge is also part of the price recovered by all other types of capacity in the system operating at those times.

Chart 2 illustrates how a peak-time surcharge works. The vertical line represents a given capacity. At the beginning, the demand is less than capacity, which translates into spot prices equal to marginal running costs (point A). Demand grows with time, so the demand curve bounces to the right. Eventually, the demand curve reaches the zone where it intersects the vertical line representing capacity. The

Chart 2.
A Framework for Electricity Pricing in High Use Hours

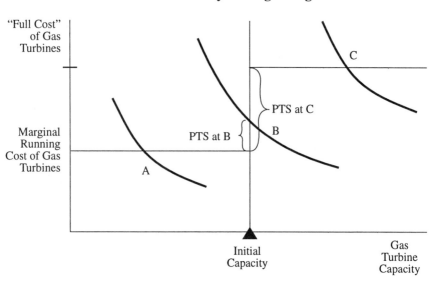

Point A =   Demand is below installed capacity. The rule is to charge marginal running cost of the highest-cost (i.e., gas turbine) units actually in use.

Point B =   Demand strikes capacity line at a price between "marginal cost" and "full cost." The rule (rarely followed) is to charge a peak-time surcharge (PTS) at B determined by the precise location of the demand curve.

Point C =   Once demand in high-use hours would call for a price higher than the "full cost" of gas turbines, the proper rule is to add new capacity to meet that demand *at* the full-cost price (as at point C), rather than to charge a higher price. The pragmatic rule is to omit points like B altogether — and to charge marginal running cost in off-peak hours and a peak-time price based on the "full cost" of gas turbines.

Source: Created by the author.

price then would be at the intersection of the initial full capacity line with the shifting demand curve (point B). That produces a rent to capacity. If demand keeps growing, that rent keeps growing. However, when demand gets to the point where the price measured back at the vertical initial capacity line is equal to the full-cost price of the gas turbines, then instead of letting the price go up farther, more gas turbines will be acquired and used.

Most electricity enterprises or systems actually go directly to point C. (See Chart 2.) They calculate the peak-time surcharge that will justify investment in additional gas turbine capacity. They ignore the short periods of time in which they might be in situations like B. This system of "marginal cost pricing" was invented in France, and it has been applied extensively in the United Kingdom as well as in some other countries. The practice fits the theory best in predominantly thermal systems. In this kind of system, peak time is defined in terms of both the hours of the day and the season of the year.

It is trickier to deal with systems that have substantial hydro capacity as well as thermal capacity. The problem is that years can go by in such a system without the system's reaching full use of its thermal capacity. Such full use is reached only when the storage dams are nearly empty, which usually happens after two or three dry years in a row. In countries like Chile, Mexico, Peru, and Costa Rica, strict application of marginal cost pricing would charge just marginal cost nearly all the time. After a third dry year in a row, it would become necessary to use all the available thermal capacity for much of the year. This would result in very high peak-time surcharges for huge numbers of hours in the year — charges that could be as high as US$0.25 to US$0.35 per kilowatt-hour to all users of energy. Nobody likes this.

The systems of countries like Mexico, Chile, Peru, and other Andean countries really do not have full applications of marginal cost pricing. They are unwilling to go that last step, enacting huge surcharges for the second and third dry year. The end result is an application of something like marginal cost pricing for the day-to-day and hour-to-hour movements. Then there are demand charges and capacity charges as well as what I call insurance policies, in which a small charge is added to the rate per kilowatt-hour to build up a surplus to pay the cost of having the standby capacity to cope with a sequence of dry years. There is some loss of economic efficiency involved, and there may be further problems in economic pricing of electricity.

Good economics tells us that sunk costs are sunk. If you invest in a technology that becomes obsolescent, you are supposed to take the hit and write down that asset to a new lower value because it has been rendered less valuable by some new technology that is causing the market price to fall. It appears that modern combined-cycle technology has rendered a lot of old generating equipment really obsolete in this sense. But in how many countries have the electricity enterprises taken a big financial hit as a consequence of the new dominance of combined-cycle technology? They have probably made good returns on the old assets as well as on the new ones, and somewhere along the way a major economic principle has been violated.

At this point, it is appropriate to examine other energy sector problems. Of particular interest is Chile's public sector generating entity, Endesa, which was not broken up at the time of its privatization. It was a successful enterprise with fine management. There was a concern that the process of privatization would cause a few traumas, so the emphasis was mainly on a comfortable transition. To break up the enterprise would have required new management for all the various pieces. It was inertia more than anything else that kept it from being divided.

When Endesa was privatized, it was still the owner of the main transmission lines in Chile. A modern electricity system lets anyone be a competitor at the spot prices. It is essential to have a neutral referee to receive the energy from the generators and deliver it to the distributors. However, this was not the case in Chile. The referee was and still is one of the participants — in fact, the biggest participant — in the generating game. There have been many accusations that Endesa uses all sorts of tricks to undercut its competitors. The division responsible for transmission should have been separated out. It could have been and probably should have been kept as a quasi-public body together with the dispatch center that decides which plants will be turned on, in which order, working from low-cost to high-cost plants.

Mexico's handling of electrical generation also is interesting and quite different from Chile's. Mexican generating capacity was badly de-optimized in the wake of the 1980s debt crisis. This story shows how different pieces of economic policy can sometimes work against each other — one of them fouls up another. Mexico had practically no money for investment. Its electricity enterprise, the Comisión Federal de Electricidad, realized that the country was in the trough of a big depression, that demand for electricity would be growing fast in future years, and that it was not being allowed to build to meet the future demand. So it played a trick. It used very expensive energy, gas turbine energy, to feed the current demand during this depression. It did not use energy from its dams and instead allowed the dams to fill all the way up to the top. In this way, it stored power now for future use. It was a very ingenious way of dealing with the constraint it faced, not being given funds to expand capacity "right now." In the process of all of this, it introduced peak-time surcharges for large users of energy. These charges were unlike England's or Chile's, where the charges were meant to cover just the running costs plus the capital costs of the marginal capacity during the hours of full use. Mexico raised the peak-time charges to levels that would stop peak-time demand. Some enterprises ended up paying US$0.30 to US$0.35 per kilowatt-hour for peak-time energy. It is amazing that once this system was in place, it stayed.

A look at the privatization of highways in Mexico is also of interest. The process has been referred to as the Mexican Highway Disaster. The people who constructed the expressways (*autopistas*) became the owners of them. The government guaranteed certain minimum traffic volumes. The constructors then set tolls that were virtually prohibitive. As a result, it was not unusual to find a stretch of tollway like that from Mexico City to Puebla practically empty. The main reason was that there was a free parallel road, while the toll road charged something like US$0.25 per kilometer. The toll road simply did not have an advantage sufficient to support such a high toll. This resulted in traffic levels that were far below the guaranteed minimum. In the end, the government caved in and began buying back most of these roads from the constructors. It was a scandal, a mess.

There is absolutely no advantage to private sector ownership of roads. There is an advantage to the private sector's building and managing roads, but not to its owning them. A private owner does not have the incentive to widen or upgrade a road at the time it is economically warranted. The private incentive is to raise the price in such circumstances. Also, the private owner has little incentive to straighten out dangerous curves or otherwise follow where good cost-benefit analysis leads.

The Double Auction approach is a solution for governments that need roads but do not have money to construct them. In the first auction, each constructor or bidder submits two envelopes. One of these envelopes contains a cash price, and the other contains a credit price with payments spread over 10, 15, or 20 years, whatever the government asks for in the bid. This faces head-on the main reason why governments ever thought about privatizing roads: they did not have the money to construct them.

Governments were simply short of money. They badly wanted roads to be built, and they found "build-own-operate" (B-O-O) a very tempting alternative. However, the auction with two envelopes solves the problem, because governments can always pick the credit envelope and not have to lay out any cash. The second auction in the double auction system is for the administration and maintenance of the road once it is built. There is no reason why the constructor should be any good at this. Such a contract should be for a three- to five-year period and no longer. At the end of the contract, the government can make necessary adjustments, such as widening the road or straightening out the curves. During the period when the road is being adjusted, management can be handled through a patch contract. A new full auction for another three- to five-year period would take place once the needed adjustments had been completed. The Double Auction system accomplishes what a B-O-O system does, but without its disadvantages.

Proper highway pricing should be based mainly on congestion tolls. This is where economic theory comes into the picture. Congestion tolls are meant to make drivers recognize the costs that they impose on others as they add themselves to the list of traffic on the road. Congestion tolls are first-best road pricing. There is no reason why congestion tolls should cover costs, at least not in the first instance. They just compensate for whatever congestion there may be. There are, of course, other reasons to consider a set of charges that extract from users the full economic cost of the road. The users may be asked to bear the full costs of the road rather than have the taxpayers pay all or part of these costs. If such charges are implemented via tolls, they are distinctly second best, but they can certainly be considered as the government auctions the maintenance and administration of the roads. However, full-cost pricing of roads is a second-best and not a first-best alternative. What does not make much sense is giving private road owners a free or almost free hand in setting tolls. Roads need economic safeguards.

My conclusion is that in designing economic policy, there is nothing more important than thinking in terms of costs and benefits. It leads to new ways of looking at certain issues and inevitably impacts decisions, helping guide the authorities toward sound economic policy.

CHAPTER 2

Law and Post-Privatization Regulatory Reform: Perspectives from the U.S. Experience[1]

PETER H. SCHUCK

INTRODUCTION

L aw plays many diverse roles in the regulatory state. It begins by defining property and contract rights and the substantive regulatory limitations on those rights. Law also specifies the regulatory structures that impose, administer, and enforce those limitations, as well as the procedures that both the regulator and the regulated must observe in their mutual dealings, and the modes of formal conflict resolution that each can invoke against the other. Law also defines the duties that the regulator and the regulated owe consumers, competitors, contractors, governmental entities and other third parties, and it prescribes the remedies through which the third parties can enforce those duties.

Privatization does not dispense with these roles; it merely alters the precise mix of private and public law through which they are played out. Whether the state spins off a previously state-run activity to private entities, as is now common in Latin America,[2] or subjects a traditionally private activity to regulation, as has been a common pattern in the United States, the state will deploy its public law to exercise some continuing degree of regulatory authority over the activity. The newly privatizing state will be under political pressure to ensure that the public is served at least as well under the new regime as it was under the old one, while the newly regulating state in effect declares, as a justification for regulation, that the previously private activity is "affected with a public interest" and that the private regime did not serve this public interest sufficiently well because of market failure or other reasons, including the demands of distributive justice.

In this chapter, I discuss three paradigmatic roles that public law can play in the kind of reformist, post-privatization political and policy environment in which many emerging liberal democratic states are now situated. These roles are 1) to create and institutionalize a strong (but rebuttable) presumption in favor of market solutions to social problems; 2) to maximize the effectiveness of regulation where it is used; and 3) to establish extra-regulatory institutions and processes that can help monitor, augment, and discipline the resulting hybrid system of markets and regulation.

In exploring these three roles, I shall draw largely on the U.S. experience, and the institutions and processes that I shall analyze are largely those at the federal (national) level. I emphasize the American case not because the United States is a typical state (which it is not), not because it is a model that Latin America should mimic (something Latin America should not and probably could not do), not because it is the system that I know best (although that is certainly true), nor because the United States has all the answers (which it does not). Instead, I do so because I believe that all of us can learn a great deal from its struggle to construct a political economy that fully exploits the economic advantages of flexible markets, technocratic expertise, and innovation while also enjoying the social advantages of legality, political accountability, distributional fairness, and other nonmarket values. This struggle has been a long and difficult one; the necessary institutions, infrastructure, and values that I shall discuss have developed quite slowly and unevenly. The current robustness of the U.S. economy — and, I would argue more controversially, the strength of the American polity (Schuck 1997; Schuck 1998, 354-358) — should not obscure the fact that the struggle is a perpetual one.

THE PRO-MARKET PRESUMPTION

There is no reason a priori to favor markets over regulation or vice versa. Only after specifying a society's values and history can we begin to construct a justification for one kind of political economy rather than another. A priori, there is no reason to believe that market failures are greater and more harmful than government failures or vice-versa. Fortunately, however, we do not live in complete normative, historical, and empirical ignorance but instead inhabit an a posteriori world deeply inscribed with values, history, and knowledge of empirical consequences. Political economies are certainly not path dependent in any strict sense; a society can choose (or may be compelled) to transform its ways of doing business, as the United States has done since the 1960s and as Russia and many Latin American and Asian states are doing now. Nevertheless, different states do exhibit distinct, socially conditioned patterns of political economy.

The political ideology, legal culture, and social institutions of the United States today mutually reinforce a presumption in favor of market allocations of goods and services and market solutions to public policy problems, at least where such solutions are feasible. The presumption is a strong one — and increasingly so — but it is also rebuttable, as I discuss below. This strong presumption in favor of markets has existed for most of American history. Recall that Adam Smith's *The Wealth of Nations* was published in 1776, the year of U.S. independence and a time when it could influence the constitutional framers. (The historical evidence suggests that Smith's ideas did indeed influence the framers, along with other ideas of the Scottish Enlightenment.)

The U.S. Constitution did not expressly privilege market approaches to public policy problems. In at least four ways, however, it did so indirectly. First, several constitutional provisions explicitly protected property and contract rights against various kinds of government infringement. Second, the Supreme Court for more than a half century (from the 1880s to 1937) interpreted another provision, the Due Process Clause, to elevate liberty of contract into a constitutional right that even political majorities could not restrict. Third, and perhaps more important in the long run, the Constitution created a highly fragmented, decentralized, and internally competitive system of governmental authority that even today fortifies the status quo, which has tended to be friendly to markets. This governance structure makes it difficult for proregulation forces to assemble political coalitions strong enough to overcome this inertia — difficult but not impossible, as demonstrated by the increase in market-constraining regulatory activity during the New Deal and 1960-1980 periods.

More interesting, the regulatory agenda has flourished even during the recent era of unbridled enthusiasm for the market. For example, political scientist R. Shep Melnick has shown how a dynamic of institutional competition among Congress, agencies, and the courts increased regulation in some policy areas even as deregulation became a central theme in U.S. political economy (Melnick 1994). Most of the new regulation has been in the nature of "social" regulation — that is, it pursues nondiscrimination, health and safety, and redistributive goals rather than seeking to control market prices, entry, exit, service, and competition, as with traditional "economic" regulation. However, there are important exceptions, such as the growing restrictions on managed care organizations in the health services industry.

Fourth, the Constitution entrenches the market by protecting the autonomy and activities of private interest groups that strongly influence the political process. Even as these groups often pursue public subsidies, economic rents, and other forms of governmental support for their narrow interests (disparaged as "corporate welfare" or "corporate socialism"), they also seek to minimize governmental interference with private decisionmaking. Their success in doing so thus reinforces the structural and ideological biases favoring market autonomy.

At a subconstitutional level, the law undergirds this privatistic, promarket presumption in several additional ways. Most fundamentally, the law defines individual entitlements and duties, and it establishes institutions and procedures for enforcing those entitlements and duties. The rights to hold and use property, to exploit original ideas, and to engage in voluntary exchanges with others are regulated by property, intellectual property, and contract law; the rights to physical, economic, and emotional integrity are protected by tort law; the rights to freedom from arbitrary governmental intrusion are protected by public law (constitutional and administrative law); and the rights to environmental quality and other public goods are protected by regulatory law. In the course of defining these entitlements and duties, the law, in effect, marks the boundaries between the private and public domains.

The presumption in favor of markets means that private providers in the United States supply many of the goods that governments in other advanced industrial democracies supply. Health care and education, especially at the university level are examples. Private provision of these goods is made possible in part by another distinctive, market-reinforcing feature of U.S. law: the nurturing of a vast, rapidly growing nonprofit, or "third," sector that provides many of the goods and services that lie near the shifting border between what is public and what is private.

In addition to health care and education, these goods and services include charity for the indigent, other philanthropy, care for pre-school children and the infirm elderly, professional organizations, cooperative activities, scientific research, museums, the performing arts, a vast array of other cultural and social service activities, and community action and advocacy efforts. Even the political parties in the United States are decidedly private in their financing and governance compared with those in other countries.

This intermediation by nonprofit organizations between the public and private sectors is an important, fascinating, and complex motif in U.S. life (Hansmann 1980). For present purposes, it suffices to say that the public's trust in the integrity, effectiveness, and selflessness of the nonprofit sector crucially affects the American political economy. By providing a "softer," nonmarket alternative to a public that relies heavily but uneasily on the profit motive to provide certain highly valued social goods, the nonprofit sector often deflects and suppresses what might otherwise be strong public demands for direct government provision or regulation. This public trust is sometimes misplaced; in fact, many nonprofit providers operate much as private, for-profit providers would. Nevertheless, the settled acceptance of, and even preference for, this alternative is a pivotal factor in many debates about the appropriate role of government, such as ministering to the needs of the poor.

It is axiomatic that in order for the law to facilitate the voluntary exchange of property and to support other rights, it must define these rights with clarity and precision. To the extent that the law fails to do so, potential buyers and sellers must bear the deadweight losses generated by the need to ascertain and negotiate what those rights are, who holds them, and how they can be traded; these costs will deter otherwise socially valuable exchanges. U.S. law, by surrounding the nature and allocation of entitlements with considerable uncertainty, often is both inefficient and ineffective.

Technical, political, and institutional factors help to explain these failures (Schuck 1984). First, there are limitations of language; ambiguity pervades legal discourse, and much of this ambiguity inevitably requires legal interpretation. Moreover, lawmakers possess only a limited ability to predict the consequences and specific applications of their legal rules; they must, therefore, use language that is general enough to provide the necessary flexibility to those who must apply these rules. Ambiguity, of course, also has important political functions. When lawmakers seek to balance conflicting values and interests, general language helps them to persuade each of the contenders that they have won something and that the law will project their victory into the future. This, however, produces definitions of entitlements that are compromised and indeterminate.

The institutional processes of lawmaking and law application greatly magnify this uncertainty. The common law method of adjudication entails case-by-case development of legal doctrine, which is both defined and limited by the particular facts of decided cases. Only weak hierarchical controls constrain the highly decentralized American judiciary, which is further fragmented into federal, state, and local court systems, and private tribunals that increasingly divert important litigation away from public courts and public norm-creating processes. Thus, conflicting lines of doctrine resisting authoritative resolution persist between and within each jurisdiction. The ambiguity and compromise of legislation are compounded by the intricate, frustrating, and often constitutionally uncertain division of authority between the state and the federal governments. Lawmaking and law administration by executive officials, while usually more specific than statutes, nonetheless, leave many important questions unresolved. Bureaucrats, more frequently than legislators and judges, use general language in order to maximize their discretion, permit flexible solutions, compromise conflicting interests, and avert legal challenges. All of these uncertainties, of course, are greatly compounded by the separation of powers at each level of American government, which multiplies the number of institutional participants in decisionmaking and requires the constant negotiation of recurrent conflicts, producing indeterminate and unpredictable outcomes.

By defining private entitlements, the law not only promotes markets but also prescribes how government must proceed if it wants to regulate them. As noted earlier, the presumption in favor of markets and against regulation is often overcome. The New Deal and Great Society eras imposed vast regulation, and the relatively conservative administration of Richard Nixon extended federal regulation to many new areas, such as pensions, occupational health and safety, environmental protection, energy, and health care. Under Presidents Gerald Ford and Jimmy Carter, regulation expanded in environmental and consumer product safety, even as a regulatory reform movement prompted substantial deregulation in the surface transportation and airline industries, as well as in the energy sector. The Ronald Reagan and George Bush years also brought deregulation to certain policy areas — some agencies were even abolished altogether — yet Congress and the administration also extended the reach of environmental controls, antidiscrimination law, air bag requirements, import restrictions, and other market restraints. Employers were also subjected to new immigration enforcement requirements, assuming a novel gatekeeping role.

During Bill Clinton's administration, new regulatory programs requiring plant closing notification, employee leaves, managed health care, and other practices have been established. At the same time, however, Congress and the Federal Communications Commission have taken important steps to deregulate the immense telecommunications industry, and international trade restrictions have been relaxed. Without waiting for Congress to deregulate financial services, the Federal Reserve Board administratively facilitated much deregulation of the banks under its jurisdiction, while other financial institutions, in effect, dismantled many long-standing regulatory barriers. The 1998 merger of Citicorp and Travelers Group accelerated this process, presenting Congress with a fait accompli that it ratified through far-reaching deregulation of the financial services sector in 1999, breaking a political stalemate of almost 20 years. Regulatory reform, including deregulation and privatization, has proceeded even in areas of traditional social regulation. Examples include housing, through the expansion of the Section 8 "voucher" program; public education, through federal and state authorization on a limited scale of "charter" schools and education vouchers; and affirmative action. Another form of deregulation has occurred as federal courts have gradually lifted long-standing desegregation orders that had tightly controlled the public school bureaucracies.

Viewed more generally, the period since the 1960s has exhibited a number of common themes. I shall briefly mention six of them. First, an interesting and in some ways puzzling mixture of regulatory expansion, regulatory retrenchment, deregulation, procedural limits on regulation, and other kinds of regulatory reform have developed. Much *economic* regulation was curtailed; a notable exception is the current movement toward new controls on service and pricing decisions of managed health care firms. In contrast, *social* regulation has expanded (Posner 1997).

Second, many states have expanded their own regulatory authority, especially in areas such as health care, insurance, consumer protection, land use, and occupational licensing. This increased diversity in regulatory requirements has generated new conflicts between federal and state regulators, which the courts must resolve by applying ambiguous "federal preemption" principles.

Third, federal controls over the decisions of other levels of government have increased dramatically. Federal intergovernmental regulation imposed high costs on state and local governments while yielding questionable benefits. Regulating governments is often more difficult than regulating private entities, while new hybrid forms combining public and private organizational features create their own impediments to democratic accountability. In the 1994 unfunded mandates law, Congress tried to limit the growth of this federal intergovernmental regulation, with doubtful results.

Fourth, far-reaching judicial regulation, although of a less visible, unsystematic kind, has increased. Courts expanded common law tort liability in many areas, particularly in products liability, employment relationships, and charitable institutions such as hospitals. (Some observers, however, believe that the products liability expansion may recently have slowed or ceased altogether.) Courts increasingly adjudicate under common law tort principles disputes in which the parties are in a direct or indirect contractual relationship with one another. Courts often uphold these tort claims, which are more complex to litigate but offer plaintiffs the possibility of recovering greater damages, even though the courts traditionally confined them to a simple contract claim. Such a trend would contradict the law's traditional preference for contractual allocations of risk, at least where the parties possess roughly comparable bargaining power. Many legal scholars criticize this development (Rubin 1993).

Fifth, deregulation, once enacted, has proved very durable; remarkably little re-regulation of previously deregulated industries has occurred. Deregulation's staying power is all the more impressive in light of the intense criticisms leveled at it by powerful interests in the airline, cable broadcasting, telecommunications, and financial services industries.

Sixth, much federal regulatory reform since 1975 has taken the form of procedural controls on the federal regulatory process itself (Mashaw, Merrill, and Shane 1998, 147-160, 252-285). This development, which is probably less familiar to most regulatory reformers elsewhere, represents a pattern, perhaps distinctive to the United States, in which reformers attempt to employ process reforms in order to achieve substantive policy ends. They often view this approach as politically and substantively attractive. It effects a compromise between proregulation and deregulation positions; it seems less threatening to regulated interests; it operates across-the-board rather than applying only to particular industries; and it seeks to be prophylactic, preventing and improving regulation before it goes into effect rather than undertaking the more difficult task of reforming regulation after it is already in place.

Through a series of executive orders, all U.S. presidents since Gerald Ford have required regulators subject to executive branch control (as distinguished from the so-called "independent" regulatory agencies subject to greater congressional control) to submit proposed regulations for review by officials in the Executive Office of the President, principally what is now the Office of Information and Regulatory Affairs (OIRA) in the Office of Management and Budget. This review includes preparation of a regulatory calendar disclosing regulatory priorities and timetables, as well as submission of analyses that seek to compute and compare the private sector costs and benefits of proposed regulations and alternative approaches. A recent congressional investigation criticized the quality of these analyses (U.S. General Accounting Office 1999). Congress, for its part, has enacted a variety of statutory controls on the process of regulatory development. These are designed to force agencies to predict and evaluate how proposed regulations, at least "significant" ones, will affect environmental protection (the first requirement of this kind, enacted in 1969), small business development, competition, paperwork reduction, and other politically popular goals. In some cases, these laws require or encourage regulators to adopt the least costly or restrictive regulatory alternative — an emphatic affirmation of the traditional presumption in favor of market approaches to the solution of public policy problems (Mashaw, Merrill, and Shane 1998, 252-285). Two leading Washington, D.C. think tanks representing somewhat different political perspectives — The Brookings Institution and the more pro-market American Enterprise Institute — recently launched a study of regulatory cost-benefit analysis (Crandall et al. 1997). Its initial reports are highly critical of how government conducts such analyses (Hahn 1999).

IMPROVING THE EFFECTIVENESS OF REGULATION

The presumption in favor of markets in the United States has foreclosed a great deal of regulation for which there is always considerable political support — regulation that not only the federal government but also state and local governments might otherwise have been required or permitted to impose. This same pro-market presumption, of course, has driven the deregulation movement and caused government to privatize activities that were publicly administered,[3] such as prisons and education. Important as these market-oriented initiatives have been, however, they have left a vast body of economic and social regulation firmly in place. Indeed, the overall quantity of regulation in the United States has probably grown during this era of deregulation because of growing public concerns about the environment and public health, access to medical providers, occupational health and safety, discrimination, immigration, pensions, land use, and many other regulated activities. Most current regulatory reform efforts are concerned with this body of existing, pending, and future regulation.

This section discusses how regulatory reformers in the United States have attempted to employ legal techniques, rules, and institutions in order to improve the quality of regulation — not to eliminate it. By using the question-begging word "quality" here, I mean to call attention to the fact that regulation, which assumes many different forms and operates in many different policy domains, also operates with different goals, justifications, and constraints. A given regulatory program, however, is likely to be concerned with one or a few but not all of these goals. Moreover, reforms must be tailored to the goals and characteristics of particular regulatory programs and to the nature of the markets with which the regulations are concerned.

For these reasons, it may be useful to distinguish these goals briefly before I proceed to discuss the legal instruments used to improve regulatory quality. Some regulatory regimes seek to increase the efficiency (as commonly understood by economists) of an externality-generating activity by ensuring that actors consider all relevant costs (and benefits). Alternatively, or in addition, they may be designed to reduce health or other risks, regardless of externalities; to control monopoly, oligopolistic, or monopsony market power or the effects of such power; to protect firms or industries from competition; to allocate resources thought to be too scarce and precious to be left to unregulated markets; to facilitate the functioning of markets by improving information or by redressing inequalities of bargaining power; to conscript private actors into the government's law enforcement efforts; to prevent insolvency or increase public confidence in markets; to further substantive equality; to advance other distributional goals (for example, regionalism); to allocate resources and authority among different levels of government; and to increase public participation or procedural fairness. This long list of regulatory purposes, moreover, is far from complete.

In pursuit of these goals — but also in due recognition of their elusiveness — reformers have devised many specific legal strategies or techniques that are designed to improve regulatory effectiveness, that is, the ability or propensity of a regulatory program to achieve its goals, whatever they may be. I shall briefly discuss 12 of these strategies or techniques, in no particular order: public remedies, private litigation, public advocates, information disclosure, improved regulatory information, gatekeepers, market testing, antitrust law, private regulation, public auction of regulatory rights, private trading of regulatory obligations, and enhancement of the credibility of regulatory commitments. This list, of course, is not an exhaustive set of regulation-imposing approaches.

Public Remedies

Regulatory statutes almost invariably provide for criminal and civil penalties for regulatory violations. The agency's arsenal of sanctions, which usually require it to obtain a court decree enforcing the administrative order, may include fines, imprisonment (for serious, intentional violations), loss of licenses and other regulatory rights, and administrative penalties. The statute may lodge the power to prosecute in the agency, in the Department of Justice, or in some combination of authorities, often leading to disputes about enforcement strategies and priorities. Indeed, such disputes commonly occur even *within* a single department or agency.

The argument for public remedies, of course, is that they enable the government to use public power to vindicate public rights by compelling social actors to comply with the regulations. Such remedies are especially important when the putative beneficiaries of the regulatory program are relatively powerless and when their private remedies would take a non-monetary form or would be so limited that private contingent fee lawyers would be unlikely to represent them. Public enforcement, however, is often criticized as weak, dilatory, unimaginative, and politicized by the "capture" of the regulatory agency by the regulated industry. Hence, the case for augmenting public remedies with private remedies.

Private Litigation

Certain regulatory schemes are enforceable through private individuals, groups, or firms seeking money damages (compensatory and, in some cases, punitive) or some form of injunctive relief. To establish this remedy, the legislature must provide for the private "cause of action" in the statute, or the courts must find such a remedy by implication from the statute. After a brief period during the early 1970s when federal courts found implied causes of action in many statutes, the Supreme Court in *Cort v. Ash* and subsequent cases in effect imposed a presumption against implied private causes of action, leaving to Congress the policy choice of whether to create such a remedy (Mashaw, Merrill, and Shane 1998, 1113-1226; Stewart and Sunstein 1982).

As a policy matter, the principal argument in favor of private causes of action is that they can supplement the regulatory agency's limited enforcement resources and enable the intended beneficiaries of regulation to circumvent a passive or "captured" agency and enforce regulatory obligations through the courts. The principal arguments against them are that the legislature and the expert regulatory agency are in the best positions to select the optimal level and pattern of enforcement, while private enforcers pursuing their self-interest may distort these regulatory choices and priorities and actually weaken regulatory effectiveness in the process. In addition, enforcing regulation through a diverse, decentralized system of federal courts will tend to increase inconsistencies in the applicable legal rules and hence magnify regulatory uncertainty. (This objection can sometimes be met, as it is under the Voting Rights Act, by requiring private litigants to bring their claims in a single court in which the agency also litigates.) Private litigation through the courts may also alter the balance of constitutionally separated powers among the three branches in the development of regulatory principles.

Public Advocates

Some jurisdictions create offices of public counsel, ombudsmen, or public advocates in an effort to magnify the voices of interests that would not otherwise be adequately represented, perhaps because of organizational costs, free rider problems, and other reasons well discussed in the public choice literature. The statutory powers of these advocates vary considerably, as do the definitions of the interests that they are supposed to represent. Some of these agencies are limited to processing citizen complaints, while others are authorized to conduct investigations, obtain information from agencies, testify at legislative and administrative hearings, participate as a party to regulatory proceedings, seek judicial review of agency decisions, and have an opportunity to review regulatory actions before they become final. Most are required to represent the "public interest" — citizens, ratepayers, or consumers, generally. I am unaware of any rigorous evaluation of the effect of public advocacy organizations on regulatory outcomes, although anecdotal reports testify to their occasional influence.

Information Disclosure

Increasingly, regulatory reformers turn to information disclosure as a remedy for consumer ignorance. This, they hope, will reduce search costs by facilitating comparisons among competing products and services, thereby maximizing consumer choice. Proponents view this technique as a means of improving the functioning of consumer markets, perhaps reducing or eliminating the need for command-and-control regulation, which is widely recognized as inefficient and ineffective.

In recent years, reformers have extended disclosure, a core strategy of securities regulation since 1933, to many other policy areas. Examples include information about the rates and performance of health care providers, lawyers, and other professionals; consumer loan interest rates; insurance premiums; auto leasing terms; brokerage rates; auto fuel efficiency; toxic chemicals; home purchase settlement charges; and unit prices in grocery stores. With the advent of the Internet and other low-cost technologies that facilitate the aggregation, dissemination, and analysis of information, reformers have advanced proposals to adopt new disclosure requirements and to refine old ones. Some important prospective applications include political campaign contributions and auto dealers' costs and sale prices. More conventional information disclosure requirements, such as those for pharmaceutical labeling and warning labels on cigarettes, alcohol, and other consumer products, have generated an enormous volume of product liability litigation. Judicially imposed disclosures by health-care providers have created a common law right of informed consent that sometimes augments patients' medical malpractice claims (Schuck 1994).

Improved Regulatory Information

In a variety of ways, regulators constantly seek to enhance the quality and quantity of the information that they need to identify and define regulatory problems, lay out alternative approaches, prescribe specific solutions, and monitor outcomes. Efforts to increase public participation take many different forms and are intended in part to increase and diversify the flow of information, values, and perspectives to the regulators.

Perhaps the most systematic information-improving technique favored by many regulatory reformers, especially economists, is cost-benefit analysis (or its less demanding cognate, cost-effectiveness analysis), discussed above (Crandall et al. 1997). However, many consumer, environmental, and other interest groups bitterly oppose it on a number of methodological and other grounds, particularly as a criterion for health and safety regulation. Government agencies sometimes criticize it as well on grounds either of principle or practice (U.S. General Accounting Office 1999).

Many, although certainly not all, objections to cost-benefit analysis might be met by introducing more realistic assumptions about the cognitive capacities and behavioral patterns of individuals facing uncertain choices involving remote risks. A number of U.S. economists and legal scholars are engaged in a wide-ranging effort to refine the conventional law and economics analysis by drawing on experimental and other empirical evidence about the ways in which ordinary people actually make decisions under conditions of uncertainty. This approach, known as behavioral law and economics, brings to traditional analysis important modifications — for example, applying bounded rationality (Simon 1957, 1961) and developing such concepts as bounded willpower and bounded self-interest (Jolls, Sunstein, and Thaler 1998). Although this more behavioral approach to cost-benefit analysis is quite promising, these fresh concepts inevitably complicate regulatory policymaking by calling on regulators to consider new indeterminacies (for example, where these boundaries of rationality, will, and self-interest lie) and to make new tradeoffs (for example, between individual irrationality and governmental irrationality). Thus, it remains to be seen whether behavioral law and economics will yield significant regulatory policy payoffs that exceed those produced by the more conventional analysis.

Private Gatekeepers

In many markets, government regulators find it prohibitively costly to monitor the behavior of sellers effectively and to detect their fraudulent transactions and other legal violations, perhaps because the market is highly fragmented, highly complex, or both (as in securities sales). In such markets, however, it is sometimes possible for regulators to conscript private professionals, on whom the sellers must rely as "gatekeepers" to the market, into serving as vigilant watchdogs over their own clients by requiring them — at risk to their own professional reputations and legal status — to vouch publicly for their clients' honesty and for the accuracy of the information that the clients provide to potential buyers and to regulators. The most common examples of such gatekeepers are accountants who must certify the accuracy of tax returns, accounts, and disclosures; lawyers who must provide opinion letters about the legality of transactions; and employers who must screen potential workers for immigration status. This gatekeeping economizes on the government's own monitoring and enforcement costs but only by shifting them to private actors, altering their incentives, and necessitating monitoring of the private monitors (Kraakman 1984).

Market Testing

Regulators can also economize on monitoring and enforcement costs by using private individuals or organizations to test the market for possible legal violations. The testers, by representing, or *mis*representing, themselves as genuine buyers, can hope to elicit from the sellers their true market behaviors, thereby producing information that regulators can then employ to detect and prosecute those behaviors. This technique, which operates as a kind of random audit, is often used to detect racial or other discrimination in housing, employment, and other consumer markets, and it could readily be extended to others (Turner, Fix, and Struyk 1991).

Antitrust Law

Antitrust regulation enables both the government and private competitors to challenge the practices that produce or sustain excessive market power. This is done through regulatory promulgation of antitrust guidelines and rules, by regulatory prosecution of criminal or civil violations in administrative or judicial fora, and by private litigation by competitors or others who can demonstrate economic loss as a result of the firm's market power. In recent years, economists have expressed growing skepticism about the theoretical soundness and practical effectiveness of antitrust law, especially in light of the globalization of markets. Many antitrust regulators have come to share that skepticism, limiting their enforcement largely to horizontal mergers and other clearly anticompetitive behavior. The current controversy over the antitrust claims brought against Microsoft by federal and state prosecutors partly reflects this theoretical impasse, especially as to new telecommunications technologies (Jost 1998).

Private Regulation

Government regulators often rely on private entities to exercise some of the functions that public regulation would otherwise have to perform. The U.S. Consumer Product Safety Commission, for example, looks to private, nonprofit testing and certification organizations, such as the American National Standards Institute and the American Society for Testing and Materials to set and, to a limited extent, enforce minimum standards of safety and effectiveness for particular industries and product lines. The National Highway Traffic and Safety Administration sometimes adopts regulatory standards promulgated by private automotive engineering groups. Building codes frequently incorporate the standards established by private electrical, construction, and other groups whose members are then subject to those standards. Public regulation of hospitals and educational institutions often incorporates the standards of private accreditation groups. The legal authority to make and enforce ethical rules and standards relating to certain other practices of the legal, medical, and other professions is often delegated to professional organizations, which then "self-regulate" their members. In the early years of the Occupational Safety and Health Administration, most of the agency's important safety standards simply adopted existing standards created by private standard-setting organizations (Hamilton 1978). Regulation by the National Association of Securities Dealers (NASD) and by the various other stock exchanges also combines public regulation with substantial delegation of regulatory authority to private groups (Banner 1998).

This pervasive system of private self-regulation is subject to obvious risks of conflict of interest and other abuses, and it is often criticized for protecting the regulated industry's interests at the expense of the public interest through lax standards, self-dealing, and toothless enforcement. Nevertheless, it is widely used, as it serves a number of important public purposes. It mollifies opposition to regulation by co-opting the industry into the regulatory scheme. It draws on technical expertise and regulatory experience that the government cannot readily duplicate. And it reduces the time and public cost entailed in developing and issuing regulations.

Public Auction of Regulatory Rights

Traditionally, governments have distributed valuable regulatory rights, such as licenses and exclusive franchises, at no cost to the rights-holder, other than the costs of the application process, which can be high. Some reformers have long criticized this allocation system as economically inefficient, distributively unfair, and politically corrupt. The successful applicant receives a windfall — say, an operating license for a television station — of potentially enormous value, while the public fisc receives nothing in exchange for relinquishing it. Applicants have a strong incentive to exercise their political influence, perhaps in improper ways, in order to obtain the valuable right; those without such influence are seriously, perhaps fatally, disadvantaged. The administrative process can be very costly, especially if the application is contested; it may be protracted and can involve substantial expenditures for legal, accounting, consulting, and other services. When an applicant finally wins, the successful applicant (now rights-holder) has a reduced incentive to fulfill the conditions of licensure because renewal of an incumbent's license will be denied only if its performance is unusually poor. An additional defect of the system is that the absence of a market price conceals the right's true value.

For all these reasons, some state governments have experimented with auctions of some of these regulatory rights, especially in the areas of federally regulated telecommunications and environmental pollution. Thus, the U.S. Federal Communications Commission has auctioned off a number of broadcasting operating rights, often raising substantial revenues in the process. A number of difficulties have arisen in connection with the design and administration of these auctions, such as ensuring that there are enough bidders and that the bidders can actually come up with the cash if they are successful (Ayres and Cramton 1996). The U.S. Environmental Protection Agency (EPA) has been auctioning off emission rights under the Clean Air Act for almost a decade. And on April 1, 1998, California became the first state to permit the auctioning off of electricity as part of its novel program of deregulation of electric utilities; some 16 other states plan to follow California's lead (Salpukas 1998). The auction approach has also been proposed for more exotic policy areas, even including the allocation of human organs and immigrant visas.

Private Trading of Regulatory Obligations

Once regulators determine what the regulatory rights and duties are and initially distribute them, they can authorize the rights-holders and duty-bearers to engage in market transactions, subject to more or less constraining regulatory trading rules. The most important policy area in which this approach has been employed is the trading of emission rights initially distributed to polluters by the EPA under the Clean Air Act. While the market for emission rights has sometimes been thin, the auction approach is credited with reducing the costs of achieving a given level of emission reduction. Given this success, reformers are now proposing to permit such trading in other regulatory areas. For example, I have proposed a system for the trading of refugee protection burdens among nations under international rules and supervision (Schuck 1998, chapter 13).

Credible Regulatory Commitments

As noted earlier, a central criticism of the regulatory state is the unpredictability of its decisions and the uncertainty costs that this generates. Regulatory unpredictability, which is common if not ubiquitous in the United States, probably reflects a number of different factors: the dynamic political environment in which agencies operate; the rapid turnover of their appointed leadership; the fast-changing markets and technologies that they attempt to regulate; the relatively poor quality and provisional character of the information on which regulators must base their decisions; and the multiple, indeterminate, and conflicting nature of most agencies' policy goals.

Regulatory uncertainty is especially pernicious in policy areas in which the agency seeks to encourage the regulated entities to make large, long-term investments in technology, expansion, or infrastructure or other capital assets. This problem arises, for example, with antitrust policies whose twists, turns, and ambiguities have made it difficult for firms to know whether they can adopt certain practices or make certain decisions — often in situations in which delay is very costly. Unless the agency can make credible, durable, and enforceable commitments to adhere to a consistent regulatory policy, the entities will try to avoid these investments or will adopt costly strategies for minimizing the regulatory risks associated with uncertainty. For this reason, some reformers emphasize the need for regulators to employ techniques that clearly signal their policy commitments and make deviations from those commitments costly to the agency in political, fiscal, or other terms. Such techniques might include the agency entering into enforceable, long-term contracts with regulated entities; giving those entities fiscal or policy "hostages" that can only be released if the agency hews to a specified course; developing regulatory policy through rulemaking rather than through case-by-case adjudication; adopting bright-line rules rather than ambiguous standards; or announcing policy commitments or fiscal investments that would be politically risky for the agency to reverse (Blackmon and Zeckhauser 1992; Rossi 1998).

An inevitable feature of this approach, of course, is that it limits the agency's future flexibility — indeed, this is its very objective — and it thereby risks locking the agency into a policy that may prove to be misguided either at its inception or as a result of changing circumstances. Therefore, a prudent agency will search for the optimal balance between regulatory flexibility and predictability, which is difficult because that balance point will itself change as regulatory conditions, needs, and information change.

EXTRA-REGULATORY INSTITUTIONS AND PROCESSES

I have been describing a complex system of political economy in the United States, one that privileges markets both legally and culturally but that also integrates these markets in a multitude of ways with administrative regulation and private self-regulation in different combinations and to varying degrees in diverse policy domains. What remain to be discussed, then, are the other extra-regulatory institutions and processes that monitor, augment, and discipline this hybrid system.

In the remainder of this chapter, I consider five of the most important of these extra-regulatory institutions and processes: 1) legislative oversight; 2) an independent judiciary; 3) administrative law, including rulemaking, adjudication, and "regulatory equity"; 4) interest group competition; and 5) adversarial media. It is important here to repeat a point made at the outset: All of these institutions and processes were established and strengthened only over a long period of time and after incessant political struggle. None of them has yet fully realized the goals and ideals ascribed to them.

Legislative Oversight

Of all the world's legislative bodies, the U.S. Congress is almost certainly the most powerful. Its power is constitutionally based to some extent but is also a product of other factors: long political tradition, the U.S. party system; a history of strong, skillful, and entrepreneurial leaders; and a history of the U.S. public's deeply ingrained suspicion of concentrated authority, especially when exercised by bureaucrats.

This congressional power is manifested not only through its enactment of authorizing and appropriations legislation but also through the energetic exercise of its power to investigate, monitor, oversee, and influence the views of the key officials in the agencies and other executive branch organs. It is a striking fact that the level of congressional oversight activity appears to have kept up with the rising level of federal regulation (Strauss 1997, 969). One might imagine that congressional investigations of the executive branch would be more frequent and intense during the periods of divided government when different parties control the White House and Congress. A study by David Mayhew, however, demonstrates that this is not ordinarily true; the level of investigatory activity is unrelated to whether there is divided government (Mayhew 1991).

In part, this may be because Congress has institutionalized the oversight process. The General Accounting Office (GAO), acting at the request of its members, conducts and publishes numerous studies of agency policies, practices, and performance. The GAO, which also performs financial auditing of agencies for Congress, generally enjoys a reputation for nonpartisanship and in recent years has become one of the most powerful organizations in the federal government. Congress, interest groups, scholars, and the media avidly read its reports. In addition, Congress has established in each of the major agencies an "office of the inspector general" with considerable independence from the agency head and with a duty to inform Congress of most of its investigative findings.

Congress also conducts oversight by influencing agency leadership through its power to confirm most presidential appointees and through its staff's frequent informal interactions with agency officials. It has the right to demand from the executive branch whatever unprivileged information and in whatever form it wants, and it can enforce this right by enforcing subpoenas, threatening officials with contempt citations, and withholding funds or legal authority from the agency. Congress's influence, of course, is so notorious that disputes seldom reach that point. In almost all cases, the agency capitulates to the congressional committee or negotiates a compromise with it (Aberbach 1990). By enacting the Small Business Regulatory Enforcement Fairness Act of 1996, which requires agencies to lay every new rule before Congress for a period of time for possible disapproval before the rule takes effect, Congress has forged a new and particularly far-reaching instrument of oversight, one whose significance will be measured not by the number of rules disapproved but by the informal influence over rules that it will afford to congressional committees and staff. This approach is also exemplified by the pending Mandates Information Act, which would allow any member of Congress to raise a parliamentary objection to any bill whose provisions would impose costs of at least $100 million on private businesses, thereby cutting off debate on the bill unless the objections were immediately overruled by the chamber (Cushman 1999).

Congress often uses its oversight power as to agencies to exert indirect influence on private actors — even and perhaps especially after privatization or deregulation — with the government eager to demonstrate that relinquishing its ownership or regulatory control will not harm the public. This indirect influence may occur when a congressional committee seeks to shape an agency's enforcement agenda by pressing it to prosecute, or refrain from prosecuting, a private individual or firm neither owned nor regulated by the government. Recently, for example, Congress was angered by persistent increases in the fares charged by deregulated airlines and urged antitrust and transportation officials to investigate these practices and prosecute any anticompetitive conduct. Another example is the congressional investigation of the tobacco industry, whose products are sold in private, largely unregulated markets. This investigation, along with negotiated settlements between the industry and lawyers representing the states, produced legislative proposals to regulate its advertising, sales practices, and exposure to litigation.

Independent Judiciary

No single institution is more central to the rule of law and to the efficient functioning of markets than an independent judiciary, one in which judges purport to decide disputes on the basis of general laws rather than narrow partisan or political considerations. Judges' decisions are usually more constrained by principles, precedents, and traditions than are the decisions of legislators and bureaucrats, which tend to be more discretionary, more open-ended, and hence more unpredictable. It is especially vital that the public *thinks* that judges are independent, as this enhances the legitimacy of, and habitual compliance with, their decisions. Independence, of course, is in the eye of the beholder, but it is a continuous variable that can be measured along a number of different dimensions. For federal judges, it is encouraged by a constitutional guarantee of lifetime tenure during good behavior and undiminished salary. Perhaps more important, almost all U.S. judges, even elected ones, think of themselves and their role as independent.

Judicial independence serves the interests not only of judges and litigants who seek impartial treatment but also of legislators, bureaucrats, and special interest groups. This may seem somewhat paradoxical; after all, courts exercising judicial review often frustrate legislators' desires by, in effect, rewriting or invalidating legislation on constitutional and statutory grounds. Courts can also alter bureaucratic rules. In principle, however, independent judges act as the politicians' agents, monitoring compliance with constitutional, legislative, and bureaucratic norms. By enabling politicians and bureaucrats to make binding, durable agreements, courts help them to bargain cheaply and effectively, which is crucial to a fluid, consensual policymaking process. Indeed, public choice theorists like Richard Posner (now a distinguished judge himself) argue that by creating and maintaining an independent judiciary, lawmakers serve their own political interests by ensuring that their promises will be kept and their bargains will be enforced. "A judiciary that was subservient to the current membership of the legislature," Posner writes, "could effectively nullify, by interpretation, legislation enacted in a previous session of the legislature. Judges are less likely to do this if the terms of judicial tenure make them independent of the wishes of current legislators" (Posner 1992, 533).

Independence in judges, however, does carry some costs to policymakers. Lacking direct accountability to the public, independent judges are more likely to make, find, and interpret law according to their own political preferences — a common complaint in the United States. If their rulings rest on constitutional grounds, the legislature cannot reverse them without amending the Constitution, but even their statutory rulings, which the legislature can and often does reverse (Eskridge 1991), enjoy the status quo-reinforcing advantage of this shift in the burden of political intiative.

Administrative Law

Assuming that privatized firms and entities remain subject to regulation, the system of administrative law, applied by agencies and enforced by reviewing courts, is a central lever for controlling both bureaucratic discretion and private compliance in accordance with the rule of law. The vast, complex body of U.S. administrative law is based largely on the federal Administrative Procedure Act (APA), augmented by constitutional principles of due process. Although the daily work of regulation is dominated by informal activity and constant give-and-take between the regulator and the regulated, the APA is primarily concerned with the more formal decision-making processes through which agencies develop most of their regulatory policies (Mashaw, Merrill, and Shane 1998).

Three of these processes are especially important: adjudication, rulemaking, and what I call "regulatory equity." Agency adjudication is modeled on the judicial process. It consists of an adversary hearing presided over by an administrative law judge, and it employs trial-type evidentiary and procedural rules, albeit often in somewhat looser forms. All agency enforcement proceedings initially take this form, as do most other formal agency actions that decide the rights or duties of particular entities. Parties to agency adjudications enjoy the right to invoke judicial review, and the standard and scope of that review are usually quite broad: *de novo* review with respect to issues of law and "substantial evidence" review of the record as a whole with respect to issues of fact. In agency adjudication, the agency proceeds on a case-by-case basis that is similar in some ways to common law adjudication. Like a court, the agency is generally, but not wholly, bound in principle by its own precedents. Because the adjudication process has proved to be relatively slow, costly, narrow, often unrepresentative, and inflexible in developing regulatory policy, most agencies prefer to proceed through rulemaking when possible.

Indeed, one of the major thrusts of regulatory reformers during the 1960s and 1970s was to encourage or even require agencies to develop more of their policies through rulemaking rather than through the case-by-case adjudication that most of them were emphasizing. Reformers maintained that rulemaking has many advantages as a policy-making instrument. It would be quicker, cheaper, more expert, more participatory, more visible and legally transparent, better informed, less "lawyerized" and "judicialized," and more oriented to the pursuit of broad policy considerations. Modeled on the legislative process, "informal" rulemaking is the most important form of agency rulemaking directed at the development of rules of general applicability. ("Formal" rulemaking, which is more adjudicative in character, is primarily reserved for ratemaking.)

An agency usually initiates informal rulemaking by publishing a notice of proposed rulemaking that briefly summarizes the nature and purpose of the rules that the agency intends to promulgate, sets forth the text of the proposed rule, and invites the public to submit detailed written comments on it. Sometimes, the agency will also convene a legislative-type hearing in which members of the public may appear to testify as live witnesses but usually without cross-examination. The agency, having considered these public reactions, may modify its proposed rule and invite another round of public comments before publishing its final rule. Interested parties who are dissatisfied with the final rule may seek judicial review before it goes into effect or can be enforced against them. As the legislation analogy implies, the reviewing court's standard is usually more deferential for review of the agency's rule than in adjudication. The rule presumably is a product of the agency's expertise, and assuming that the rule is not legally defective, the court will ordinarily uphold it unless its policy is found to be "arbitrary and capricious."

Despite the greater deference that reviewing courts are supposed to pay to rules that agencies develop through informal rulemaking, some courts have been so exacting that the agencies have found even rulemaking too slow, costly, vulnerable to judicial second-guessing, and otherwise burdensome for effective policymaking. As a result, they have often turned to other, more informal processes or even returned to case-by-case adjudication. Unfortunately, however, these alternative processes lack many of the virtues of rulemaking and entail many problems of their own (Mashaw and Harfst 1990).

What is desired, of course, is an approach to policymaking that draws on the strengths of both rules and adjudication while avoiding their limitations.[4] At least since Aristotle defined different conceptions of justice, decisionmakers have understood that general rules and individual case-by-case adjudications possess competing advantages and disadvantages as instruments for achieving justice. To vastly oversimplify, rules are more hard-edged and clear-cut; they usually provide more advance notice, guidance, and certainty both to those who are subject to them and to those who must apply them in specific cases. Depending on their generality, rules also tend to resolve more cases than adjudication does; hence, they can be an efficient way to order behavior. However, rules suffer from limitations of form, knowledge, comprehensiveness, and articulation. In contrast, adjudication tends to be more contextual and highly fact-sensitive, allowing the official to tailor decisions to the special circumstances of particular cases. However, decisions from adjudication provide less guidance for the generality of cases than rules do.

In Anglo-American law, the highly distinctive courts and doctrines of "law" and "equity" were separated in order to capture these two competing conceptions of justice. The separate systems of law and equity evinced a recognition not only that each possesses virtues that the other lacks but also that attempting to combine these different conceptions in one system could end up undermining both of them. Nevertheless, the ideal policy-making system would be one that somehow managed to provide clear and coherent direction in the generality of cases while also remaining responsive to the unique and compelling equities of individual situations.

Elsewhere, I have called this the ideal of "regulatory equity" and have analyzed its nature, the various forms through which it can be pursued, its institutionalization in a particular federal agency, and its relationship to four cognate techniques that are designed to make rule-based systems fairer by increasing their responsiveness to special circumstances: discretion, judicial equity, agency adjudication, and an exceptions process (Schuck 2000, Chapter 5).

Interest Group Competition

Regulation in a post-privatization environment entails a complex system of competition among special interest groups, including government bureaucracies, regulated firms, industry associations, suppliers, employee groups, consumer organizations, and specialized media. To what extent does this group competition produce policy outcomes that are in the public interest?

Beginning with James Madison's justly famous Federalist 10, mainstream democratic theory has vilified special interest groups. The usual critiques emphasize their narrowness of motive and vision, their unfair advantages in the political process, and their promotion of inefficient and inequitable public policies. I have argued that, as applied to the United States, this negative assessment is false or at least dangerously incomplete and that special interest groups have improved the effectiveness of the American polity (Schuck 2000, Chapter 7).

Adversarial Media

The role and public responsibilities of the media are heightened in a post-privatization world. In the United States, at least, the media enjoy very broad access to public records, proceedings, meetings, and decisions as a matter of legal right (for example, under the First Amendment, the Freedom of Information Act, the Government in the Sunshine Act, the Federal Advisory Committee Act, and state law counterparts) and as a matter of political cultural tradition. However, media access to the transactions of private individuals or groups largely depends on the private parties' willingness to relinquish their privacy and agree to media scrutiny. As previously public functions are increasingly performed by private entities, this scrutiny will become essential to public understanding and assessment of those privatized activities, indeed to the very legitimacy of the privatization project itself.

Although U.S. citizens often denounce the media for assuming what appears to be an adversarial stance toward the public and private institutions on which they report, this stance, on balance, serves the public well. Almost all powerful decisionmakers and institutions wish to avoid public monitoring and criticism of their activities. Only aggressive media that are by nature suspicious of power holders possess both the incentives and the skills to penetrate the shell of privacy and to ferret out the information that the public needs to determine where its interests lie. The media are themselves powerful institutions that prefer secrecy to public exposure, a fact that underscores the importance of the ancient conundrum, "Who will watch the watchmen?"

To discharge their public duty effectively, the media must be fiercely independent — not only of the government but also of the private power centers that they must scrutinize. Industry publications are often dependent on the firms they cover for advertising, subscriptions, patronage, and news. Hence, they may not be as aggressive as their public responsibilities demand. In a privatized environment, some other means must be devised to develop independent monitors of private activities about which the public needs to be informed. Legal rights of access to those activities are essential, but those rights are meaningless without the institutionalization of the monitoring and reporting functions. In the United States, responsibility for these functions is increasingly being shared by public institutions, private media organizations, and nontraditional "new media" spawned by the Internet, including informal chat groups and individual watchdogs.

CONCLUSION

B ased on the U.S. experience, a democratically accountable, legally controlled regulatory regime in a post-privatization environment will require a private law that scrupulously defines and enforces property rights. It will also require a public law that creates the appropriate mix of market and regulatory solutions to social problems (Schuck 2000, Chapter 13). Where the government chooses a regulatory solution, it must devise regulatory mechanisms and procedures that are fair, efficient, participatory, and subject to the rule of law. This means establishing political and legal institutions — such as legislative oversight, an independent judiciary, and a body of administrative law — that can monitor and discipline the regulators. It also means protecting social institutions, such as private interest groups and an adversarial media, that can supply regulators with the social intelligence and political legitimacy that they will need for effective governance.

Notes

1. This chapter also appears under the same title in Peter H. Schuck, 2000, *The Limits of Law: Essays on Democratic Governance* (Boulder, Colo.: Westview Press). While the substance of the chapter is the same in both books, this version reflects suggestions from the volume editor and the academic editorial style of the North-South Center Press at the University of Miami.

2. For a recent journalistic account of the problems of a privatized electric utility industry in Brazil, see Moffett 1998.

3. Privatization in the United States has proceeded in many different areas of public activity, often in a piecemeal or experimental fashion. For a recent journalistic review of these efforts, see Wessel and Harwood 1998, which discusses the privatization of uranium production, health care, airports, foster care placement, prisons, highways, schools, fire departments, sanitation and janitorial services, social services, welfare eligibility screening, and even a government personnel recruitment agency purchased and privatized by its former employees.

4. The remainder of the discussion in this section draws heavily on Schuck 1984.

References

Aberbach, Joel. 1990. *Keeping A Watchful Eye: The Politics of Congressional Oversight.* Washington, D.C.: The Brookings Institution.

Ayres, Ian, and Peter Cramton. 1996. "Pursuing Deficit Reduction Through Diversity: How Affirmative Action at the FCC Increased Auction Competition." *Stanford Law Review* 48: 761-815.

Banner, Stuart. 1998. "The Origin of the New York Stock Exchange, 1791-1860." *Journal of Legal Studies* 27: 113-140.

Blackmon, Glenn, and Richard J. Zeckhauser. 1992. "Fragile Commitments and the Regulatory Process." *Yale Journal of Regulation* 9:73-105.

Crandall, Robert W., Christopher DeMuth, Robert W. Hahn, Robert E. Litan, Pietro S. Nivola, and Paul R. Portney. 1997. *An Agenda for Federal Regulatory Reform.* Washington, D.C.: American Enterprise Institute for Public Policy Research and The Brookings Institution.

Cushman, John H. 1999. "House Passes Bill to Curb Laws that Impose Costs on Businesses." *New York Times,* February 11: A25.

Eskridge, William N. 1991. "Overriding Supreme Court Statutory Interpretation Decisions." *Yale Law Journal* 101: 331-455.

Hahn, Robert W. 1999. *Regulatory Reform: Assessing the Government's Numbers.* Working Paper 99-6. July. Washington, D.C.: AEI-The Brookings Institution Joint Center for Regulatory Studies.

Hamilton, Robert W. 1978. "The Role of Nongovernmental Standards in the Development of Mandatory Federal Standards Affecting Safety or Health." *Texas Law Journal* 56: 1329-1484.

Hansmann, Henry B. 1980. "The Role of Nonprofit Enterprise." *Yale Law Journal* 89: 835-901.

Jolls, Christine, Cass R. Sunstein, and Richard Thaler. 1998. "A Behavioral Approach to Law and Economics." *Stanford Law Journal* 50: 1471-1550.

Jost, Kenneth. 1998. "The Microsoft Antitrust Case." *CQ Researcher* (June): 1-2.

Kraakman, Reinier H. 1984. "Corporate Liability Strategies and the Legal Controls." *Yale Law Journal* 93: 857-898.

Mashaw, Jerry L., and David L. Harfst. 1990. *The Struggle for Auto Safety.* Cambridge, Mass: Harvard University Press.

Mashaw, Jerry L., Richard A. Merrill, and Peter M. Shane. 1998. *Administrative Law: The American Public Law System,* 4th ed. St. Paul, Minn: West Group.

Mayhew, David R. 1991. *Divided We Govern: Party Control, Lawmaking, and Investigations, 1946-1990.* New Haven, Conn.: Yale University Press.

Melnick, R. Shep. 1994. *Between the Lines: Interpreting Welfare Rights.* Washington, D.C.: The Brookings Institution.

Moffett, Mark. 1998. "Sour Juice." *The Wall Street Journal,* April 27: A1.

Posner, Richard A. 1992. *An Economic Analysis of Law,* 4th ed. Boston: Little, Brown & Co.

Posner, Richard A. 1997. "The Rise and Fall of Administrative Law." *Chicago-Kent Law Review* 72: 953-963.

Rossi, Jim. 1998. "The Irony of Deregulatory Takings." *Texas Law Review* 77:297-320.

Rubin, Paul H. 1993. *Tort Reform by Contract.* Washington, D.C.: AEI Press.

Salpukas, Agis. 1998. "Deregulation of Utilities in California." *The New York Times,* April 2: D4.

Schuck, Peter H. 1984. "When the Exception Becomes the Rule: Regulatory Equity and the Formulation of Energy Policy Through an Exceptions Process." *Duke Law Journal* 1984: 163-300.

Schuck, Peter H. 1994. "Rethinking Informed Consent." *Yale Law Journal* 103:899-959.

Schuck, Peter H. 1997. "Against (and For) Madison: An Essay in Praise of Factions." *Yale Law and Policy Review* 15: 553-597.

Schuck, Peter H. 1998. *Citizens, Strangers, and In-Betweens: Essays on Immigration and Citizenship.* Boulder, Colo.: Westview Press.

Schuck, Peter H. 2000. *The Limits of Law: Essays on Democratic Governance.* Boulder, Colo.: Westview Press.

Simon, Herbert A. 1957. *Models of Man.* New York: John Wiley & Sons.

Simon, Herbert A. 1961. *Administrative Behavior.* New York: The Macmillan Co.

Stewart, Richard B., and Cass R. Sunstein. 1982. "Public Programs and Private Rights." *Harvard Law Review* 95: 1193-1322.

Strauss, Peter L. 1997. "Presidential Rulemaking." *Chicago-Kent Law Review* 72: 965-986.

Turner, Margery A., Michael Fix, and Raymond J. Struyk. 1991. *Opportunities Denied, Opportunities Diminished: Racial Discrimination in Hiring.* Washington, D.C.: Urban Institute Press.

U.S. General Accounting Office. 1999. "Analysis of OMB's Reports on the Costs and Benefits of Federal Regulation." (GAO/GGD-99-59): 1-76.

Wessel, David, and John Harwood. 1998. "Selling Entire Stock!" *The Wall Street Journal,* May 14: A1.

CHAPTER 3

Transaction Costs, Politics, Regulatory Institutions, and Regulatory Outcomes

ANTONIO ESTACHE AND DAVID MARTIMORT

INTRODUCTION

With the wave of infrastructure privatization that has spread throughout the world, many countries are working to create new regulatory institutions to monitor the behavior and performance of their newly privatized infrastructure monopolies. There is little conceptual work on the optimal design of these new institutions. A review of the work on organizational design that grew with developments in principal-agent theory in the 1980s should improve our understanding of the design of regulatory institutions and suggest some policy lessons. In this literature, regulation is generally viewed as a game between various players with different degrees of knowledge and information required to make the choices that lead to the efficient and fair allocation of resources. Analysis of the incentive problems underlying these games provides some useful lessons on the optimal design of regulatory regimes, but this is not enough. We also need to improve our understanding of the internal organization of government to assess the importance of the institutions responsible for implementing regulatory regimes.

To progress in this direction and to provide better analytical support for practitioners' recommendations, we have to move away from the standard normative approach that has been the cornerstone of public sector economics. In the standard normative context, the government has generally been viewed as a single entity with a clear objective function (the maximization of social welfare), a large set of possible policy tools, and a perfect ability to commit.[1] Refocusing this perspective on regulatory transactions also is not enough. Analysis should extend to the internal organization of a government.

Understanding incentive problems in regulation requires, in the perspective suggested by Ronald Coase (1937) and developed by Oliver Williamson (1975; 1985), recognizing that the organization of hierarchies is the result of a minimization of transaction costs.[2] Applying *transaction cost* theory to policy would begin by isolating the transaction costs. The first transaction costs we will look at depend at once on the extent of the information problem faced by a government and on how broad a scope governments have in relying on the market to implement regulatory responsibilities. For instance, the right to regulate an industry cannot be sold to outsiders. Yet, as the state exerts regulatory rights, aspects of this responsibility — among them, auditing and detailed studies leading to rate or price-cap revisions — sometimes are subcontracted.

A second set of transaction costs deals with difficulties in writing fully contingent contracts. Contracts often cover only a finite length of time and are not necessarily binding to future generations and future governments. A renegotiation of administrative and incentive costs often results. Moreover, a unified, centralized government body ruling the economy in its entirety does not exist. Politics is, at its core, competition among the several principals involved in public decisionmaking. As noted by Terry Moe (1986) and James Q. Wilson (1989), bureaucrats are subject to a multitude of influences and regulatory rights, and often several agencies share work on an issue.[3]

Further, no government intervention occurs without an attempt by coalitions to manipulate its outcome. Regulatory contracts and institutions have to account for the possibility of a capture of the bureaucracy by interest groups. (The word "capture" means control or influence.)

Our thesis is this: *In taking transaction costs into account, structures and processes will affect regulatory outcomes and, hence, should be recognized explicitly in the design of incentive-based regulation.* The *structures* that affect the regulatory outcome include the distribution of regulatory rights among different levels of the government, the objectives given to agencies, and the voting procedures used to elect political principals, all of which influence regulatory decisions.[4] This is not recognized by the normative approach to public sector economics. The *processes* that matter to regulatory outcomes include the timing of government intervention, the setting of the length of term and the span of control of different regulatory bodies, and the design of communication channels within the regulatory hierarchy. A failure to address these influences is bound to overestimate or underestimate the effective impact of incentive-based regulation on regulatory outcomes.

The following sections of the paper explain more clearly how structure and processes matter to regulatory outcomes. The second section sets up the stages of our analysis. It describes the four-layer hierarchy (voters-political principals-regulators-regulated agents) that has been the fundamental focus of New Regulatory Economics so far. At each of these layers, transaction costs can influence the optimal design of the organization of the government. The rest of the paper demonstrates how the main types of transaction costs can influence this design. The third section describes the government failures that arise from contract incompleteness. The fourth section proposes possible solutions to each of these failures, beginning with the observation that structures and processes matter. The point of this section is to show how different forms of contract incompleteness may countervail each other. The fifth section concludes the paper by developing some applications.

A STYLIZED MULTI-LAYER VIEW OF THE REGULATORY PROCESS IN RESTRUCTURED INFRASTRUCTURE

Restructuring processes in infrastructure generally leaves monopolistic providers in the distribution of electricity, gas, and water. In the absence of any regulation of price, quantity, and quality, monopolists would restrict output and would charge consumers an excessively high price. Regulation is needed to reach a higher level of social welfare, but consumers themselves cannot accomplish this directly because of the free-rider problem in collective action (Olson 1965).[5] Regulation must therefore be designed and enforced by institutional regulators who act in the name of voters and who are limited in the number of tasks they can handle because of bounded rationality problems (Simon 1957, 1961). The control of service quality and of price structure as well as the decision regarding rate of return on investment is left to a utility regulator.

This control is imperfect. Regulators face information asymmetries in their relationships with the firms they regulate. They do not know the exact technologies of a firm or the elasticity of its demand. They have little knowledge about the internal incentive structure of a firm and the contracts that a firm may have with nonintegrated input suppliers. Regulators' tasks may be limited; regulators also may have only limited instruments to carry out their functions. For instance, the Environmental Protection Agency (EPA) in the United States is limited to regulating emissions of only some chemical products, although in principle it could use more fine-tuned incentives to limit overall pollution damages.

Control imperfections also stem from the way that regulators are accountable for their acts not directly to consumers but to "political" principals, who may belong to the legislative or the executive branch of the government. Regulators can be endowed with a federal or a state mandate, and they can have tenures with quite different lengths. Political principals have difficulties in controlling regulators who are generally at an informational advantage because of their expertise or simply because of their access to historical information.[6] In most countries, the control exercised by the national legislature on these regulators is indirect. There is a system of committees and subcommittees representing various constituencies that is subject to various influences. In some cases (as in the United States), part of the control is not under the legislature directly but under a government budget office that implements budgetary control of these agencies.

Political principals themselves can hardly be put on explicit incentive schemes for maximizing social welfare because of the free-riding problem that voter-consumers would then face in controlling these political entrepreneurs.[7] Instead, consumers use the rather rough and imperfect procedures inherent in voting to impose some accountability on the political principals. Only career considerations and the threat of political takeovers can adjust the political decisionmakers' incentives. It should be noted that the political arena is not a perfectly competitive market. Enormous fixed costs must be incurred before entering this market. This reduces the scope for an efficient control of the incumbents.[8] Moreover, voters are often only imperfectly informed regarding the effort and efficiency of the political decisionmaker. They must, therefore, rely on rather imperfect measures of their own level of satisfaction in deciding on their voting strategy.[9]

Each layer of government — voters, political principals, regulators, and regulated agents — can be viewed as a principal-agent relationship with its own informational problem. The simplified overview of society that we get from this picture is that society and its government are based on a sequence of vertical contracts that solve, more or less easily, a number of agency problems. Loss of control results as incentives trickle down the hierarchy through a system of delegation. However, control problems in government are not only vertical; as discussed in the introduction, many peculiarities come from government's multiprincipal nature.[10] Regulators share the control of the firm. Political principals share the control of the regulatory policies not only with each other at a given date but also with their successors. Legislatures are divided into numerous committees and subcommittees, each having its own objectives and each trying to influence the bureaucracy.[11] Moreover, the bureaucracy itself is not a unified body. Often agencies and bureaus compete with one another for resources, and at the same time bureaucrats compete for influence within a given industry.

With this complex description of the regulatory organization in mind, we can move to an analysis of the different kinds of contractual incompleteness that impede the efficiency of the government's intervention.

TRANSACTION COSTS IN GOVERNMENT ORGANIZATIONAL STRUCTURE

The overall organization of government can be seen as a nexus of more or less explicit contracts linking stakeholders. Without a grand, overall, complete regulatory contract, many opportunities for hidden gaming occur, each game bringing its own set of transaction costs. The contractual externalities that arise from the incompleteness of regulatory contracts is a reality that departs from the more idealized view of society in which unified control is feasible. This section reviews the relevance to the institutional design of transaction costs that stem from three types of government failure: lack of government commitment, the multiprincipal nature of government, and the excessive discretion of the various decisionmakers in the regulatory process.

Lack of Commitment and the Need for Renegotiation

Because all future contingencies may not be foreseen when the government proposes a regulatory contract to the firm — and because new information becomes available as the regulator learns about earlier realizations of the contractual targets — renegotiation of the contract matters and can improve ex post efficiency. This may, however, lead to some counterintuitive results for practitioners. To understand why, it is useful to compare situations with and without full commitment.

Under full commitment, the optimal regulation of a public utility repeats the way the optimal static contract deals with the fundamental tradeoffs between efficiency and rent extraction. To reduce the costly informational rent that efficient firms can obtain by mimicking less efficient firms when both choose from the same menu of cost targets and lump sum transfers, regulators distort the cost and production targets to make less efficient values less attractive to an efficient firm.

Without full commitment, to improve second-period efficiency, the regulator is willing to renegotiate the regulatory contract after the first period of the relationship, when the regulator knows more about the private information of the firm and is willing to renegotiate the contract. This search for increases in ex post efficiency may, however, introduce some perverse incentives from an ex ante point of view. Anticipating an increase in the power of incentives later on, efficient agents may behave less than optimally in the earlier periods of the relationship. In particular, they tend not to reveal their information, and the revelation of information is further slowed down in the bureaucratic hierarchy.[12] This is where the counterintuitive results show. For instance, rates of return may best be increased following a good performance. Yet, regulated firms may best be allowed to plan new investments or to change their prices as new information on demand is learned. Otherwise, a public utility, anticipating that a regulator will use the information revealed in the first period of the regulatory relationship to readjust the contractual terms, has fewer incentives to reveal any information that can help improve the rent extraction versus efficiency tradeoff ex post.

The main point is that incentive compatibility constraints are hardened by the mere possibility of renegotiation. As a result, inefficient choices are made in the first period: choices related to transaction-specific asset problems (assets that might not be of use under future contracts); choices of inefficient technologies; and pricing far above marginal cost to manipulate the beliefs of the regulator about the firm's marginal cost before the renegotiation stage. More generally, the inability to commit increases the transaction costs of contracting, which is often underestimated by practitioners. These higher transaction costs may be justified by the need to retain some flexibility in order to ensure that past regulators or political principals are not allowed to bind the future of society to a given regulation. This is important because consumers' tastes may change in the future, or the political principals themselves may change after an election, and these new decisionmakers may favor other groups. Hence, society as a whole agrees on imposing limited terms for the mandates of its political principals to limit the possible intertemporal abuse of powers.[13]

The Multiprincipal Nature of Government

An important step toward assessing the real nature of the rent-extraction versus efficiency tradeoff is to consider government intervention as a result of a whole set of different principals, each with his or her own objective.[14] Jointly, these principals may have for a collective objective the maximization of the same social welfare function as that of a single benevolent regulator. However, each principal has only a limited mandate to fulfill. For instance, the EPA is concerned with protecting the environment, which is only one aspect of consumers' welfare, while a utility regulator is concerned with controlling the rates of return or with controlling the price cap and price structure of the utility. Each agency has only a partial view of the regulatory stake.[15]

The importance of this complex structure of government can be illustrated by four main themes in the literature on multiprincipal-to-agency relationships: allocative inefficiency, rent distribution and regulatory rights, the optimal levels of regulatory decentralization, and the timing and voting rights of the various agencies. These factors are all influenced by the design of regulatory institutions.

Allocative Inefficiency. Under this complex structure, the regulatory process introduces new distortions with respect to what would have been implemented under unity of command. The rent-extraction versus efficiency tradeoff that results from the regulators' interactions must capture the fact that a regulator typically does not take into account what other regulators' schemes are when he or she offers a regulatory incentive scheme. The separation of powers among regulators affects allocative efficiency.

Rent Distribution and Regulatory Rights. The noncooperative behavior of rival regulators also results in the firm's being offered excessively low-powered or excessively high-powered incentives, depending on the sets of activities that the regulators control. When several regulators control *complementary* activities of the firm, they extract too much informational rent from it, and the power of incentives tends to become excessively low.[16] Each regulator exerts a negative externality on the other. Cost-plus arrangements result from this overregulation.[17] When regulators instead control *substitute* activities, the reverse phenomenon happens as a result of regulatory competition. Regulators compete with the others to attract the agent toward the activity under their own control. The common agent can play one principal against the other to escape their global control. In equilibrium, because now a principal exerts a positive externality on the others, higher powered incentives than would have been collectively optimal are offered. Decision rules are then closer to their full information values, and allocative efficiency improves.[18] However, the firm keeps a larger amount of informational rent than what would be socially optimal.[19]

Optimal Levels of Regulatory Decentralization. The number of agencies in control of the firm and the timing of their interventions affect the outcome of this structural separation. Administrative processes and structures affect the outcome of the regulatory interventions. The larger the number of agencies controlling a given firm (permitting, subsidizing, and monitoring), the greater the inefficiency of the regulatory outcome. Indeed, an extreme version of the free-rider problem may arise when control is highly decentralized. It may not be worth allowing a project if one expects other agencies to restrict their own contributions to its financing. There is at least casual evidence in the United States that such outcomes arise.[20] The experience of the European Economic Community provides other examples in which local decisions were financed by the supranational institutions in an environment in which goals and incentives often were not compatible.

Timing and Voting Rights of Agencies. Sequential intervention of different agencies calls forth excessive rent extraction and allocative distortions that are even larger than those in the simultaneous game.[21] For instance, the Stackelberg leader position of the EPA vis-à-vis local and state agencies in designing environmental taxes weakens the case for the separation of the regulatory responsibilities on environmental issues between state and federal levels of the government. Regulation becomes extremely stringent. An interesting interpretation of these sequential timings is that the Stackelberg leader benefits somewhat from a veto right and only accepts regulations that guarantee its constituency a minimal utility. As long as the regulators have quasi-linear utility functions independent of the regulated firms' private information, the identity of the vetoing principal has no effect on the regulatory distortions. But when this assumption is rejected, the decentralization of regulatory responsibilities can lead to an optimal assignment of regulatory instruments that is also hierarchical.[22]

With an open rule system, Congress is free to amend any proposals made by a committee. This means that the regulators face multiple political principals. In this type of setting, regulatory agencies are able to exploit one of these principals against another and increase their own powers regarding the decision they are to implement. To shift the policy closer to its most preferred outcome, which turns out to be that of the median voter, the veto of the presidency is needed as an institutional option.[23]

Discretion of the Decisionmakers

In the regulatory hierarchy, discretion matters at two different levels — first, at the level of the political principal; second, at the level of the regulatory agency itself. We sometimes distinguish between formal and real authority. As discussed in Philippe Aghion and Jean Tirole (1997), real authority lies in the hands of agents implementing the final regulatory decision — in our case, the regulators and bureaucrats — although political decisionmakers are endowed with the formal authority to make public decisions. Both political and regulatory decisionmakers are important, and one must recognize both to understand how the overall design of regulatory institutions influences regulatory outcomes.

Discretion of the Political Principal. Perspectives on the political principal's discretion represent the power of interest groups and the influence of contributions as a rational system linked to an aggregate measure of society's satisfaction. Alternatively, they also represent median constituency results in a voting procedure influenced by ideology as well as direct economic interests.

The Received Theory of Frictionless Influence. A line of research commonly associated with the Chicago School of economics is often quoted by practitioners to argue the importance of political risks and discretion in the design of regulatory institutions. This line of research illustrates very clearly the idea that political principals who have some discretion regarding the set of policies that can be implemented are subject to a number of conflicting influences exerted by different pressure groups — for example, consumers, firms, and taxpayers.[24] The perspective of this line of research is that the political principal values the contributions, or the "bribes," that he or she receives from the interest groups but also considers social welfare. Contributions are needed to help political decisionmakers finance their electoral campaigns, and, further, these bribes may be purely perks. Social welfare matters because political decisionmakers have reelection concerns, and it gives an aggregate measure of the satisfaction of society.

This line of research predicts that the interest groups are powerful. Interest groups affect economic outcomes because they can circumvent the celebrated free-riding problem in collective action. The outcome of the game is almost immediate:

Lobbies influence the policy outcome by moving the choice of policy toward their own preferred outcomes, and the political decisionmaker maximizes a welfare function that favors interest groups.[25] This research is, however, unable to assess the true reasons why free riding is less an issue for some group forming than for other group forming. The true parameters of the influence of an interest group are not characterized. Notably, nevertheless, Richard A. Posner (1976), although he does not provide a formal treatment of this issue, stresses that the force of an interest group may depend on an institutional setting. Structures matter in defining the power of a group. The main problem is that it is also difficult to see how the contract between an interest group and the political decisionmaker is more enforceable than any other contract aimed from the outset at controlling the political decisionmaker. Because it ignores the agency problem that makes the control of these political principals impossible, this line of research does not give a clear account of the role of the regulatory institutions in constraining the political principals' behavior, much as it does not give an explicit view of the different pressure groups. Hence, the frictionless influence view has little to offer in terms of specific policy advice.

Political Principals and the Distribution of Rents. An interesting alternative approach is proposed by David P. Baron (1989) and also by Jean-Jacques Laffont (1995). Although Baron and Laffont do not restrict a priori the set of instruments available to the political decisionmakers, they make explicit the assumption that the choice of the political principal is made through a voting procedure. Society is composed of voters with different preferences about the level of regulation that should be implemented. In fact, these preferences may come from ideology or may come directly from the different shares of the regulated firm that each group of voters gets individually. The regulatory choice of the median voter is implemented as a result of the voting procedure. The case to reduce discretion is that the political principal maximizes social welfare — defined not as an aggregate of the voters' utilities but as the welfare of the median voter — within the principal's constituency rather than within the society as a whole.

An important corollary of this line of research is that suboptimal contracts, such as average cost pricing or simple quotas, can now find a rationale. Although these tools are imperfect ways of transferring wealth between groups, they can be used to tie the hands of a political principal by reducing his or her discretion. However, a full endorsement of these instruments would require a better understanding of the way in which different constituencies can try to align the preferences of the political decisionmaker with their own. In other words, what is lacking is a full-fledged treatment of how campaign contributions and other forms of influence by interest groups affect the outcome of the political game and, therefore, affect the incentives of a political candidate to align his or her policy with that of an interest group. Indeed, these political principals are putting a value on reelection that may depend on the number of voters who choose them, and the voters' preferences are likely to be affected by the stringency of the regulation.[26] Another unsolved issue is the exact role institutions play in the final economic outcome. The voting procedure used to select the political principal is somewhat exogenous. Yet, it would seem important to know how districts affected differently by regulation aggregate their preferences through the voting procedure.

Discretion of the Regulators. An interest group can be active not only before the enactment of a regulatory policy, as discussed above, but also when it is implemented. In other words, interference with the regulatory process can also arise within the regulatory institution — something that practitioners tend to be very much concerned with. This concern is the main anchor to the debate on accountability, independence, and autonomy. Problems can arise from three main sources: internal versus external influences on the regulators, conflicts between the legislative powers and the bureaucracy, and the complex dynamics of bureaucratic behavior.

Internal and External Influences. Bureaucracies are the nexus of conflicting influences. Regulatory agencies are no different; they are subject particularly to the internal influence of a political principal representing the voters' interests and to the external influence of interest groups. As a result of multiple efforts to curb their behavior, the "regulator-bureaucrats" become vested in the status quo, and it becomes extremely hard to provide any incentives.[27] There are two ways to influence the bureaucrats' incentives: first, wages; second, implicit incentives or career concerns. In addition, exogenous restrictions on the set of instruments available to the different political principals controlling the bureaucracy may help to reduce the scope of the bureaucrats' action in regard to rent extraction.[28] When different principals, for instance, different committees, affect substitute activities of the bureaucrat-regulators, the bureaucrat-regulators can play one principal against the other to gain more freedom. The bureaucracy goes its own way. The solution is to increase accountability by exposing the bureaucrat and making private information on the effectiveness of the bureaucrat's behavior available. Simple institutional rules like the public release of regulatory information may allow this kind of information sharing between multiple principals. In a nutshell, regulatory processes can successfully curb the bureaucracy, and practitioners are right to emphasize this point.

Conflict between Legislative Power and the Bureaucracy. An agency problem between the political principal (the Congress) and the regulatory agencies can also create the conditions necessary for the capture of these regulators by an interest group.[29] Congress uses the agency as a monitoring system to observe signals regarding the private information of the public utility. Such discretion in the hands of the regulator gives the regulatory agency some power or, expressed differently, some real authority.[30] Indeed, by bribing the regulator, a firm could insure a misuse of the regulator's power. An individual regulator will prefer to take perks or to take a position in the industry later on rather than to obey the regulatory mandate received. Again, this is why it makes so much sense to restrict future interactions between a regulatory agency and the firms it is regulating.

This means that a regulatory contract, on top of satisfying the usual incentive constraints, must also satisfy a set of collusion-proof constraints to insure that the regulator does not misuse power. This does not come cheaply to society.[31] Communication costs in the formation of the capturing coalition or transaction costs due to the nonenforceability of side-contracts will generally prevent the regulator from getting the full informational rent of the firm. Capture can only be effective when a stake exists in concealing from the political principal information whose concealment is favorable to the regulated agent. This happens quite often, for instance, in the context of utility privatization.

The problem is that the constraints needed to avoid collusion or corruption affect the terms of the tradeoff between efficiency and rent extraction. To limit the regulator's incentives to collude with an efficient firm that earns some informational rent from regulation, the political principal has to reduce the regulatory stake further. This, however, increases distortions in production decisions above the level that might occur in a problem-free environment. Moreover, these distortions have to be greater when collusion is relatively more efficient — that is, when the transaction costs of side contracting are low. Low-powered regulation is then called for to limit the scope for collusion. Low-powered incentives indeed imply lower levels of rent for efficient types and, therefore, fewer possibilities for corrupting regulators. These low-powered incentives also correspond to the choice of more bureaucratic rules for the agency, which is given less power and less discretion. The point is that processes also matter and can be quite costly to an efficient outcome.

The Dynamics of Bureaucratic Behavior. Part of the reality of regulation is that there are side contracts between a regulator and the interest group being regulated. Since side contracts are illegal, they cannot be enforced by a court of justice.[32] The regulator is lenient with the firm as long as the regulator's prospects for getting "bribes" or future employment opportunities in the industry are high. The firm is ready to "bribe" the regulator as long as its stances remain lenient. Modeling capture by or influence of the interest group as an enforceable side contract hides some features of the dynamics of capture. David Martimort (1997b) shows that side-contract agreements become easier to enforce when the regulator is better informed about the firm or when preferences for the future of the administrative branch of the government are more pronounced than preferences for the future of the political principal. The discrepancy between the long-term objectives of the bureaucracy and those of the political principals matters and does affect the regulatory outcome. In sum, transaction costs of side-contracting are endogenous and depend on mere regulatory institutions. Again, the point is that *structures matter to regulatory outcomes*.

THE WHOLE PICTURE: TRANSACTION COSTS AT PLAY

In this section, we take a broader perspective on regulatory institutions to try to see how a more coherent design of regulatory institutions can reduce the influence on regulatory outcomes of the government failures discussed in the previous section. Following Williamson's (1985) argument regarding the theory of the firm, already applied with some success, we argue that the optimal regulatory institutions are those that minimize the overall transaction costs of contracting. To test the implications of this paradigm for the internal organization of the government, we use the results highlighted in the last section and develop the idea that playing contractual externalities against one another may help improve social welfare. This second-best approach is obviously subject to the same weaknesses as any other second-best analysis. We, nevertheless, think that this second-best approach turns out to be extremely useful for getting a richer picture of the internal organization of the government.

How to Improve Commitment?

The first step in the search for a regulatory institution that minimizes transaction costs and, hence, reduces interference with desirable regulatory outcomes is to look for an approach that guarantees a commitment by all parties involved to deliver on their responsibility. Since contracts among the firms, the regulators, and the executive and legislative powers are likely to be quite incomplete, *the specification of renegotiation rules is quite critical*, as are the systems of checks and balances discussed below.

Renegotiation Rules and Separation of Powers. A well-known result among political scientists and part of the recent folklore of the industrial organization economists is that the design of rules and processes at the renegotiation stage can improve commitment.[33] One choice is the separation of powers among different regulatory agencies. This is not something that practitioners like to recommend. Indeed, the idea of unifying regulatory responsibilities under a single umbrella institution is quite a common recommendation. Theoretical research suggests that this may not be the best strategy when commitment capacity by the government to the regulatory contract is limited or when renegotiation is a likely outcome of the reform process.

No Commitment at All. Under an extreme form of incompleteness, in which regulatory contracts are limited to cover only the current period, because of some type of constitutional constraint, for instance, Trond Olsen and Gaute Torsvick (1993a) show that it may be better to split up the control of the firm between two regulatory agencies rather than to leave all the control rights in the hands of a single omnipotent regulator.[34] Under separation, both regulators control the firm's output. As a result of complementarity between their regulatory tools, their free riding in providing incentives to the firm implies that the firm would extract excessive rent in the second period of the relationship. The firm receives excessively low-powered incentives under separation. The main benefit is that it is less valuable for an efficient firm to hide its type in the first period of the relationship. As a result, there is more information revelation in earlier periods, and total intertemporal welfare may increase. It should be clear that benefits of increased knowledge in negotiating for the second period should be traded off against the cost of the first period competition between the different agencies. In sum, the overall benefits of separation are ultimately unclear when one assesses its impact from an intertemporal point of view. The more general result is that there may be an optimal degree of decentralization in a regulatory charter, that is, an optimal number of agencies in control of a given firm. This number optimally trades off the cost of a larger static inefficiency coming from the coarser sharing of regulatory rights against the dynamic benefits of coarser sharing.[35]

Renegotiation improves ex post efficiency; however, the free-rider problem among regulatory agencies at the time of renegotiating the contract makes this ex post improvement harder to achieve.[36] Separation improves the commitment ability of the government, but there is a twist. Intertemporal welfare increases with separation only when the separation takes place at the renegotiation stage. The optimal regulatory charter requires, therefore, a cooperative offer of the regulatory contracts when regulation of a firm starts and a splitting up of the regulatory rights among various agencies at the renegotiation stage occurs. Generally, this type of optimal regulatory charter is infeasible.[37] The more important result that practitioners may want to keep in mind is that the excessive splitting of the responsibilities of regulatory agencies may be good for regulatory outcomes.

The solution may be to go for sequential moves of the regulatory decisions. For instance, the federal government may act as a leader in renegotiating regulatory contracts. Then local governments would follow by offering complementary regulations. This type of institutional framework corresponds to what is used in the Common Agricultural Policy in the European Union. In sum, the case for separation as a way to improve commitment through the precise fine-tuning of the regulatory process is an ambiguous one. Nevertheless, we believe that it has strong relevance.

Checks and Balances. The recommendation in favor of separation also comes up in discussions of checks and balances. Sometimes the lack of commitment comes from the inability to contract ex ante on a variable that provides a valuable signal of the firm's performance, one that becomes available only at the interim stage. For instance, the future profitability or product quality of a firm cannot be assessed at the time the contract is written.

Jean Tirole (1994) shows that creating different agencies, each with a specific objective function, improves commitment. Indeed, these agencies intervene differently, depending on the realizations of signals. For instance, an agency concerned with consumer's surplus intervenes following evidence that the firm will charge a high price in the future. A ministry of finance concerned with the profitability of the firm will terminate projects that turn out to have intermediate cost overruns. Allocating the right to intervene between "tough" and "soft" agencies, according to the ex post realization of the signals, readjusts the ex ante incentives of the firm and improves intertemporal welfare. In a similar vein, Tracy R. Lewis and David E. Sappington (1991) analyze the intertemporal separation of powers between two short-lived principals. They take the allocation of tasks between both regulators as given but show that characteristics of this separation — for example, preventing firms from transferring money from one period to the other when control shifts to a different regulator — may be helpful in protecting the nonverifiable investment of the regulated firm.

Tirole (1994) and Lewis and Sappington (1991) construct a system of checks and balances in which different agencies react differently to the information they may receive. The design of the objective function of the regulators then becomes an important tool both to control the regulated firm and to readjust the incentives of the regulator to intervene. The discussion of the specific objectives is, however, something practitioners seldom deal with explicitly.

Elected Political Principals and Independent Agencies. The above discussion focused only on the case of a benevolent principal unable to commit to an intertemporal behavior. The splitting of the social welfare function among several agencies was helpful, but things become different in the case of a political principal. Elected political principals cannot commit society to a particular regulation in the future. However, when they have a majority, they often can create independent agencies and relinquish some of their powers and responsibilities to them. Of course, the threat of losing future elections makes them create independent agencies that will still represent their constituencies even in the case of political defeat. Examples abound in regulation, but perhaps the most striking one belongs to the macro-economics arena. The choice of relinquishing the control of monetary policy to an independent central bank is a way for a government in favor of a monetarist policy to commit future generations to it even when future governments might be more willing to allow higher levels of inflation.

We are not aware of any formal theoretical analysis along these lines in the framework of the New Regulatory Economics. Nevertheless, we conjecture that relinquishing regulatory rights to independent agencies may have social benefits, at least from an ex post point of view. More groups are represented in the regulatory decisions that are taken ex post, and future minorities are somewhat protected. The ex post regulatory outcome is close to what would have been chosen by a benevolent regulator. However, when a non-benevolent government gives a regulatory agency objective functions similar to its own, the government creates its own competition. As we have shown earlier, this competition entails inefficiency. Competition among government bodies extracts too much rent from the constituency the government is supposed to protect. Relinquishing regulatory powers also has ex ante costs.

Credibility of Commitment to a Regulatory Charter. An important problem of the models we have just surveyed is that they assume that regulatory players interpret a commitment to creating an agency (and incurring the administrative costs that it requires) as a credible signal that the newly defined objectives and responsibilities of this agency are not going to be overruled in the future. Institutional designs have to be credible to have any bite.

The credibility of the separation between various agencies can be enforced by standard reputation-like arguments. As argued in the reputation literature, agencies, because they are long-term players, should be able to impose their most preferred regulatory outcome — that is, they should be able to render their structural separation credible. This argument is a little loose and suffers in two ways in its underpinnings: First, agencies could build reputations to improve their collective commitment abilities, and a single agency could certainly build a reputation for not renegotiating any regulatory contracts. Second, although agencies may be long-term players, bureaucrats often have limited tenures. One should understand how collective reputations could be established among cohorts of regulators, especially when they sometimes have different intrinsic preferences on the stringency of regulation.

How to Limit the Scope for Non-benevolence?

Since non-benevolence is to be expected, it seems reasonable to look for ways to limit its scope. One way of doing so is by focusing on simplicity in the instruments of regulation. We already discussed this possible remedy to nonbenevolence of political principals. Regulatory contracts could be simplified to leave less leeway to the political decisionmakers. This suggests that simple rules like constraints on the use of discretionary transfers and short-term mandates of political principals can be written as constitutional rules aimed at controlling non-benevolent principals. More generally, using instruments that are not sensitive to information, like quotas, is a way to curb non-benevolence of political decisionmakers. However, using these instruments creates other problems when contract enforcements are a problem, as is typical in many reforming countries and in environments in which information is limited.

Another way of dealing with non-benevolence, which is important in countries with an inefficient public sector in need of reform, is to figure out the optimal speed of reform. Mathias Dewatripont and Gerard Roland (1992) show that a benevolent principal willing to impose some layoffs on an industry is likely to impose these layoffs gradually rather than right away when its policy has to be accepted by a majority of voters or workers within the sector. Under unanimity, it is a well-known result from the incentive literature that the optimal policy should be implemented with full commitment.[38] Under majority rule, the political principal prefers to impose reform gradually; workers leave an industry at different dates, depending on their efficiency. By doing so, the principal learns some information about the workers' efficiency and can use it in credible threats to shift majorities in the future. The principal can impose some concessions from some groups in the majority today by threatening them with being in the minority tomorrow. Allowing the political principal to use such credible threats increases his or her bargaining power. The processes of reform are important when the political game imposes only majority voting.

Separation of Regulatory Powers as a Way to Prevent Capture

Under integration of the regulatory powers, collusion is quite efficient, and society must incur a large cost of capture. For instance, bad projects are allowed too often, and the budgetary burden on society increases. Information asymmetries between partially informed regulators and the firm they regulate weaken regulators' ability to extract advantages from the firm. Asymmetric information implicitly increases the transaction costs of capture. The overall cost of capture borne by society is diminished by introducing competition between asymmetrically informed bureaucrats.

The structural separation between different regulatory agencies can act as a commitment to prevent regulatory capture by an interest group. For instance, splitting the control rights on the firm's output between a public utility commission and an environmental protection agency helps prevent the capture of the regulatory process by the producer. Several regulatory agencies with specific missions now each control only one dimension of the overall performance of the firm. However, their incomplete knowledge about the dimensions that they do not observe directly puts them at a disadvantage vis-à-vis a firm in the collusion game. Their individual ability to extract rents from the firm is thus weakened. If the regulators were merged, they would be able to observe fully the performance of the firm, but their demands for bribes could perfectly match the supply, that is, the informational rent left to the firm if the regulator behaves in a lenient way.

The argument for separation has to be considered much more carefully than simply following the suggestions in this quick assessment. The various interactions between separation and regulatory outcomes are discussed next in some detail.

The Efficiency and Distributional Consequences of Separation. The efficiency and distributional consequences of structural separation are somewhat ambiguous. On the one hand, the interest group can escape control under separation of powers if regulators are incompetent or corrupt. This is the standard argument given by practitioners about why a public utility commission, for instance, is better than sector-specific regulators.[39] However, efficient firms can then get rents from every dimension of information observed by the regulators and can fool them more easily than regulators who do not cooperate. On the other hand, the discretion of partially informed regulators who are corrupt may justify a reduction in the individual power regulators obtain through separation. Because of the asymmetric information they face, regulators exert their individual power by trying to capture benefits from the industry only when the industry is inefficient. Hence, only the informational rent of the less efficient firms needs to be reduced to diminish the discretion of regulators who may be corrupt. Therefore, less efficient firms unambiguously lose from the structural separation of powers, and this is how regulatory outcomes improve under the separation of regulatory powers. Inefficient firms may suffer from the more bureaucratic rules followed by each single agency to reduce the cost of collusion-proofing, yet separation argues for the use of more bureaucratic rules. The choice of communication channels and the choice of more bureaucratic rules are two complementary tools used to improve the design of the internal organization of the government. Again, structures and processes move hand in hand.

Separation and the Firm's Budget Constraints. Separation has not only ambiguous distributional consequences but also an ambiguous allocative impact. Indeed, separation may harden or soften the firm's budget constraints, depending on the extent of the adverse selection problem that the government faces. Separation may indeed call for fewer or more projects being accepted by the regulatory charter than when several agencies are used to help the decision-making process. Few projects with relatively large uncertainty and more projects with relatively little uncertainty are still allowed under separation. Rules are not too bureaucratic under integration. The single regulator under integration would have enough discretion to allow the pursuit of some bad projects. However, even if the single regulator gets captured, the stake of collusion and the cost for society remain small. As we discussed above, rules are more bureaucratic under separation, and bad projects are more likely to be stopped by a charter with several regulatory agencies.

This result is in sharp contrast with the one obtained by Dewatripont and Maskin (1995). These authors show that some form of decentralization of the rights of refinancing projects hardens the firm's budget constraint.[40] Similarly, Andrei Shleifer and Robert W. Vishny (1993) discuss how corrupt regulators holding complementary permits are able to extract an excessive amount of bribes from the firm, leading to insufficient entry to the market — that is, leading to hardening of its budget constraint.[41] In sum, the theoretical jury is still out on the impact of separation on specific regulatory outcomes. Practitioners generally have already decided against it in developing countries with limited institutional capacity.

Separation and Communication Problems. Until now, we have assumed that communications between each regulator and the principal were taking place simultaneously. The benefits of separation also exist when we allow one regulator to observe other regulators' information before deciding on the degree of collusion with the firms regulated. This hierarchical organization captures the often observed asymmetry in the role of different regulators intervening at different stages of the regulatory process. For instance, the procedures for merger control differ across countries but in general require two stages, notification and investigation, to be completed sequentially. According to Nutall and Seabright (1993), who compare the different organizations of regulation, in some countries the tasks are separate responsibilities of two distinct bodies — for example, the Director General for Fair Trading and The Monopolies and Merger Commission in the United Kingdom. In the European Union, a unique body, the Merger Task Force performs both activities. Even if one could agree with these authors and recognize that a concentration of the tasks speeds up the regulatory process, it may also involve greater costs in terms of capture. J.J. Laffont and David Martimort (1995) show that a sequential separation between regulators still helps in fighting capture. However, the gains of reducing the cost of collusion-proof constraints are only obtained vis-à-vis the first intervening agency, which is only partially informed and, therefore, at a disadvantage in the bribery game with the regulated firm. The sequential separation between the regulators comes with an asymmetry between their real authority and the level of bureaucratic procedures they follow. Regulators moving first follow more bureaucratic procedures and are entitled to less formal authority than regulators moving last. Again, structure and processes matter and affect the regulatory outcome.

The Life Cycle of Regulatory Agencies and Transaction Costs. Institutions affect the efficiency of the collusion game between the interest groups and the regulatory agencies. The key to getting a richer vision of the capture transaction is to see it as a self-enforceable side-contract between the regulator and the firm being regulated. This is the natural theoretical framework for analyzing such collusion, and it is the most realistic way, as the formalism of regulatory processes and rules is often dominated by less formal processes and rules.[42] This occurs because there is no court of justice to enforce these illegal agreements and the parties must rely on "words of honor" for fulfillment of their agreements. The common view argues that the repetition of the regulatory game is good because it allows for fewer opportunistic behaviors by the regulator.[43] This is, in fact, not the case in a repeated game environment in which the regulator is always the same. The regulator's expectations regarding future advantages deriving from friendly behavior toward the industry and the industry's expectation of lenient behavior from the regulator are the glue that allows these illegal agreements to be self-enforcing.[44]

These informational rents, which will be under the control of the regulator in the future, create the stakes for starting collusive relationships immediately. The higher the stakes in the future, the higher the cost of capture today. Since more and more opportunities for collusive behavior may emerge over time, the optimal regulatory charter calls for smaller and smaller regulatory stakes as time goes on. Therefore, more bureaucratic rules should be imposed as agencies grow older. In other words, the bureaucratization of government intervention is an unavoidable outcome.[45] Agencies follow a so-called "life cycle." They begin by behaving in the public interest and then become increasingly influenced by interest groups. They then become vested in the status quo and overly bureaucratized (Bernstein 1955).

This life cycle view of regulatory agencies' modeling of capture also gives firmer theoretical foundations to the Laffont and Tirole (1993, Chapter 13) model of capture, which assumes enforceable side-contracts, although the long-term outcome of the regulation is the same as that obtained with a static model of capture.[46] The key novelty of the analysis is to derive the efficiency of the side-contracts from the institutional structure. These side-contracts, because they are not enforceable and are established through a dynamic process, suffer from some transaction costs. The transaction costs of capture change with simple institutional constraints: 1) Transaction costs decrease with the amount of information that the regulator gets on the firm; 2) they decrease with the discount factor of the principal, that is, with the discrepancy between the time horizon of the political principal and that of the firm; and 3) they decrease with the discount factor of the bureaucracy. Changing these parameters increases the value of the continuation of capture for the regulator and for the firm. The capture transaction is now more easily enforced.

The consequences of this endogenization of the transaction cost of capture for institution design are immediate. First, arm's length regulation, in which the political principal exerts the regulatory rights itself where there is little room for an active bureaucracy could be preferred to a closer day-to-day relationship with the firm, which occurs under regulation. The recent move away from regulation, toward antitrust policies as observed in European countries, can be given a rationale along these lines. Indeed, antitrust policies make little use of ex ante monitoring devices and correspond, in fact, to the use of ex post monitoring controls. Courts and (often) poorly informed judges are given large degrees of discretion in an absolutely unpredictable way in order to break any scope for capture by the industry. The reinforcement of antitrust agencies throughout Latin America, for instance, could be seen as a significant possible improvement of the potential efficiency of regulatory outcomes for the same reason.

The life-cycle view of regulatory agencies also shows that the composition of the agency itself matters. As discussed by James Q. Wilson (1989), we can isolate three different types of regulators: the so-called "careerists," who are more likely to move to the industry they regulate once they have finished their tenure in the civil service; the "professionals," who are former industry managers willing to continue to exercise some influence on the regulatory process; and the "politicians," who see their civil service as a first step before taking a political position. All these types respond to different implicit incentives. Clearly, the two first groups are more likely to give a high continuation value on collusion with the firm. This suggests that shifting the balance of power toward the "politicians" within the regulatory agency itself is optimal, which is not quite consistent with standard recommendations given by practitioners, as suggested by the overview prepared by William T. Smith (1996). Alternatively, playing on the tenures of the bureaucrats helps to fight capture. Short-term involvement in the civil service should, nevertheless, be traded off with the gain of longer lasting relationships like a better learning of the industry conditions.

Limited Commitment and the Degree of Honesty of the Policymakers. Simple "constitutions" that limit the intertemporal mandates of a government can be used as constraints to prevent capture.[47] At the time of designing a constitution, the writers have to decide whether a government should be able to bind the future of society to a given policy or whether the government's regulatory rights should be given for shorter periods. The cost of commitment is that a badly composed government could extract more rent from its ability to commit. Instead, short-term mandates are such that a badly composed government can be replaced by an honest one that is more willing to prevent capture by the industry. Political competition acts as a potential threat to regulatory capture. The cost of short-term contracts is, instead, that they are prone to the standard hold-up problem.[48] Firms underinvest if they are ex post expropriated from their investment at the time of change in the regulatory policy.

When political decisionmakers are likely to be dishonest, the optimal complete intertemporal contract or constitution calls for collusion-proof regulatory mechanisms. In contrast, when dishonesty is less likely, letting collusion happen is optimal for firms because it allows them to avoid paying the increased costs of fighting collusion. This outcome can also be implemented as a simple constitution which chooses ex ante between long-term and short-term contracting. In particular, a more efficient technology of collusion, that is, a lower transaction cost of capture, calls for the choice of short-term contracts. Indeed, the deadweight loss due to capture is less important under short-term contracting. This result is reinforced by Olsen and Torsvick (1995), who show that the benefits of offering a sequence of two short-term contracts with respect to writing a long-term contract increase with the transaction costs of side-contracting. A more efficient ex post capture induces a tougher reaction of the political principal, and the regulatory stake is strongly reduced. In other words, there is an implicit competition between the political principal for the second period and the regulator when they make deals with an interest group. An increase in the efficiency of side-contracting hardens this competition. Playing the bureaucracy against a political principal who is unable to commit helps to improve social welfare. The increase in the efficiency of the bureaucracy becomes a commitment device.[49] Collusion-proofing calls for little discretion, which is good when only short-term contracts can be written.

Delegation and Decentralization. One question that remains largely unanswered in the theory of government is the optimal degree of decentralization. The shrinking share of the government sector in western economies, the failures of the socialist economies, and the discussion of the costs and benefits of federalism are all evidence that this debate is ongoing.[50]

The folklore of the public economics literature argues that decentralization is good because it allows local powers entitled with regulatory rights to use their local information to improve the provision of regulation and redistribution and to protect the public good at the local level. The standard argument is that these benefits of decentralization must be traded off against the costs of lack of coordination in the regulatory policies of the competing states. Externalities arise from this decentralized exercise of regulatory rights.[51]

This argument is, at best, incomplete because it implicitly assumes that local principals are unable to communicate the information they learned at the local level to the upper levels of the regulatory hierarchy. If such communications were available, a large centralized mechanism would be enough to coordinate all jurisdictions. Moreover, under seemingly innocuous assumptions, such as risk-neutrality, unrelated local shocks, and acceptance of federal contracts at the interim stage (after local governments have learned their own information), there are decentralized ways of implementing the optimal, coordinated regulatory policy. With a convenient set of budget allocations and grants at the local level, the federal level can achieve an efficient policy by letting local jurisdictions have the formal authority for implementing local regulation.[52]

There are three possible ways to prove the optimality of decentralized structures. The first argues that the main benefit of decentralization comes from the ability of the local governments to collude with specific interest groups at local levels.[53] This collusion is indeed socially optimal because it allows the overall contractual arrangement to use the shared information of the local behavior to improve on the centralized arrangement. Capture is not a curse for society; on the contrary, it allows regulatory contracts to be completed.[54] A second solution is to recognize that communication between the local and the centralized governments implicitly is assumed to be limited because, for instance, the so-called revelation mechanisms are not available.[55] Contracts are then incomplete. The mere existence of a communication constraint creates scope for collusion at the local level between the regulated firm and its regulator. The structural asymmetry that decentralization introduces between these two layers of the hierarchy helps the central level use the local regulators to complete their regulatory contract. A third, less normative, perspective about the optimal organization argues that delegation may also help in the case of nonbenevolent political principals elected through voting procedures. The basic idea is that the optimal organization trades off the incentive costs of decentralization (modeled as a moral hazard problem between the local regulators and the centralized one) and the benefits of decentralization, which is a better representation of the preferences of the local median voter by the local elected principals.

LESSONS FOR A PRAGMATIC APPROACH TO THE DESIGN OF REGULATORY INSTITUTIONS

Table 1 summarizes the main discussions covered in this paper. It suggests that there is a reasonable degree of consensus between practitioners and theorists on many of the issues covered here. Everyone seems to agree that utility regulation has to promote (static and dynamic) efficiency while it protects consumers from potential monopolist abuses and investors and operators from political influence. Everyone also agrees that there is a trade-off between the credibility of the regulatory commitments and the flexibility required to rebalance, as needed, the interests of the various actors. Some degree of flexibility is desirable, but the track record of governments in their use of flexibility is generally perceived as being so problematic that the rules built in the various privatization instruments are designed to limit this flexibility.

Some degree of discretion is always available. Since regulatory contracts cannot foresee all future occurrences, safeguards are needed. One of the key components of these safeguard mechanisms analyzed in some detail by practitio-

Table 1.
Summary of the Main Approaches to Minimizing
Transaction Costs in the Design of Regulatory Frameworks

	Impact on Regulatory Outcome if Not Taken into Account	How to Minimize Transaction Costs
Lack of Commitment of Government and Need for Renegotiation	With more information in second period, regulators want to improve incentive. This reduces incentive for efficiency in first period.	"Overincentivate" in period one. Maintain flexibility to renegotiate to avoid overbinding commitments to private operators.
Multiprincipal Nature of Government	Allocative inefficiency and more or less incentive because of horizontal coordination problems.	Improve information and monitoring (formal yardstick competition will be a useful tool).
	Sub-optimal degree of decentralization and vertical coordination problems; reduced efficiency rent to firms and move toward cost-plus regime.	Reduce number of players. Let regulators share information to soften their competition.
	Too little incentive built in contract when multiple regulators cover complementary activities because of overregulation.	Give a veto right to head of state or institutions to which regulators are accountable.
	Too much incentive built in contract when multiple regulators cover substitute activities because of regulatory competition.	
	Sequentiality of regulatory decisions matter.	
Discretion of Political Principal	Structure-driven direction of incentives, because incentives drive the distribution of power of interest groups. Politicians favoring median voter rather than majority of voters.	How to fix structures? separation? Fix process by specifying decision-making processes (including voting mechanism to ensure proper representation in decision-making process). Suboptimal contracts (average cost pricing or quota) can be useful ways of tying the hands of politicians.
Discretion of Regulator	Internal influences: wages and promotions can be used to alter rent distribution; increased internal incentive to perform to reduce external influence and risk of collusion.	Increase accountability (disseminate information any way possible, including through the media, which also requires educating the media). Cut rent and move toward cost-plus.
	Conflict between legislature and regulators; need to reduce rent to cut risks of collusion.	Fix structures to reduce risks.
	Regulatory dynamics: side payments.	

ners is the specific design of regulatory institutions. One of the key points made in this paper is that these safeguards sometimes reflect and imply transaction costs that influence or should influence the optimal rent-efficiency trade-off in ways sometimes ignored by practitioners.

The first generic issues practitioners usually cover concerning institutional design are the importance of the independence, autonomy, and accountability of regulatory institutions for the sustainability of reforms within the regulated sectors. Most of the literature on transaction costs due to government failures would agree with the need to meet these three criteria. However, the literature emphasizes that the ways the criteria are met are determined by the ways the transaction costs are minimized, which, in turn, drive the desirable design of the regulatory framework. The time dimension, for instance, is crucial. In practice, it means that if there are commitment problems, short-term institutional contracts between the various players are more likely to ensure independence and autonomy. This has an impact on the duration of the nomination of the regulators. Short-term contracts may be better; yet, typically, contracts for regulators are between four and eight years, often with possibilities of renewal.

The empirical debate on the design of the regulators' job goes further, which is a potential source of tension. According to one of the schools of thought discussed above, it would seem that what practitioners typically recommend, ensuring that the regulators are appointed on the basis of professional rather political criteria, may not be the optimal strategy to minimize capture because the professional experts are likely to come from the sector they are supposed to regulate and are likely to return to it sooner or later. This is the case in most developing countries. Most practitioners would reply that the idea of electing regulators may be just as dangerous in developing countries. Unless the democratic process is well oiled and has the required transparency and accountability, elected regulators are unlikely to be much more independent than professional regulators; they will simply represent different interests. What is interesting to note, however, is that while practitioners and theorists emphasize different sources of capture, both agree that one way of dealing with this risk of capture is to ensure that the selection process involves both the executive and the legislative branches.

Autonomy covers various issues. Practitioners will generally argue that agencies need to have access to their own funding sources. Relying on budgetary transfers decided by politicians is often viewed as a threat to the independence of the regulators, as an easy way to reduce the effectiveness of a regulator would be to cut its budgetary allocation. Levies on the regulated firms or the consumers of the regulated services are the most common alternatives and can be viewed as user fees to be paid for the protection services provided by the regulators. To some extent, the regulatory fee approach also increases the accountability of the regulators because there is a more direct link between the source of their financing and what is expected from them.[56]

However, autonomy has to be more than financial. Regulatory agencies must be able to recruit their own staff. The achievement of staffing autonomy will often require an exemption from civil service salary and recruitment rules and may also imply that the regulatory agencies have to be able to recruit external consultants when the required skills are not available locally to address specific needs. Autonomy in monitoring of compliance and enforcement deserves to be highlighted because it requires that specific instruments be assigned to the regulators. This match between instruments and institutions is also a recurring theme addressed by the theoretical literature, which does not provide closure, so there is little policy advice to be drawn beyond what practitioners have to say. To be effective in their role, the regulators must be able to impose penalties according to clearly defined rules. This is consistent with the emphasis on simple, transparent rules that have emerged from the literature reviewed in this chapter. The other theme addressed here is that there is an ideal sequence in the decision-making process that depends on the distribution of information among the actors.

Both practitioners and theoreticians agree that accountability requires transparency in the decision-making process, which, unfortunately, too often is counterintuitive to many bureaucrats. Accountability also requires an operating environment subject to simple and clear procedural rules, including stipulated deadlines for reaching decisions, detailed justifications of decisions, nonpolitical reviews of decisions, opportunities for all concerned parties to be heard through public hearings (and hence greater interactions with consumer defense groups), and venues for appeal and provisions permitting removal of regulators in case of proven misbehavior. The practical challenge, however, is no longer the staffing. The challenge is to ensure that the information generated by this process is relevant to allowing the required accountability. This is, unfortunately, not the case in many countries, as process-oriented regulators tend to deal with details that have little to do with the distribution of the rent generated by the private or public monopolies providing utilities services. These regulators deal with the formal regulatory issues rather than the real regulatory issues, so that transparency requirements become an alibi rather than an instrument to be used by regulators.

Finally, practitioners tend to discuss their views on the optimal number of agencies. For all or most infrastructure sectors, practitioners tend to recommend creating multisectoral agencies (a single regulatory agency such as the state-level regulators in the United States, Canada, and Australia and national regulators in Costa Rica and Jamaica) rather than a sector- or industry-specific agency. This is one of the recommendations that appears to be at odds with what theory suggests. The case for *some* degree of separation of regulatory roles is made strongly by many of the papers surveyed for this study; however, too much separation can lead to unclear and complex overlapping of divisions of responsibilities. This apparent inconsistency can be reconciled in two ways. First, the practitioners' concern with the need to share regulatory resources (regulatory economists and lawyers) to deal with the limited regulatory capacity is generally not addressed by the theorists surveyed in this chapter, who focus on the United States or the United Kingdom, probably the largest producers of "regulatory skills."[57] Second, the fact that some degree of overlapping of responsibilities is unavoidable (such as the regulation of environmental issues, which typically involves multiple government institutions) guarantees that the gains achieved through some degree of separation are achieved.

Considered jointly, the impact of transaction costs resulting from the difficulties involved in organizing governments often implies that less rent and fewer incentives need to be built into the regulatory frameworks if transaction costs in general and collusion problems in particular are to be minimized. This is an important conclusion, as it rejoins the recommendation from theory on the optimal strategy to deal with excessively high risk levels in privatization projects. There seems to be some truth in the saying that there can be "too much of a good thing" when considering the appropriate level of incentives to build into regulatory regimes.

Notes

1. Baron and Myerson (1982) and Laffont and Tirole (1993).

2. It is important to note that transaction costs only matter because government intervention takes place under asymmetric information. Under symmetric information, the internal organization of the government has no bites on the outcome of its intervention. Coasian bargaining within the government makes the internal distribution of regulatory rights within the government irrelevant. Transaction costs, therefore, are dependent on the extent of the informational problem faced by the government at the time of intervening. When different institutions are associated with different values of these transaction costs, there is scope for their comparison and for a somewhat rough optimization over regulatory structures.

3. Landis (1960), in his report to the newly elected president, offered a remarkable survey of these overlapping responsibilities. See also Kahn's (1988) seminal book on regulation.

4. In the United Kingdom, for instance, the electricity regulator was given specific ranking of its responsibilities. He/she is responsible for securing all reasonable demands, for securing proper financing, and for promoting competition. The defense of the interest of consumers is subject to these three primary responsibilities. (See Electricity Act 1989.)

5. Even if governments sometimes subsidize consumer associations to create a bilateral monopoly.

6. See Kiewiet and McCubbins (1991) for a thorough discussion of the issues raised by the delegation of some powers from the Congress to the bureaucracy.

7. There is a clear parallel between this discussion and discussion of the firm as a monitoring technology, according to Alchian and Demsetz (1972) and Holmstrom (1982).

8. See Myerson (1979) for a discussion of entry in the political market.

9. See the discussion of sociotropic voting rules of voting in Ferejohn (1986).

10. See Moe (1986), Baron (1985), and Martimort (1996b).

11. Weingast and Moran (1983) show empirically that the Congress has much of the bargaining power when dealing with the bureaucracy.

12. The intertemporal inconsistency and its impact on decision rules have been forcefully made in the macroliterature, which has analyzed the issue of rules versus discretion. See the seminal contribution of Kydland and Presscott (1977) and the survey of the literature presented in Persson and Tabellini (1994, Introductory Chapter). In an agency context, it has been more fully understood with the works of Dewatripont (1989) and Laffont and Tirole (1990).

13. Constitutional rules exist that impose these limits. In France, there is no limit to the number of consecutive mandates that a political decisionmaker may

have. The only limitations are on his/her span of control — that is, on the number of simultaneous mandates permitted. In the United States, a president can have only two consecutive mandates.

14. This difference may not be so clear-cut for the reasons that within the firms the central management is also part of a group of bilateral, explicit contractual relationships with different stakeholders (creditors, customers, regulators, owners, and others) who have their own specific interests in the firm.

15. Baron (1985) and Martimort (1996b) analyze contractual settings describing these situations. Their basic assumption is that the splitting of responsibilities among the various regulatory agencies comes from a splitting of their monitoring technologies. As a result of this distribution of regulatory rights, each of these agencies is only able to contract on its own sphere of responsibilities. Their noncooperative behavior in regulating the industry follows. The regulation implemented is then a Nash equilibrium among various regulations offered in a decentralized way.

16. Stole (1990) and Martimort (1992, 1996a, 1996b) present a general theory that analyzes the contractual externalities that appear under adverse selection when regulatory powers are shared by noncooperating agencies.

17. See also Bernheim and Whinston (1986) for an analysis of a common agency game under a moral hazard case that also exhibits this under-provision of effort. Dixit (1996) also discusses a moral hazard model with linear schemes, featuring many of the insights of the present model. He applies it to the organization of the bureaucracy. We discuss this model in the subsection of this chapter entitled "Discretion of the Regulators."

18. This is true when a pure equilibrium of the contracting game between the principals exists. Martimort and Stole (1997) show that it may be possible to find information structures such that only mixed-equilibria exist with substitutes. In this case, only distributions of regulatory rules are offered in equilibrium by each principal. This suggests that the policy outcome may be quite fuzzy.

19. This discussion in terms of positive versus negative externalities between different government centers may offer a unifying framework for reading the emerging literature on federalism and budget constraint (see Qian and Roland 1994). This literature argues that the allocation of fiscal and monetary policies to the regional and national levels is due to the nature of the externalities (positive and negative) respectively, that decentralizing these policies implies for the budget constraint of local firms.

20. For instance, in the United States, the transports sector also has been said to be under an extremely inefficient regulation (Kahn 1988). Noticeably, it is under several overlapping jurisdictions, including those of the Interstate Commerce Commission, the Civil Aeronautics Board, the Federal Marine Commission, the Federal Trade Commission, the Bureau of Public Roads, and the Department of Commerce. See also, Landis (1960) for a discussion of the externalities associated with this separation of powers among agencies and their consequences on regulatory efficiency, such as delays in decisionmaking, overloads due to inter-regulatory agency conflicts to be settled, and so on.

21. See Martimort (1996b) for a formal proof of this assertion.

22. See Estache and Zheng (1995) for a model discussing the optimal instrument assignment in the context of multiple lawyers of regulators playing the Stackelberg game.

23. This veto can be modeled easily in an agency framework as a constraint on the well-being of the president.

24. Grossman and Helpman (1994).

25. See Helpman (1997) for a survey of this literature.

26. Laffont and Boyer (1995) build such a model. They assume that a political decisionmaker is reelected with a probability that is proportional to the amount of campaign contributions he receives. This amount is, in turn, linked to the informational rent that the interest group gets from regulation. Grossman and Helpman (1996) try to endogenize the weight that political decisionmakers give an interest group as a result of a campaign contributions game.

27. Spiller (1991) and also Wilson (1989).

28. Dixit (1996).

29. Laffont and Tirole (1993, Chapter 13). Kiewiet and McCubbins (1991) make the important point that the process of delegation from Congress to the bureaucracy leads surely to the abdication of any power.

30. As Niskanen (1971) has forcefully argued, information is the key that allows the bureaucracy to pursue objectives other than social welfare maximization.

31. The regulatory agency is assumed to have all the bargaining power in offering the side-contract to the interest group. In other words, there is little competition within the bureaucracy for the exercise of power.

32. A noticeable exception is given by political campaign contributions.

33. This point has, for instance, been made forcefully by McCubbins, Noll, and Weingast (1986 and 1989). See also Spiller (1991) and Levy and Spiller (1996).

34. More exactly, their model deals with the issue of privatization and the consequences of the structural separation between the owners of the firm and its regulator.

35. Olsen and Torsvick (1995).

36. Martimort (1997b) shows why and how the separation of powers acts as a commitment at the renegotiation stage to have a tough renegotiation among the different noncooperating agencies controlling the regulatory agenda.

37. See Kahn (1988) for a discussion of the expansion of regulation over time.

38. See Baron and Besanko (1992).

39. Laffont and Martimort (1995) show how efficient firms advantageously may be able to play one regulator against the other.

40. The main focus of Dewatripont and Maskin (1995) is the organization of the banking sector. They show that a banking sector in which lenders are constrained in the size of the loans they offer can be used as an effective incentive device. When lenders have a limited ability to finance projects, a venture needs to look for refinancing by other lenders who are at an informational disadvantage vis-à-vis the

initial lender. As a result, the cost of capital increases, and this hardens the ex ante incentives of the firm to complete projects earlier. Obviously, the logic of their argument also applies to regulatory agencies with limited budgets.

41. Their approach is cast in terms of exogenous stakes of collusion and exogenous bribery strategies. We already addressed, in the section of this chapter entitled "The Multiprincipal Nature of Government," the excessive rent-extraction that arises in multiprincipal models when the principals control only complementarity activities of the agent. The weakness of this approach is that it overestimates the problem of control of the bureaucracy by modeling no control at all. Because it has no normative underpinnings, there is no place for a welfare comparison among regulatory institutions.

Multiplying the number of regulators to induce inefficiencies in the bribery game is also an argument that the Public Choice literature has put forward (Miller, Shughart, and Tollison 1984). This approach suffers, nevertheless, from the same weaknesses as Shleifer and Vishny (1993).

42. See Tirole (1992) and Martimort (1997a and 1997b) for models along these lines.

43. Salant (1992), Salant and Woroch (1992), and Gilbert and Newbery (1993).

44. See Fudenberg and Maskin (1986) for a general proof of the Folk Theorem in repeated games.

45. As suggested not only by numerous political scientists, including Lierson (1949), Bernstein (1955), Huntington (1966) and Downs (1967), among others, and also by sociologists and practitioners (Kahn 1988).

46. Martimort (1997b).

47. Laffont and Tirole (1993), Chapter 16.

48. See Williamson (1975) and Grossman and Hart (1986).

49. Sappington (1987) builds a related model.

50. See Stiglitz (1994, Chapter 10) for a discussion of the centralization versus decentralization problems in this context.

51. We do not aim here at discussing the huge literature that, following Tiebout (1956), has analyzed these externalities. Few of these papers have really taken the agency perspective, which is necessary for an institutional analysis. Klibanoff and Morduch (1995) is a valuable exception. The authors provide a model of decentralization based on informational constraints and discuss the meaning of residual regulatory rights in this context. Additional ideas are discussed in Estache (1995).

52. Baron and Besanko (1992) and Moockherjee and Reichelstein (1996) show this result in the context of the theory of the firm.

53. Caillaud, Jullien, and Picard (1995).

54. See Itoh (1993) for this point in the framework of the theory of the firm.

55. See Laffont and Maskin (1987). Also, Laffont and Martimort (1995) explicitly takes this route and models collusion and limits of communication together.

56. Also, there are potential problems here because regulation is a public good, and this will probably lead to some degree of free riding.

57. Exceptions include Spiller (1991) and Levy and Spiller (1996), Guasch and Spiller (1997), and Kahn and Kessides (1997).

References

Aghion, Philippe, and Jean Tirole. 1997. "Formal and Real Authority in Organizations." *Journal of Political Economy* 105: 1-29.

Alchian, Armen, and Harold Demsetz. 1972. "Production, Information Costs and Economic Organization." *American Economic Review* 62: 777-795.

Atkinson, Anthony Barnes, and Joseph E. Stiglitz. 1980. *Lectures in Public Economics.* London: McGraw Hill.

Baron, David P. 1985. "Non-Cooperative Regulation of a Non-Localized Externality." *Rand Journal of Economics* 16: 269-282.

Baron, David P. 1989. "Regulation and Legislative Choice." *Rand Journal of Economics* 20: 467-477.

Baron, David P. 1995. "The Economics and Politics of Regulation: Perspectives, Agencies and Approaches." In Banks and Hanushek, eds. *Modern Political Economy*, eds. Jeffrey S. Banks and Eric A. Hanushek . Cambridge: Cambridge University Press.

Baron, David P., and David Besanko. 1992. "Information, Control, and Organizational Structure." *Journal of Economics and Management Strategy* 1: 237-276.

Baron, David P., and Roger Myerson. 1982. "Regulating a Monopolist with Unknown Costs." *Econometrica* 50: 911-930.

Becker, Gary S. 1983. "A Theory of Competition among Pressure Groups for Political Influence." *Quarterly Journal of Economics* 98: 371-400.

Bernheim, B. Douglas, and Michael Whinston. 1986. "Common Agency." *Econométrica* 54: 923-943.

Bernheim, B. Douglas, and Michael Whinston. 1987. "Menu Auctions, Resource Allocations, and Economic Influence." *Quarterly Journal of Economics* 101: 1-31.

Bernstein, Marver H. 1955. *Regulating Business by Independent Commission.* Princeton: University Press.

Boyer, Marcel, and Jean-Jacques Laffont. 1995. *Environmental Risks and Bank Liability.* Departement de Sciences Économiques. Montreal: Université de Montreal.

Buchanan, James. 1980. "Rent-Seeking under External Diseconomies." In *Towards a Theory of the Rent-Seeking Society*, eds. James Buchanan, Robert Tollison, and Gordon Tullock. College Station, Texas: Texas A&M Press.

Caillaud, Bernard, Bruno Jullien, and Pierre Picard. 1995. "Competing Vertical Structures: Precommitment and Renegotiation." *Econométrica* 63 (May): 621-646.

Coase, Ronald. 1937. "The Nature of the Firm." *Económica* 4: 386-405.

Congleton, Roger P. 1984. "Committees and Rent-Seeking Effort." *Journal of Public Economics* 25: 197-209.

Cremer, Jacques, Antonio Estache, and Paul Seabright. 1996. "Decentralizing Public Services: what can we learn from the Theory of the Firm?" *Revue d'Économie Politique* 106 (1).

Damien, Neven, and Robin Nutall. 1993. *Merger in Daylight: The Economics and Politics of the European Merger Control.* London: Centre for Economic Policy Research.

Dasgupta, Partha, Peter Hammond, and Eric Maskin. 1979. "The Implementation of Social Choice Rules." *Review of Economic Studies* 46: 185-216.

Dewatripont, Mathias. 1989. "Renegotiation and Information Revelation over Time." *Quarterly Journal of Economics* 103: 589-620.

Dewatripont, Mathias, and Eric Maskin. 1995. "Credit and Efficiency in Centralized and Decentralized Economies." *Review of Economic Studies* 62: 541-555.

Dewatripont, Mathias, and Jean Tirole. 1994. "A Theory of Debt and Equity: Diversity of Securities and Manager-Shareholder Congruence." *Quarterly Journal of Economics* 109: 1027-1054.

Dewatripont, Mathias, and Gerard Roland. 1992. "Economic Reform under Political Constraints." *Review of Economic Studies.* 59: 595-620.

Dixit, Avinash. 1996. *The Making of Economic Policy: A Transaction Cost Politics Perspective.* Cambridge: MIT Press.

Downs, Anthony. 1967. *Inside Bureaucracy.* Boston: Little Brown and Company.

Estache, Antonio, ed. 1995. "Decentralizing Infrastructure, Advantages and Limitations." World Bank Discussion Paper 290.

Estache, Antonio. 1997. *Designing Regulatory Institutions for Infrastructure — Lessons from Argentina.* Viewpoint No. 114, Private Sector Development Department, The World Bank Group.

Estache, Antonio, and Kamgbin Zheng. 1995. "Controlling Brazil's Pollution: Federal versus State Taxes and Fines." *Journal of Infrastructure Systems.* 2 (2: June).

Ferejohn, John. 1986. "Incumbent Performance and Electoral Control." *Public Choice* 86: 5-26.

Fudenberg, Drew, and David Levine. 1989. "Reputation and Equilibrium Selection in Games with a Patient Player." *Econométrica* 57: 759-778.

Fudenberg, Drew, and Eric Maskin. 1986. "The Folk Theorem in Repeated Games with Discounting or with Incomplete Information." *Econométrica* 54(3): 533-554.

Fudenberg, Drew, David Levine, and Eric Maskin. 1994. "The Folk Theorem with Imperfect Public Information." *Econométrica* 62: 997-1039.

Greenwald, Bruce C., and Joseph E. Stiglitz. 1986. "Externalities in Economies with Imperfect Information and Incomplete Markets." *Quarterly Journal of Economics* 101: 229-264.

Grossman, Gene M., and Elhahan Helpman. 1994. "Protection for Sale." *American Economic Review* 84: 833-850.

Grossman, Gene M., and Elhahan Helpman. 1996. "Electoral Competition and Special Interest Politics." *Review of Economic Studies* 63: 265-286.

Grossman, S., and Oliver Hart. 1986. "The Costs and Benefits of Ownership: A Theory of Lateral and Vertical Integration." *Journal of Political Economy* 94: 691-719.

Guasch, J. Luis, and Pablo Spiller. 1997. Managing the Regulatory Process: Design, Concepts, Issues and the Latin American and Caribbean Story. Mimeo.

Hart, Oliver, and Jean Tirole. 1988. "Contract Renegotiation and Coasian Dynamics." *Review of Economic Studies* 45: 509-540.

Helpman, Elhanan. 1997. "Politics and Trade Policy." In Kreps, David, and Kenneth Wallis, eds., *Advances in Economics and Econometrics: Theory and Applications.* New York: Cambridge.

Holmstrom, Bengt. 1982. "Moral Hazard in Teams." *Bell Journal of Economics* 10: 74-91.

Holmstrom, Bengt, and Jean Tirole. 1989. "The Theory of the Firm." In *Handbook of Industrial Organization*, part 1, eds. Richard L. Schmalensee and Robert D. Willig. Amsterdam: Elsevier Science Pub. Co.

Holmstrom, Bengt, and Jean Tirole. 1998. *LAPM: A Liquidity-Based Asset Pricing Model.* National Bureau of Economic Research Working Paper No. 6673. Cambridge, Mass.: National Bureau of Economic Research.

Holmstrom, Bengt, and Paul Milgrom, 1991. "Multitask Principal Agent Analyses: Incentive Contracts, Asset Ownership, and Job Design." *Journal of Law, Economics and Organization* 7: 24-52.

Huntington, Samuel. 1966. "The Marasmus of the ICC: The Commission, the Railroad and the Public Interests." In *Public Administration Policy: Selected Essays*, P. Woll, ed. New York: Harper and Row.

Itoh, Hideshi. 1993. "Coalitions, Incentives, and Risk Sharing." *Journal of Economic Theory* 60: 410-427.

Kahn, Alfred E. 1988. *The Economics of Regulation: Principles and Institutions*, 2d edition. Cambridge, Mass.: MIT Press.

Kahn, Alfred E., and Ioannis Kessides. 1997. *Regulating Network Industry in Argentina.* Working Paper. Washington, D.C.: World Bank.

Kiewiet, D. Roderick, and Matthew McCubbins. 1991. *The Logic of Delegation: Congressional Parties and the Appropriations Process.* Chicago: Chicago University Press.

Klibanoff, Peter, and Jonathan Morduch. 1995. "Decentralization, Externalities, and Efficiency." *Review of Economic Studies.* 62: 223-247.

Kofman, Fred, and Jacques Lawarree. 1993. "Collusion in Hierarchical Agency." *Econométrica* 61: 629-656.

Kydland, Finn, and Edward C. Prescott. 1977. "Rules rather than Discretion: The Inconsistency of Optimal Plans." *Journal of Political Economy* 85: 3.

Laffont, Jean-Jacques. 1994. "The New Regulatory Economics: Ten Years After." *Econométrica* 62: 507-538.

Laffont, Jean-Jacques. 1995. "Industrial Policy and Politics." *International Journal of Industrial Organization* 14: 1-27.

Laffont, Jean-Jacques, and David Martimort. 1995. Separation of Regulators against Collusive Behavior. Mimeo, IDEI.

Laffont, Jean-Jacques, and David Martimort. 1998. "Collusion and Delegation." *Rand Journal of Economics*, forthcoming.

Laffont, Jean-Jacques, and Eric Maskin. 1987. "Monopoly with Asymmetric Information about Quality: Behavior and Regulation." *European Economic Review.* 31 (1-2: Feb.-March).

Laffont, Jean-Jacques, and Jean Tirole. 1990. "Adverse Selection and Renegotiation in Procurement." *Review of Economic Studies* 75: 597-626.

Laffont, Jean-Jacques, and Jean Tirole. 1991. "The Politics of Government Decision Making: A Theory of Regulatory Capture." *Quarterly Journal of Economics* 107: 1089-1127.

Laffont, Jean-Jacques, and Jean Tirole. 1992. "Should Government Commit?" *European Economic Review* 36: 345-353.

Laffont, Jean-Jacques, and Jean Tirole. 1993. *A Theory of Incentives in Procurement and Regulation.* Cambridge, Mass.: MIT Press.

Landes, William, and Richard A. Posner. 1975. "The Independent Judiciary in an Interest-Group Perspective." *Journal of Law and Economics* 18: 875-901.

Landis, John. 1960. *Report on Regulatory Agencies to the President Elected.* U.S. Senate, Committee on the Judiciary. Committee Print.

Leiserson, Avery. 1946. "Interest Groups in Administration." In *Elements of Public Administration*, ed. F. Morstein Marx. New York: Prentice Hall.

Levy, Brian, and Pablo Spiller. 1993. Regulation, Institutions and Commitment in Telecommunications: A Comparative Analysis of Five Country Studies. Annual Bank Conference on Development Economics, The World Bank. May 3-4.

Levy, Brian, and Pablo Spiller. 1996. *Regulations, Institutions, and Commitment: Comparative Studies of Telecommunications.* New York: Cambridge University Press.

Lewis, Tracy R., and David E. Sappington. 1991. "Oversight of Long-Term Investment by Short-Lived Regulators." *International Economic Review* 32: 579-600.

Martimort, David. 1992. "Multi-Principaux avec Anti-Selection." *Annales d'Économie et de Statistiques* 28: 1-38.

Martimort, David. 1996a. "Exclusive Dealing, Common Agency and Multiprincipal Incentive Theory." *Rand Journal of Economics* 27: 1-31.

Martimort, David. 1996b. "The Multiprincipal Nature of the Government." *European Economic Review* 40: 673-685.

Martimort, David. 1997a. "A Theory of Collusive Behavior." *Scandinavian Journal of Economics* 99: 555-579.

Martimort, David. 1997b. The Life Cycle of Regulatory Agencies: Dynamic Capture and Transaction Costs. Mimeo.

Martimort, David. 1998. Renegotiation Design with Multiple Regulators. IDEI, Toulouse. Mimeo.

Martimort, David, and L. Stole. 1997. A Note on the Revelation Principle in Common Agency Games. Mimeo.

McAfee, Preston R., and John McMillan. 1995. "Organizational Diseconomies of Scope." *Journal of Economics and Management Strategy* 4: 399-426.

McCubbins, Matthew, Roger Noll, and Barry Weingast. 1987. "Administrative Procedures as Instruments of Political Control." *Journal of Law, Economics, and Organization* 3: 243-277.

McCubbins, Matthew, Roger Noll, and Barry Weingast. 1989. "Structure and Process, Politics and Policy: Administration Arrangements and the Political Control of Agencies." *Virginia Law Review* 75: 431-482.

Melumad, Nahum D., Dilip Mookherjee, and Stefan Reichelstein. 1995. "Hierarchical Decentralization of Incentive Contracts." *Rand Journal of Economics* 26: 654-692.

Miller J., William F. Shughart, and Robert Tollison. 1984. "A Note on Centralized Regulatory Review." *Public Choice* 43: 83-88.

Mirrlees, J. A. 1971. "An Exploration in the Theory of Optimum Income Taxation." *Review of Economic Studies* 38: 175-208.

Moe, Terry. 1984. "The New Economics of Organization." *American Journal of Political Science* 28: 739-777.

Moe, Terry. 1986. "Interests, Institutions, and Positive Theory: The Policies of the NLRB." Studies of American Political Department.

Moockherjee, Dilip, and Stefan Reichelstein. 1996. *Budgeting and Hierarchical Control.* Paper in series, Industry Studies Program. Boston: Boston University.

Myerson, Roger. 1979. "Incentive Compatibility and the Bargaining Problem." *Econométrica* 47: 61-73.

Neven, Damien, Robin Nutall, and Paul Seabright. 1993. Regulatory Capture and The Design of European Merger Policy. In *Merger in Daylight*, eds. Damien Neven, Robin Nutall, and Paul Seabright. London: CEPR Press.

Niskanen, William. 1971. *Bureaucracy and Representative Government*. New York: Aldine-Atherton.

Olsen, Trond, and Gaute Torsvick. 1993a. "The Ratchet Effect in Common Agency: Implications for Privatization and Regulation." *Journal of Law, Economics and Organization* 9: 136-158.

Olsen, Trond, and Gaute Torsvick. 1993b. "Collusion and Ratcheting in Hierarchies." Norwegian Research Center in Organization and Management. Mimeo.

Olsen, Trond, and Gaute Torsvick. 1995. "Intertemporal Common Agency and Organizational Design: How much Centralization." *European Economic Review* 39: 1405-1428.

Olson, Mancur. 1965. *The Logic of Collective Action: A Theory of Interest Groups in Public Goods*. Cambridge: Harvard University Press.

Olson, Mancur. 1982. *The Rise and Decline of Nations: Economic Growth, Stagflation and Social Rigidities*. New Haven: Yale University Press.

Peltzman, Samuel. 1976. "Towards a More General Theory of Regulation." *Journal of Law and Economics* 19: 211-240.

Persson, Torsten, and Guido Tabellini, eds. 1994. *Monetary and Fiscal Policy, Vol. 2: Politics*. Cambridge, Mass.: MIT Press.

Posner, Richard A. 1976. "Theories of Economic Regulation." *Bell Journal of Economics* 5: 335-358.

Qian, Yingyi, and Gérard Roland. 1994. Regional Decentralization and the Soft Budget Constraint: The Case of China. ULB Bruxelles. Mimeo.

Salant, David J. 1995. "Behind the Revolving Door: A New View of Public Utility Regulation." *Rand Journal of Economics* 26: 362-377.

Sappington, David Edward. 1987. *Privatization, Information and Incentives*. Cambridge, Mass.: National Bureau of Economic Research.

Salant, David J., and Glenn A. Woroch. 1992. "Trigger Price Regulation." *Rand Journal of Economics* 23: 29-51.

Shleifer, Andrei, and Robert W. Vishny. 1993. "Corruption." *Quarterly Journal of Economics* 109: 599-617.

Simon, Herbert A. 1957. *Models of Man*. New York: John Wiley & Sons.

Simon, Herbert A. 1961. *Administrative Behavior*. New York: The Macmillan Co.

Smith, William T. 1996. "Utility Regulators: Creating Agencies in Reforming and Developing Countries." Paper presented to the International Forum for Utility Regulators, Oxford, England, June.

Spiller, Pablo. 1991. "Politician, Interest Groups, and Regulators: A Multiple-Principals Agency Theory of Regulation, or 'Let Them Be Bribed.'" *Journal of Law and Economics* 33: 65-101.

Stigler, George J. 1971. "The Theory of Economic Regulation." *Bell Journal of Economics* 2: 3-21.

Stiglitz, Joseph E. 1994. *Whither Socialism?* Cambridge, Mass.: MIT Press.

Stole, Lars. 1990. "Mechanism Design under Common Agency." University of Chicago. Mimeo.

Tiebout, Charles. 1956. "A True Theory of Local Public Expenditures." *Journal of Political Economy* 64 (5) 416-424.

Tirole, Jean. 1986. "Hierarchies and Bureaucracies: On the Role of Collusion in Organizations." *Journal of Law, Economics and Organization* 2: 181-214.

Tirole, Jean. 1992. "Collusion and the Theory of Organizations." In *Advances in Economic Theory*, Vol. 2, ed. J.J. Laffont. Cambridge: Cambridge University Press. 151-206.

Tirole, Jean. 1994. "The Internal Organization of Government." *Oxford Economic Papers* 46: 1-29.

Weingast, Barry, and Mark Moran. 1982. *The Myth of Runaway Bureaucracy: The Case of the FTC*. St. Louis: Center for the Study of American Business, Washington University.

Williamson, Oliver. 1975. *Markets and Hierarchies*. New York: The Free Press.

Williamson, Oliver. 1985. *The Economic Institutions of Capitalism*. New York: The Free Press.

Wilson, James Q. 1989. *Bureaucracy: What Government Agencies Do and Why They Do It*. New York: Basic Books.

CHAPTER 4

The Political Economy of Regulatory Policy

LUIGI MANZETTI

INTRODUCTION

While there are plenty of studies looking at why and how countries privatize, there is little research to date on the impact that privatization has had in terms of competition and regulation, primarily because the state divestiture of monopolistic state-owned enterprises (SOEs) in public utilities has taken place only recently in most of Latin America. On the issue of regulation vis-à-vis privatization, especially in the context of developing countries with little or no experience regulating utility infrastructure markets, there is substantial agreement in the scholarly community. Works on privatization (Baumol, Panzar, and Willig 1982; Yarrow 1986; Gray 1996; Kwoka 1996) propose a hypothesis that I have summarized as follows:

> Competition and regulation should be introduced in the market, particularly when affecting SOEs enjoying a monopoly status, prior to state divestiture. If this is not done, chances are that after privatization the new company will be able to abuse its monopoly status by extracting rents through the restriction of supply and the charging of high prices for services rendered. This, in turn, will negatively affect economic efficiency gains from privatization, as the potential benefits ensuing from lack of competition are lost.

An important corollary to this hypothesis would be that if regulation is not in place with competition from the start, it will be difficult to alter a monopolistic structure after privatization because companies in the privatized industry will resist any changes in advantageous ownership rights that the government granted during privatization (Guislain 1997).

The goal of this chapter is to bring empirical evidence to the above hypothesis by examining regulation and post-privatization structures in the electricity and telecommunications markets in Argentina and Chile. Electricity prices plummeted in Argentina, while they remained comparatively high in Chile. In telecommunications, however, the roles were reversed: Chilean long-distance telephone rates dropped dramatically compared with those in Argentina. This chapter will show how regulation vis-à-vis competition is at the core of the discrepancy in market behavior after privatization took place across these countries and sectors and, arguably, beyond these countries and sectors. Equally important, I will argue that this discrepancy, in turn, has more to do with political calculations than economic factors. Usually, when SOEs were sold to the private sector under monopolistic clauses, the privatization process was marked by lack of transparency and collusion between government officials and interested private tenders. This collusion continued after privatization because, under such conditions, the regulatory framework, instead of fostering competition, usually guaranteed the monopolistic status quo ensuing from the sell-off.

Chile and Argentina were selected for the following reasons. Both countries pioneered privatization policies in Latin America. Chile privatized in two rounds: 1974-1979 and 1985-1989.[1] Argentina's privatization program started in mid-1989 and was nearly complete by 1997. Factors other than pioneering status and incremental approach were also crucial in these two cases. Both countries were more than early privatizers; both have been hailed by multilateral lending institutions, such as the World Bank and the International Monetary Fund (IMF), as models not only for Latin America but also for the rest of the developing world. Argentina and Chile were the first countries in Latin America to privatize monopolistic companies in electricity and telecommunications. These sectors have been in private hands for several years now, allowing the gathering of enough data to make a meaningful post-facto evaluation.[2] By the same token, we can draw upon a substantial amount of literature that has developed on regulation and privatization in these countries and can contribute to it. The second round of the Chilean privatization process (1985-1989), the more important of the two, took place only five years before Argentina's, which considerably reduces scholars' time-lag problems when comparing the Chilean and Argentine cases.

The chapter is organized as follows. The first section explains the political and economic reasons why establishing regulation prior to privatization was only a minor concern at the outset of the state divestiture programs in Argentina and Chile. The second section analyzes how the different characteristics of the regulatory frameworks enhanced or prevented competition in the electricity and telecommunications sectors. The third section discusses what can be learned from the experiences of both countries in terms of regulatory policies. The conclusion wraps up the argument about the importance of establishing competition with regulation at the start of privatization.

WHY WAS REGULATION DOWNPLAYED?

Privatization policies in Latin America occasionally have been driven by ideological motives mixed with political exigencies, as they were in Chile under General Augusto Pinochet. The economists of the Pinochet regime — the so-called "Chicago boys" — implemented reforms that went beyond the economic sphere and aimed at transforming Chilean society in a conservative direction. Pinochet's conservative revolution rested on the ideological principle that the market was the main instrument of economic decisionmaking (Hachette and Lüders 1993, 31).

Yet, what interested Pinochet the most in the market reform agenda was that it could emasculate the bargaining power of traditional political parties, which had used government resources to create patronage networks, as well as diminish the bargaining power of such influential vested interests as trade unions and business organizations. The only institution left untouched was the military, which could then act as the ultimate arbiter in the political arena.[3] Thus, privatization in Chile reformulated "the nature of political coalitions and compromises. It also reshap[ed] the political scene, setting the framework of a more narrow public domain, one in which there would be less room for politics to occur" (Schamis 1992, 62). Seen in this light, "popular capitalism," a program devised in the mid-1980s to make people small shareholders in former SOEs, was an overt effort by the Pinochet regime to lure middle-class and working-class people away from their traditional patrons — that is, from labor, left-wing, and Christian democratic parties.

Although Pinochet's economic team presented the second wave of privatizations (1985-1989) as a means not only to promote long-term-like efficiency gains but also to spread ownership, strengthen domestic capital markets, and ease the financing of public investment projects, it is clear that what mattered most to the administration was maximizing short-term fiscal revenues (Sáez 1993). The relative emphasis placed upon the quick achievement of these goals hampered the transparency of the whole privatization process (Marcel 1989; Schamis 1999), a fact that was recognized by some of its own proponents (Hachette and Lüders 1993, 6).

Unlike the Chilean economic team, which could enforce policy with no public contestation due to the authoritarian nature of Pinochet's regime, the privatizers in Argentina found a more politically complex situation. In the weeks preceding his inauguration, President Carlos Saúl Menem (1989-1999) realized that five decades of misguided import-substitution industrialization and welfare policies initiated by the founder of his Partido Justicialista, Juan Perón, had driven the Argentine state into insolvency. Menem's government, in dire straits, desperately needed foreign aid and investments to revitalize an economy that had grown only about 1 percent annually since 1975. He and his closest advisers clearly understood that to receive a substantial reduction of the country's debt under the auspices of the Brady Plan, Argentina first had to regain the support of the United States, the IMF, the World Bank, and the European Union. Testifying before the Bicameral Commission on Privatization in 1990, Minister of Public Works and Services Roberto Dromi described Argentina as a country on its knees that had to beg foreign investors to come in and multilateral agencies to supply financial aid.[4]

Given Argentina's economic condition when President Menem took office in mid-1989, the administration made no real pretense of using privatization as a means of improving economic efficiency (Aspiazu and Vispo 1994). According to Menem's strategy, the state-divestiture program became an instrument to accomplish two objectives: creating fresh revenues and attracting new supporters for his political coalition. First, in the initial round of privatization engineered by Minister Dromi during the 1989-1991 period, revenue maximization was essential to close the fiscal deficit (Hachette and Lüders 1993, 38). Second, to broaden his support coalition, Menem offered a share of the privatization business to potential losers. These were companies that had thrived as suppliers of goods and services to SOEs, namely the country's largest domestic conglomerates. Menem assured the conglomerates that the upcoming bids would require the creation of consortia among foreign banks holding Argentine debt papers, foreign utility companies with the expertise to run the SOEs to be privatized, and domestic partners with the "necessary political connections" (Majul 1993, 1994; Palermo and Novaro 1996; Schamis 1999).

The Argentine privatization program was characterized by its amazingly quick pace and its lack of transparency, particularly under Minister Dromi, who eventually had to resign amid charges of corruption in early 1991 (Natale 1993).[5] Although successful privatization entails time-consuming and careful planning, Menem decided that there was no time to waste. For example, he allotted only 14 months for privatization of the telephone company (Petrazzini 1995, 119). Due to the Argentine government's need to maximize fiscal revenues and to achieve political goals that had nothing to do with economic efficiency, the creation of an effective regulatory framework that would be in place prior to the telephone company privatization was doomed from the start (Petrecolla, Porto, and Gerchunoff 1993). For Argentina, regulation was eventually left to special agencies in several (but not all) public utility sectors within the framework of a very weak antitrust legislation.

In Chile, the Pinochet regime, beginning in 1973, redesigned regulation to minimize government intervention. As we shall see in more detail later, the Chileans, unlike Argentina's privatizers, did not opt to establish a unified system of sector-specific agencies. Instead, they designed individual sector-specific laws that would be enforced by superintendencies and special commissions with powers of intervention that varied appreciably and depended upon the executive branch (Fernández Fredes 1996). Furthermore, unlike Argentina, Chile began to establish several institutions in charge of antitrust law, including the National Prosecution Office (appointed by the executive) and two antitrust commissions; the Central Preventive Commission, and the Resolutive Commission (which serves as a board of appeals for the Central Preventive Commission).[6] Unfortunately, the Chilean legal framework often proved inadequate as time went by.[7] A close examination of the Argentine and Chilean administrations' official documents and policy statements from the outset of their respective privatization programs shows, unequivocally, a government assumption that as soon as private owners took over SOEs, the market — almost by magic — would solve all economic problems.[8]

In a conversation with a high-ranking Argentine official, I told him that there was no true causal relationship, at least in theory, between type of ownership and economic performance. His response was, "No, sir, private ownership is always better."[9] This statement is in sharp contrast with the European Competitiveness Advisory Group's conclusion in 1995, which says, "What matters most is not so much that the ownership — and management — of public utilities moves from the state to the private sector, as that competition is introduced and extended wherever possible."[10] Nonetheless, responses like the Argentine official's were quite common among the government officials I interviewed. Mine was not an isolated experience. In a published report, a World Bank official noted that when he tried to advise a government about how to regulate the power sector of that country before privatization could take place, he received the following response: "But this is nothing new! Our government has always controlled the activities of state-owned enterprises through different ministries. And these controls have created many problems. We don't need to reinvent the past and put a label on it" (Tenenbaum 1995, 1).

For the new zealots of market reforms, particularly the politicians among them, what mattered the most was not creating steady rules that assured fair competition after privatization was completed but getting the cash to bridge fiscal imbalances — and to forge new political coalitions and destroy old coalitions with domestic and international vested interests.[11] As a result, governments only paid lip service to promoting competition.

The predictable outcome of privatization within a weak regulatory framework was the transfer of monopolistic market control from the public to the private sector. Commenting about the regulation problems of the telecommunications sector in Latin America, one analyst stated:

> [T]he problem lies ahead because most countries did not create strong regulatory institutions. . . . Despite pressure from the World Bank to do so, the regulatory agencies were riddled with political meddling and bureaucratic constraints. . . . In every country, within the first five years, agreements struck with the government at the time of privatization had to be modified, sometimes informally (Ramamurti 1995, 33).

COUNTRY ANALYSES

Chile

The privatization of the electricity sector in Chile began in 1985 and was virtually completed by 1989. Chile is divided into four grids, of which the central one, the Sistema Interconectado Central (SIC), serving about 90 percent of the Chilean population, accounts for roughly 80 percent of the country's installed capacity. The two largest state electricity companies, Empresa Nacional de Electricidad (Endesa) and Chilectra (operating in the SIC), were first purchased in part by their own managers and employees through a buyout scheme that swapped severance payments for company shares (Galal et al. 1994). Subsequently, additional shares were sold to private pension funds (Administración Fondos de Pensiones — AFPs) and to small investors through public auctions. Foreign companies showed little interest in this privatization at the time, partly because the country was just coming out of the severe economic crisis of 1982. However, Chile's electricity privatization was much heralded as an innovative form of "popular capitalism" (Hachette and Lüders 1993). Ironically, as ownership became widespread, it became clear that shareholders were unable to make management accountable because shareholders' voting rights were restricted, leaving the executives with too much management discretion (Marcel 1989; Bitrán and Sáez 1994, 347). The former SOEs' executives, now turned entrepreneurs, created two major holding companies, Enersis and Chilgener, through which they were able to gain control of the majority of the former SOE's shares, as well as of their management operations (Lauro 1996).[12]

The Pinochet regime created most of the regulatory framework prior to privatization. In 1978, the National Energy Commission, a special office dependent upon the Ministry of the Economy, was set up to coordinate private investment activities and regulate prices for the entire sector. In June 1982, Decree-Law No. 1/ 82 established the electricity regulatory framework, stipulating "definitive" concessions for an indefinite period and granting the new private companies the right to exploit their respective markets ad infinitum. Such legislation was rather rigid in conception; it was meant to restrain government intervention while reassuring investors but made little room for future changes that could be necessary in changed market conditions. As could be expected, the regulatory regime soon proved deficient for a number of reasons. First, the new companies quickly acquired a monopolistic position in the market because they were allowed to pursue both horizontal and vertical integration. For example, Enersis became the largest shareholder of Endesa, which dominates the market in electricity generation; of Chilectra, the biggest Chilean power distribution company; and of Transelec, a major electricity transmission provider. Consequently, Enersis gained a monopolistic market position in the SIC in all aspects of the electricity business. Not surprisingly, this situation favored a steady increase in prices between 1984 and 1990 (Blanlot 1993; Bitrán et al. 1999). As shown in Table 1, tariffs steadily rose, starting in the last year of state ownership (1984), as did profits. According to Chilean government officials, the fact that Chile's electrical rates increased to levels among the highest in Latin America is due to the monopolistic structure of the market.[13] Thanks to the hefty profits made under such conditions, Enersis and Chilgener became two of the most profitable electricity companies in the region.[14] By the mid-1990s, the companies were so well capitalized that they were major bidders in the privatization of electricity SOEs in Argentina, Peru, Bolivia, and Brazil (Lauro 1996). Second, Enersis, once it took control of Endesa, also acquired the water rights for most of the territory that the SOE owned, thus inheriting a powerful rent.[15] This meant that prospective investors in hydroelectric plants would pay dues to Endesa to acquire water rights. The situation created a de facto entry barrier: new investors would be discouraged from entering the market because they would not have the water rights to undertake the most "efficient projects" (Bitrán and Serra 1994, 184).

In 1994, to bypass the water rights stumbling block, the consortium TransGas, made up of Tenneco (United States) and British Gas, started plans to build a pipeline to bring Argentine gas across the Andes. The consortium's gas was expected to power a new electricity generating company to be built by three U.S. firms that would have competed with Chilgener for the most lucrative industrial market of the country, which is located in the Concepción-Valparaiso-Santiago area (*Lagniappe Letter* August 1995, 4). The use of gas as an alternative source of power generation was expected to cut electricity prices by 15 percent to 20 percent.[16] Chilgener immediately responded by simultaneously making up plans for a competing pipeline and contesting in court the environmental soundness of the TransGas project. Allegedly, domestic electricity companies fought the entry of competitors with three arguments to politicians and regulators. First, if Chilean companies were to become leaders in the sector and expand their operations abroad, they had to maintain a monopolistic position at home. Second, Chilean private pension funds were heavily invested in the Chilean companies' stocks, as were small investors, so opening up the sector to competition would likely have undesirable social and political consequences.[17] Third, both government and opposition parties were reminded that electricity companies had been generous contributors to their political campaigns.[18] By the end of 1996, frustrated by mounting political, legal,

Table 1.
Endesa's Average Electricity Prices
(US$/100kWh) and Profits (1984-1990)

Year	Residential Tariff	Small Industry Tariff	Large Industry Tariff	Profits in Millions of US$
1984	6.18	5.31	3.84	33
1985	6.40	5.56	3.78	-65
1986	6.48	5.62	3.81	50
1987	7.06	6.19	4.29	62
1988	8.23	7.60	4.78	179
1989	9.24	8.62	5.45	106
1990	8.77	8.18	5.17	104

kWh = kilowatt-hour

Source: Pablo Spiller and Luis Viana Martorell, 1994, "How Should It Be Done? Electricity Regulation in Argentina, Brazil, Uruguay, and Chile," unpublished manuscript, University of California, Berkeley.

and financial roadblocks, Tenneco and British Gas reasoned that the investment was not worth fighting for and abandoned it, leaving the Chilean companies in their dominant position.[19] These events seem to suggest that the collusion between policymakers and business interests at the time of the electricity privatization under the Pinochet regime (Schamis 1999) continued after the country returned to democracy.

All these factors together have helped create entry barriers for other companies willing to invest in the market. As a result, they have also discouraged allocative efficiency because the monopolistic nature of the market provides no incentives in that direction (Bitrán and Sáez 1994; Guislain 1997; Bitrán et al. 1999). Barriers to entry were indeed sustained; until 1996, Chile attracted the lowest amount and number of foreign investments in South American electricity markets that were privatized. The lack of competition allowed prices to remain high enough that inefficient producers stayed in business at a profit (Heller and McCubbins 1996). In short, the hastiness of the electricity privatization, the need to provide investors with a lucrative business opportunity, and the government planners' lack of experience in electricity privatization made it possible for Enersis and Chilgener to monopolize the sector and to acquire tremendous economic and political clout (Paredes 1992). Bitrán and Serra summarized the situation in these terms:

> The regulatory process is increasingly becoming a bargaining process, where the relative power and influence of interest groups is having a great impact on the outcome of the regulatory process. This environment has led to the development of rent-seeking activities, as it becomes profitable to devote resources to develop influences with the purpose of favorably affecting the regulator's decisions. Also, important amounts of resources are devoted to settling disputes arising in an ambiguous regulatory framework between regulators and firms and between firms (1995, 30).

The privatization of the Chilean telecommunications sector had a very different outcome. It took place between 1986 and 1990. Until that time, SOEs had controlled most of the domestic telephone markets, although two small regional companies had been sold to Chilean investors in 1981. The General Telecommunications Law No. 18168 of 1982 set up the regulatory framework. This law was amended in 1987 to pave the way for privatization of both the Telephone Company of Chile (Compañía de Teléfonos de Chile — CTC), the largest domestic service provider, and the National Telecommunications Company (Empresa Nacional de Telecomunicaciones — ENTEL), the other SOE operating in Chile's long-distance service market. In 1988 Bond, an Australian company, acquired 50.1 percent of CTC, which controls 94 percent of Chilean telephone lines. Company employees and AFPs, who, as we have seen, acquired important stakes in the electricity holding companies, were relegated to only 4.3 percent and 7.7 percent of the shares, respectively (Molano 1997, 60).[20] Eventually, in 1990, Bond sold its shares in CTC to Telefónica de España (a monopoly in Spain, then controlled by the Spanish government), which had become the largest shareholder of ENTEL in 1989.[21]

In terms of shareholding composition, the main difference between the two Chilean utilities' privatizations is that the government made a deliberate effort to lure foreign investors in the case of telecommunications. The fact that Bond, with no previous experience in the business, beat the competition also demonstrates that in 1988 large foreign companies were still reluctant to come to Chile as long as Pinochet remained in charge. (He left office in March 1990.[22]) One major problem in telecommunications after privatization was that the new companies were granted monopoly status in their respective markets, as was true in the electricity sector. Again, the government made no effort to promote competition, and the privatization contracts established legal entry barriers by creating new monopolies under private ownership. The distortions caused by this state of affairs were particularly evident in the case of ENTEL, which experienced yearly rates of return on capital that exceeded 40 percent on average. Moreover, the methods of regulating long-distance rates penalized consumers, as the prices that ENTEL charged were substantially above marginal costs (Bitrán and Serra 1995). As for CTC, the local service provider, its later acquisition of the rights to enter the cellular phone market in its concession area also raised some concerns. According to Eduardo Bitrán and Raúl Sáez, "For technical reasons only two companies can operate in the same geographical area, and in the long run cellular phones may become an important competitor in the local and domestic long-distance market" (1994, 365).

In 1992, the Chilean Antitrust Commission ruled that government regulators had to remove legal barriers preventing the entry of new companies into long-distance service. The Commission also stated that cross-shareholdings were unlawful and that, therefore, Telefónica had to sell either its CTC shares or its ENTEL shares. This decision was crucial, as it forced competition into a lucrative market that had earned ENTEL profits in 1993 alone worth US$80 million. At the end of 1994, Chile adopted a multi-carrier system that today has eight major long-distance companies fiercely competing for market shares. Not surprisingly, prices have dropped dramatically since then. A call from Santiago to New York that in 1993 cost US$1.50 per minute plummeted to as low as US$0.23 by the end of 1995 and then stabilized at an average of $0.75 per minute in 1996 (Guislain 1997, 211). In contrast, a call from New York to Santiago in 1996 was more expensive, at about US$0.90 per minute (*Latin American Monitor: Southern Cone* May 1996, 9). These developments prompted an enthusiastic commentator to state, "more than any place in the world, Chile is the testing ground for how to succeed in telecommunications" (*Journal of Commerce* 1995: 12).

Increased competition resulted in better customer service and increased traffic; monthly international calls rose from an average of 6 million minutes prior to liberalization to an average of 11 million minutes afterward. By the same token, increased competition squeezed profit margins, compared with those in the "pre-deregulation" period (Bitrán and Serra 1995). Nonetheless, contrary to industry fears, the telecommunications sector achieved an average annual growth rate of 19.5 percent between 1990 and 1995, which was three times faster than the growth rate of the economy as a whole.

Argentina

In Argentina, upon assuming office, in 1989, the Menem administration implemented a sweeping privatization program and did so faster than the Chilean privatization. Before proceeding further, it is important to note that most experts (see, for example, World Bank 1995) suggest that privatization should begin with companies in the industrial and commercial sectors, as occurred in Chile, Brazil, and Mexico. Companies in these sectors are usually smaller and easier to restructure than public utilities, and they often do not require the development of a regulatory framework if they operate in competitive markets. Moreover, as was pointed out earlier, governments in developing countries embarking on privatization often do not have experience in this area and need to develop expertise through smaller divestitures before attempting to sell off large utility infrastructures, which require prior solution of complex legal, technical, and financial issues. Nonetheless, for both fiscal and political reasons, Menem started by privatizing the large public utilities first.

The sale of Argentina's state telephone company, Empresa Nacional de Telecomunicaciones (ENTel), was the second large auction that Menem undertook. (The sale of the national airline, Aerolíneas Argentinas, was the first one). Unfortunately, ENTel's sale was marred from the start by problems and a seemingly endless series of changes in the rules regulating its transfer to the private sector. No regulatory scheme had been conceived before the sale. ENTel was eventually divided into northern and southern regions, splitting the Buenos Aires metropolitan area, to make the stock more attractive to investors.[23] When potential investors began to withdraw, reacting to the government's chaotic handling of the sale, Minister of Public Works and Services Dromi created some additional incentives. He awarded the two new regional companies exclusive rights for both local and long-distance service — and stretched the original terms of exclusive concession from five to seven years, adding a three-year extension in the event that the investment targets were achieved. (The seven-year period ended in November 1997.)

The initial terms of transfer stipulated a 16-percent rate of return guaranteed by the government to the new private owners (Petrazzini 1995). As the sale neared a close, the government changed both the initial price floor and the regulatory structure in response to political pressure. In April 1990, the Menem administration devised a new regulatory scheme that detailed the rights and obligations of all parties involved, including the creation of a National Commission of Telecommunications (Comisión Nacional de Telecomunicaciones — CNT) to be responsible for regulating the sector. CNT was theoretically meant to be an independent agency, with financing to come from a 0.5 percent sales tax on the new private companies. However, the CNT did not become operational until two years after the telephone monopoly had passed into private ownership.

The price regime was again changed a few weeks before ENTel was auctioned, and its content was disclosed to the public at the very last minute. Because of these constant changes, the rush that characterized the whole process, and the uncertain macroeconomic environment affecting Argentina at the time, the sale attracted only three bidders. Finally, in November 1990, Telefónica de España took control of the more lucrative southern region, while Telecom, a French-Italian consortium made up of France Telecom and Stet (of Italy), won the bid for the northern region. Telefónica de España and the Telecom consortium then set up a joint venture, Telintar, to provide long-distance service. The Argentine minority shareholder for Telefónica was the Pérez Companc group and for Telecom the Techint and Soldati groups. None of the Argentine partners had any experience in the telecommunications business but played an important role in lobbying the Menem administration on behalf of their partners before and after the sell-off (Majul 1993, 1994).

The immediate result after the telephone company privatization was a sharp increase in the pulse price (the unit in seconds of conversation by which prices are determined); it rose an average of 96.57 percent. While transfer pulse prices had averaged between US$.015 and US$.028, by the end of 1990 they had risen to US$.042 (Abdala 1994, 62). In April 1991, a new factor altered the situation. The enactment of the Convertibility Law made illegal any price adjustments through the indexation mechanism contained in the privatization contract. This forced the government and the private telephone companies to stipulate a new agreement in November 1991, which set the pulse price at US$.038 and granted a number of concessions to Telefónica and Telecom that more than compensated for the loss in diminished pulse rates (Abdala 1994).

In 1992, the Menem government negotiated a reduction in domestic long-distance rates with the private companies. Although the reduction cost the two companies an estimated loss of US$145 million each, with this reduction the companies obtained a concession for the booming cellular phone business that was expected to yield profits far beyond what they had given up. In 1994, Telefónica and Telecom tried to renegotiate local and international tariffs. As in prior instances, the two companies dealt directly with the government, while ignoring the CNT, which in theory was the "independent" regulatory agency granted authority to "apply, interpret, and enforce laws, decrees, and other norms in the telecommunications sector."[24] The CNT was chaired by a trustee nominated by the executive branch of government. However, in early 1993, it was overhauled, and a competent board of directors was appointed through a competitive examination system. When the private telecommunications companies tried to make a deal with the Ministry of the Economy and Public Works, which completely bypassed the CNT, consumer groups took them to court. Members of the CNT board (but not its president, who was a political appointee and had tacitly agreed to the direct dealing between the government and the telephone companies) eventually testified that the price hikes were unwarranted. Consequently, the appeals court ruled against any price increases. A few months later, the executive branch dismissed the whole CNT board by executive order as a retaliatory measure.[25] From that point on, all major decisions on telecommunications issues were made by the Ministry of Economy and Public Works in open defiance of the law that ascribed to the CNT the jurisdiction over telecommunications matters. Indeed, undeterred by the appeals court decision, the government in January 1997 issued a new executive order restructuring local and long-distance tariffs, as if it had been agreed with the telephone companies all along. The executive order established that international call rates would be cut by an average of 42 percent and local call rates would be increased by 50 percent (*Latin American Monitor: Southern Cone* March 1997, 3).[26]

Telefónica and Telecom welcomed the government initiative and started to apply the new rates immediately. However, consumer groups succeeded in having an administrative court issue an injunction against the charging of the new rates until a public hearing could be held. To appease both critics and telephone companies, the government issued a new decree (264/98) in April 1998. The decree terminated the Telefónica and Telecom monopoly at the end of 1999, in violation of the 1990 concession contract, which stipulated that if the companies fulfilled their contractual obligations by 1997, they would be eligible for an extension up until 2000. To offset the decree, the government allowed the telephone companies to enter the lucrative cable television market, from which they were previously excluded. In June 1998, the Supreme Court, which Menem had "packed" with sympathetic judges in 1989, upheld the legality of the executive order of January 1997. In the end, the telephone companies and the government were able to obtain what they wanted all along. As of the last quarter of 1999, despite a reduction in the price for international and long-distance calls, the Argentine rates remain among the highest, not only in Latin America but also compared to the rest of the world (*Latin American Monitor: Southern Cone* June 1998, 3-4). Furthermore, the supposed liberalization of the telecommunications sector in 2000 will take place under strict conditions. Two additional licenses will be awarded to countries currently doing business in Argentina in the cellular phone service sector, meaning that the consortium composed of the U.S. conglomerate GTE and the Argentine media group Clarín as well as the Movicom composed of Bell South, Motorola, and Citicorp will all be operating in Argentina in 2000.

In retrospect, the handling of privatization first and regulation later seems to have concealed a strong collusion between government and business.[27] The British consulting firm Nero, hired by the Argentine government to give support to the tariff restructuring, estimated that the guaranteed 16-percent return established in the original contract actually had yielded a net return on assets of 48 percent in 1993 alone, when all factors were considered. The new private companies posted high profits throughout their concession period. In 1998, Telecom and Telefónica had net earnings of US$260 million and US$370 million, respectively. These figures represented respective increases of 17 percent and 19 percent over the previous year.[28]

The difference between the Chilean and Argentine trends can be understood easily. After deregulation, a phone call between Santiago and New York cost US$0.75 a minute. In comparison, a similar call from Argentina to the United States cost $3.69 a minute (ADELCO 1995, 13). The higher profit margins posted by the Argentine companies compared to their Chilean counterparts have much to do with the conditions of their monopolistic environments. Until deregulation, ENTEL of Chile yielded returns of 40 percent, which analysts regarded as the result of overpricing, not of increased efficiency (Maloney 1993, 373). The Argentine telecommunications companies, as the Nero study found, have been posting net returns on assets even greater than their Chilean counterparts. Thus, there seems to be a clear association between monopolistic market conditions and high profits.

A further indication that overpricing is at the core of high profit margins is the two Argentine telecommunications companies' tenacious court battle against the use of call-back cards; individuals and companies were beginning to use the cards (issued by telephone companies in other countries, mainly the United States) to reduce costs. Telefónica and Telecom contended that call-back card system usage was illegal because it broke the 1990 monopoly agreement with the government. In 1995, a federal appeals court in Buenos Aires ruled that the telecommunications companies' argument was unfounded because the 1990 transfer contract did not cover call-back operations.[29]

The privatization of the Argentine electricity sector, begun in 1991, was quite a different story. Government planners tried to make the best use of other countries' experiences to avoid past mistakes, such as those made in the ENTel privatization. Much influenced by external factors, authorities introduced competition and transparency of rules in the electricity market. The World Bank, which heavily financed the project, exercised strong pressure along with international investors who feared a repetition of the ENTel privatization saga.[30] In 1992, the Argentine Congress passed Law No. 24065, which established a new regulatory framework. The law, complemented by Decree 1398/92, left the enforcement of regulation to Ente Nacional de Regulación de Energía (ENRE), a new agency that started operating in 1993 and was financed much as the CNT was.

The Menem administration initiated the sale of controlling interests in the electric power services sector in Buenos Aires and its metropolitan area, as well in other less lucrative markets in the interior. Following a procedure tried in England, existing monopolies were divided into power generation, transmission, and distribution companies and then auctioned separately. Under this scheme, companies operating in power generation compete among themselves to sell electricity to a power pool supervised by Cammesa, a nonprofit agency jointly owned by the government, power companies, and major users. The transmission companies then charge a fixed rate to send power to distribution companies that, in turn, compete fiercely to attract customers, as their prices are subject to consumers' demand and efficiency criteria. Large users were left with the option of contracting directly with power generators, bypassing distributors.

In 1992, Servicios Eléctricos del Gran Buenos Aires (SEGBA) was split into three different companies — one for generation, which kept the name Servicios Eléctricos del Gran Buenos Aires, and two for distribution, Empresa de Electricidad del Norte (EDENOR) and Empresa de Electricidad del Sur (EDESUR); 51 percent of the shares were auctioned to interested bidders. French and Chilean consortia won EDENOR and EDESUR, respectively. These two privatizations were generally regarded as exemplary because of the competent and transparent manner in which the government achieved them. They also attracted quite a number of very competitive bids. The EDENOR and EDESUR privatizations exemplified the premise that having a good regulatory framework in place prior to state divestiture increases the attractiveness of sales rather than deterring bidders.

In the end, the 32 electricity generation companies that resulted from the Argentine privatization process engaged in competitive tactics so cutthroat that, by 1993, the companies' tariffs were lower than before privatization.[31] Companies' profit margins turned into deficits between 1992 and 1993.[32] Eventually, in 1995, tariffs rebounded but were still 40 percent below their pre-privatization levels. Competition also was enhanced by the fact that barriers to new entrants were lifted. As a result, investors, taking advantage of the abundance of natural gas in Argentina, built new gas-powered generators that began to compete with older hydroelectric and coal-fueled plants. Of course, consumers were the main beneficiaries of this new trend, as they received cheaper and better services than they had ever imagined.

In sum, freed from the urgency and political manipulations that characterized the ENTel privatization, the Menem administration, with the technical assistance of foreign consultants, proceeded with the electricity sector privatization in a professional manner, maximizing revenues and efficiency gains. Moreover, the electricity sector's clear regulatory framework attracted many investors — just the opposite trend from that seen in the privatization of ENTel, where unclear rules actually discouraged foreign companies.

SOME INITIAL LESSONS

Far from eliminating the problem of regulation, privatization has created new challenges. This chapter has shown how political factors were paramount in shaping the development of the regulatory frameworks in Chile and Argentina. Clearly, at least in the beginning of the privatization process, the goal of ensuring competition through privatization was, at best, a secondary goal for policymakers in both countries, as their primary goals of retaining political control and maximizing short-term fiscal revenues took precedence.

Two different trends were also underlined. As hypothesized, when privatizations were poorly executed and lacked credible regulatory frameworks, they usually caused rent-seeking behavior by the new private owners that resulted in high prices. In contrast, when good regulation was in place from the beginning or when deregulation took place only after privatization, efficiency gains were clear. In addition, where there were privatizations without regulation in place, there were strong suspicions of collusive practices involving government and private companies to the detriment of the public interest. Such collusion defies the idea behind market reforms in general and privatization in particular, which is the creation of competitive, transparent markets.

Only in one case, electricity privatization in Argentina, were competition and regulation both present at the time of privatization. Understandably, Argentina's electricity privatization is usually mentioned as an example of an effective privatization process and is now being studied not only by other developing and post-Communist countries planning to divest their electricity sectors but also by U.S. regulators.[33] The privatization of Argentina's electricity industry has produced excellent results by significantly lowering prices, bringing in large foreign investments, and tremendously expanding supply. In addition, ENRE's enforcement of regulations has become easier, as partial self-regulation of the market occurred through healthy competition.

In the other three cases, concessions were granted under monopolistic clauses. Among these, competition was introduced later on only in the Chilean telecommunications market, and this occurred only thanks to the intervention of an external agency, the Antitrust Commission. To date, the telecommunications sector in Argentina and the electricity sector in Chile remain highly monopolistic markets.

As hypothesized, sectors whose concessions were privatized under monopolistic clauses within a weak regulatory framework did exhibit rent-seeking behavior by the companies in the privatized markets. This seems to explain why, for example, electricity prices rose after privatization and remained high in Chile, while the opposite trend was observed in Argentina. Figure 1 clearly illustrates this situation. In Chile, electricity generators predominantly use "node" rather than "spot" prices to charge distribution companies because node prices are much more stable. Conversely, in Argentina, spot prices are the only ones used. Indeed, prices have been so high in Chile that, in June 1997, the Superintendency of Electricity and Fuel finally acted and asked electricity companies to refund clients about US$18 million

Figure 1.
Trends of Three Set Prices for Electricity in Argentina and Chile

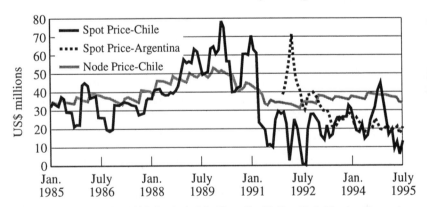

Source: Flemings Securities, 1997, *Survival of the Fittest* (April). New York: Flemings Research.

Table 2.
Net Electricity Prices Received by Generators
(1993-1995) in US$/MWh

Year	Endesa	Chilgener	Central Costanera	Central Puerto
1993	54.9	47.9	37.40	37.48
1994	57.0	52.0	37.40	36.73
1995	54.4	50.8	36.41	35.83

MWh = megawatt-hour

Source: Flemings Securities, 1997, *Survival of the Fittest* (April). New York: Flemings Research.

in excess fees for the first half of 1997 alone.[34] Equally illuminating is the fact that in Argentina in the mid-1990s, where electricity companies were forced to compete, the subsidiaries of Endesa (Central Costanera) and Chilgener (Central Puerto) charged lower prices than they charged at home in Chile (Table 2). However, there are also indications that rent seeking crosses the boundaries of national regulatory regimes; for example, the Chilgener in 1996 disclosed plans to link the generators it owns in the Argentine province of Neuquen to its network in Chile to satisfy increasing demands in Chile. According to the proposal, which was implemented, the generators on the Argentine side would work under Chilean regulations, allowing the distribution project to operate on the same marginal cost criteria used in Chile but to charge Chilean consumers more lucrative prices than it charged in Argentina. "Thus," as a sector analyst concluded at the time, "there is a distinct attraction in playing by Chilean rules" (*Lagniappe Letter* August 1996, 10).

Much of the same can be said about the telecommunications sector in Argentina, where, according to a World Bank analysis, "tariffs are very high by international standards and are hampering the competitiveness of the Argentine economy. Meanwhile, competing countries like Chile, where privatization has gone with strong competition in the market, have seen telephone tariffs plummet and have increased the penetration rate (teledensity) much faster" (Guislain 1997, 231).

As shown in Table 3 (see next page), Argentine rates for domestic long-distance and international calls are the highest among the six Latin American countries surveyed. In contrast, in Chile, where the sector is competitive, domestic long-distance rates tie for the second cheapest, and international long-distance rates are the cheapest. As noted, the monopolistic rent-seeking attitude of the Argentine telephone companies is also evident in the tenacity with which they tried to stop the use of call-back cards, when this type of service was not even contemplated in the concession contract.

For the Argentine telephone companies and the Chilean electrical companies, with firms earning annual net returns on assets averaging 20 percent and even 30 percent, increased earnings are not solely due to increases in efficiency but have much to do with rent-seeking behavior.[35] Evidence that rent seeking is a plausible explanation for such large payoffs comes from the only one of the cases in which

Table 3.
Telephone Tariff Comparison in Latin America in US$
(first quarter of 1997)

	Venezuela	Peru	Brazil	Chile	Argentina	Mexico
Connection, residential	54.3	344.2	250	170.1	302.5	125.3
Connection, business	61.7	559.4	250	170.1	302.5	448.7
Subscription (monthly), residential	4.6	9.6	12.9	13.1	10.8	9.4
Subscription (monthly), business	18.0	15.1	18.1	13.1	37.5	14.8
Number of free units	100	25	90	0	100	100
Local call, length of a unit	1 min	3 min	4 min	1 min	2 min	per call
Price per local call unit	0.02	0.07	0.08	0.04	0.03	0.10
Domestic long distance, average per minute	0.21	0.24	0.15	0.21	0.74	0.26
International long distance, average per minute	1.76	1.45	1.54	0.68	2.69	0.88

Source: Flemings Securities, New York, unpublished data.

the market started as a monopoly and eventually became competitive, the Chilean telecommunications market. In 1993, under monopoly status, ENTEL had net profits of US$80 million. In 1995, after deregulation, profits were squeezed to $15 million (Bitrán and Serra 1995, 27).

Early on in this chapter, I also argued that a corollary to the hypothesis advocating the introduction of regulation with competition in privatization is that post-facto regulation of a government monopoly transferred to private ownership is ineffective, as it becomes difficult to prevent rent-seeking behavior on the part of the privatized companies once the ground rules are set and property rights are granted. The evidence for the corollary is less clear than that for the hypothesis but still seems to support the point to a large degree. Once again, the electricity sector in Argentina shows that if a good regulatory framework, coupled with competition in the market, is set in place at the time of privatization, things proceed more smoothly because part of the regulation is actually performed by the market via competition, and litigation among the parties involved is less likely.

In the case of Chile, for instance, quite detailed sector-specific laws were meant to leave little discretion for government bureaucrats and politicians. Pinochet's economists chose this approach in reaction to the interventionist policies that had characterized the Salvador Allende administration in the early 1970s (Hachette and Lüders 1993). Later, the Pinochet regime established sector-specific "superintendencies" with limited powers of intervention. This approach "is appealing because it is perceived as the regulatory equivalent of going 'autopilot,' but it is likely to work only when a government has a clear idea of the industry structure it wants, moves quickly to this structure, and then doesn't change its mind" (Tenenbaum 1995, 3). This "straitjacket" characteristic is also a major weakness, precisely because, due to its rigidity, a government has little room for maneuvering if market conditions change. This is what Chilean policymakers had to confront in the post-Pinochet era.

Given that sector-specific laws left no way out, Chilean government officials used antitrust legislation, which was only scarcely employed under Pinochet, as an alternative means to break up monopolistic markets.[36] As noted earlier, this effort succeeded in the case of telecommunications, but what about electricity? In 1990, the government accused Enersis of monopolistic practices. The case went all the way to the Supreme Court, which, in a controversial decision, found the evidence presented unconvincing. In June 1997, the government brought a similar case before the Antitrust Commission, arguing that Enersis's monopolistic control of the SIC was responsible for the absence of new power companies investing in Chile's central region for the previous ten years. Again, Enersis won the legal battle, although the company was required to observe some new conditions.[37] Government prosecutors considered this second ruling "abusive" and damaging to the Chilean economy because it solidified the monopolistic nature of the electricity sector. However, they were quick to add that it had been, since the beginning, "a battle between David and hundreds of Goliaths."[38] A pro-government Congressman, Ramon Briones, was even blunter when he declared that the Antitrust Commission was virtually a "hostage" to domestic economic interests.[39] The Antitrust Commission's different stances toward telecommunications regulation and toward electricity regulation, as the comments above suggest, have a political rather than an economic explanation. By breaking up the telecommunications sector, the Antitrust Commission was negatively affecting foreign investors, namely Telefónica de España. However, domestic investors benefited from the decision only to the extent that they could create joint ventures with other major telephone companies and get a piece of the business. Instead, Enersis and Chilgener are Chile's largest companies and are becoming important players in the electricity market in South America. For the reasons discussed earlier, they tend to have tremendous political clout, which their managements adroitly use to maintain their privileged status.

The Argentine telecommunications privatization is a textbook case of what can go wrong when regulation is implemented after privatization. Lacking a clear regulatory framework from the start, this privatization resulted in never-ending negotiations between the government and the telephone companies. The situation became so chaotic that, in an unusual move, the World Bank strongly advised the

Menem administration that the appointment of a new, highly qualified group of CNT commissioners would be indispensable for bringing transparency to the sector's management (Edwards 1995). Yet, when the CNT tried to gain some control over the sector, Telefónica and Telecom stonewalled, preferring to cut a deal directly with the executive branch. What followed was the emasculation of the CNT's prerogatives and the resumption of a highly political manipulation of the sector's regulation on the part of the Menem administration.[40] This further development allowed the government and the telephone companies to strike new agreements; however, it resulted in a series of embarrassing setbacks in successful court challenges, thus creating even more confusion and uncertainty.

CONCLUSION

This brief analysis of the Chilean and Argentine cases brings up considerations of a more general nature, given that the kinds of problems described are far from limited to these two countries. In retrospect, it appears clear that the best way to avoid many regulatory problems is to create competition in the market prior to privatization. In the preceding case analyses, prices are invariably high where competition is weak — for example, for electricity in Chile and for telephones in Argentina. Weak competition penalizes consumers and diminishes existing firms' incentives to increase efficiency, to the detriment of the economy as a whole. Further, Argentina's telephone experience and Chile's electricity experience demonstrate that post-facto regulation of a public monopoly transferred to private ownership is ineffective, as it cannot prevent strong rent-seeking behavior on the part of the new companies after the ground rules are in place and property rights are granted. A recent World Bank study estimates that ineffective regulation in public utilities is responsible for a US$1 billion loss for society in Argentina alone, or 0.35 percent of Argentina's gross domestic product. This situation created a 16-percent hidden tax for consumers (Chisari, Estache, and Romero 1997).

By the same token, this chapter suggests that there is a clear relationship between SOEs transferred to the private sector under monopolistic conditions and the lack of transparency and collusion that characterize such transactions. These kinds of transfers not only run counter to the economic rationale behind privatization, as the lack of competition undermines efficiency gains, but also from a political standpoint, are at odds with the democratic principles that are supposed to be at the ideological core of market reforms. Monopolies foster privilege and unfairness, not democracy. This is an important point, as we cannot artificially separate the economic aspects of privatization from its broader political implications. Governments told their people in Chile and Argentina, as well as in other Latin American countries experiencing similar policies, that state divestiture would bring along better services, larger opportunities to become an active part of the market by spreading ownership, and greater attention to the individual's rights both as a consumer and a citizen. Unfortunately, not all these promises have been fulfilled, and we must be aware that when governments raise expectations and are unable to live up to them, disappointment can turn into protest movements that can be easily exploited by demagogues who, once in power, may reverse the positive accomplishments that market reforms have attained. Collusion and lack of transparency in some public utility privatizations almost invariably, not only in Chile and Argentina but in other countries such as Brazil, Peru, and Mexico, have prompted a new public debate in recent times over the need for greater regulation, some of which resemble the interventionist policies of the past.

However, on the positive side, it must be said that multilateral institutions like the World Bank and the IMF are now urging countries to make the regulatory issue a priority prior to privatization, in light of past mistakes. This new trend can be clearly seen in Brazil, which has privatized telecommunications and electricity in the last few years and set up regulatory institutions prior to sell-offs. The hope is that the Brazilian example will become the rule rather than the exception in the years to come.

In conclusion, privatization, to live up to its promise, must promote competition and transparency. To paraphrase Milton Friedman, only in this way can economic freedom translate into political freedom. A capitalist economy can certainly thrive under monopolistic or oligopolistic conditions. However, it will never fulfill its potential if economic power is held in the hands of a few to the detriment of the rights of individuals, as monopoly "inhibits effective freedom by denying individuals alternatives" (Friedman 1962,14). The task of the new regulatory state in the years to come indeed will be to find ways to protect such freedom without abusing its own discretionary powers.

Notes

1. Experts are usually unanimous in regarding electricity and telecommunications as benchmark examples for government regulatory policy as a whole. This is because they are large infrastructures that are vital to the economic growth of any economy as well as to people's everyday lives. Moreover, these sectors' market nature often exhibits monopoly or quasi-monopoly features that require government regulation.

2. The need to have countries that had privatized and regulated both electricity and telecommunications for an appreciable time period led to the exclusion of Mexico, which is only now beginning to privatize electricity, and Brazil, which only recently privatized telecommunications. Peru has privatized both sectors, but it has done so later than Argentina and Chile, and I was unable to gather enough meaningful data for comparison.

3. Interview with Rolf Lüders, former finance minister of the Pinochet regime. Santiago de Chile, August 1996.

4. *Página/12*, 1990, 8-11.

5. Dromi allegedly pocketed about US$7 million for the privatization of the highways alone. *Buenos Aires Herald*, September 14, 1999, 3.

6. In both Argentina and Chile, antitrust agencies are understaffed and have little capacity to gather data independently, which limits their ability to pursue offenders effectively. Of the two, the Argentine antitrust institution is the weakest. It was created in 1980 with limited jurisdiction and no authority to sanction penalties since all decisions on this matter belong to the Ministry of the Economy, on which it depends directly. Interviews with Mario Bacman, Comisión Nacional para la Defensa de la Competencia, Buenos Aires, July 1996.

7. Interview with Rodrigo Asenjo, head of the National Economic Office (Fiscal Nacional Económico), Santiago de Chile, August 1996. See also Peredes (1993) and Blanlot (1993).

8. On Argentina, see Ministerio de Economía y Obras y Servicios Públicos (1993). On Chile, see Foxley (1983), Marcel (1989), and Meller (1993).

9. Interview with José Guillermo Capdevila, director of the Comisión Nacional de Correos y Telégrafos, the national mail regulatory agency, Buenos Aires, August 1995. Capdevila was part of the legal council that designed Argentina's state divestiture legislation under Minister Dromi.

10. *Financial Times*, December 13, 1995, 2.

11. On the politicization and lack of transparency of the Chilean privatization process, see Marcel (1989).

12. Enersis's largest shareholders were AFPs, 34.4 percent; employees, 28.7 percent; other institutional stockholders, 15.3 percent. Endesa's stock ownership followed a similar pattern: AFPs, 28 percent; foreign investment funds, 29 percent; Enersis, 25.3 percent; and

employees, 16 percent. Chilgener's shareholding structure was AFPs, 46 percent; regular stockholders, 14 percent; domestic stockholders, 15 percent; foreign investors, 7 percent. No individual was allowed to own more than 20 percent of a company's total stocks (Lauro 1996, 78). The disproportionate power of management vis-à-vis shareholders was demonstrated in 1997 when Enersis's Chief Executive Officer, José Yuraszeck, and the company board allowed Endesa of Spain to purchase an important stake in the company without convening a shareholders' meeting. After a prolonged legal battle, a judge ruled in 1998 against Yuraszeck and several board members, who, in the meantime, had been forced to resign. *La Tercera*, November 12, 1998, 1.

13. In 1990, according to the Organización Latinoamericana de Energía, residential rates measured in US$ per 100 kWh were as follows: Chile, $8.7; Brazil, $8.6; Argentina, $8.1; Mexico, $4.1; Colombia, 2.6; Ecuador, 2.0; and Venezuela, $1.6.

14. Only the Brazilian giant Electrobras was more profitable in 1996, *Latin Trade*, September, 1997, 43.

15. Former government officials who worked on the electricity privatization process at the time acknowledged the seriousness of this problem and candidly admitted that they simply overlooked it. Interview with former Finance Minister Rolf Lüders, Santiago de Chile, August 1996.

16. Data provided by Flemings Securities. Interview with Flemings officials. May 1995, New York.

17. Immediately after the TransGas project was announced, Enersis and Chilgener's stocks fell appreciably. Interview with TransGas officials. Santiago, August 1996.

18. In Chile, political campaign financing is basically unregulated. Big domestic companies tend to make large donations to the most important parties. Electricity companies are the country's most important campaign contributors and exercise a tremendous lobbying power. Interview with Professor Oscar Godoy, former member of the National Commission on Ethics, and representative Carlos Centero, Santiago de Chile, August 1996.

19. Interviews with TransGas officials, Santiago de Chile, August 1996.

20. Starting in 1987, the government allowed telephone employees to turn their severance pay into company shares, as it had been the case in the electricity privatization.

21. At the time, Telefónica de España was a monopolistic SOE in Spain.

22. This point was stressed in correspondence that I had with diplomats from the United States, France, Italy, and Spain who served in Chile at the time.

23. Originally, the government wanted to split ENTel into five regional companies, but potential buyers made it clear that only the Buenos Aires metropolitan area, where 59.2 of the country's telephone traffic was concentrated, was of interest to them (Petrazzini 1995, 121).

24. Decree 1185/90, Article 6.

25. Interview with Andrea Rodríguez, consumer news correspondent for *Clarín*, Argentina's largest daily, Buenos Aires, July 1996.

26. The idea behind the tariff restructuring was that both Telefónica and Telecom-Stet, aware of the fact that the exclusive long-distance service concession would be lifted either in 1997 or in 2000, thought that a gradual reduction of rates for such a service was in order to prepare themselves for future competition. However, to offset the lost revenues in long

distance, they needed a corresponding increase in local call rates. Interview with Professor Augustín Gordillo, Buenos Aires Law School, Buenos Aires, August 1996.

27. Interview with Andrea Rodríguez, Buenos Aires, April 1997.

28. Data provided by Flemings Securities and Telefónica.

29. Interview with Appeals Court Judge Luis Uslenghi, member of the three-panel court that ruled on the case, Buenos Aires, May 1996.

30. Interviews with senior officials at the Ministerio de Economía y Obras y Servicios Públicos, Buenos Aires, July 1995 and August 1996. Interviews with World Bank officials, May 1995 and September 1996. All the public officials interviewed had managed several aspects of the electricity privatization process directly.

31. Electricity tariffs between September 1992 and November 1994 dropped as follows: small users, 9.0 percent; medium users, 6.2 percent; large users, 7.5 percent. Only small users under the category T1-R-1 saw an increase. Data provided by the national energy regulatory agency ENRE. Interview with ENRE officials, Buenos Aires, May 1995.

32. Post-privatization losses were $52 million in 1992 and $65.8 million in 1993. Profits started to emerge in 1994 ($1.3 million) and 1995 ($46.5 million). Data provided by the national energy regulatory agency ENRE. Interview with ENRE officials, Buenos Aires, May 1995.

33. *Wall Street Journal*, June 19, 1996, A1, A12.

34. *El Mercurio,* June 16, 1997, 1.

35. For the Argentine case, see Chisari, Estache, and Romero (1997). For the Chilean case, see Meller (1993).

36. Interview with Rodrigo Asenjo, Santiago, August 1996.

37. The Antitrust Commission barred Enersis from changing the amount of shares in its subsidiaries and from increasing its own market share in the electricity sector. It also asked the government to revise ambiguous regulations and price-setting schemes. *Latin American Monitor: Southern Cone*, July 1997, 2.

38. *Financial Times*, June 18, 1997, 19.

39. *El Mercurio*, June 17, 1997, 1.

40. This was confirmed in an interview with Henoch Aguiar, who was a CNT board member at the time these events took place, Buenos Aires, August 1996.

References

Abdala, Manuel. 1994. "The Regulation of Newly Privatized Firms: An Illustration from Argentina." In *Privatization in Latin America: New Roles for the Public and Private Sectors,* eds. Werner Baer and Melissa Birch. New York: Praeger.

Aguiar, Henoch. 1996. Interview. Mr. Aguiar was a CNT board member at the time these events took place, Buenos Aires (August).

Asenjo, Rodrigo. 1996. Interview. Head of the National Economic Office (Fiscal Nacional Económico), Santiago de Chile (August).

Aspiazu, Daniel, and Adolfo Vispo. 1994. "Algunas enseñanzas de las privatizaciones en la Argentina." *Revista de la CEPAL,* December: 129-147.

Bacman, Mario. 1996. Interviews. Comisión Nacional para la Defensa de la Competencia, Buenos Aires (July).

Baumol, William, John Panzar, and Robert Willig. 1982. *Contestable Markets and the Theory of Industry Structure.* New York: Harcourt Brace Jovanovich.

Bitrán, Eduardo, Antonio Estache, José Luis Guasch, and Pablo Serra. 1999. "Privatizing and Regulating Chile's Utilities, 1974-2000: Successes, Failures, and Outstanding Challenges," In *Chile: Recent Policy Lessons and Emerging Challenges,* eds. Guillermo Perry and Danny M. Leipziger. Washington, D.C.: World Bank. 327-392.

Bitrán, Eduardo, and Raúl Sáez. 1994. "Privatization and Regulation in Chile." In *The Chilean Economy,* eds. Barry Bosworth, Rudiger Dornbusch, and Raúl Labán. Washington, D.C.: The Brookings Institution.

Bitrán, Eduardo, and Pablo Serra. 1994. "Regulatory Issues in the Privatization of Public Utilities: The Chilean Experience." *The Quarterly Review of Economics and Finance* 54 (Summer): 179-197.

Bitrán, Eduardo, and Pablo Serra. 1995. "The Chilean Experience on Regulating Privatized Infrastructure." Unpublished manuscript. Santiago de Chile.

Blanlot, Vivian. 1993. "La regulación del sector eléctrico." In *Después de las privatizaciones: hacia el estado regulador,* ed. Oscar Muñoz. Santiago: CIEPLAN.

Buchanan, James. 1980. "Rent Seeking and Profit Seeking." In *Toward a Theory of the Rent-Seeking Society,* eds. James Buchanan, Robert Tollison, and Gordon Tullock. College Station: Texas A&M University Press.

Capdevila, José Guillermo. 1995. Interview. Director of the Comisión Nacional de Correos y Telégrafos (the national mail regulatory agency). Buenos Aires (August).

Chisari, Omar, Antonio Estache, and Carlos Romero. 1997. *Winners and Losers from Utilities Privatizations: Lessons from a General Equilibrium Model of Argentina.* Policy Research Working Paper 1824. Washington, D.C.: World Bank.

Edwards, Sebastian. 1995. *Crisis and Reform in Latin America: From Despair to Hope.* New York: Oxford University Press.

El Mercurio. June 16, 1997, 1.

El Mercurio. June 17, 1997, 1.

Fernández Fredes, Francisco. 1996. "La regulación de la actividad económica y los derechos del consumidor. La experiencia Chilena." Mimeo. Santiago de Chile.

Financial Times. June 18, 1997, 19.

Flemings Securities. 1995. Interview with Flemings officials. New York. (May).

Flemings Securities. 1997. *Survival of the Fittest*. April. New York: Flemings Research.

Foxley, Alejandro. 1983. *Latin American Experiments in Neoconservative Economics*. Berkeley, Calif.: University of California Press.

Friedman, Milton. 1972. *Capitalism and Freedom*. Chicago: University of Chicago Press.

Galal, Ahmed, Leroy Jones, Pakai Tandon, and Ingo Vogelsang. 1994. *Welfare Consequences of Selling Public Enterprises: An Empirical Analysis*. New York: Oxford University Press.

Glade, William. 1989. "Privatization in Rent-Seeking Societies." *World Development* 17 (5): 673-682.

Godoy, Oscar, and Carlos Centero. 1996. Interviews. Former member of the National Commission on Ethics and representative, respectively, Santiago de Chile (August).

Gordillo Augustín. 1996. Interview. Professor, Buenos Aires Law School, Buenos Aires. (August).

Gray, Phillip, ed. 1996. *Industry Structure and Regulation in Infrastructure: A Cross-Country Survey*. PSD Occasional Paper 25. Private Sector Development Department. Washington, D.C.: World Bank.

Guislain, Pierre. 1997. *The Privatization Challenge: A Strategic, Legal, and Institutional Analysis of International Experience*. Washington, D.C.: World Bank.

Hachette, Dominique, and Rolf Lüders. 1993. *Privatization in Chile: An Economic Appraisal*. San Francisco: ICS Press.

Heller, William, and Mathew McCubbins. 1996. "Politics, Institutions, and Outcomes: Electricity Regulation in Argentina and Chile." Unpublished paper. San Diego, California.

Kwoka, John. 1996. *Privatization, Deregulation, and Competition: A Survey of Effects on Economic Performance*. PSD Occasional Paper 27. Private Sector Development Department. Washington, D.C.: World Bank.

La Tercera. November 12, 1998, 1.

Latin American Monitor: Southern Cone. July 1997, 2.

Latin Trade. September 1997, 43.

Lauro, Adriana. 1996. "Las Empresas Chilenas Invaden la Argentina." *Apertura* (July): 72-101.

Lüders, Rolf. 1996. Interview. Former finance minister of the Pinochet regime. Santiago de Chile (August).

Majul, Luis. 1993. *Los dueños de la Argentina*. Buenos Aires: Sudamericana.

Majul, Luis. 1994. *Los dueños de la Argentina II*. Buenos Aires: Sudamericana.

Maloney, William. 1993. "Comments." In *The Chilean Economy*, eds. Barry Bosworth, Rudiger Dornbusch, and Raúl Labán. Washington, D.C.: The Brookings Institution.

Marcel, Mario. 1989. "La Privatización de Empresas Públicas en Chile, 1985-88." *Revista Cieplan* 26 (June): 5-60.

McCraw, Thomas, ed. 1981. *Regulation in Perspective*. Cambridge, Mass.: Harvard University Press.

Meller, Patricio. 1993. "A Review of the Chilean Privatization Experience." *Quarterly Review of Economics and Finance* 33 (Special Issue): 95-112.

Ministerio de Economía y Obras y Servicios Públicos. 1993. *Argentina en crecimiento.* Buenos Aires: Ministerio de Economía y Obras y Servicios Públicos.

Ministerio de Economía y Obras y Servicios Públicos. July 1995 and August 1996. Interviews with senior officials. Buenos Aires.

Mitnick, Barry. 1981. *The Political Economy of Regulation.* New York: Columbia University Press.

Molano, Walter. 1997. *The Logic of Privatization: The Case of Telecommunications in the Southern Cone of Latin America.* Westport, Conn: Greenwood Press.

Natale, Alberto. 1993. *Privatizaciones en privado.* Buenos Aires: Planeta.

National Energy Regulatory Agency (ENRE). 1995. Interview with ENRE officials, Buenos Aires (May).

Organización Latinoamericana de Energía. <www.olade.org.ecl>

Palermo, Vincente, and Marcos Novaro. 1996. *Política y poder en el gobierno de Menem.* Buenos Aires: FLACSO.

Paredes, Ricardo. 1992. "Privatización y Regulación: Lecciones de la Experiencia Chilena." In *Hacia el estado regulador,* ed. Oscar Muñoz. Santiago: CIEPLAN.

Petrazzini, Ben. 1995. "Telephone Privatization in a Hurry: Argentina." In *Privatizing Monopolies,* ed. Ravi Ramamurti. Baltimore: The Johns Hopkins University Press.

Petrecolla, Alberto, Alberto Porto, and Pablo Gerchunoff. 1993. "Privatization in Argentina." *Quarterly Review of Economics and Finance* 33 (Special Issue): 67-93.

Ramamurti, Ravi. 1995. "The New Frontier of Privatization." In *Privatizing Monopolies,* ed. Ravi Ramamurti. Baltimore: The Johns Hopkins University Press.

Rodríguez, Andrea. 1996. Interview. Consumer news correspondent for *Clarín,* Buenos Aires (July).

Rodríguez, Andrea. 1997. Interview. Buenos Aires. April.

Sáez, Raúl. 1993. "Las privatizaciones de empresas en Chile." In *Hacia el estado regulador,* ed. Oscar Muñoz. Santiago: CIEPLAN.

Schamis, Héctor. 1992. "Conservative Political Economy in Latin America and Western Europe: The Political Sources of Privatization." In *The Right and Democracy in Latin America,* eds. Douglas Chalmers, Maria do Carmo Campello de Souza, and Atilio Borón. New York: Praeger.

Schamis, Héctor. 1999. "Distributional Coalitions and the Politics of Economic Reform in Latin America." *World Politics* 51 (January): 236-268.

Smith, Warrick. 1997. *Covering Political and Regulatory Risk: Issues and Options for Private Infrastructure Arrangements.* Private Sector Development Department. Washington, D.C.: World Bank.

Sonneschein, Mabelle G., and Patricia A. Yokopenic. 1996. "Multinational Enterprises and Telecommunications Privatization." In *Privatizing Monopolies: Lessons from Telecommunications and Transport Sectors in Latin America,* ed. Ravi Ramamurti. Baltimore: The Johns Hopkins University Press.

Spiller, Pablo, and Luis Viana Martorell. 1994. "How Should It Be Done? Electricity Regulation in Argentina, Brazil, Uruguay, and Chile." Unpublished manuscript. University of California, Berkeley.

Tenenbaum, Bernard. 1995. "The Real World of Power Sector Regulation." *World Bank Viewpoint,* Note No. 50. (June): 1-4.

TransGas officials. 1996. Interview. Santiago (August).

Uslenghi, Luis. 1996. Interview. Appeals Court Judge, member of the three-panel court that ruled on the case, Buenos Aires (May).

Wall Street Journal. June 19, 1996, A1, A12.

World Bank officials. May 1995 and September 1996. Interviews.

Yarrow, George. 1986. "Privatization in Theory and Practice." *Economic Policy* 2 (April): 324-377.

CHAPTER 5

Structuring Prudential Bank Regulation to Promote Efficiency and Safety

GEORGE G. KAUFMAN

INTRODUCTION

B anking is prominent among the sectors that most affect the health of a country's macro economy. A large and growing body of evidence indicates that an efficient financial system contributes significantly to both aggregate and per-capita economic growth. An even larger and older body of evidence indicates that breakdowns in a nation's financial sector, particularly in banking, likely magnify and, possibly, ignite breakdowns in the domestic macro economy and even beyond. Indeed, a survey (Lindgren, Garcia, and Saal 1996) by the International Monetary Fund (IMF) reported serious banking problems in some two-thirds of its 180-plus member countries since 1980. The domestic transfer cost of resolving the insolvent banks, in terms only of government funding of the negative net worths of the insolvent institutions, whose deposit liabilities the governments generally protected from loss either explicitly or implicitly, has not infrequently exceeded 10 percent of the country's gross domestic product (GDP). This estimate excludes losses from any unused labor and capital resources that reduce GDP, the misallocation of employed resources from at least ex-post poor investments, and adverse exchange rate effects.

It follows that an efficient and safe banking and financial system is a prerequisite for an efficient and expanding macro economy. Partially because of this relationship between the financial sector and the macro economy, banks, and, to a lesser extent, other financial institutions and financial markets have been subject to government regulation in nearly all countries almost throughout their history. But the types and intensity of the regulation have changed greatly through time and vary greatly across countries. This chapter will 1) review the theory and evidence linking the economic health of the financial and real sectors of the economy, 2) discuss and evaluate the arguments for banking regulation, 3) evaluate the success and failure of prudential regulation and reasons for failure, and 4) suggest a framework for structuring prudential bank regulation to enhance efficiency and safety as well as to improve macroeconomic performance through a regulatory approach enacted recently in the United States, one that can be adapted for other countries.[1]

BANKING AND ECONOMIC ACTIVITY

Although the evidence suggests that the behavior of banks significantly affects the macro economy for both good and bad, the predominant focus to date has been on the bad — on breakdowns in banking spreading to breakdowns in the macro economy. A large number of studies report that the frequency of bank failures in the United States, the United Kingdom, and a number of other industrial countries is inversely correlated with the stage of the business cycle, rising during recessions and falling during expansions. (A review of this literature appears in Benston and Kaufman 1995; Kaufman 1994.) The studies differ on how banking crises begin — whether bank problems exogenously ignite the macroeconomic problems or whether bank problems are ignited by the macroeconomic or other forces exogenous to banking and then intensify the magnitude and duration of problems related to these forces. Among contemporary economists, Hyman Minsky (1977) and Charles Kindleberger (1985, 1996) are the major proponents of the view that banks exogenously ignite problems that spread first throughout the banking and financial sectors and then spread beyond, causing downturns in the macro economy. Like most economic agents, banks get caught up in the euphoria of budding economic expansions and expand credit rapidly to finance the increase in economic activity, particularly in areas subject to the greatest increase in demand and, consequently, in prices — for example, the stock market and real estate. Moreover, the credit is often collateralized by the assets purchased. The credit expansion fuels and accelerates the economic expansion, accelerates asset price increases, and encourages additional speculation. Both lenders and borrowers fall victim to "irrational exuberance." Through time, borrowers become more highly leveraged and turn increasingly to shorter-term debt, and their margin of safety in covering their debt service payments from operating revenues or continued increases in asset prices declines and approaches zero. Increasingly, debt servicing is financed out of new debt (Ponzi finance). Any slight decline in expected revenues or even a slowdown in expected revenue growth, no less the bursting of asset price bubbles, can then cause defaults. The financial system crashes off its own weight. Through a sequence of distress-selling, fire-sale losses, further defaults, business failures, bank runs, and bank failures, the expansion turns into a macroeconomic downturn.

Most contemporary analysts, however, view the bank problems during macroeconomic downturns as problems caused primarily by the accompanying business failures and rising unemployment, which in turn are often caused by an exogenous shock — including government policies' reducing aggregate bank reserves and, therefore, reducing the money supply or the bursting of asset price bubbles (Bordo, Mizrach, and Schwartz 1997; Hubbard 1991). The banking problems follow the downturn in the macro economy. Increases in business failures and unemployment as well as declines in asset prices increase defaults on bank loans and the perceived risk of performing bank loans. Depositors find it increasingly difficult to evaluate the financial health of their banks and to differentiate financially healthy institutions from sick ones. As a result, in the absence of deposit insurance, they are encouraged to shift (run) from deposits at their banks into currency outside of banks rather than into deposits at other, "safe" banks. Unless the accompanying loss in aggregate bank reserves is offset by a central bank lender of last resort, a multiple contraction in money and credit is ignited (Kaufman 1988). This, in turn, feeds back to the macro economy, transmitting and magnifying the initial downturn.

In either scenario, regardless of the cause of the illness, sick banks in large numbers have adverse implications for macroeconomic stability. To the extent that the poor performance of banks is perceived as a market failure, government prudential regulation is often suggested as a cure that will restore and maintain health. However, as we discuss later, such regulation is not necessarily performance enhancing. It may even contribute to the banking problem, and it is often motivated by objectives other than prudential ones.

Recent empirical research has tended to confirm the theoretical arguments of earlier analysts that efficiency in the banking and financial systems enhances per-capita economic welfare in a country (Levine 1997a, 1997b). Efficient financial markets reduce the cost of marshaling savings, channeling them at lowest cost to the most potentially productive uses as determined by market forces and monitoring and disciplining the users to maintain the most efficient allocation of real resources. The recent studies also suggest that long-term economic welfare is enhanced most when the efficiency extends to the banking markets (an indirect financing channel) and the capital markets (a direct financing channel), so that there is competition both within each channel and between the two channels. Such a structure is particularly helpful in periods of macroeconomic or financial problems. If problems arise in one channel, borrowers will be able — albeit not necessarily instantaneously, costlessly, or efficiently — to switch to the alternative channel; the aggregate flow of savings and investment will be damaged less than if this option did not exist. The mix of participants would, however, be altered. Moreover, if one channel is operating inefficiently for any number of reasons, including overregulation, the transfer of funds to the competing channel is likely to exert pressure on the first channel to improve efficiency (Kaufman and Kroszner 1997). The relative size of each channel in a number of countries is shown in Table 1.

Table 1.

Financing of Private Nonfinancial Sector by Direct (Capital Market) and Indirect (Banking System) Channels, Selected Countries, 1993

Country	Indirect Channel Banks	Direct Channel Other Institutions	Foreign Sources Capital Markets
	(%)	(%)	(%)	(%)
Brazil	80	20	—	—
Germany	65	—	28	7
Hungary	23	—	28	49
India	22	34	39	5
Israel	52	—	42	7
Japan	43	24	34	—
Korea	25	35	37	4
Mexico	91	9	—	—
Singapore	87	13	—	—
U.K.	42	—	52	6
U.S.	17	21	62	—

Source: Bank for International Settlements (BIS), 1998, *The Transmission of Monetary Policy in Emerging Market Economies*, Policy Paper No. 3 (January), 24, (Basle, Switzerland: BIS).

The advantages of having two competing channels of intermediation are gaining wider recognition. Alan Greenspan, chairman of the Board of Governors of the Federal Reserve System, has recently noted problems in focusing on banking in isolation: "Recent adverse banking experiences have emphasized the problems that can arise if banks are almost the sole source of intermediation. Their breakdown induces a sharp weakening in economic growth. A wider range of nonbank institutions, including viable debt and equity markets, are important safeguards of economic activity when banking fails" (Greenspan 1998, 8).

Similarly, David Reid of the Bank of England believes that the robustness of financial markets, particularly in emerging economies, can be improved by relying less on banks as financial intermediaries. He notes that in such economies,

> . . . a high proportion of financial intermediation tends to be channeled through the banking system. Banks are highly geared organizations with a high proportion of their liabilities being capital certain. . . . The risk-bearing liabilities of banks (capital) are often not as strong as they seem because of unwillingness to account realistically, connectedness of business or other reasons so that gearing can often be higher than it appears. When shocks hit such an economy they have to be absorbed through adjustments to asset values, the incidence of which tend to fall disproportionately on bank owners because of the dominant position of banks as financial intermediaries and their high gearing. Owners of banks tend to be politically well connected and when the solvency of their institutions is undermined can often exert strong pressure for public support which, if conceded, can be hugely expensive and send wrong market signals, failing to penalize management mistakes, reinforcing the incorrect notion that banking does not require much capital and generating moral hazard throughout the system (Reid 1998, 2; also see Working Party on Financial Stability 1997).

A recent study by Ross Levine (1997b) found that among 38 countries examined, those with both a highly developed and liquid capital (stock) market and a highly developed banking system experienced an average annual real per-capita growth rate of 3.7 percent between 1976 and 1993. This was more than twice the 1.5 percent annual rate experienced by the countries with the least developed banks and capital markets. Countries with a highly developed capital market but an undeveloped banking sector and countries with an undeveloped capital market but a highly developed banking sector experienced intermediate-term per-capita growth of about 2 percent annually.[2]

These results were surprising to some analysts, who only shortly earlier had touted the superiority of universal banks that both provided a wide range of financial services and were linked with nonfinancial firms either through ownership or lasting business relationships — for example, banks in Germany. Recent evidence suggests that although such universal banks provided liquidity to related entities over a variety of economic conditions, they frequently did so at high interest rates and expropriated any gains (Edwards and Fischer 1994; Weinstein and Yafeh 1998). Also, in Japan, the banks, as major creditors, imposed more conservative polices on their more highly leveraged debtor firms than nonbank creditors were able to impose on their less leveraged debtor firms. As a result, the highly leveraged firms with banks as major creditors were no more profitable and grew no faster than their industry peers. Nor did universal banks appear, on average, to provide superior corporate governance through time.

Evidence also suggests that where and when banks were permitted to become large and were protected from competition, they became inefficient and less profitable than banks in countries with more competitive banking systems (Barth, Nolle, and Rice 1997; McCauley and White 1997). In addition, through excessive political influence over government or regulators, or both, banks frequently managed to stymie the development of capital markets — for example, in Germany and Japan.[3] This reduced competition further and eliminated a funding channel at the very times that the banks were experiencing problems that curtailed their own ability to extend credit. As a result, the macroeconomies in these countries often performed more poorly than did those in countries with functioning bank and functioning capital market channels. Evidence from a large number of countries with transitional, emerging, and even developed economies (for example, New Zealand and, recently, Japan) also suggests that most countries have enhanced their competitive environments by permitting foreign ownership of banks.

RATIONALE FOR GOVERNMENT REGULATION OF BANKING

All firms in all countries are regulated either by the marketplace or by the government. In a market economy, most firms are primarily regulated by the marketplace; in a socialist economy, they are primarily regulated by government. In many economies, the two forms of economic regulation are in continuous competition with each other. When one is perceived not to be working well, by whatever criteria, support develops for a change to the other. Market failures in banking are often seen as more damaging than market failures in other industries, in large part because the public appears to understand less well the industries, such as banking, that deal in intangibles than those that deal in tangibles, such as manufacturing and mining. The operations of banks appear shrouded in mystery. As a result, failures are more frightening and become a cause of alarm about system breakdown. These failures readily become the stuff that journalists and, in particular, novelists and movie scriptwriters use as a base for "horror" stories. This is likely to hasten the changeover from one form of regulation to another — particularly the change from market to government regulation. The market-government regulation cycle may be depicted as follows:

Market regulation→market failures→ "horror" stories→ government intervention (regulation)→government failures (less frequent than market failures but higher cost)→government deregulation →market regulation→ market failures→ . . . .

It may be argued that in economies in which market and government regulation coexist, the tension between them provides protection against excessive government regulation on the one hand and insufficient market regulation on the other. Such beneficial tension is missing in most developing and transitional economies, where state-owned banks and credit allocation through the banking system are important.

Reasons for government regulation of banks include implementing government credit allocation, increasing the financial system's safety, and increasing competition and efficiency.

Assisting Government

From its earliest days, bank regulation has often focused on using banks to pursue the economic, political, or social goals of the government through directed credit — that is, credit allocation — and provision of revenue to the government. Banks have been regulated by the government more than other firms in almost all countries almost from the time banks were first established, because they were frequently viewed as serving a greater public interest and purpose than other firms. Banks provide a major source of credit to households and business enterprises as well as governments and, indeed, were almost the sole source of that credit in earlier days in many countries and still are in some countries today. A major percentage of what serves as money in nearly all countries is provided through banks. Because banks were conducting the "government's business," almost all countries required them to be specially chartered with limited specified powers.

In many countries, the first banks were chartered by the government to make loans to itself, chartered in exchange for part of the revenues the banks would generate, or chartered for both purposes. To maximize the government share of bank revenues, at least in the short run, the charters were generally limited in number to provide monopolies in given geographic areas. Thus it was with the chartering of the Bank of England in 1694 (West 1997). Similarly, the first banks in the United States after independence were chartered by the individual states. A number of the states received more than one-quarter of their revenues from owning or taxing banks (Sylla, Wallis, and Legler 1996; Wallis, Sylla, and Legler 1994). Richard Sylla has noted that in early U.S. history, banks were widely viewed as public utilities and given monopoly franchises: "The earliest state-chartered banks [in the United States] were thought by legislators, shareholders, bankers, and the general public as public utilities. They were given exclusive privileges, namely monopolies of banking in their towns, in return for providing financial services to the state and the public" (Sylla 1995, 212). The tradition of state-owned and state-controlled banks carries down to today. Most large banks in many emerging countries are state-owned banks, and even the state-owned banks privatized in recent years often effectively became state-controlled banks. State-owned banks exist even in some industrial countries, such as France and Italy (see Table 2 and Table 3).

Governments have found state-owned banks and state-controlled banks an excellent off-budget, thereby, hidden dispensatory of credit, not only for specific firms or industrial sectors to finance the government's industrial polices (directed credit) but also for financial political favors to supporters, cronies, friends, and fence sitters. In the extreme, such funding resembles grants more than loans, and credit cultures at these banks are often weak if not nonexistent (Kaufman 1997b). As a result, governments are generally willing to privatize or decontrol almost any other industry before banking. Indeed, as a rule, state-owned banks and even state-controlled banks in many countries are economically insolvent and survive only because governments guarantee their deposit liabilities that prevent runs by deposi-

Table 2.
Percent of Total Assets of Banking System Held by State-Owned
Banks, Selected Countries, 1997

Developing Countries	Percent	Developed Countries	
Argentina	36[1]	Japan	0
Brazil	48	Germany	50
Chile	14	United States	0
Colombia	23		
Hong Kong	0		
India	87[2]		
Indonesia	48		
Korea	13		
Malaysia	8		
Mexico	28		
Singapore	0		
Taiwan	57		
Thailand	7		
Venezuela	30		

[1]1993   [2]Not strictly comparable

Source: Morris Goldstein and Philip Turner, 1996, *Banking Crises in Emerging Economies: Origins and Policy Options*, Economic Paper No. 46 (October), 19, Basle, Switzerland: Bank for International Settlements.

Table 3.
Importance of State-Owned Banks By Region, 1994

	Percent of Total Banking Assets
West and Central Africa	91
Gulf Cooperation Council	67
SEANZA Countries*	60
Arab Countries	60
Central and Eastern Europe	57

*Eighteen Southeast Asian countries, including Japan, Australia, New Zealand, and Singapore.

Source: Tommaso Padoa-Schioppa, 1996, Address to the Ninth International Conference on Bank Supervision, June 12-14, Basle Committee on Banking Supervision, Stockholm, 20.

tors. Guaranteed deposits are effectively off-balance-sheet debt of the government and should be recognized as such in the reported government deficit. It is not surprising, therefore, that the largest bank losses in recent years were suffered by state-owned banks. Forty billion dollars and counting appear to have been lost to date both by the Credit Lyonnaise (France) and by the State Bank of São Paulo (Banco do Estado de São Paolo — BANESPA). Many other state-owned banks are not far behind, particularly in Asia, including China. However, government priorities were financed! State-owned banks and state-controlled banks are likely not only to generate operating losses but also to cost taxpayers further through misallocating resources and retarding economic development and growth in the long term.

Prudential

Banks are also regulated to enhance their safety and minimize their failures. Banks are widely believed and feared to be inherently unstable because they are structurally fragile. The perceived fragility arises from three sources:

1. Low cash-to-assets ratio (fractional reserve banking);
2. Low capital-to-assets ratio (high leverage); and
3. High demand debt (deposit)-to-total debt (deposit) ratio.

Each one of these sources by itself is perceived to reflect fragility, but the three in combination are perceived as particularly fragile and dangerous. At the first signs of doubt about their banks' ability to redeem deposits in full and on time, demand and other short-term depositors can run on the banks in order to be first in line and get their funds out without loss. Because banks hold cash equal to only a fraction of their deposits, they are likely to have to sell some earning assets quickly to accommodate the fleeing depositors. In the process, they are likely to suffer fire-sale losses, the more so the more opaque the assets. These losses, in turn, are likely to exceed the small capital base of the banks and to drive them into insolvency.

Not only were banks perceived to fail more frequently than other firms, but their failures were also perceived to be more detrimental and costly to the economy for a number of reasons. Among other things, the failures would:

1. Reduce deposits and thereby reduce the aggregate money supply and hamper trade;
2. Reduce the most liquid wealth holding of a large number of lower-income and middle-income households;
3. Reduce the availability of the major source of credit to households, business enterprises, and governments; and
4. Give rise to fears that the failures would spread to other banks and beyond to the financial system as a whole, to the macro economy, and to other countries — that is, produce systemic risk.

But fragility per se does not necessarily imply breakage or failure. Rather, it implies "handle with care." And, when encouraged to do so, the market does so, just as the breakage rate for fine wine glasses and china is likely to be lower than for ordinary drinking glasses and dishware. The same is true for banking. U.S.

experience in this area is useful for a number of reasons. First, reasonably accurate historical data is available. The United States has had a large number of privately owned banks. Until recently, most were particularly fragile because restrictions on geographic and product-line expansion hindered them from reducing their risk exposures through diversification as much as they might otherwise have done. In addition, with the exception of the repudiation of gold contracts in 1933, the U.S. government did not expropriate or devalue deposits, as occurred in Argentina in 1989, and, with the exception of the South after the Civil War, the United States did not experience changes in governments that resulted in the new government's repudiating the debt or money of the old government or in confiscating bank balances. This permits us to analyze the performance of the U.S. banking system over a sufficiently long period of time to derive a meaningful number of observations both before and after the introduction of the safety net.

The U.S. experience also permits us to analyze the effects of imposing government guarantees on a previously basically uninsured banking system.[4] Before the Federal Deposit Insurance Corporation (FDIC) safety net was introduced in 1933, U.S. banks were primarily regulated by the marketplace. In contrast, the ongoing debate on deposit insurance reform in many current developing and transitional economies involves reducing government regulation by reducing insurance coverage from complete coverage of all liabilities of currently or previously state-owned and even state-controlled banks. That is, the debate focuses on partially replacing government discipline with market discipline.

From soon after the Civil War (1870) through 1995, the average annual failure rate for banks in the United States was greater than that for nonbanks (Kaufman, 1996b). However, all the difference is attributable mainly to the large number of bank failures, nearly 10,000, from 1929 through 1933, the onset of the Great Depression. With the exception of this period, the annual bank failure rate was about the same as the annual nonbank failure rate. Indeed, for the period 1870 to 1914, before the establishment of the Federal Reserve System, when prudential regulation was minimal, the annual bank failure rate was lower than that for nonbanks.[5] However, in all periods, the variance in the annual bank failure rate was greater than the variance in the nonbank failure rate; the bank failures were clustered in only a few years. Such clustering is consistent with the presence of bank contagion and systemic risk and contributes to the widespread public fear of bank failures.

Further, more thorough analysis of the numerical values of the three bank ratios widely perceived to reflect fragility indicates just the opposite, particularly in the period before the bank safety net. These values were determined by the marketplace. Despite the perception otherwise, cash ratios were not lower for banks than for other firms nor were, or are, banks' earning assets necessarily more opaque. Although demand deposits facilitate runs on banks, the very fact that they do serves as a powerful form of market discipline on bank management to curtail risk taking (Calomiris and Kahn 1991). That is, while runs on banks may be detrimental to bank stability, the threat of runs may serve to enhance stability by making management more cautious.

Finally, the low capital ratios in use before deposit insurance (even after adjustment for double liability) could have existed only if the market perceived banks to be less risky instead of riskier than other firms. Indeed, the evidence suggests that in the United States, in this period, not only was the failure rate lower for banks than for nonbanks, but bank insolvencies were resolved more quickly with less loss to depositors or creditors than were nonbank insolvencies (Kaufman 1992, 1994, 1996a). In the absence of deposit insurance, depositor runs on banks perceived to be insolvent quickly produced liquidity problems and forced the banks to suspend operations. Bank examiners determined whether the bank was experiencing liquidity or solvency problems. If they concluded that the bank was insolvent, the problem was resolved through recapitalization by existing shareholders, by merger, by sale, or by liquidation. The bank did not have much opportunity to operate while insolvent and further increase its losses, as could happen after federal government-provided deposit insurance was introduced and the need for depositors to run was reduced. Decisions about whether and when to resolve insolvencies were effectively transferred from the marketplace to the regulatory agencies. In contrast, nonbank insolvencies are resolved through the bankruptcy process, which is much slower and, in the United States, not favorable to creditors. Thus, creditors demand higher capital ratios at nonbank firms to protect themselves from failures that are associated with relatively larger losses.

It should be noted that the runs before deposit insurance and the accompanying liquidity problems were largely the result, not the cause, of the bank insolvencies. That is, with rare exceptions, the solvency problems caused the liquidity problems, rather than the liquidity problems' causing the solvency problems (Kaufman 1996a). An analysis by J.F.T. O'Conner, who served as Comptroller of the Currency from 1933 through 1938, of the causes of some 3,000 national bank failures before deposit insurance reported that runs accounted for less than 10 percent of all causes listed for these failures (with some failures having multiple causes) and were a cause in less than 15 percent of all failures (1938).

Despite this evidence on the small number and low cost of bank failures on average, the large numbers of bank failures in a few years before deposit insurance were frightening when they occurred and gave rise to fears of a systemic risk. The failures were widely perceived to represent serious market failures. This led to calls for improvements. In response, the government imposed a government-provided safety net under the banks. The first net was in the form of a discretionary Federal Reserve lender of last resort. When this failed to prevent the severe banking crisis of the early 1930s (less than 20 years after the net was introduced), the less discretionary, at least on the downside, form of deposit insurance by the FDIC was established. Gerald Corrigan, former president of the Federal Reserve Bank of New York, has emphasized the importance of systemic risk in justifying the safety net: "More than anything else, it is the systemic risk phenomenon associated with banking and financial institutions that makes them different from gas stations and furniture stores. It is this factor — more than any other — that constitutes the fundamental rationale for the safety net arrangements that have evolved in this and other countries" (Corrigan 1991, 3).

However, when the government provides deposit insurance, it has, like any insurer or guarantor, a financial stake in the financial condition of the bank and will act to protect its interest through regulating prices and making rules or both.

Government-provided deposit insurance is by necessity accompanied by government regulation. Ironically, therefore, when banking is considered "special," requiring special regulation, it is not because banking is inherently more fragile than other industries and market discipline on it is less effective and efficient, but because part of the special regulation generally imposed — deposit insurance — has increased banking's fragility and weakened market discipline, requiring additional, special offsetting regulation. Believing that banks are special is a self-fulfilling prophecy that will make them so.

Other Rationales

Bank regulation has also been justified on grounds other than credit allocation and safety, which are unique to banking. Avoiding natural monopolies, protecting competition, and increasing efficiency are goals common to other regulated industries (Benston and Kaufman 1996). There is no evidence from any country at any time that banking has continuously declining cost curves and is a natural monopoly in which individual banks will continuously combine until there is only one bank left. Indeed, much recent evidence suggests not only frequent continued entry of new banks and strong bank competitors but also diseconomies of scale for the largest banks.

More frequently, particularly because control over money and credit is widely viewed as more dangerous than control over other sectors, regulation in banking is directed at preventing excessive economic concentration, which may lead to excessive political power, and at encouraging competition. In the United States, regulation attempted to achieve this objective by limiting banks' ability to grow through additional offices or products. In addition, when banks threatened to circumvent these barriers, additional regulations that restricted mergers and geographic extensions through holding companies were imposed. In the United States, these regulations were slowly removed, starting in the 1980s, as technology eased their circumvention and permitted nonbanks to offer competing products — primarily information and management of risk — with less regulation. As a result, at least on-balance sheet bank growth slowed, and many banks experienced severe financial difficulties in the 1980s. This helped reduce the fear of large banks. However, to many it appeared as if the regulations were restricting rather than promoting competition, by protecting individual banks from inroads into their market areas. Nor is there evidence that government regulation was successful in reducing excessive risk taking. Indeed, there is evidence that regulation frequently encouraged risk taking that resulted in large losses and insolvencies, through encouraging activities that furthered government policies in other areas and through failing to monitor or discipline banks on a timely and effective basis. For example, money center banks in the 1970s were encouraged to lend heavily to less developed countries, and S&Ls throughout the 1970s were encouraged to take large interest-rate risk exposures by funding long-term, fixed-rate mortgages with short-term deposits.

REGULATION AND STRUCTURE

B ecause regulation affects the structure of banking, it is useful in evaluating alternative regulatory regimes to consider the implications of alternative banking structures for the major objectives of the financial system, which are summarized in Table 4. The structure ranges from narrow banks (and broader capital markets) at one end of the spectrum to broad (universal) banks (and narrower capital markets) at the other end (Kaufman and Kroszner 1997). It is evident that neither of the two extreme structures satisfies all the objectives. Each structure has advantages and disadvantages (Steinherr 1996; Steinherr and Huveneer 1994). Individual countries need to pick and choose among structures to find one that best satisfies their needs. No one size is likely to fit all, but the optimum for most countries may lie closer to the center of the spectrum than at either end.[6] One recent study of financial regulation and structure concluded, "Financial regulation — being the result of politics, ideology, and culture — does have a significant impact on the structure of the financial system" (Scholtens 1997, 321).

Because no country starts from scratch, the design of the optimal structure must be based on the existing structure. It follows from the earlier analysis that countries whose banking structure lies relatively close to the narrow bank end, such as the United States, could improve their structure by adopting regulations that broaden their banks' powers, while countries that lie closer to the broad bank end could improve the efficiency and safety of their banks by narrowing their powers and encouraging the development of capital markets. However, recent examinations of the differences between samples of generally identified narrow and broad bank countries in the 1990s revealed that the differences were not as great and that the structures were more complex than the stylized representations (Rajan and Zingales 1998; Scholtens 1997).

EVALUATION OF PRUDENTIAL REGULATION

G overnment regulation of banks in almost all countries in recent years has been a flop, at least with respect to safety. Directly as a result of poorly structured and implemented regulation, banks in many countries have assumed greater risk exposures, have generated greater losses, and have been a greater burden to the macro economy and particularly to the taxpayers than was the case in earlier periods with less regulation. As noted earlier, even before the current severe banking problems in Asia, some 130 countries, among them a number of South American countries, were identified by the IMF as having experienced severe banking problems since 1980, with costs of resolutions to the taxpayers in these countries often exceeding 10 percent of GDP (Lindgren, Garcia, and Saal 1996; Caprio and Klingebiel 1996). Argentina's resolution costs topped 10 percent of GDP three times in the past 20 years: in the early 1980s, with an estimated resolution cost of about 55 percent of GDP; in the late 1980s, with an estimated cost of 15 percent; and in 1994-1995, with 2 percent (Caprio and Dooley 1996). Resolution costs for Chile in the early 1980s were at 41 percent of GDP; for Venezuela in the mid-1990s, at 18 percent; and for Uruguay in the early 1980s, at 24 percent. The estimated resolution costs in a number of countries are shown in Table 5.

Table 4.
Relationship of Banking Structure to Financial System Objectives

Objective	Banking Structure	
	Narrow	**Broad**
Stability		
Without effective intervention and closure rules	Restrictions on bank portfolios lead to fewer bank failures and lower losses to depositors, but may not provide greater overall financial stability.	Larger losses are possible as permissible activities widen and assets become more volatile, but diversification can promote stability.
With effective intervention and closure rules, when bank net worth is positive	Few failures and low overall, but the effect of structure depends on the ability to monitor; if rules are credible and monitoring is largely independent of the riskiness of assets, there is no relationship between structure and stability. If risky assets are more difficult to monitor, losses may be greater for broader banks, which may require more sophisticated supervisors.	
Economies of scale and scope	Less likely, particularly scope economies.	More likely to be realized.
Competition	Less concentration likely, but greater segmentation of markets.	Higher concentration likely.
Avoidance of regulatory capture	Less likely, if bank is not part of a financial conglomerate.	Banks are more likely to try to stifle competition from new institutions and markets. Greater potential for "too big to fail" syndrome.
Avoidance of conflicts of interest	Less potential, if bank is not part of a financial conglomerate.	More potential, without privately chosen or mandated firewalls.
Avoidance of political manipulation	Banks are susceptible to credit control through regulatory definition of "safe" assets.	Banks are susceptible to credit control under implicit industrial policy.
Corporate control	Weak role for banks.	Important role for banks, particularly in managing financially distressed companies.
Monetary control	No relationship to structure, except for 100 percent reserve banks, which offer the central bank total monetary control.	

Table 5.
Estimated Transfer Cost of Selected Banking Crises*

Country	Period	Estimated Cost ÷ GDP (%)
United States	1980s	2.5
Japan	1990s	NA
Norway	1987-1989	4.0
Spain	1977-1985	16.8
Sweden	1991	6.4
Bulgaria	1990s	14
Hungary	1991-1995	10
Israel	1977-1983	30
Mexico	1990s	12-15
Argentina	1980-1982	55.3
Argentina	1989-1990	13
Brazil	1994-1995	5-10
Chile	1981-1983	41.2
Uruguay	1981-1984	24.2
Venezuela	1994-1995	18
Turkey	1982-1985	.5
Finland	1991-1994	8.4

*Includes all depository institutions; costs are to governments and depositors.

Sources: Caprio Jr. and Klingebiel 1996; Lindgren, Garcia, and Saal 1996; Rojas-Suarez and Weisbrod 1996; *Wall Street Journal* October 22, 1998.

An analysis of bank failures by the IMF indicated a number of common causes (Garcia and Saal 1996). These include the following:
- macroeconomic instability and shocks, particularly asset price bubbles;
- rapid bank asset and credit growth;
- weak internal bank controls;
- poor credit assessment culture;
- high loan concentration;
- poor accounting and disclosure practices;
- poor laws and regulation, particularly regarding supervision of banks and bankruptcy;
- late and weak intervention by regulators;
- political interference with regulators to disguise problems; and
- lagged and poorly implemented deregulation, liberalization, and privatization.

It follows that the design of bank regulation and financial sector structure must address and correct these problems. As noted earlier, in the United States, without poorly structured government deposit insurance, the government could not have effectively encouraged savings and loan associations to finance their long-term, fixed-rate mortgages with short-term deposits. What depositors would have left their funds in such exposed institutions without guarantees against loss? Indeed, S&Ls were much more interest-rate risk balanced before deposit insurance was introduced. Likewise, credit allocation operations of state-owned banks and directed credit operations of state-controlled banks could not occur without government guarantee of deposits.

The highly concentrated structure of banking, either nationally or in regional market areas in most countries, does not so much reflect market forces as it reflects restrictive regulation of new charters, new powers, and new competitors — for example, in the development of capital markets.

REGULATORY AND DEPOSIT INSURANCE REFORM IN THE UNITED STATES

The issue of appropriate prudential regulation cannot be separated from the issue of appropriate deposit insurance. A number of alternative prudential regulatory and deposit insurance structures have been proposed, including the following:

- replacing government-provided deposit insurance with private insurance,
- scaling back government-provided deposit insurance,
- reregulating control of bank risk,
- narrow or "fail-safe" banking,
- risk-based deposit insurance premiums, and
- structured early intervention and resolution (SEIR).

History in most countries, including in Argentina, supports the belief that some form of explicit or implicit government-provided deposit insurance for some, basically "small" depositors is a political reality (Miller 1996). Private insurers may achieve and retain depositor confidence when a single bank fails or a small number of relatively small banks fail but will quickly lose credibility when a larger number of banks fail or when large banks fail. Moreover, it is unlikely that the government would give private insurers unrestricted ability to resolve banks quickly when their capital declines to zero. Thus, the private insurers would not be able to control their losses, as the insolvent banks would continue to operate and frequently would even increase their risk exposure by "gambling for resurrection." If this is so, then explicit government-provided insurance, in which the rules are specified in advance of any crisis, with some reasonable probability of being adhered to, is preferred to implicit insurance, in which the rules are not specified in advance and the parameters of who is and who is not covered are fought in the political arena after the crisis.

Although narrow banking has initial intuitive appeal, more thorough examination reveals a number of fatal flaws. Institutions that invest in higher yielding, "nonsafe" assets would be able to outbid narrow banks for deposits. Broad banks that offer a range of financial products would also be able to take advantage of any economies of scope that may exist. As these institutions grow, the depositors would wield the same political power for obtaining insurance as did the depositors in the previous broad banks. Nowhere in the world have market forces produced narrow banks as the preferred bank structure. Moreover, by requiring government to designate what are "safe" assets, the narrow structure encourages governments to use the banks for credit allocation; the government may designate certain types of favored loans — for example, long-term Treasury securities or mortgage loans or loans to industry X or Y— as safe or eligible loans regardless of their actual risk. The history of the politics of the Basle capital-risk classifications provides little evidence to the contrary. Narrow banks are likely to become state-controlled banks quickly. Lastly, because even safe assets can decline in market value, without a firm closure rule, regulators could keep insolvent narrow banks in operation, generating continued losses, albeit relatively small losses.

Reregulating risk is unlikely to be successful. Financial deregulation and liberalization was, in large measure, in response to the failure of regulation and to widespread avoidance of regulation. Once the technology genie is out of the bottle, it is difficult to put it back in. Risk-based insurance premiums, while desirable per se, would not solve the agency problem and prevent regulators from keeping insolvent institutions in operation without an accompanying closure rule. The alternative is SEIR, which, used with both risk-based insurance premiums and scaled-back, government-provided deposit insurance coverage, should reduce the moral hazard and principal-agent problems that plague most if not all deposit insurance structures now in use. SEIR assumes that these problems are not inherent in deposit insurance to any greater extent than in private markets. Rather, they appear more serious because governments often price their services based on considerations other than economic ones — for example, political considerations. As a result, government-provided deposit insurance generally has been mistructured and often underpriced. However, governments could provide insurance without excessive moral hazard or principal-agent problems if it were structured correctly. And that is what SEIR is designed to do. It leaves in place the existing banking and regulatory structures, which makes it more politically feasible and quicker to adopt.

SEIR in weakened form is contained in the prompt corrective action (PCA) and least cost resolution (LCR) provisions of the fundamental deposit insurance and regulatory reform structures included in the U.S. FDIC Improvement Act (FDICIA) of 1991, which was enacted at the depth of the banking and thrift crises. The main features of the structure are summarized in Table 6. The particulars of this program, its history, and experience with it to date have been discussed elsewhere (Benston and Kaufman 1997, 1998; Kaufman 1997a). Suffice it to say that this scheme attempts 1) to structure government regulation (which is required by the limited and explicit government deposit insurance provided) to mimic private market regulation and 2) to supplement government regulation with market regulation, which is encouraged by not insuring "large" depositors, who are accustomed to engaging in credit evaluations in their everyday investment decisions and to suffering periodic losses. In the process, SEIR introduces explicit regulatory sanctions on financially troubled banks; the sanctions become progressively harsher and progressively more mandatory as a bank's performance deteriorates and as it approaches insolvency.

Probably most important, SEIR introduces a mandatory "closure" rule, through which banks are resolved by recapitalization, merger, sale, or liquidation before their economic (market value) capital is fully dissipated, say, when their capital declines to some small but positive percentage of their assets.[7] In theory, if a bank could be resolved at such a point, losses would be confined to shareholders and would not affect depositors. Deposit insurance would be effectively redundant. As all bank deposits are, in effect, fully collateralized in terms of market values, the bank assumes the advantages of a narrow bank without most of the disadvantages. Moreover, if losses from bank failures can be eliminated or at least minimized, fears either of a competitive banking system, which may encourage individual bank failures, or of systemic or contagion risk, which occurs only when large negative net worths cascade from bank to bank, wiping out the next counterparty's capital, are no longer warranted. The primary focus of the remaining regulation can be on efficiency. Unlike other insurance companies, which can limit but not eliminate all losses, for example, fire and automobile insurance companies, a government deposit insurance agency can completely eliminate its losses by monitoring and strictly enforcing its closure rule at no lower than zero economic capital. That is, except for major fraud, losses from bank failures would effectively be under the agency's own control.

The incentive for banks to engage in excessive moral hazard behavior is restrained by copying the constraints that private insurance companies impose through insurance contracts and creditors impose through covenants. Risk exposure is priced by risk-based insurance premiums. In addition, increasingly harsher and broader sanctions that reduce the ability of the firm to shift losses to its creditors or insurance firms are imposed as insolvency approaches. The use of multiple performance zones or tranches, measured, say, by capital-asset ratios, permits the sanctions to be strengthened gradually rather than sharply and abruptly. This increases the credibility of regulators that impose the sanctions and decreases incentives for the financial institution to increase its risk exposure as its performance deteriorates to near the bottom of a zone. To supplement the sanctions (sticks), incentives (carrots) in such forms as additional powers or fewer and faster examinations are specified to encourage banks to perform well.

Regulatory discipline is reinforced by market discipline exerted from uninsured larger depositors and other creditors, who are accustomed to engaging in credit evaluations. These creditors may be expected to charge higher interest rates or to run from these banks to safer banks as the financial condition of a bank deteriorates. Evidence from the United States and Canada strongly indicates that larger depositors, at least, are able to differentiate financially strong from weak banks (for example, Calomiris and Mason 1997; Kaufman 1994; Carr, Mathewson, and Quigley 1995). Likewise, a comparative analysis of deposit behavior during the 1994-1995 banking crisis in Argentina showed that banks' deposit declines were greater as the banks' nonperforming loans were greater (Moore 1997). This is shown in Figure 1.

Regulators' incentives to delay and forbear from imposing sanctions in response to political pressures or other agendas are restrained by specifying that minimizing losses from bank insolvencies will be the sole objective of prudential

Table 6. Summary of Prompt Corrective Action Provisions of the Federal Deposit Insurance Corporation Improvement Act of 1991

Leverage Zone	Mandatory Provisions	Discretionary Provisions	Capital-Asset Ratios (%) Risk Based Total	Risk Based Tier 1	Non-Risk Based Tier 1
1. Well capitalized			>10	>6	>5
2. Adequately capitalized	1. No brokered deposits except with FDIC approval		>8	>4	>4
3. Undercapitalized	1. Suspend dividends and management fees 2. Require capital restoration plan 3. Restrict asset growth 4. Approval required for acquisitions, branching, and new activities 5. No brokered deposits	1. Order recapitalization 2. Restrict inter-affiliate transactions 3. Restrict deposit interest rates 4. Restrict certain other activities 5. Any other action that would better carry out prompt corrective action	<8	<4	<4
4. Significantly Undercapitalized	1. Same as for Zone 3 2. Order recapitalization* 3. Restrict inter-affiliate transactions* 4. Restrict deposit interest rates* 5. Pay of officers restricted	1. Any Zone 3 discretionary actions 2. Conservatorship or receivership if institution fails to submit or implement plan or recapitalize pursuant to order 3. Any other Zone 5 provision, if such action is necessary to carry out prompt corrective action	<6	<3	<3
5. Critically Undercapitalized	1. Same as for Zone 4 2. Receiver/conservator within 90 days* 3. Receiver if still in Zone 5 four quarters after becoming critically undercapitalized 4. Suspend payments on subordinated debt* 5. Restrict certain other activities				<2

*Not required if primary supervisor determines action would not serve purpose of prompt corrective action or if certain other conditions are met.
Source: Board of Governors of the Federal Reserve System and author.

regulation and then imposing explicit and visible rules that mandate sanctions, including resolution, when banks fail to respond to earlier discretionary sanctions. The sanctions become progressively more mandatory as the performance of a bank deteriorates. The threat of mandatory sanctions increases the credibility and effectiveness of discretionary sanctions, supplementing rather than replacing the discretionary sanctions. The mandatory sanctions also increase certainty, equalize treatment of the banks, and help free regulators from political pressures. Identifying insolvency loss minimization as the objective in prudential regulation establishes the same objective that private insurers and creditors have. By achieving objective compatibility, deposit insurance becomes incentive compatible, so that all players — private and government — will row in the same direction.[8] At the same time,

Figure 1.
Real Deposit Growth and Bank Asset Quality in Argentina and Mexico
December 1994-June 1995

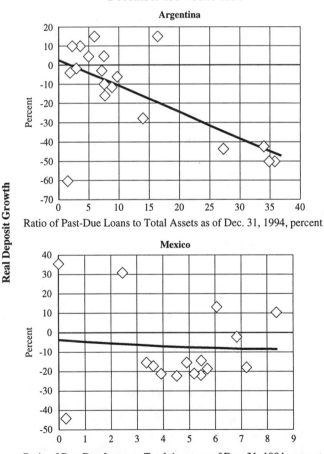

Source: Robert R. Moore, 1997, "Government Guanrantees and Banking: Evidence from the Mexican Peso Crises," Financial Industry Studies, Federal Reserve Bank of Dallas (December):18-19.

increased transparency enhances regulatory agency compliance and accountability. It is important to note that, while SEIR should reduce the number of bank failures, it is designed primarily to reduce, if not eliminate, the costs of bank failures; the exit of banks that fail either through bad management or bad luck is required to attain and maintain an efficient banking industry.

To date, the PCA and LCR structure in FDICIA appears to have been successful in the United States. However, the precise contribution of FDICIA is difficult to isolate because of the combined effects of the prolonged recovery of the U.S. economy, the virtual elimination of product inflation, the avoidance of asset price bubbles in energy and real estate (where U.S. banks are big lenders), and an upward-sloping yield curve in enhancing the recovery of banks and thrifts from the debacle of the 1980s to their healthiest level since the 1960s. There were strong indications that market discipline had been awakened, at least temporarily. Bank capital ratios built up rapidly through the sale of new shares in the early 1990s to their highest levels since the 1960s, before bank profitability was established. In addition, shared losses were imposed on uninsured depositors at resolved banks in almost all resolutions in which the FDIC suffered a loss (Benston and Kaufman 1997, 1998). However, because no major money center bank has failed or even deteriorated sharply in performance since 1992, a true test of "too big to fail" (TBTF) — or, more accurately, too big to impose pro-rata losses on uninsured deposits — has not yet occurred.

It is important to note, however, that TBTF has become substantially more difficult for the regulators to impose. With one exception, the FDIC is prohibited from protecting uninsured depositors in insolvencies in which doing so will increase its losses. To protect uninsured deposits at these insolvent institutions, a determination must be made in writing by two-thirds of the FDIC directors and the Board of Governors of the Federal Reserve System and by the Secretary of the Treasury in consultation with the President of the United States that not protecting the uninsured depositors "would have serious adverse effect on economic conditions or financial stability" and that protecting these depositors would "avoid or mitigate such adverse effects" (FDIC Improvement Act of 1991). If the protection does result in a loss to the FDIC, a special assessment must be levied on all banks, based on their total assets. Thus, most of any cost would be borne by other large and likely competitor banks, who may be unenthusiastic about using their monies to keep an insolvent competitor in operation. In addition, the Secretary of the Treasury must provide documentation underlying the decision to Congress, and the General Accounting Office must review the documentation. This requirement should discourage aggressive use of the TBTF exception.

Moreover, TBTF would be invoked only if a very large bank had been unresponsive to the series of PCA sanctions that had been imposed on it earlier to prevent it from failing. If the sanctions were imposed on a timely basis, few if any banks would get to the point of requiring protection. Before deposit insurance was introduced in the United States at the national level in 1933, only relatively small banks failed. A number of very large banks in the United States have failed, including Continental Illinois, the seventh-largest bank in the United States, in 1984 (Kaufman 1995). Deposit insurance effectively transformed bank failures in the

United States from a small-bank to an all-size phenomenon. Large banks may, however, be able to exert strong political pressure for TBTF.

It is also important to understand how pro-rata losses could be imposed on uninsured deposits without affecting the economy adversely. In the United States, insolvent banks are resolved by the federal regulators without having the banks go through the bankruptcy courts. The FDIC generally acts as receiver. Insured depositors have full access to their funds on the next business day, either at the bank that assumed these deposits or at the bank in receivership until it is liquidated. Under FDICIA's PCA requirements, the regulators become increasingly involved with a troubled institution before it requires resolution in an attempt to turn it around. Through identifying and notifying potential bidder banks of a possible insolvency, the FDIC has the opportunity to value the insolvent bank's assets before resolution. Thus, at the time of resolution, the FDIC is in a position to make a reasonably accurate estimate of the recovery value of the assets and the loss it will incur in protecting insured depositors. The FDIC then provides an advanced portion of the pro-rata, albeit conservative, estimated recovery value to the uninsured depositors, available the next business day. In effect, the uninsured depositors will have immediate access to funds equivalent to the par of their deposits amount less the pro-rata estimated loss, which under FDICIA should be relatively small. If such provisions were not in place, it is likely that long delays would result in uninsured depositors' receipt of their funds. Substantial unnecessary economic harm might occur, as pressure to protect uninsured deposits fully would become too strong to resist.[9]

In 1993, the United States also enacted depositor preference legislation that could further reduce the probability of loss to the FDIC in large bank failures and thus also reduce the need to invoke TBTF (Kaufman 1997c). This legislation gives the FDIC and uninsured depositors at domestic offices of insured banks equal standing as well as priority over depositors at foreign offices of these banks and such other creditors as sellers of Fed funds. Because large U.S. banks raise a meaningful percentage of their funds through such sources, the FDIC and domestic depositors will suffer losses only if a bank's losses are so great that they exceed the total amount of the subordinated funds. However, in a dynamic environment, this protection could be reduced and even eliminated if the subordinated claimants protected themselves by running or by collateralizing their claims. To the extent that these measures would strip the troubled banks of their best assets, deposit preference could actually increase losses to the FDIC and uninsured domestic depositors.

Exporting of SEIR to Other Countries

SEIR has a large number of advantages over other prudential regulatory structures that also make it attractive for countries other than the United States. These include the following:

- maintaining existing banking structure;
- maintaining insurance for "small" depositors only;
- reducing number of failures;

- reducing losses from failures (making deposit insurance effectively redundant);
- reducing bank insurance premiums and incorporating risk-based premiums;
- reducing the probability of systemic (contagion) risk;
- reducing too-big-to-fail responses (reducing protection of uninsured depositors);
- encouraging market discipline from "large" depositors to supplement regulatory discipline;
- reducing moral hazard behavior by banks;
- reducing agency problem for regulators;
- providing for carrots as well as punishments or sanctions to improve bank performance;
- permitting a wide range of product powers for well-capitalized banks;
- reducing regulatory micro-management of banks.

However, because countries differ in significant ways, it is important to tailor the SEIR structure to the particular characteristics of the country. The effectiveness of SEIR depends on the abilities of both the regulators and the marketplace to impose discipline to curtail bank risk taking and losses, on bankers to manage their operations in a way that maximizes value for shareholders and the economy, and on governments to accept loss minimization in insolvencies as the primary goal of bank regulation. If these parties can agree to these preconditions, SEIR may be modified to be effective in the particular countries. The most important modifications would depend on the following characteristics of a country:

- macroeconomic instability;
- strength of private market and tradition of market discipline;
- structure of banking, including solvency and the importance of state-owned banks and state-controlled banks;
- sophistication of bankers;
- sophistication of bank regulators, supervisors, and examiners;
- sophistication of market participants;
- credit culture;
- equity culture;
- bank control of nonbanks and nonbank control of banks;
- loan concentration in banks;
- quality of accounting information and disclosure;
- bankruptcy and repossession laws; and
- bank reliance on foreign currency deposits.

More specifically, the following features need to be tailored carefully to the country:

- values of the trip wires for PCA and LCR;
- types of regulatory sanctions;
- division between regulatory rules and discretion;

- definition of "small" depositors;
- regulation of foreign currency exposure; and
- bankruptcy (resolution) process for insured banks.

In many countries, deposit insurance reform is being introduced at the same time as financial deregulation or liberalization and for the same reasons. The two reforms are not independent of each other. Because SEIR retains some government-provided deposit insurance, it retains the need for some government regulation, in particular, for government supervision and examination to be able to monitor banks on an adequate basis. Deregulation does not imply de-supervision. Indeed, super-vision may need to be intensified after liberalization, since many banks, after laboring for years under a repressed system, are often ill prepared to operate suddenly in a market structure with penalties as well as rewards. In particular, they are likely to have weak if any credit cultures and to be unlikely to engage in sufficient credit analysis and monitoring. Thus, bank risk exposures likely will virtually explode following a sudden changeover from financial repression to financial liberalization unless the liberalization is structured correctly (Working Party on Financial Stability 1997). Unfortunately, there was insufficient recognition of this tendency in many countries — for example, in the United States in the early 1980s and in Japan in the late 1980s; this was an important cause of the banking debacles. Banking liberalization must be phased in or sequenced in such a way that regulatory discipline is never reduced by more than what market discipline reasonably can replace. The weaker the sum of market and regulatory discipline or total discipline on banks, the higher the required private capital ratios required to achieve the same degree of stability.

As the macroeconomic and political instability in a country increase, the values of the final trip wires for the PCA and LCR tranches need to be raised, particularly for resolution of potential insolvencies. If these zones are stated in terms of capital-asset ratios, it is important to note both that assets must include off-balance-sheet as well as on-balance-sheet activities and that the Basle capital ratios are minimum requirements for large international banks in industrial countries with relatively high macroeconomic and political stability. For most other banks and countries, the capital ratios for each zone need to be considerably higher. These values also need to be higher as the quality of accounting information is poorer. Although poor quality accounting information may either overstate or understate the true information, the incentives are to overstate values. Thus, banks almost universally under-reserve for loan losses and find additional ways of at least temporarily hiding losses. Because the value of the trip wire for resolution determines the potential for losses to the insurance agency, assigning a value that is too low to prevent or minimize losses can defeat the objective of SEIR.

What are the appropriate capital ratios for banks in a particular country? Because deposit insurance insulates banks from full market discipline, the market solution in an insurance environment implicitly incorporates a provision for loss sharing and, therefore, understates the capital ratio that the market would require in the absence of insurance. A proxy for this value may be obtained in each country by observing the value that the market requires of noninsured bank competitors — for example, independent finance companies or insurance companies. In most countries, these ratios are significantly higher. Thus, increasing bank capital ratios to these levels does not increase their costs unfairly; instead, it primarily removes a subsidy. Moreover, because capital is effectively any claim that is subordinated to the insurance agency, it can include subordinated debt, which in some countries has tax advantages over equity. Because debt holders have more to lose than to gain, they tend to monitor their debtors carefully. As a result, requiring part of the banks' capital requirements to be in the form of subordinated debt with a remaining maturity of, say, at least two years, so it cannot run, serves to intensify market discipline. At the end of 1996, Argentina required its banks to issue subordinated debt equal to 2 percent of their deposits.

Resolving a bank before its capital becomes negative does not represent confiscation or expropriation. Current shareholders are given the first right to recapitalize the institution. It is only if they prefer not to do so, most likely because they believe that the bank's true capital position is even worse than the reported position, that resolution through sale, merger, or liquidation goes forward. Any proceeds remaining after resolution are returned to the old shareholders.

It also follows that the values of the capital ratio trip wires for each zone need to be higher as 1) the credit and equity cultures in a country are weaker; 2) as the bankers, regulators, and market participants are less sophisticated; 3) as bank loan portfolios are more concentrated; 4) as the definition of "small" depositor becomes broader; and 5) as bank reliance on foreign currency deposits is greater.[10] Likewise, these conditions also suggest greater emphasis on regulatory rules than on regulatory discretion.

The definition of "small" depositor is likely to be a political rather than an economic one and to vary from country to country. It would include depositors to whom any losses from insolvency would be sufficiently large to move them to protest politically and to gain the sympathy of a large percentage of the country's population. Also, these are depositors who may be incapable of doing meaningful credit evaluations of their banks or depositors for whom the cost of doing so is high enough that they would be likely to shun using banks. Requiring them to evaluate the credit worthiness of banks would result in a deadweight loss to the economy. Moreover, it is primarily the relatively small depositors who are capable of carrying out their day-to-day financial business with currency rather than deposits. Because runs on banks from deposits to currency, which reduce aggregate bank reserves and deposits, are far more serious than runs from troubled to safe banks, which primarily reshuffle aggregate bank reserves and deposits, full deposit insurance coverage is desirable for depositors who are capable of such behavior.

Foreign currency-denominated deposits are particularly important in smaller open economies. There, exchange-rate problems and banking problems are often interrelated and easily confused. Foreign currency problems can spill over and ignite banking problems. Banks that offer deposits denominated in foreign currencies assume exchange-rate risk, unless these deposits are offset by foreign currency-denominated assets or otherwise hedged; the shorter term the deposits are, the "hotter" the money, and the greater the risk. Banks are tempted to raise funds in foreign currencies particularly when domestic interest rates greatly exceed those on the foreign currencies. Economic theory, however, indicates that in equilibrium such rate differences should be matched by equal differences in the opposite direction between spot and forward exchange rates. This condition is referred to as interest rate parity.[11]

Any downward pressure on the country's exchange rate will impose losses on unhedged banks and, if large enough, these losses may cause banking problems in previously strong banking systems or exacerbate problems in weak banking systems, as has occurred recently in many Asian countries. In addition, downward pressure on the exchange rate in a country with a financially strong banking system may encourage depositors in domestic currency to run to deposits in foreign currencies, possibly even at the same "safe" banks. This is a run on domestic currency, not on banks. However, the run exerts downward pressure on the country's exchange rate. If the country attempts to protect its exchange rate, it needs to sell foreign reserves. This reduces aggregate bank reserves. Unless this decrease is offset by infusions of reserves from other sources by the Central Bank, which would be difficult to accomplish in these countries without intensifying the problem, it will ignite a multiple contraction in money and credit. This is likely to impair the financial solvency of the banks and may ignite bank runs.

This appears to have happened in Argentina from 1994 to 1995, following the devaluation of the Mexican peso in December 1994. The devaluation caused depositors of Argentine pesos in Argentine banks to become concerned about the exchange rate of the peso, and at least one Argentine bank suffered large losses from investments in Mexican bonds. The Mexican crisis served as a "wake-up" call for investors to examine countries that may have the same risk exposures. Argentina was apparently one of these. In response, some depositors switched from peso-denominated deposits to U.S.-dollar-denominated deposits (see Table 7) and from weaker Argentine banks to stronger Argentine banks (Carrizosa, Leipziger, and Shah 1996; Schumacher 1996). Because Argentina had a currency board, which required the Central Bank to support the dollar-peso exchange rate, the run into dollar deposits caused the Central Bank to lose dollar reserves. This, in turn, reduced total reserves in the banking system, igniting a multiple contraction in all bank deposits, and, as shown in Figure 2, forced interest rates, particularly on peso deposits, to rise sharply, in part to compensate for the fear of peso devaluation. In the aftermath, a large number of primarily smaller and weaker banks failed, with some losses to private depositors (Caprio and Dooley 1996; Pou 1997). Thus, a run on domestic currency turned into a run on the banking system and a serious banking problem. The "tequila effect" ended when the Argentine government's actions to maintain the peso-dollar exchange rate gained widespread credibility and stopped the Central Bank's loss of dollar reserves.

Table 7.
Percent Changes in Deposits at Argentine Banks
December 1994 to July 1995 by Denomination of Deposit

Month	Peso Deposits	Dollar Deposits	Total
	(%)	(%)	(%)
December	-0.85	0.84	0.02
January	-6.33	1.53	-2.27
February	-6.01	-0.31	-2.95
March	-8.63	-8.05	-8.31
April	1.09	-8.14	-4.01
May	0.38	-2.00	-0.88
June	1.93	2.09	2.02
July	4.38	5.80	5.12

Source: Liliana Schumacher, 1996, *Bubble or Depositor Discipline? A Study of the Argentine Banking Panic*, Ph.D. dissertation, University of Chicago, 32.

To the extent that the Mexican-Argentine events reflected systemic contagious risk, they represented common-shock or indirect systemic risk, where third parties searched for countries situated similarly to Mexico. These events did not represent direct systemic risk, where A causes B, which causes C, and so on, in domino or cascading fashion, with the Mexican crisis directly causing the Argentine crisis. Instead, common-shock systemic risk is based on third parties' inability to differentiate quickly enough among countries. This type of risk is rational and information based and reflects market forces at work. The risk ends if and when economic agents become convinced that the other countries are not situated similarly — economically, financially, or politically — to the country experiencing the initial shock. At that point, the banking, exchange rate, and other changes will stabilize and reverse. This was the case in Argentina after the Mexican crisis and again, even more rapidly, after the crisis in Southeast Asia in mid-1997. (As shown in Figure 3, interest rates in 1997-1998 followed a pattern similar to that of 1994-1995.) After comparing the two crises, investors saw few similarities. When investors do find similarities, the changes will continue until a new equilibrium is reached. Appropriate government policy response to what it perceives to be common-shock risk would focus on increasing the availability and decreasing the cost of reliable, timely, and useful information, in part by encouraging transparency and disclosure.

If a country with a strong foreign currency position but a financially weak banking system experiences depositor runs to domestic currency deposits at "safe" banks or into domestic currency, the banking problem will not spread to foreign currency problems. However, if the runs are from domestic currency deposits to foreign currency deposits at even the same "safe" banks, downward pressure will

Figure 2.
Argentine Short-Term Interest Rates on Peso and U.S. Dollar Securities
1994-1995

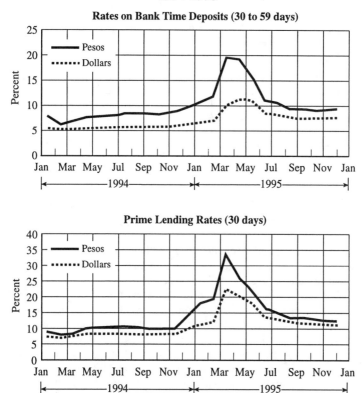

Source: Central Bank of Argentina, *Statistics Bulletin.*

be exerted on the exchange rate and will ignite an exchange-rate problem. Thus, exchange-rate problems can cause banking problems, and banking problems can cause exchange-rate problems. However, because the causes differ, the solutions also differ.

Correcting national banking problems first requires the recapitalization of insolvent or undercapitalized banks and, second, the introduction of SEIR-like deposit insurance provisions. Because state-owned banks and, at times, also state-controlled banks are perceived to have complete government protection, they provide unfair competition to private banks and are likely to prevent these banks from gaining or even maintaining market share, unless equal protection is provided for them either explicitly or implicitly. Indeed, it is difficult to have a system of limited deposit insurance in a banking system that includes major state-owned banks or state-controlled banks. Major state-owned banks and state-controlled banks should be completely privatized, with sufficient capital to be economically

Figure 3.
Argentine Short-Term Interest Rates on Peso and U.S. Dollar Loans
1997-1998

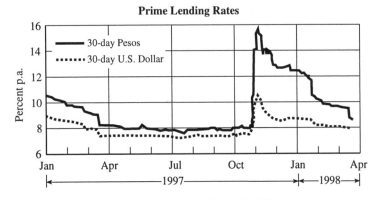

Source: J.P. Morgan, *World Financial Markets,* March 27, 1998, 56.

solvent and politically independent. Because their insolvencies or negative net worths are likely to be greater than their going concern or franchise values, it is unlikely that private parties will bid on these banks unless the capital deficits are reduced. This requires the use of public (taxpayer) funds. Because the sale will change bank management and ownership, and value will not accrue to the old shareholders, such a use of public funds is necessary and appropriate. It differs significantly from the inappropriate use of public funds to prop up existing shareholders and managers, as is being practiced in a number of countries, including Japan.[12] Imposing SEIR on already insolvent banks would be, for the most part, ineffective, as the incentives for market discipline would be distorted.

Permitting well-capitalized foreign banks to purchase state-owned banks in competitive bidding is desirable for at least four reasons. First, in some countries, the foreign banks will be relatively small units of much larger well-capitalized organizations that may be perceived to be able to protect their small affiliates more securely than the domestic government can protect deposits at domestically owned banks through deposit insurance. Second, foreign banks are likely to bid a higher premium than domestic bidders bid for insolvent or barely solvent institutions to get a toehold in the country — thereby reducing the amount of public (taxpayer) funds that need to be injected to reduce or eliminate the negative net worths of the banks or to reduce them to a level that private bidders are willing to absorb. Third, the foreign banks are likely to enhance competition and encourage a more efficient domestic banking system, particularly in countries dominated by a few large, domestically owned banks. Entering foreign banks tend to be financially strong institutions that can successfully challenge local monopolies and cartels. Fourth, large international banks are likely to be more diversified than smaller domestic banks and will reduce the vulnerability of the banking sector to adverse shocks. A recent World Bank study reports that the greater the percentage of foreign banks in emerging economies, the lower the intermediation costs, and the stronger all banks are (Goldstein 1998). Argentina's experience in opening its market to foreign banks appears to be working well.

Foreign currency problems reflect macroeconomic problems that central banks have traditionally dealt with. The solution does not require changes in prudential bank regulations, although the scheme discussed in this chapter is helpful if governments permit these problems to deteriorate into banking problems.

Because differences in economic, political, and other characteristics are generally greater between the developing countries and the industrial countries than they are among industrial countries, SEIR is likely to require greater modification when it is applied to developing countries. However, the necessary modifications may be relatively smaller than those required for alternative deposit insurance reform schemes under discussion.

SUMMARY AND CONCLUSIONS

B anking matters. The quality of banking is a significant factor in economic growth. Poor banking performance hinders economic growth and development in a country. Financial instability, characterized by widescale bank insolvencies, magnifies and prolongs any instability in the macro economy that may have initially ignited the banking problems. Good banking and financial sector performances enhance macroeconomic performance. A country's financial performance is generally enhanced if the country has a developed banking sector and a liquid capital market and if the country encourages competition between the two channels and among institutions operating in each channel.

Because of its importance and as well as its perceived fragility, banking is viewed as different from other industries and is regulated by almost all governments everywhere for a number of reasons, including enhancing the safety of governments themselves. If the government provides any deposit insurance or other parts of a safety net under banks, it has a financial interest in the health of the banks and will regulate, supervise, and examine them to protect its own interest. However, to date, prudential regulation has often been counterproductive in its net effects. Through time, prudential regulation appears to have contributed to the widespread banking crises of recent years as much as it has prevented such crises, if not more so. The poor performance stems primarily from misstructuring these regulations, particularly government-provided deposit insurance and the other parts of the safety net, thus permitting governments to pursue objectives other than minimizing the losses of bank insolvencies to taxpayers. This should not be a surprise. Governments are poor at replacing market discipline with regulatory discipline for basically the same reasons that they are poor at replacing market allocation of resources, including credit, with directed allocation. Not only is efficiency a lower priority, but also too much information must be processed centrally even for the smallest countries and the largest computers.

This chapter has described a prudential regulatory scheme of structured early intervention and resolution, designed to minimize the costs of bank failures by constraining both the moral hazard behavior of banks and the poor principal-agent behavior of regulators that plague most current programs. The scheme combines regulatory and market discipline and, as a result, is incentive compatible. Much of this scheme has been incorporated in the United States in the prompt corrective action and the least-cost resolution provisions of the FDIC Improvement Act of 1991. The U.S. experience to date is promising and suggests that SEIR may be appropriate for other countries, including transitional and developing economies. However, to maximize its effectiveness, SEIR must be tailored to the economic, political, and cultural characteristics of each country as well as to the financial and regulatory structures in place in each country. Lastly, the chapter discussed what is required to do so and how this may be done.

Notes

1. A somewhat similar task was undertaken by the Working Party on Financial Stability in Emerging Market Economies, 1997.

2. I have been unable to replicate Levine's study completely. Using a slightly different data set for the same 38 countries, I find the same general pattern as Levine does, but a considerably narrower spread in per-capita real GDP growth rates among the four groups of countries. Argentina is included among the countries with the least developed banking and capital markets and also the lowest average growth rate. However, the sample period ends in 1992, before Argentina's strong growth of more recent years. Nevertheless, Argentina appears to have a relatively undeveloped banking sector, even in comparison with other South and Latin American countries.

3. Very large banks may also be better able than smaller ones to exert political and public relations pressure for full government protection of their depositors and other creditors when they encounter solvency problems. This danger is discussed in a later section.

4. Some government guarantees did exist before 1933. Although deposit insurance had not been provided by the federal government, deposit insurance schemes had been introduced in a number of states, but almost all had failed. Also, national bank notes issued by nationally chartered banks were required to be fully collateralized, and any deficit was to be paid by the U.S. Treasury Department (Calomiris 1989; Kaufman 1987).

5. Anna J. Schwartz (1988) reports similar evidence for other countries.

6. Some researchers have suggested that broader banks may be relatively better for developing economies until their financial markets develop further. On the other hand, broader banks may be successful in slowing the development of alternative capital markets.

7. Liquidation or physical closing of insolvent banks should be employed only rarely and only when the demand for banking services at the locations involved appears insufficient to promise competitive returns.

8. Incentive-incompatible deposit insurance structures occur frequently because multiple and conflicting goals are specified for policymakers. For example, a recent analysis of bank regulatory reform by the OECD lists four "enduring objectives of financial services regulation":

"Maintaining a safe and sound financial system

Correcting market failures and enhancing competition

Providing an environment for effective implementation of financial policy

Achieving redistributive social goals."

It is apparent that although the first three goals may be compatible, the fourth goal may not be compatible with these. Thus, a deposit insurance scheme based on these goals is unlikely to be incentive compatible (Organization for Economic Cooperation and Development 1997, 33).

9. In the 1989 banking crisis, Argentina froze some bank deposits and substituted 10-year government bonds with below-market interest rates that traded below par (Pou 1997).

10. The Basle Committee on Banking Supervision, established in 1975, has developed a number of principles for effective prudential regulation and banking supervision (1997). These may be used as minimum guidelines for evaluating the sophistication of the supervision.

11. Before the recent crisis, banks in a number of Asian countries were borrowing heavily in short-term foreign currencies (primarily dollars) at low interest rates and lending in domestic currency at much higher rates in amounts that may have suggested that they were operating under the illusion that their governments could and did repeal the law of interest-rate parity.

12. The use of taxpayer funds in supporting banks is often misunderstood. (See, for example, Working Party on Financial Stability 1997, 41.)

References

Bank for International Settlements (BIS). 1998. *The Transmission of Monetary Policy in Emerging Market Economies.* Policy Paper No. 3 (January). Basle, Switzerland.

Barth, James R., Daniel E. Nolle, and Tara N. Rice. 1997. "Commercial Banking Structure, Regulation, and Performance: An International Comparison." *Managerial Finance* 23(11): 1-39.

Basle Committee for Banking Supervision. 1997. *Core Principles for Effective Banking Supervision.* Basle, Switzerland: Bank for International Settlements (BIS) (April).

Benston, George J., Robert A. Eisenbeis, Paul M. Horvitz, Edward J. Kane, and George G. Kaufman. 1986. *Perspectives on Safe and Sound Banking.* Cambridge, Mass.: MIT Press.

Benston, George J., and George G. Kaufman. 1995. "Is the Banking and Payments System Fragile?" *Journal of Financial Services Research* (December): 209-240.

Benston, George J., and George G. Kaufman. 1996. "The Appropriate Role of Bank Regulation." *Economic Journal* (May): 688-697.

Benston, George J., and George G. Kaufman. 1997. "FDICIA After Five Years." *Journal of Economic Perspectives* (Summer): 139-158.

Benston, George J., and George G. Kaufman. 1998. "Deposit Insurance Reform in the FDIC Improvement Act: The Experience to Date." *Economic Perspectives* 22(2): 2-20. Federal Reserve Bank of Chicago.

Bordo, Michael D., Bruce Mizrach, and Anna J. Schwartz. 1997. *Real vs. Pseudo International Systemic Risk: Some Lessons from History.* Working Paper, Rutgers University.

Calomiris, Charles W. 1989. "Deposit Insurance: Lessons from the Record." *Economic Perspective.* Federal Reserve Bank of Chicago (May-June): 10-30.

Calomiris, Charles W., and Charles M. Kahn. 1991. "The Role of Demandable Debt in Structuring Optimal Banking Arrangements." *American Economic Review* (June): 497-513.

Calomiris, Charles W., and Joseph R. Mason. 1997. "Contagion and Bank Failure During the Great Depression: The June 1932 Chicago Banking Panic." *American Economic Review* (December): 863-883.

Caprio Jr., Gerald, and Michael Dooley. 1996. "The Lender of Last Resort Function Under a Currency Board: The Case of Argentina." *Open Economies Review* 7(19): 625-650.

Caprio Jr., Gerald, and Daniela Klingebiel. 1996. *Bank Insolvency: Bad Luck, Bad Policy, or Bad Banking.* Working Paper, World Bank (April).

Carr, Jack, Frank Mathewson, and Neil Quigley. 1995. "Stability in the Absence of Deposit Insurance: The Canadian Banking System 1890-1966." *Journal of Money, Credit, and Banking* (November): 1137-1158.

Carrizosa, Mauricio, Danny M. Leipziger, and Hemant Shah. 1996. "The Tequila Effect and Argentina's Banking Reform." *Finance and Development* (March 1996): 22-25.

Central Bank of Argentina. *Statistics Bulletin.*

Corrigan, E. Gerald. 1991. "The Banking-Commerce Controversy Revisited." *Quarterly Review.* Federal Reserve Bank of New York (Spring): 1-13.

Edwards, Jeremy, and Klaus Fischer. 1994. *Banks, Finance and Investment in Germany.* New York: Cambridge University Press.

García, Gillian, and Matthew Saal. 1996. "Internal Governance: Market Discipline and Regulatory Restraint: International Evidence." In *Rethinking Bank Regulation: What Should Regulators Do?* Federal Reserve Bank of Chicago.

Goldstein, Morris. 1998. *The Asian Financial Crisis.* Washington, D.C.: Institute for International Economics.

Goldstein, Morris, and Philip Turner. 1996. *Banking Crises in Emerging Economies: Origins and Policy Options.* Economic Paper No. 46. Basle, Switzerland: Bank for International Settlements (October).

Greenspan, Alan. 1998. Remarks at Annual Convention of the Independent Bankers Association of America, March 3, Washington, D.C.: Board of Governors of the Federal Reserve System.

Hausmann, Ricardo, and Liliana Rojas-Suárez, eds. 1996. *Banking Crises in Latin America.* Washington, D.C.: Inter-American Development Bank.

Hubbard, R. Glenn, ed. 1991. *Financial Markers and Financial Crises.* Chicago: University of Chicago Press.

Kaufman, George G. 1987. "The Federal Safety Net: Not for Banks Only." *Economic Perspectives.* Federal Reserve Bank of Chicago (November/December): 19-28.

Kaufman, George G. 1988. "Bank Runs: Causes, Benefits, and Costs." *Cato Journal* (Winter): 539-587.

Kaufman, George G. 1992. "Capital in Banking: Past, Present, and Future." *Journal of Financial Services Research* (April): 385-402.

Kaufman, George G. 1994. "Bank Contagion: A Review of the Theory and Evidence." *Journal of Financial Services Research* (April 1994): 123-150.

Kaufman, George G. 1995. "The U.S. Banking Debacle of the 1980s: An Overview and Lessons." *The Financier* (May): 9-26.

Kaufman, George G. 1996a. "Bank Failures, Systemic Risk, and Bank Regulation." *Cato Journal* (Spring/Summer): 17-45.

Kaufman, George G. 1996b. *Bank Fragility: Perception and Historical Evidence.* Working Paper Series No. 96-18. Federal Reserve Bank of Chicago (September).

Kaufman, George G. 1997a. *Banking Reform: The Whys and How Tos.* Working Paper, Loyola University, Chicago.

Kaufman, George G. 1997b. *Preventing Bank Crises: Taking the "State" Out of State Banks.* Working Paper, Loyola University, Chicago (July).

Kaufman, George G. 1997c. "The New Depositor Preference Act: Time Inconsistency In Action." *Managerial Finance* 23(11): 56-63.

Kaufman, George G., and Randall S. Kroszner. 1997. "How Should Financial Institutions and Markets be Structured? Options for Financial System Design." In *Safe and Sound Financial Systems: What Works in Latin America,* ed. Liliana Rojas-Suárez. Washington, D.C.: Inter-American Development Bank.

Kindleberger, Charles P. 1985. "Bank Failures: the 1930s and 1980s." In *The Search for Financial Stability: The Past Fifty Years.* Federal Reserve Bank of San Francisco.

Kindleberger, Charles P. 1996. 3rd ed. *Manias, Panics, and Crashes: A History of Financial Crises.* New York: Wiley.

King, Robert G., and Ross Levine. 1993. "Finance Intermediation and Economic Development." In *Capital Markets and Financial Intermediation*, eds. Colin Mayer and Xavier Vives. New York: Cambridge University Press.

Levine, Ross. 1997a. "Financial Development and Economic Growth: Views and Agenda." *Journal of Economic Literature* (June): 688-726.

Levine, Ross. 1997b. "Stock Markets, Economic Development, and Capital Control Liberalization." *Perspective.* Investment Company Institute (December): 1-7.

Lindgren, Carl-Johan, Gillian García, and Matthew I. Saal. 1996. *Bank Soundness and Macroeconomic Policy.* Washington, D.C.: International Monetary Fund.

McCauley, Robert N., and William R. White. 1997. *The Euro and European Financial Markets.* Working Paper No. 41, Basle, Switzerland: Bank for International Settlements (May).

Miller, Geoffrey D. 1996. "Is Deposit Insurance Inevitable? Lessons from Argentina." *International Review of Law and Economics* (June): 211-232.

Minsky, Hyman P. 1977. "A Theory of Systematic Financial Fragility." In *Financial Crises: Institutions and Markets in a Fragile Environment*, eds. Edward Altman and Arnold Sametz. New York: Wiley.

Moore, Robert R. 1997. "Government Guarantees and Banking: Evidence from the Mexican Peso Crisis." *Financial Industry Studies.* Federal Reserve Bank of Dallas (December): 13-21.

Morgan, J.P. 1998. *World Financial Markets* (March 27).

O'Conner, J.F.T. 1938. *The Banking Crisis and Recovery Under the Roosevelt Administration.* Chicago: Callaghan and Co.

Organization for Economic Cooperation and Development. 1997. "Regulatory Reform in the Financial Services Industry: Where Have We Been? Where are We Going?" *Financial Market Trends* (June): 31-96.

Padoa-Schioppa, Tommaso. 1996. Address to the Ninth International Conference on Banking Supervision, June 12-14, Basle Committee on Banking Supervision, Stockholm, Sweden.

Pou, Pedro. 1997. "What Lessons Can Be Learned from Recent Financial Crises?" *The Argentine Experience in Maintaining Financial Stability in a Global Economy.* Federal Reserve Bank of Kansas City (August): 141-167.

Rajan, Raghuram, and Luigi Zingales. 1998. "Debt, Folklore, and Cross-Country Differences in Financial Structure." *Journal of Applied Corporate Finance* (Winter): 102-107.

Reid, David. 1998. "Measures Proposed by the G10 and Basle Committee." Presentation at ICM Conference on Systemic Risk, April, London.

Rojas-Suárez, Liliana, ed. 1997. *Safe and Sound Financial Systems: What Works for Latin America.* Washington, D.C.: Inter-American Development Bank.

Rojas-Suárez, Liliana, and Steven R. Weisbrod. 1996. "Banking Crises in Latin America: Experiences and Issues." In *Banking Crises in Latin America*, eds. Ricardo Hausmann and Liliana Rojas-Suárez. Washington, D.C.: Inter-American Development Bank.

Scholtens, Bert. 1997. "Bank and Market-Oriented Financial Systems: Fact or Fiction?" *BNL Quarterly Review* (September): 301-323.

Schumacher, Liliana. 1996. Bubble or Depositor Discipline? *A Study of the Argentine Banking Panic.* Ph.D. dissertation, University of Chicago.

Schwartz, Anna J. 1988. "Financial Stability and the Federal Safety Net." In *Restructuring Banking and Financial Services in America,* eds. William S. Haraf and Rose Marie Kushmeider. Washington, D.C.: American Enterprise Institute.

Steinherr, Alfred. 1996. "Performance of Universal Banks." In *Universal Banking,* eds. Anthony Saunders and Ingo Walter. Chicago: Irwin Professional.

Steinherr, Alfred, and Ch. Huveneers. 1994. "On the Performance of Differently Regulated Financial Institutions: Some Empirical Evidence." *Journal of Banking and Finance* 18(2:March): 271-306.

Sylla, Richard. 1995. "The Forgotten Private Banker." *The Freeman* (April): 210-214.

Sylla, Richard, John J. Wallis, and John B. Legler. 1996. "Historical Economics: U.S. State and Local Government." *NBER Reporter* (Spring 1996): 11-16.

Wall Street Journal. 1998. (October 22).

Wallis, John J., Richard E. Sylla, and John B. Legler. 1994. "The Interrelation of Taxation and Regulation in Nineteenth-Century U.S. Banking." In *The Regulatory Economy,* eds. Claudia Golding and Gary D. Lidecap. Chicago: University of Chicago Press.

Weinstein, David E., and Yishay Yafeh. 1998. "On the Costs of a Bank-Centered Financial System: Evidence from the Changing Main Bank Relation in Japan." *Journal of Finance* (April): 635-672.

West, Edwin G. 1997. "Adam Smith's Support for Money and Banking Regulation: A Case of Inconsistency." *Journal of Money, Credit and Banking* (February): 127-134.

Working Party on Financial Stability in Emerging Market Economies. 1997. *Financial Stability in Emerging Market Economies.* Basle, Switzerland (April).

PART II.

PUBLIC UTILITY AND FINANCIAL MARKETS REGULATION

CHAPTER 6

Reforming Urban Water Systems: A Tale of Four Cities

MARY M. SHIRLEY[1]

INTRODUCTION

In recent years, some analysts have seen the growth of private contracts in urban water systems and pronounced it a worldwide trend (World Bank 1994b, Frischtak 1997). Others, however, are less sure, focusing instead on the reasons why private participation may be less likely in water than in other natural monopolies. Is water different?

This study finds that water is indeed different. Important externalities mean that government involvement will be larger in water than in other utilities and that it will be harder for government to establish the credibility of its promise not to confiscate returns by, for example, failing to allow promised price increases. Moreover, the nature of the sector means that information problems will be greater, unbundling will be less feasible, and enforcement will be more difficult. The rewards to political actors and private investors from reforms are likely to be smaller than in other network utilities, even where the social welfare gains may be large. As a result, the introduction of promised reforms often will be delayed, and contracts with private parties will be prone to renegotiation.

These factors help explain why promised private participation was postponed in Lima, Mexico City, and Santiago — but not in Buenos Aires. In Buenos Aires' case, a private contract was implemented because the franchise could be offered to the firm proposing the largest reduction in water tariffs. In the other cities, private participation would have required a tariff increase to cover costs, making a private contract less politically palatable. In the two cases where the potential gains to social welfare were arguably the highest, Lima and Mexico City, the political risks were also high. In these two cities, raw water was costly and scarce, and providing new connections was an important way to reward political supporters; politicians were reluctant to lose control over this important political currency.

This chapter finds large net benefits from the Buenos Aires concession, despite renegotiation of the contract and subsequent price increases. If Lima could have introduced the concession as planned, it would have done well also. Although some important reforms were introduced in Lima without private participation, they have only barely allowed the company to keep water coverage expanding at the same pace as the city's rapid growth. Mexico City introduced service contracts with private providers but delayed the start of promised management contracts indefinitely. While important improvements were introduced, they have not gone very far toward alleviating the water crisis situation in Mexico City. Additionally, although Santiago had the least net benefit from reform, because its system was the best run to begin with, it remains the top performer of the four.

The problems of privatizing water make Chile's success in running a water company as a state-owned enterprise (SOE) very appealing. The strength of Chile's institutions, however, suggests that its success may be hard for other countries to emulate. Private participation, when it can be introduced, may help countries that lack Chile's institutional strengths introduce and sustain water reforms.

This chapter first considers why private participation in natural monopolies may be desirable and then analyzes the ways in which water may be different from other utilities. It next compares the water reform experiences of four cities, within the context of four countries' privatization programs: Buenos Aires, Argentina; Santiago, Chile; Lima, Peru; and Mexico City, Mexico. It asks why Buenos Aires privatized and why Lima, Mexico City, and Santiago did not, and it compares the gains from reform in each case. It concludes with some policy implications from the experience of the four cities.

PRIVATIZATION OF NATURAL MONOPOLIES

Water is a natural monopoly, where declining long-run average costs mean that it is most efficient for only a single firm to serve the market; however, unless that firm is regulated or controlled, it will restrict output to levels where it maximizes its rents. While new technologies have reduced the natural monopoly characteristics of other sectors, no such developments have occurred in water. For example, wireless phone service can compete directly with wire line, and competition can be introduced in long distance, even where local telecommunications service is a monopoly. In power, such countries as Argentina and Chile have separated transmission from distribution and generation to allow direct competition in generation and to increase contestability in distribution. In dense urban settings, however, the only practical way to bring water into people's homes and remove wastewater from them is through a system of pipes that are costly to lay and maintain and is likely to remain, as discussed further below. The substitutes for piped water and sanitation are either impractical and unsafe in cities, such as boreholes or latrines, or very costly, such as bottled water.

The existence of a natural monopoly argues for government intervention but not necessarily for government ownership. Carl Shapiro and Robert Willig (1990) and Klaus Schmidt (1996) argue that state ownership reduces information asymmetry, but Jean-Jacques Laffont and Jean Tirole (1993) point out that lack of information about the operations of private enterprises may be a good thing if it commits the regulator to a reduced expropriation of the firm's investment. Laffont and Tirole further note that state ownership reduces the information that would otherwise be available to shareholders through the stock market.[2] Theory tells us that another advantage of state ownership is that a benevolent government will use its power as owner to maximize social welfare rather than profits, but a characteristically benevolent government is a mythical creature found only in economics texts. In practice, government agents act to maximize their own agendas (Shapiro and Willig 1990) or those of politicians or interest groups (Olson 1965), which sometimes may advance social welfare but other times does not. Public choice theories (Buchanan et al. 1980; Niskanen 1971) also argue that public managers, bureaucrats, and politicians use their control of SOEs to further their own interests rather than the state firm's efficiency and that any positive effect on social welfare becomes only a secondary motive or an unintended consequence. Matthew D. McCubbins, Roger Noll, and Barry R. Weingast (1987) show how politicians craft rules and regulations to make sure that their constituents' interests are protected.

Privatization of a monopoly improves its performance if competition can be increased or if regulation can be improved. The private owners will maximize their welfare, as the managers will, but the private owners will have a stronger incentive than government bureaucrats to control the management in order to maximize profits, as they are the claimants on any surplus funds the firm generates (World Bank 1995). As a result, an unregulated private monopoly will operate efficiently, charge high prices, and serve only a portion of demand. As John Vickers and George Yarrow point out, much depends upon the nature of the regulatory game between the firm and the government; indeed, regulation might even "reinstate the problems of public officials acting in their own interest that privatization was intended to sidestep" (1991, 114).

The choice between a regulated state monopoly and a privately owned monopoly is not the only set of options. Harold Demsetz (1968) showed that regulation was not, in principle, necessary for a natural monopoly, since a franchise to offer the service for the lowest price could be put up for competitive bidding, driving the price down to competitive levels. Oliver Williamson (1976) and Victor P. Goldberg (1976), however, noted that competitive bidding over price would not solve important problems of quality, reliability, and the like. They further argued that private investors would be reluctant to sink a large amount of investment into nonredeployable assets without a long-term contract that offered credible assurances that their quasi-rents would be protected from ex post facto appropriation. Such assurances would only be credible if there were formal dispute resolution mechanisms as well as arrangements for price adjustments and other changes, all of which could require an administrative apparatus as extensive and complex as those associated with regulation. As Keith Crocker and Scott Masten (1998) point out, "The choice between franchise contracting and regulation turns on whether court enforcement or regulator administration is the more effective way of bolstering commitment, effecting adaptations, and resolving disputes in the settings that characterize the supply of public utility services." In practice, the cost of courts and their weakness in developing countries has meant that most franchise arrangements are regulated in much the same way as private monopolies are regulated.

Countries, thus, can choose between operating their natural monopoly as a state agency or enterprise, as a regulated franchise with a private operator, or as a regulated private enterprise. However, there are also alternatives within these three options that entail less important but, nonetheless, nontrivial choices. Under the state agency or enterprise option, the government may choose to treat the water utility as a government agency or a government corporation. This agency or corporation may be owned by the federal, provincial, or local government; a further choice is that the agency or corporation may be operated as a subordinate part of the government hierarchy or much like a regulated private firm. In addition, parts of the agency's or corporation's activities or even the entire management of the state enterprise may be run by a private firm under contract for a fee.

There are also important choices in franchising. A franchise arrangement could take the form of a lease, where the private contractor rents facilities from the government and then operates and maintains the facility. In the franchise lease case, the government is responsible for new investment, replacement of major works, and debt service. Under a concession, the private operator is responsible for investment as well as operations and maintenance. For both franchising and concessions, the contractor is paid on the basis of profits and assumes all commercial risks.

In addition, the assets of the monopoly could be privately owned and operated under government regulation.

Table 1.
Contractual Options for the Provision of Urban Water Supply

	Ownership of Assets	Operations & Maintenance	Investment	Current Financing	Capital Financing
Gov't. Department or Agency	Public	Public	Public	Subsidies	Transfers
State Corporation	Public	Public	Public	Revenues	Government-guaranteed loans
Management Contract	Public	Private	Public	Public	Public
Lease	Public	Private	Public	Private	Public
Concession	Public	Private	Private	Private	Private
Private Enterprise	Private	Private	Private	Private	Private

Source: Adapted from World Bank, 1994b, *World Development Report: Infrastructure for Development*, New York: Oxford University Press.

The consequences of these choices for how risk is shared between government and utility can be inferred from Table 1. A government department gets its funds from the budget; a state corporation has a financing structure modeled on that of a private firm, even though risk is still public. With a management contract and, even more, with a lease, some or most of the operating risk is shifted to the private sector; under a concession, the private sector bears the investment risk as well as the operating risk.

Within each contractual form, there is another large array of decisions about how to fix prices, what sort of regulatory body to create, how disputes will be resolved, and how contract terms will change over time. As Claude Crampes and Antonio Estache (1997) note, the choice of regulatory structure depends on a country's hierarchy of concerns, including those of users (price, quality, and reliability); those of firms (profits, risks, and market power); those of government (fiscal burden, redundancies, environment and distributional issues); and those of regulators (reputation and remuneration). While some concerns will be the same in any monopoly, others will be affected by the nature of the service, which brings us to the question of water.

Is Water Different?

This section considers how water's potential differences from other utilities would affect the decision about and design of private contracts. One way in which water differs from other natural monopolies is in the importance of the externalities present; thus, government involvement would probably be needed even if the sector were perfectly competitive. While consumers of gas, electricity, or telecommunications might be able to substitute wood, candles, or mail — or even go without them — water is an essential and unique good with no substitutes. Although water meets the economist's definition of a private good, in that its use is rival and excludable, there are important externalities to supplying clean water.[3] Since water is capable of carrying dangerous diseases, some of which, such as cholera, are infectious and can cause epidemics, there is a strong public interest in making clean water for human consumption available and affordable.

The health effects of water and sanitation are one reason for higher public interest in the sector, but health is not the only externality associated with water. Another is depletion of aquifers, which can have many adverse consequences. Mexico City, for example, has been rapidly drawing down the aquifers under the city, and between 1986 and 1994 alone, the level of the aquifer under the central sections of the city dropped by 10 to 14 meters (Haggarty, Brook-Cowen, and Zuluaga 1999). Because of the nature of the soil under Mexico City, which sits in a dry lakebed, the depletion of the aquifer has caused the downtown area to sink by an average of 7.5 meters since the beginning of the twentieth century. This has caused cracks in buildings and unsafe structures. Other externalities arise from the pollution of streams, rivers, and the ocean with untreated wastewater, which adversely affects not only public health but also agriculture, tourism, fishing, and the property values of affected areas.

The externalities associated with water are a rationale for regulation but not necessarily for state ownership. There is little evidence that state-owned companies protect health and the environment better than private firms do, and some evidence that they are worse polluters than private enterprises (World Bank 1995). However, these externalities do make it more complicated, although not impossible, to write a regulatory contract that will attract private investment, be enforceable, and protect consumers and the environment.

A second, related challenge for private participation is that water poses greater information problems than other utilities and resources. Consumers cannot easily tell if water is safe to drink, since many dangerous pollutants do not affect the smell or the taste of water. The closest parallel is in electricity; consumers cannot know about power surges until the damage has been done. This argues for regulation of quality and monitoring of health effects, but not necessarily for state ownership. A greater information problem for private participation in water is that most of the network is buried underground, which has adverse effects on both private investment and regulation. The invisibility of water assets makes it costly and time consuming for a potential private operator to ascertain the quality of the water network before bidding and for a regulator to ascertain that a private operator is maintaining the system properly. Buried phone or power lines are similarly invisible, but a break in these lines is more obvious and does not lead to leaks. Gas is the closest parallel to water, in that a break in a gas line causes loss of product, but gas line breaks are more easily detectable because a strong and harmless odor can be added. The information problems in water raise the likelihood that either the regulator or the private supplier will try to renegotiate the contract at a later date, as more information becomes known. Were it not for these information problems, renegotiations would be less problematic in water than in sectors where technology is changing more rapidly, such as telecommunications.

Pricing of water presents a third difficulty for private participation. Crocker and Masten (1998) point out that pricing for cost recovery, which is necessary to attract private investors in water, raises issues that are somewhat different from those faced in other utilities. Since much water is not used for consumption but for washing or gardening or is wasted, it is sensible to price water to cover its marginal cost and permit a reasonable return to capital. However, consumers may not be well informed about the health risks of unsafe water or may undervalue clean water for consumption. It may not be desirable to price water high enough to permit the firm to recover its costs, if such high prices would increase the incidents of illnesses caused by consumption of such unsafe alternatives as contaminated river or well water.

An alternative is to keep prices low for some minimum volume of consumption and give a direct budgetary transfer to the firm for recovering costs associated with providing the minimum consumption volume. Still, there is risk even in pricing below marginal cost that people will consume too much of the good. Moreover, in practice, transfers to cover subsidies are usually impractical and, by giving the enterprise a soft budget, have adverse effects on operational efficiency (for evidence, see World Bank 1995). These disadvantages arise whether the firm is public or private. Private operators, moreover, may not regard government's promise to sustain a budgetary transfer in the face of political opposition as credible and thus may be unwilling to invest. Cross-subsidies that put a heavy burden on nonresidential users have disadvantages, too; they raise business costs, with adverse effects on new investment and job creation. Pricing to recover costs may be seen as more politically credible, since beneficiaries pay for expanded service; also, this pricing will discourage waste and reduce sewerage, especially in locations where water is in scarce supply, the system is close to capacity, or sewerage treatment and disposal are inadequate.

One way to tackle these problems is to set prices to recover marginal costs, including investment and external costs, and then provide direct income support to low-income consumers who might otherwise use dangerous alternatives. Such support can prove very costly unless it is carefully targeted, something Chile has done but something other countries might find administratively difficult, as I discuss later. Furthermore, the deadweight losses from the inefficient tax systems typical of most developing countries would make this form of subsidy more costly than cross-subsidies (Laffont 1998).

There are further problems in structuring water prices. In most utilities, some or all of the fixed costs are recovered through access fees, by user charges set to include some capital costs, or through some combination of the two. Metering is necessary for usage fees that will affect the quantity of water demanded. But metering costs are high compared with water's very low, short-run marginal costs. Costs are also high compared with costs of utilities, such as telephones, for which monitoring can be done from a central office instead of with on-site meters. As a result, water often has not been metered, even in many developed countries, including the United Kingdom. Where capacity is ample, the cost of metering may outweigh the benefits that might be achieved in reducing the need to expand the infrastructure, conserving raw water, and reducing wastewater contamination. Nor is it obvious who should pay for metering — the consumer, the company, or the taxpayer (Armstrong, Cowan, and Vickers 1994).

A fourth related issue complicating private participation in water is the difficulty of introducing any form of competition. Direct competition from water vendors is a way to assure access in areas not served by the network. This form of distribution is more costly, but prices are often many times the cost of supply. Prices could diminish if governments can reduce collusion among vendors and their ability to exclude entry. Distribution is even more inefficient in water than in other network monopolies except for gas and some forms of transport, such as subways. This is because, in addition to the costs of laying competing networks, there are costs of disrupting and damaging existing roadways (Crocker and Masten 1998).

Unbundling water from sewerage is costly because of the complementarities between the two. Wastewater can contaminate water supplies if it is not properly removed and treated, and a sanitation system can only operate properly if there is an adequate supply of water to flush it out.[4] Further, economies of scope are lost in that the experience gained in maintaining and operating water mains is useful for sewers (Armstrong, Cowan, and Vickers 1994). Moreover, after separation, both the water company and the sewerage company would remain monopolies in their areas, in contrast with separation of electricity generation from transmission, for example (Clarke and Cowan 1998).

Horizontal competition of the sort being tried in electricity, where suppliers compete via access to a single grid, is somewhat hampered by the need to strictly and continually monitor the quality of water each company supplies and by the information problems in monitoring quality mentioned earlier (Clarke and Cowan 1998). These problems have been overcome in electricity, however, and do not rule out competition in water. The high cost of pumping water long distances and the increases in leakage with distance mean that water will remain a local or regional business (Cowan 1994), which limits the potential for horizontal competition to a municipal area. There are also economies of scale in some locations, such as when a city is most efficiently served by a single reservoir. Where more than one reservoir can serve a city or where a considerable amount of water is pumped, there may be potential for competition.

Yardstick competition, through comparison of similar companies operating in different locations, assumes that the exogenous factors that affect company costs are to some extent correlated. However, given the local nature of water, this may often not be the case (Clarke and Cowan 1998). Validity of yardstick competition also depends on the companies' not colluding. Accordingly, the water operators within a country should have different owners; however, achieving ownership diversity may be a problem because the market for operation of water companies has not been very competitive until quite recently. Comparison is further complicated in countries with one very large urban center, where all other urban agglomerations are much smaller, a typical situation in many developing countries.

Competition to participate in the water market may occur through competitive bidding for the franchise or management contract. Here, gains are likely to be smaller than in utilities other than water because externalities and information problems raise regulatory risk in a sector with very large capital costs, almost entirely in sunken assets. This may explain why there have been so few experienced international operators willing to bid on franchise contracts, while there has been active competition among international operators bidding in electricity and telecommunications. Thus far, the water franchise market has been dominated by two French operators, Suez Lyonnaise des Eaux and Vivendi (formally Generale des Eaux) and, in the 1990s, also by some U.K. water companies. A related problem is that bidding for such long-lived investments is likely to be infrequent, which was an important consideration in the United Kingdom. There it was felt that capital markets could encourage productive efficiency, since inefficient companies would be threatened with a takeover bid. An active market for corporate control would have resulted in mergers, however, and that conflicted with the regulator's aim to keep a sufficiently large number of companies for yardstick competition (Armstrong, Cowan, and Vickers 1994).

Thus, the economics of water combines several factors to make private participation more difficult in water than in other utilities: first, externalities require government intervention; second, information problems make contract negotiation and monitoring more difficult; third, pricing and metering issues make regulatory design more complicated; and fourth, technological and informational barriers make competition less feasible. These factors in no way preclude a welfare-enhancing private contract. However, they raise the transaction costs and regulatory risk of private participation.

The political economy of water is another factor that may work against private participation. Since water systems are typically less valuable than those in electricity or telecommunications, their sale or lease would raise less revenue to reward supporters or compensate opponents. The main political benefit is likely to come from new capital for expanded investment and better maintenance and service both from private investors and from consumers paying higher prices. The beneficiaries from the increases in capacity that would result are likely to be the urban lower classes in most developing countries. Many of these people are recent migrants from rural areas to sections of the city not yet served by water infrastructure. These urban poor are typically unorganized groups with low political power.

While these potential winners may have little political weight, the potential losers are typically more powerful. The main rents in water are in construction, not operation, and the private suppliers interested in operating urban water systems are often affiliated with construction companies. Domestic construction companies may not necessarily favor private participation in water if they expect to earn less rent than under public procurement, as a result of the private operator's giving preferences in contracts to its affiliated construction company.

Consumers who are already connected to a water supply typically have to pay more for water in order to allow a private investor to recover quasi-rents. They can be expected to oppose private participation, especially if the increased costs outweigh the value to them of reducing their risk of communicable diseases. These consumers are likely to have higher incomes, to be more organized, and to have more political options than the urban poor. Other potential losers are workers who are made redundant in the public water company, although their opposition may be reduced through severance pay or share ownership. Politicians who use local infrastructure investments as a way to reward their supporters would oppose any form of private participation that would reduce their capacity to control the timing and the location of new investments.[5] The fact that water is a unique good, necessary for human life, has meant that public ownership, low consumer prices, and continued service to those who fail to pay their bills are often legally enshrined and that popular opposition to monopoly rents or even quasi-rents may be especially strong in this sector.

For all these reasons, we expect that countries will be slow to involve the private sector in water, even when they are undertaking privatization in other natural monopolies. Where private participation is allowed, we expect that the initial pricing formula will minimize the cost to existing consumers and that information problems will make contracts more incomplete. None of these problems mean that countries that do chose to involve the private sector will be worse off than they would be under continued state ownership. Rather, to the extent that private participation reduces information asymmetries and increases incentives to invest in and operate the sector efficiently, we expect to see welfare gains.

EMPIRICAL EVIDENCE THAT WATER IS DIFFERENT

The experience of water and sanitation in four capital cities — Buenos Aires, Lima, Mexico City, and Santiago — supports the presumption that private contracts are less likely in water and sewerage systems than in other utilities.[6] All four countries implemented a major privatization program that included the sale of telecommunications and, except for Mexico, the sale of electricity. In three of the four countries, the decision about private participation was largely the responsibility of the central government; thus, the same authority that had opted to privatize other utilities made the decision whether to privatize water.[7] In two cases, Lima and Santiago, a number of preparative steps were taken, but the decision was ultimately reversed. In Mexico City, service contracts were introduced with four private companies, with the aim of eventually contracting out operation and maintenance of the network. However, in 1998, the management contracting stage was already three years behind schedule, and there was no clear signal of when, if ever, it would be implemented. Only in Buenos Aires was substantial private involvement implemented — through the signing of a concession contract with Aguas Argentinas in 1992.

COMPARATIVE NEED FOR WATER REFORM IN FOUR LATIN AMERICAN CITIES

Why did Argentina implement private participation in water as planned, while the other three countries did not? The benefits from private participation would have been at least as high in Lima and Mexico City as in Buenos Aires and arguably higher. Only in Santiago would the benefits of a private operator have been relatively small. One benefit would be additional private capital for investment in expansion. Table 2 shows that Buenos Aires had the lowest connection rate before reform (70 percent), but Lima's (75 percent), which may in fact have been lower if all slum areas had been included, was almost as low. As for Mexico City, although connection rates were high, efforts to reduce depletion of the aquifer relied on development of water sources outside the basin that entailed large investment costs. For example, current plans are for a source 140 kilometers from the city with an investment cost of around US$500 million. In contrast, Santiago had high connection rates (see Table 2) and no need for major new investments in water supply for the medium term.

Table 2.
Conditions in the Water System Before Reform: Four Cities

	Buenos Aires 1992	Mexico City 1992	Lima 1991	Santiago 1988
Population in Service Area (millions)	8.2	8.3	6.1	4.4
Population Connected (%)	70%	96.1%	75%	99%
Unaccounted-for Water	44%	33-47%	42.1%	34%
Workers/1000 connections	3.4	13.8	4.7	2.2
Connections Metered	2%	NA	10%[1]	100%
Billed Amounts Collected	85.1%	NA	43%[2]	93%
Water Consumption Per Capita[3]	352	236	220	192

1. Metered and read; about 30 percent are metered.   2. 1985.   3. Liters per day.

Source: Author's compilation.

Another potential benefit from private participation, more funds for better maintenance, also would have been higher in Lima and Mexico City than in Buenos Aires or Santiago. Unaccounted-for water was high in all the cities before reform, but the cost of waste varied because of large differences in the cost of raw water. Although numbers are not available, the cost of raw water appears to have been much higher in Lima and Mexico City than in Buenos Aires or Santiago. In Buenos Aires, relatively clean water from the adjacent Río de la Plata is in ample supply; Santiago also has ample water, from the Río Maipo and a natural reservoir that is gravity-fed from the sources to the treatment plants. In contrast, Lima is in a desert and depends on a badly polluted river for two-thirds of its water; the other third is pumped from an aquifer that becomes contaminated when the water table near the ocean drops. Water scarcity contributed to a cholera epidemic in 1989. Mexico City relies for two-thirds of its raw water on wells from 70 to 200 meters deep, which tap into the city's rapidly depleting aquifer.[8] The other third is pumped uphill from distant rivers; for example, one site is 127 kilometers distant and 1,200 meters below the city. The costs of pumping water from sources outside the Mexico City basin and pumping sewerage beyond the basin are high; also, the pumping of the aquifer is causing the city to sink, damaging many buildings and causing pipes to buckle and break. Since rainwater and sewerage are not separated, the runoff cannot be used to replenish the aquifer. Instead, all wastewater is dumped and treated beyond the basin.

Another likely effect of private participation is reduced per-capita consumption because increased metering, higher bill collection rates, and pricing to provide a return to investment motivate consumers to reduce waste. Reduced waste has larger benefits in cities where water is scarcer and has larger externalities. Hence, Lima and Mexico City would arguably have benefited more from better metering and billing and efficiency pricing than Buenos Aires or Santiago would have. Per-capita consumption is 236 liters per day in Mexico City, very high compared with European rates of 150 to 200 liters per day, although still less than Buenos Aires' 352 liters per day. Before the service contracts, water in Mexico City was free to many users; metering was low, about a third of all connections were not registered, and many of those who were registered did not receive a bill or did not pay their bills when they received them. Sixty-eight percent of total collections were from large industrial or commercial users who represented only about 2 percent of the customer base. In Lima, only 30 percent of connections were metered, few meters were read, less than half of billed amounts were collected, and the average tariff was very low, only US$0.13 M^3 (per cubic meter) in 1988. Consumption of water in Lima, 220 liters per capita per day, was lower than in Buenos Aires or Mexico City, but this was largely because water service was so poor. Water shutoffs averaged 15 hours per day in Lima, with rationing in the summer.

Of course, adequate investment, metering, bill collection, and scarcity pricing do not necessarily require private participation, as Santiago shows. The benefits there from private investment would have been less than in the other three cities. Nevertheless, the main explanation for the choice of ownership in Santiago and in the other cities was political, as we discuss in the next section.

POLITICAL ECONOMY OF WATER IN THE FOUR CITIES

Ultimately, the privatization decision in the four cities is best understood in terms of the political economy of water. The political benefits from private participation in water are usually low, even though the social welfare benefits, such as better public health, water conservation, and environmental improvements, can be quite high. This is because the beneficiaries from an expanded system often have low political clout, and the additional revenues available to reward supporters or compensate losers are relatively small. The political costs, including higher tariffs to existing consumers and loss of the ability to channel rents to political supporters, may thus be higher than the benefits.

A crucial difference between Buenos Aires and the other cities was that the Menem government was able to change the political cost-benefit equation because the average amount paid for water was not only high compared with the marginal cost but also high compared with other cities. Average price paid, shown in Table 3, that is, revenues collected divided by cubic meters distributed, was higher in Buenos Aires before reform than it was in the other cities before reform, despite Buenos Aires' relatively lower water cost.[9] The price paid was high in Buenos Aires in part because the costs of the state-owned company were very high. Private companies buying into water service estimated that they could reduce costs enough to make reasonable returns despite the price reduction.[10] (For example, after reform, the labor force of Aguas Argentinas fell from 7,666 to 4,678.) As a result, Buenos Aires could bid its concession for the lowest tariff and expect that consumer prices might go down; all the other cities would have had to increase prices to cover costs in order to attract private investors. Thus, even though Lima's water company was at least as inefficient as Buenos Aires' SOE, major savings from efficiency gains could not have averted a tariff increase there. Lima's tariffs were very low compared with its high raw water costs and its need for major new investments to cope with water scarcity. Not surprisingly, Lima's proposed concession contract would have allowed up to a 40-percent real increase in water tariffs.

Effective prices eventually did go up in Lima, Mexico City, and Santiago, partly from increased collections and partly from tariff increases. However, prices still do not cover costs to permit a reasonable return to investment in Lima and Mexico City. It is significant that these cities could not offer a price decrease as a selling point for privatization. Large increases in water tariffs would be politically contentious and threaten the credibility of a private contract. In contrast, the winning bid in Buenos Aires offered a tariff 26 percent lower than the price charged by the state enterprise, although the contract was renegotiated later, as is discussed in the next section.[11]

Price increase was not the only reason that the other cities did not proceed with their plans for private participation. Since most of Santiago's population was already connected and the water company was functioning well, the benefits from privatization were much smaller than in the other cities. As a result, the sale of the Metropolitan Enterprise of Sanitary Works (Empresa Metropolitana de Obras de Sanitarias – EMOS) received little attention until quite late in the privatization program. The administration of General Augusto Pinochet, which began in 1973 from a military coup, did not begin to enact the legislation to set up the regulatory

Table 3.
Average Revenues Collected/M^3 Distributed[1]
(US$)[2]

Average Revenues per M^3 Water	Buenos Aires	Lima[3]	Mexico City	Santiago
Pre-Reform	$0.18	$0.15	$0.22	$0.11
Post-Reform	$0.16	$0.18	$0.27	$0.14

1. Dates are the following: Buenos Aires – pre-reform, 1992; post-reform, 1993; Lima – pre-reform, 1991; post-reform, 1992; Mexico City – pre-reform, 1992; post-reform, 1993; Santiago – pre-reform, 1989; post-reform, 1990.

2. Revenues adjusted for collection rates net of indirect taxes/M^3 produced, adjusted for unaccounted-for water (UFW).

3. Includes sewerage.

Source: Author's compilation.

framework for privatizing water until 1988.[12] Instead, it focused first on privatizing manufacturing, where public ownership was reduced to zero, then on banking, then on telecommunications and electricity.[13] When attention finally turned to water, it was too late; the government was negotiating with a potential private buyer when it was surprised by its defeat in an October 1988 plebiscite and had to call elections, and the military-backed candidate subsequently lost. The new, democratically elected president was ideologically opposed to privatizing water. Moreover, the new government could reap the economic benefits of reform by implementing the water legislation already passed under the dictatorship without changing ownership. Indeed, by keeping water public, they could reward political supporters with seats on the boards of the state-owned water companies.

In contrast to the timing of the planned EMOS sale in Santiago, the Drinking Water and Sewerage Service of Lima (Servicio de Agua Potable y Alcantarillado de Lima — SEDAPAL) was included in the Fujimori government's program from when it was first announced in 1992, much like the Menem government's treatment of the Sanitary Works of the Nation (Obras Sanitarias de la Nación — OSN). This was a serious program. From 1992 to 1996, Peru sold 14 large SOEs and signed seven concession contracts, privatizing electricity, telecommunications, steel, copper, and banking. The intention to privatize water was also serious, as evidenced by the fact that three potential bidders were prequalified.

Partly because of the promise of this concession, the Lima water company received US$600 million from the World Bank, the Japan Overseas Economic Cooperation Fund, and the Government of Peru for rehabilitation of the distribution network and expansion of service to low-income consumers. Thanks to this support, a number of reforms were introduced, which may have had the unintended consequence of reducing the political benefits of going ahead with the concession. Coverage was expanded, and increases in tariffs and productivity reduced SEDAPAL's drain on the budget. The concession would have meant not only much higher tariffs but also more efficient billing, expanded metering, and better collection. President Alberto Fujimori expressed concern about the affordability of water for Lima's poor consumers.[14] Timing was also a problem. Privatization of water was becoming increasingly unpopular with the public.[15] The concession was postponed until after the 1995 elections, then further delayed; finally, in 1997, President Fujimori announced that SEDAPAL was no longer slated for a concession.

Mexico City's water system was not part of the general privatization program. Indeed, it could not be, since it was not organized as a corporate entity. Instead, water was regulated and managed through a hodgepodge of organizations set up in large part to channel water investments and employment to enhance political support. Thus, there was one municipal entity responsible for building new infrastructure, another responsible for administration, and 16 political sub-units (*delegaciones*) of the municipal government with responsibility for the operation and maintenance of the secondary distribution network. The 1992-1993 reform grouped the *delegaciones* into four zones and introduced service contracts with four private companies, with the goal of gradually increasing the private sector's responsibility for managing the secondary network, but the organization of the sector was not changed. This is because the political leaders of the country and the city had conflicting goals; they wanted to reduce the fiscal drain of water, but they also wanted to preserve water's political usefulness, at least until after the 1994 presidential elections.

The ruling party, the Institutional Revolutionary Party (Partido Revolucionario Institucional — PRI), had been losing ground in Mexico City, and in the 1988 presidential elections it won only 27 percent of the vote there. The new President, Carlos Salinas de Gortari, launched a program to win the support of local communities through better services and appointed Manuel Camacho, a member of the president's inner group of technocrats and a potential presidential candidate, as mayor of Mexico City. Camacho used control over municipal services, including water, to win constituents for the PRI. This was apparently successful, as the PRI won 40 percent of the city's vote in the 1991 congressional elections. At the same time, the federal government wanted higher rates of metering and collection since it was subsidizing about two-thirds of the costs of pumping water into Mexico City.[16] The service contracts were designed to meet these needs, but they were timed to begin only after Camacho left the mayor's office in 1993, while the management phase of the contracts was scheduled to begin only in 1994. In any event, the service contracts began in 1994-1995, and, by 1999, the management phase still had not been negotiated, in part because the political cost of ceding control over the distribution network to private contractors was higher than the benefits. The costs would be borne by the municipal government, while the benefits would accrue largely to the federal government. Since the political coalition governing Mexico City is now different from that controlling the federal government, reform is even less likely, unless the federal government decides to stop subsidizing Mexico City's water investment.

In summary, in two cities with the most pressing needs for reform, private participation was derailed (Lima) or delayed (Mexico City). Of course, private participation is not the only route to reform. Lima, Mexico City, and Santiago went on to introduce reforms under public ownership. The next section compares the results in those cities with those of the concession in Buenos Aires.

Table 4.
Comparison of Current Regulatory Regimes

	Buenos Aires	Lima	Mexico City	Santiago
Reform (start date)	Concession w/ private operator (1993)	Reform SOE (1992)	Service contracts with private operators (1993)	Reform SOE (1990)
Regulator	Agency under Public Works Secretariat. Budget autonomy, but subject to pressures.	Agency under Vice Ministry for Infrastructure in Ministry of the Presidency. Budget autonomy but low power.	3 municipal agencies regulate quality, contracts and bill collection. No political insulation.	Agency under Ministry of Industry. No budget autonomy, but protected by legal status.
Dispute Resolution	Renegotiation of contract with govt. (not regulator).	Ad hoc appeals by company to Vice Ministry for Infrastructure.	None	Neutral arbitration plus courts.
Pricing	Concession bid, then reviewed every 5 years unless cost index increases more than 7%.	Arbitrary, cost-plus, based on company request. Price is greater than marginal cost.	Regulator proposes; municipal assembly must approve. Price is less than 50% of marginal cost.	Adjusted to cover marginal cost and average costs every 5 years. Inflation adjusted yearly. Price is average cost plus enough to allow at least 7% return on assets.
1996 Tariff (US$) (average price)	$0.24	$0.35 (includes sewerage)	$0.32 (includes sewerage)	$0.30
Subsidies	Unmetered price based on housing attributes; cross-subsidy of low-volume consumption.	Cross-subsidy, business to residential.	Cross-subsidy, business to residential, metered to unmetered.	Means-targeted subsidy for (average) 60% of first 20 cubic meters.
Status of Water Company	Private company.	SOE under public law.	Four private; 16 sub-municipal, Municipal investment agency	SOE incorporated under private law.

Source: Author's compilation.

RESULTS OF THE REFORMS

As Table 4 shows, the reforms resulted in very different regulatory regimes in the four cities. An optimal regulatory system, which would maximize social welfare and would be credible to potential investors, is one that clearly sets out the rules and regulations, endows the regulator with autonomy from ad hoc political interference in the enforcement of these rules, insulates the regulator from capture by the regulated industry, and provides assurance that the water company is free from politically motivated interference in its operations and has an incentive to operate efficiently and invest. Since rules cannot cover all eventualities, there would also be a neutral mechanism for resolving disputes between the regulator and the company. Water tariffs would be designed to encourage efficiency in operations and investment, such as a cap on the amount by which prices can increase. For example, the United Kingdom sets water tariffs to rise by an amount (K) above the increase in the retail price index (RPI + K). In theory, this sort of price cap motivates efficiency because the company can keep any additional revenues it earns from efficiency gains during the period in which the cap operates. At the end of the period, the prices may be reduced so that the efficiency savings are henceforth shared with the consumer (Armstrong, Cowan and Vickers 1994). Optimal tariffs would also allow private investors to cover their cost of capital and would cover the opportunity cost of scarce water and marginal social cost — that is, marginal cost including externalities.

In the real world, there are many institutional and political barriers to creating an optimal regulatory scheme. This section briefly compares the regulatory regimes in the four cities and their outcomes, starting with Santiago.

Santiago's water system is the best managed and regulated of the four and was so even before the 1990 reforms. Market coverage is 100 percent, unaccounted-for water is a low 20 percent, quality of water is high, and service interruptions are few. EMOS earned a 10 percent return on total assets in 1996; yet, the average price paid for water that year (US$0.30 per cubic meter) was not much above Buenos Aires' (US$0.24 per cubic meter) and below Lima's ($0.35 per cubic meter, including sewerage) thanks to higher collection rates and labor productivity.[17] As a result of the reforms, Chile today has an independent water regulator insulated from politics by laws that, because of Chile's Constitution, are very hard to change. Water tariffs are designed to motivate efficiency: they are set according to the long-run marginal costs of a hypothetical efficient company adjusted to cover average costs in order to assure financial solvency.[18] Tariffs, too, are protected from political manipulation because the formulas are spelled out in the law. Furthermore, there has been little incentive for consumers to push for change, since poor consumers and many middle-income consumers are protected by a means-targeted subsidy, which covers 60 percent on average of the first 20 cubic meters of water consumption. The water company operates under private commercial law and has been largely free from politically motivated interference except in its investment decisions.

Finally, Chile's regulatory regime would be very credible with a private investor. A dispute resolution mechanism allows the company to appeal the regulator's pricing decisions to a neutral arbitration committee; other decisions can be appealed to the courts under constitutional protections against confiscation of property rights.

If there was a cost to Chile of not selling EMOS, it was the failure to build a sewerage treatment plant. Since Chile's regulation makes sewerage treatment a lucrative business because it is also subject to the rule that tariffs must cover average costs plus at least a 7-percent return on assets (ROA), many observers believe that a private operator would have built the plant. However, the government would not permit EMOS to borrow to build the plant and required the company to pay 60 percent to 100 percent of its profits as dividends, solving a fiscal problem but delaying sewerage treatment. As a result, only about 3 percent of sewerage is treated; until 1994, farmers of land adjacent to Santiago irrigated food crops with water from rivers contaminated by untreated wastewater, which explains why Santiago has had a higher incidence of cholera than the rest of the country.[19] Untreated wastewater is also adversely affecting Chile's beaches and ocean fishing.

Buenos Aires' concession is not as sound as Santiago's regulation in some respects but is still an important improvement over the previous regime and much better than that of Lima or Mexico City. Buenos Aires' reform created an independent water regulator with budget autonomy (funded from a tax collected by the concessionaire), but it has not had the autonomy and power bestowed on Chile's regulator. The regulator answers to a board of political appointees, which makes tariff setting more vulnerable to political considerations than it is in Santiago. Buenos Aires, like Chile, uses a form of price cap. However, if real increases in a set of cost indices are more than 7 percent, Aguas Argentinas can ask for an extraordinary price increase. These indices are somewhat ambiguous and can be a source of conflict. The disputes around the 1997 renegotiation of the concession contract are evidence of the vulnerability of Buenos Aires' water institutions to pressures from both the company and political forces. In contrast, decisions of Santiago's regulator can be appealed to an arbitration board or the courts but are not subject to renegotiation with the regulator.

Some observers suggest that the poor design of Buenos Aires' concession agreement and the regulator's weak capacity may have led to regulatory capture, as evidenced by tariff increases since the concession was signed (Artana et al. 1997). The original bid of a 26-percent decrease in tariffs was predicated on information about the company that proved inaccurate and on a high "infrastructure" charge for new connections, a charge that proved to be uncollectable. In 1994, the company won a 13.5 percent tariff increase through renegotiation of the contract on the basis of new information and a request by the municipality to expand water service to a new community. In 1997, the high infrastructure charge for new users was dropped, and an increased tariff of about 18 percent was introduced. The charge, which covered approximately half of the capital costs of expanding the system, had fallen largely on poor residents on the outskirts of the city who had been connected to wells and increasingly refused to pay. Further increases in 1998 led to a dispute over the increase in the company's cost index. Aguas Argentina's request for an 11.7-percent increase was reduced by the regulation to 1.6 percent, then raised by the federal ministry supervising the sector to 4.6 percent.

Another weakness of the water tariff regulation is that the price of residential water, much of which is not metered, is based on services inside the house, the type of construction, and the location—times a consumption assumption. The unmetered tariff is intended to subsidize low-income consumers, but the actual effect is hard to measure, and income is not one of the variables used. Tariffs vary widely: one household could pay as much as seven times the tariff paid by a household with a property of similar size in 1996.

Although the concession arrangement has some weaknesses, it has achieved major improvements. Annual investment by Aguas Argentinas is five times that of the state-owned OSN, water coverage has expanded to more than 80 percent, pressure and continuity are up, customer service is improved, and total factor productivity of the company showed major improvements. One study estimated that the net present value of the future stream of benefits from the concession before the renegotiation was more than US$1.5 billion, of which about 80 percent went to consumers (Abdala 1997).[20]

In contrast, the failure to conclude the concession in Peru probably left it worse off. Although Peru introduced some reforms under public ownership, such as raising prices and offering voluntary retirement to workers, the government failed to introduce a more efficient regulatory regime, leaving in place ad hoc, cost-plus pricing. (A move to a price cap has been planned.) A new water regulator was created with financial autonomy (funded through a 2-percent tax on monthly tariff revenues) and reasonably high salaries, but its ability to regulate is compromised by the high level of political interference in SEDAPAL.

Foreign assistance allowed SEDAPAL to expand investments and improve maintenance. However, this increase barely kept up with the expansion of the city, and market coverage has stayed at about where it was before reform, 75 percent, although the number of connections has increased by about 100,000. Hours of service still averaged 15 per day, and some districts in Lima received no service for more than two months in 1997. Although maintenance improved, unaccounted-for water was still high, at 36 percent. Prices increased but still do not cover marginal costs, which were US$0.45 per cubic meter, according to a 1994 World Bank estimate, compared to an effective tariff of US$0.35 per cubic meter in 1996. Because metering and billing rates are still low, increased tariffs have provided little incentive for consumers to reduce waste. Frequent cuts in service were still the main curb on excess consumption.

An estimate of the welfare gains that would have resulted if Peru had gone ahead with the concession, using the same methodology that it used for Argentina and assuming a winning bid in accord with terms of the bidding documents, suggests that the gains to Peru would have been about US$1 billion (Alcázar and Xu 1999). This is optimistic, since the bidding documents assume that a private investor will sink US$100 million over the first five years with only a 40-percent real price increase. A winning bidder would probably have tried to renegotiate the contract in favor of higher compensation if the World Bank estimate of marginal costs had turned out to be accurate or low. This would have reduced the consumer surplus, but not necessarily social welfare if prices had moved closer to a level reflecting water's scarcity value, especially if consumption for drinking by lower-income consumers could be subsidized without causing costly distortions.

Finally, the introduction of service contracts in Mexico City did not change its confused and highly politicized regulatory regime. Prices are recommended by the regulator and then must be voted on by the municipal assembly. An important improvement introduced by the service contracts is the expansion of registered consumers and metering, plus better billing, in a situation of very costly, raw water supply. This has had a one-time effect on waste, by raising prices from zero, but any sustained conservation will depend on tariff increases. Tariffs still do not cover even 50 percent of the cost of pumping water up into the city (or pumping wastewater out), and any increase is highly political, since it must be voted on by the municipal assembly. As long as federal subsidies cover most of the cost of Mexico City's water consumption, there is little likelihood of change.

CONCLUSIONS

This tale of four cities suggests that water is different from other utilities. Large externalities motivate more government intervention than in other utility monopolies. A long history of water tariffs below cost, subsidies, and lax bill collection or enforcement of penalties for nonpayment increase the regulatory risk perceived by potential private investors. Information problems make contracts hard to design and monitor. The net political benefits from private participation in water may be perceived to be lower in many cases. The revenues raised from private participation are likely to be lower than in other utilities, and the main beneficiaries may have less political voice than the opponents.

An interesting question is whether countries should try to replicate Chile's often more politically palatable route of improving performance under public ownership. Several factors would make this difficult in most countries. First, Chile has long been building efficiency in all its public services, and the 1990 water reform was only the latest manifestation of these efforts. Countries that try to reform water drastically or in the presence of a largely inefficient and corrupt public bureaucracy would not, in fact, be emulating Chile's model. Second, Chile's regulatory framework was designed with an intent to sell water assets by a military dictatorship ideologically committed to private markets. Constitutional and political institutions designed by the same dictatorship have subsequently insulated the regulation from politically motivated changes. In countries that lack Chile's institutions, it may be hard to sustain efficient and independent regulation through major political changes without a private stakeholder to fight for government to keep its promises (Levy and Spiller 1996). Third, the means-tested subsidy also helped Chile win public acceptance of water price increases. Untargeted cross subsidies, such as those used in the other cities, benefit the rich as well as the poor, and often the rich benefit disproportionately. Indeed, many of the poor are often not connected (as was the case with the Ciudades Jóvenes in Lima) and must buy their water from vendors at much higher prices. Such subsidies can quickly become unaffordable. Replacing cross-subsidies with publicly funded support, as Chile has done, is welfare enhancing, however, only if the tax system is less regressive and less inefficient than cross-subsidies. Such subsidies can also become unaffordable if targeting is too broad, and there will be pressures to broaden the targets. Fourth, Chile's excellent educational system and cadre of highly trained economists enabled it to design and implement an efficient regulatory framework and to staff the regulator and water company with competent individuals. Salaries in the regulatory body are high enough to retain good staff, and the corporatization of the water company frees it from civil service rules and allows it to bargain collectively. Finally, Chile, despite its good performance, has decided to privatize EMOS as a way to insulate the company further from political interference.

The experience of the other three cities may be more relevant for many countries, and that experience favors the case for private participation. Despite weaknesses in the Buenos Aires concession contract and regulator, and despite subsequent tariff increases, the concession has brought substantial net economic benefits to consumers. In contrast, the failure to proceed with private participation in Lima and Mexico City had major costs, which were only partially reduced by reform of the state-owned enterprise.

This tale of four cities also suggests that reform, in the sense of moving the regulatory framework closer to the optimal, is much more difficult in cities with scarce water supply and/or major externalities. Ample and accessible water in Santiago and Buenos Aires kept costs down, which increased the feasibility of setting tariffs to cover marginal social costs and capital investments. Lima and Mexico City have inherently more costly systems, complicating reforms regardless of whether private participation is involved.

Notes

1. The author thanks Claude Menard (Université de Paris I), Santiago Urbiztondo (FIEL and UNLP), Manuel Abdala (Expectativa Economic Consultants), Lorena Alcázar (Universidad del Pacífico), Antonio Estache, Luke Haggarty, and Ana María Zuluaga (World Bank) for their many useful comments and suggestions, as well as the participants in the conference on regulation (May 21-22, 1998) in Buenos Aires, organized by Luigi Manzetti (Southern Methodist University). The assistance of Omer Karasapan and Warrick Smith (World Bank) and other staff working on the private participation in infrastructure database is gratefully acknowledged. The author is Research Manager, the World Bank. The views expressed are the author's own and do not necessarily reflect those of the World Bank, its Board of Directors, or the countries they represent.

2. Laffont and Tirole, 1993, point out that even if some shares are traded and the rest are owned by the government, private investors have little incentive to acquire information in the illiquid market created by high government stakes in the company.

3. A public good is nonexcludable and nonrival. For example, information is a public good, since it is very costly to prevent others from using it (nonexcludable) and its use by one individual does not subtract from its availability to another (nonrival). When a good is nonexcludable, it cannot be marketed for a price and when it is nonrival it should not be. Water, however, is both excludable and rival. Wastewater treatment has public good characteristics in that the benefits to one consumer do not reduce benefits to others (Merrit 1997).

4. A problem in early U.S. cities (Crocker and Masten 1998).

5. I am grateful to Paul Joskow for suggesting this reasoning to me.

6. Information in this section is taken from Abdala (1997) and Alcázar and Abdala (1999) for Buenos Aires; Alcázar and Xu (1999) for Lima; Haggarty, Brook-Cowen, and Zuluaga (1999) for Mexico City; and Shirley, Xu and Zuluaga (1999) for Santiago.

7. Mexico is the exception, and even there the central government dominated decisions in Mexico City during much of the period in question.

8. The extraction rate from the aquifer is currently 42 cubic meters per second, while the replenishing rate is only around 24 cubic meters per second.

9. One commentator on this work has suggested that Buenos Aires' water prices were not higher in relative terms, given the per-capita GDP of Buenos Aires. However, the salient comparison is in water prices for low-income groups, whose relative purchasing power was not much higher in Buenos Aires than in the other cities. Moreover, it is the change in prices that matters in political debate. This is illustrated by the strong consumer protests against recent price increases, despite the fact that the average price of water in Buenos Aires is still one of the lowest in our sample, even taking into account connection charges.

10. The price bids might also have been low because of buyers' curse or because the companies expected to be able to renegotiate later.

11. Information problems could lead to overbidding or underbidding, and either the regulator or company could initiate renegotiation. While in Buenos Aires the company negotiated for change, in the UK the regulator has been negotiating down price increases below the original K factors (Armstrong, Cowan, and Vickers 1994).

12. Between March 1988 and January 1990, five laws were passed to incorporate the water companies, set up a new tariff system, institute concessions for water and sewerage, and create a water regulator.

13. The other utilities were not as well run — telecommunications suffered from large unmet demand, and electricity suffered from theft — which may partly explain their higher priority. They would also command a higher sales price.

14. Although survey evidence suggests that willingness to pay for water was high in Lima's poor communities, a bigger problem would have been affordability of connection costs unless some form of financing could be found.

15. In 1992, 63 percent of the public surveyed were in favor of private participation in water; by 1997, 78 percent were opposed.

16. The cost of new meters is paid by the federal government.

17. These tariffs, unlike those in Table 3, are not adjusted for collection rates.

18. The actual accounts of each water company are adjusted by the regulator to international or Chilean best practice for some parameters (such as unaccounted-for water or the cost of capital).

19. After the epidemic broke out in Peru, Chile prohibited the use of untreated wastewater for low-growing food crops. It continues to be used for fruit and other high-growing food crops.

20. The methodology (Galal et al. 1994) estimates a counterfactual of continued public ownership and then calculates the difference between that and the concession, in consumer surplus, workers' welfare, and increased returns to government and buyers. The sum is the net benefit, here presented as the net present value of future flows.

References

Abdala, Manuel. 1997. "Welfare Effects of Buenos Aires' Water and Sewerage Services Privatization." XXXII Reunión Anual de la Asociación Argentina de Economía Política. Bahía Blanca. (November).

Alcázar, Lorena, and Manuel Abdala. 1999. "Institutions, Politics and Contracts: Private Sector Participation in Urban Water Supply Systems: The Case of Aguas Argentinas' Concession." Draft.

Alcázar, Lorena, and Penelope Brook-Cowen. 1996. "Research Proposal: Institutions, Politics, and Contracts: Private Sector Participation in Urban Water Supply." Unpublished manuscript.

Alcázar, Lorena, Colin Xu, and Ana María Zuluaga. 1999. "Reforming Urban Water Supply: The Case of Peru." Draft manuscript.

Armstrong, Mark, Simon Cowan, and John Vickers. 1994. Regulatory Reform: Economic Analysis and British Experience. Cambridge, Mass.: MIT Press.

Artana, Daniel, Fernando Navajas, and Santiago Urbiztondo. 1997. La Regulación Económica en las Concesiones de Agua Potable y Desagües Cloacales en Buenos Aires y Corrientes, Argentina. Inter-American Development Bank Working Paper R-312.

Baldez, Lisa, and John Carey. 1997. "Budget Procedure and Fiscal Restraint in Post-Transition Chile." In "Political Institutions and the Determinants of Public Policy: When Do Institutions Matter?" eds. Stephan Haggard and Mathew D. McCubbins. Unpublished manuscript.

Clarke, George, and Simon Cowan. 1998. "Competition and Privatization in Urban Water Supply." Research Proposal. Unpublished manuscript.

Cowan, Simon. 1994. "Competition in the Water Industry." Oxford Review of Economic Policy 13: 83-92.

Crampes, Claude, and Antonio Estache. 1997. "Regulatory Trade-offs in the Design of Concession Contracts." Draft manuscript.

Crocker, Keith, and Scott Masten. 1998. "Prospects for Private Water Provision in Developing Countries: Lessons from 19th Century America." Draft manuscript.

Demsetz, Harold. 1968. "Why Regulate Utilities?" Journal of Law and Economics 11: 55-66.

Frischtak, Claudio R. 1997. "Enhancing Local Private Sector Participation in the Water Supply and Wastewater Sector: Reflections from the Latin American Experience." Draft manuscript.

Galal, Ahmed, Leroy Jones, Pankaj Tandon, and Ingo Vogelsang. 1994. Welfare Consequences of Selling Public Enterprises: An Empirical Analysis. New York: Oxford University Press.

Goldberg, Victor P. 1976. "Regulation and Administered Contracts." Bell Journal of Economics 7: 426-448.

Haggarty, Luke, Penelope Brook-Cowen, and Ana María Zuluaga. 1999. "Institutions, Politics and Contracts: Private Sector Participation in Urban Water Supply Systems. The Case of Mexico City Water Sector Service Contracts." Draft manuscript.

Kornai, János. 1992. *The Socialist System: The Political Economy of Communism.* Princeton, N.J.: Princeton University Press.

Laffont, Jean-Jacques. 1998. "Competition, Information and Development." Paper presented at Annual World Bank Conference on Development Economics. Washington, D.C.

Laffont, Jean-Jacques, and Jean Tirole. 1993. *A Theory of Incentives in Procurement and Regulation.* Cambridge, Mass.: MIT Press.

Levy, Brian, and Pablo Spiller, eds. 1996. *Regulations, Institutions and Commitment: Comparative Studies of Telecommunications.* New York: Cambridge University Press.

McCubbins, Matthew D., Roger Noll, and Barry R. Weingast. 1987. "Administrative Procedures as Instruments of Political Control." *Journal of Law, Economics, and Organization* 3(2): 243-277.

Niskanen, William. 1971. *Bureaucracy and Representative Government.* Chicago: Aldine-Atherton.

Olson, Mancur. 1965. *The Logic of Collective Action: Public Goods and the Theory of Groups.* Cambridge, Mass.: Harvard University Press.

Schmidt, Klaus. 1996. "The Costs and Benefits of Privatization: An Incomplete Contracts Approach." *Journal of Law, Economics, and Organization* 12(1), (April): 1-24.

Shapiro, Carl, and Robert Willig. 1990. "Economic Rationales for the Scope of Privatization." In *The Political Economy of Public Sector Reform and Privatization*, eds. E.N. Suleiman and J. Waterbury. Boulder, Colo.: Westview Press.

Shleifer, Andrei, and Robert W. Vishny. 1994. "Politicians and Firms." *Quarterly Journal of Economics* 109: 995-1024.

Shirley, Mary, Colin Xu, and Ana María Zuluaga. 1999. "Institutions, Politics and Contracts: Private Sector Participation in Urban Water Supply Systems. The Case of Chile." Draft manuscript.

Vickers, John, and George Yarrow. 1991. "Economic Perspectives on Privatization." *Journal of Economic Perspectives* 5(2): 111-132.

Williamson, Oliver. 1976. "Franchise Bidding for Natural Monopolies in General and with Respect to CATV." *Bell Journal of Economics* 7(1): 73-104.

World Bank. 1994a. "Peru: Lima Rehabilitation and Management Project Staff Appraisal Report." Unpublished manuscript.

World Bank. 1994b. *World Development Report: Infrastructure for Development.* New York: Oxford University Press.

World Bank. 1995. *Bureaucrats in Business: The Economics and Politics of Government Ownership.* New York: Oxford University Press.

CHAPTER 7

Reforming the Electricity Sectors in the Southern Cone: The Chilean and Argentine Experiments

ANTONIO ESTACHE AND MARTÍN RODRÍGUEZ-PARDINA

EXECUTIVE SUMMARY

Throughout Latin America, the electricity industry is undergoing a profound change, which began in the early 1990s. The combination of deregulation, aimed at bringing about competition and improving performance, and the search for private capital, to finance significant system expansion requirements, has been unprecedented. Virtually all countries in the region now acknowledge deregulation and private financing as necessary and often desirable changes. The specific regulatory structures adopted or being considered to create competition and attract private investment differ from country to country. Undoubtedly the leading lights in the implementation of such changes have been Chile and Argentina. This chapter describes the transformation of the electricity sector in the two countries and the main lessons that can be learned by other countries considering deregulation and privatization reforms. It also charts the uneasy transition of government from owner of an integrated public utility to regulator of an essentially private industry. Such a role is essential if the gains from private sector involvement and competition in segments of this industry are to be passed through to investors and consumers rather than be captured solely by the new owners.

INTRODUCTION

A dramatic change in the structure of the electricity industry has occurred since the beginning of the 1990s in Latin America. The increasing inability of governments to fund and manage this capital-intensive sector in the face of growing demand has forced them to seek private investment. With new capital inflows has come the inevitable pressure to restructure this sector to make it more transparent and foster greater competition. From the larger countries, such as Brazil, Colombia, and Peru, to the smaller, such as Uruguay, Panama, and Bolivia, the introduction of a competitive bulk pricing system has either become or is about to become reality.

Until a decade ago, the traditional view in any of the energy ministries was that generation, transmission, and distribution of electricity were best kept within a vertically integrated monopoly. The argument was that economies of scale existed among power generation, transmission, and distribution systems and that there was, thus, a need to coordinate the various components of the system. Moreover, in the context of vertical integration, the prevailing view was that financing requirements of this industry were such that the cheapest possible source of capital was the public sector.

First among the principal drivers for the changes that occurred wholesale in the United Kingdom, Chile, and Argentina was a lack of money or a lack of willingness to fund huge capital investments from the public purse. The emergence of liberal economic policies in these countries was, in effect, a bet on the private sector's better overall management track record. Also, efficiency improvements resulting from changes in the availability of gas coupled with developments in combined-cycle gas turbine (CCGT) technology precipitated a move toward renewal of the electricity generation asset base. A shorter construction cycle for power plants, greater design standardization, and advances in computers and data processing allowed reductions in transaction costs, and the standardization and data processing advances allowed significant improvements in metering. All these factors reinforced the view that generation and supply of electricity were competitive activities and should be owned by the private sector. In the face of this, institutional reforms that would allow for privatization of the electricity industry became inevitable.

The rationale for reform of the electricity industry is broadly similar throughout the Southern Cone (Chile and Argentina). The differences lie in the institutional reforms that have been and are now being adopted to foster competition and to attract private capital to finance infrastructure investments. Among these are differences in the powers of the regulator and the extent to which competition is opened to new entrants rather than just to the incumbents.

One theme that emerges from this review is the government's difficulty in embracing its newly self-imposed role as overseer of the sector through independent regulators, rather than as owner of the assets. Yet, developing this role is essential if the gains from private sector involvement and competition in certain segments of the electricity market are to be shared by consumers with those who have invested in and are to invest in assets underlying the sector — rather than be captured solely by owners of the companies created with privatization.

CHILE[1]

Chile was not only the first country in the region but also one of the first in the developing world to embrace privatization. However, the symptoms in Chile were similar to those in most countries, developing and developed alike: price controls, rationing of service, overstaffing, and loss-making public electric utilities. In reaction to difficulties in earlier privatizations, the stated goal of the government in electricity privatization was to increase the number of individual Chilean shareholders, rather than to maximize revenues or simply to introduce market forces.

The overall privatization strategy was simple enough. First, utilities had to be transformed into public companies with tradeable shares and made subject to standard commercial auditing procedures. Then the privatization could begin. This occurred in 1986, and within four years only two generation companies remained public; both of them have since been privatized. Privatization was carried out using three different sale mechanisms:

1. Smaller companies were sold by public auction and awarded to the bidder with the highest price,

2. Larger companies' stock was floated on the stock market, and

3. The largest companies were sold in small blocks of shares (popular capitalism).[2]

In Chile's National Electricity Company (Empresa Nacional de Electricidad — Endesa), for instance, the private shareholding increased from 30 percent in 1986 to 72 percent three years later. Institutional investors would eventually account for about 25 percent of the total shares of privatized utilities, providing a stable, long-term commitment to financing the sector. Also, workers within the privatized utilities were granted between 5 percent and 10 percent of the shares of the utilities to ensure their political support. A small number of former civil servants were also able to acquire significant stakes.

The industry restructuring was undertaken in two stages. The first, between 1974 and 1979, saw an adjustment in prices to allow the public utilities to be self-financing and to prepare for the future private shareholders. The second stage, between 1979 and 1990, saw the separation of generation and transmission from distribution as well as other institutional reforms, including the introduction of a new regulatory framework in 1982.

The two existing utilities, Endesa and Chilectra, were decentralized and regionalized. Endesa, the larger of the two, was divided into 14 companies, while Chilectra was divided into three companies.

Endesa:　Six generation companies with capacities varying from 35MW to 1,832MW;

Six distribution companies with between 5,000 and 143,000 customers each; and

Two vertically integrated companies (Edelaysen with 15,000 customers and Edelmag with 35,000 customers).

Chilectra:　One generating company (Chilgener with a capacity of 756MW) and

Two distribution companies (Chilectra with 1,064,000 customers and Chilquinta with 322,000 customers).

The restructuring did not fully exploit all the possibilities offered by deregulation. The most significant failure was the fact that Endesa's transmission system, the largest in Chile, was not segregated from generation and transmission at the time of privatization. The main reason was that the decision was taken to proceed with the privatization before full definitions of the pricing rules were agreed upon. This decision continues to haunt Chile's regulators.

In 1982, a law was passed to maximize social welfare by establishing conditions within which the energy system could develop and operate efficiently. The law explicitly distinguished among generation, transmission, and distribution, spelling out the main rules for regulation in each of these sectors. The law provided for license allocation, pricing, investment, quality, and safety. In addition, it clarified the rights and obligations of all players — service providers and government institutions alike. It included explicit mechanisms for settling disputes arising between the regulators and the utilities, with the judiciary as final arbiter.

Competition was introduced only in generation and in supply to large users; these were users with demand in excess of 2 MW, even though this is probably a high threshold to achieve effective competition in supply. No constraints were imposed on vertical or horizontal integration. Clearly, the access rules for generation, transmission, and distribution differ. Further, entry is free for thermal generation; entry is not free for hydro and geothermal generation, so that a concession is advisable.[3] Further, while some firms can operate without a license, most will want to have one because a license provides some exclusive rights. To obtain such a license, a bidder is required to bid competitively to the National Energy Commission (Comisión Nacional de Energía — NEC), which then ranks the bids according to cost. Each year, the NEC assesses the minimum cost expansion plan for the system and clears the conditions for entry. While entry is free for transmission, distribution requires concessions for systems in excess of 1,500 kW. These licenses are granted for an indefinite period but can be withdrawn when service quality falls below the legally imposed standard. It is possible for the service areas of two or more operators to overlap to promote competition in the sector.

The pricing system comprises regulated charges for small customers and freely negotiated rates for large users. The regulated rates must be within a 10-percent band of the average price of freely negotiated contracts. These contracts represent approximately 40 percent of the total consumption. The regulated price[4] to final customers comprises two components:

Regulated Price = node price + distribution charge.

Node price = marginal costs of energy + marginal cost of peak power + marginal cost of transmission.

The distribution charge is recalculated every four years by determining the operating costs of a hypothetical efficient firm and setting rates to provide a 10-percent real return on the replacement value of the assets. These rates are then applied to existing companies to ensure that the industry average return on the replacement value of assets does not exceed 14 percent or fall below 6 percent. If the actual average industry return falls outside this range, the rates are adjusted. The operating costs of an efficient firm and the replacement value of assets are obtained as a weighted average of estimates from the NEC and from external consultants.

The role of regulator is undertaken by three key government institutions created prior to the privatization. The NEC was established in 1978 to develop medium-term and long-term guidelines for the electricity sector independently of the potential influence of the large utilities in the sector. It is managed by a board of directors composed of seven ministers, and it has an executive secretariat, technical staff, and resources to recruit special advisors as needed. The NEC proposes policies that are implemented as laws, decrees, or ministerial resolutions. It sets tariffs and grants licenses to public service distributors for specific regions.

The electricity law also led to the creation of an Economic Load Dispatch Center (ELDC) to coordinate the activities of all generating companies. The ELDC is a generators' pool, with specific objectives to achieve the minimum total operating costs for the system as a whole and to ensure equitable market access to all generating companies. Each ELDC member is entitled to make direct supply contracts with clients for amounts up to its available firm capacity. Any shortfall must be purchased from other members at the marginal cost of peak power (equal to the annual cost of increasing installed capacity during peak demand periods by one kilowatt[5]). The ELDC plans daily production and computes the instantaneous marginal energy cost by considering the variable costs of generating units currently operating, without considering the effects of any direct supply contracts. The programming of electricity generation (disregarding supply contracts) gives rise to energy transfers between generators, and these are priced at the system's instantaneous marginal energy cost.

The third key government actor within the sector is the Superintendency of Electricity and Fuels, created in 1985 as an administrative branch of the Economics Ministry. It supervises compliance with laws and regulations, and it monitors service quality. It also deals with users' and suppliers' complaints as well as prepares the information for the price-setting process carried out by NEC.

None of these three institutional entities is truly independent. The only independent entities in the entire Chilean regulatory system are the antitrust commissions. Although these regional Comisiones Preventivas and Comisión Resolutiva that review potential conflicts appear to be independent, they have been criticized for a relative lack of detailed technical expertise.

Overall, performance has improved greatly with deregulation and privatization.[6] Coverage rates have reached 97 percent, and more than 70 percent of the required investment has been carried out by private companies. Consumption grew by an average of 8 percent per year between 1986 and 1997.[7] Energy losses — less than 8 percent lost from generation through distribution — are about one-third of their historical level. Labor productivity has doubled, from less than 300 clients per employee at the end of the 1980s to almost 600 per employee by 1997. Similarly, the GWh of output per worker (labor productivity is measured as GWh per employee) grew from less than five to almost eight.

ARGENTINA

Argentina followed the Chilean experiment, also drawing even more heavily from the United Kingdom's privatization experience. Unlike Chile, however, Argentina separated generation, transmission, distribution, and supply — and placed legal restrictions on the activities to prevent reintegration. One of the most innovative aspects of Argentina's reforms was the introduction of a rigorous set of regulatory procedures, which offered one of the most important lessons of the Argentine experiment (Bitrán, Estache, Guasch, and Serra 1999). It appears increasingly clear that establishing a regulatory framework before privatization improves the outcome of the restructuring process. A comparison of Argentina's experience in various sectors seems to confirm that the privatization of gas and electricity, where laws established the regulatory framework prior to restructuring and privatization, produced better results and less controversy than the privatization of telecommunications and transportation, where this did not occur.

The main purposes of the reform of Argentina's electricity sector were to reach efficient pricing and production levels in the short term and to generate investment sufficient to meet long-run demands. This began in 1989 and is still going on in the provinces. The laws enabling the restructuring to take place were passed in 1989, and the process began when the federal government franchised the distribution and supply activities of SEGBA, a vertically integrated utility supplying electricity to 13 million people in greater Buenos Aires. The next step occurred in 1992, when generation and transmission activities owned by SEGBA were privatized. The result of these two changes was that the original public firm was separated into seven business units: four generation and three distribution companies. These units were then sold, either outright or in the form of a concession, to the private sector through international bids (Bitrán, Estache, Guasch, and Serra 1999).

Law 24.065, passed by the Argentine Congress in 1992, provided the regulatory framework by which the electricity sector operates, including the creation of a regulator. The general objectives contained in this law, objectives now to be found in many electricity laws throughout Latin America, not only provide a design for the regulatory framework but also lay out the decision-making process for the regulator. Some objectives of Law 24065 are as follow:

- To protect users' rights;
- To promote competitiveness in both electricity generation and supply markets and to encourage investment sufficient to ensure long-term supply;
- To promote development, reliability, equality, and free access of all transmission and distribution facilities;
- To regulate electricity transmission and distribution, ensuring fair and reasonable tariffs;
- To promote efficient supply, transmission, distribution, and use of electricity by establishing the appropriate pricing systems;
- To promote private investment in generation, transmission, and distribution to ensure market competitiveness.

In making specific provisions to establish an independent regulator, the National Electricity Regulator (Ente Nacional Regulador de la Electricidad — ENRE), Law 24.065 represents a fundamental difference in Argentina's philosophy from Chile's. Further, the appointment of ENRE's senior staff is based on a public job offering, with interviews conducted by an independent adviser (Bitrán, Estache, Guasch, and Serra 1999).

It is important to note that the functions and obligations of ENRE as set out in Table 1 are vested in the regulator by the law and not by executive power. This is a necessary condition, although not a sufficient one, for ensuring the independence and accountability of the regulator. This independence is further guaranteed by the agency's method of self-financing, in which all participants pay inspection and control fees based on their size in the wholesale market. ENRE establishes and publishes its budget annually, and the budget then must be approved by Parliament as part of the national budget.

Table 1.
Functions and Obligations of ENRE

Enforce the regulatory framework, contracts, and public service obligations.

Issue rules and regulations on matters of safety, technical procedures and norms, measurement, billing, control and use of meters, interruption and reconnection of service, access, and service quality.

Prevent anticompetitive, monopolistic, and discriminatory behavior.

Define the basis for the calculation of tariffs set in contracts.

Control tariff enforcement.

Publish the general principles to be respected by distributors and transporters to ensure free access to their services.

Determine the basis and criteria for the assignment of concessions.

Organize and implement the bidding, adjudication, and signature of contracts.

Organize public hearings.

Monitor the respect of property rights, environments, and public safety.

Take the relevant issues to court.

Regulate the proceedings to impose sanctions.

Impose fines.

Publish information and advise all actors in the system.

Issue an annual report and recommend actions when needed.

Ensure that the law is followed.

Collect information from transporters.

The major changes in the unbundling of the electricity sector are summarized in Table 2. Generation and supply were transformed into competitive sectors, while distribution and transmission are regional monopolies. There is no partial integration in Argentina like that permitted in Chile.

Some form of competition was introduced in each of the three functional segments of the electricity market. The competition introduced in generation represents possibly the most important aspect of the overall reform. The 25 operators that have emerged sell electricity into a spot market that matches electricity demand and supply with an hourly and seasonally adjusted price and terms, or through contracts that can vary in quantity and price for longer-term generation. The coordination of the demand and supply is undertaken by Cammesa, a nonprofit organization owned jointly by the government and associations of generators, distributors, transmission companies, and large-scale users, which is responsible for dispatching and for implementing the operating rules issued by the

Table 2.
Sectoral Reforms in Argentina

Generation	Transmission	Distribution
Separated from distribution and transmission.	Separated from distribution and generation.	Separated from generation and transmission.
Considered a service that can operate commercially and restructured to create a competitive market.	Considered a public service, so that a concession was granted for its operation.	Considered a public service, so that a concession was granted for its operation.
25 business units created through separate sales.	Regulation based on the need to ensure open access under a toll regime.	Regulated through the setting of tariffs based on economic costs and a system of fines to protect users.

Energy Secretary. Cammesa's main role is to control exchanges in the bulk market and control operations through the transmission network. It also performs settlements for all participants in the wholesale market. It prioritizes power dispatches based on the lowest cost of generation and transmission in satisfying demand (Bitrán, Estache, Guasch, and Serra 1999).

Large consumers can contract directly with generators to increase competition between distributors and large users further. Although large users are able thus to bypass the distribution company commercially, they cannot do so physically. This requires strict rules governing access to the distributors' infrastructure and fees paid to the distributor for the access service. Gaps in these rules can affect the value of distribution companies in the eyes of potential private investors significantly.

For distribution and for transmission, auctioning of concessions allows competitive allocation. However, these activities are natural monopolies, and conditions for post-auction competition are not easily established. For this reason, the 95-year concession is divided into shorter management periods, the first one for 15 years, and then eight for 10 years each. Six months before the end of each period, the regulator organizes the sale of the concessionaire's controlling block, with the tariff regime to be applied over the following five years. A concessionaire is clearly able to participate in the bids; if unsuccessful in the re-bid, the concessionaire loses the concession, and the government reimburses the departing concessionaire from the proceeds of the sale, net of debt.

The market, as explained above, establishes the price of generation. Computed at the load center, the price equates demand and supply, guaranteeing that the price of the last kWh purchased is equal to the cost of supplying it. The energy from generating plants is dispatched by merit order, in increasing order of short-run marginal production cost, the cost of generating an additional kWh, and transporting it to the load centers. The most expensive generator used to meet demand sets the clearing price. Any generator with a lower cost makes a profit. This is what drives the incentive to cut costs. Generators are also paid for their capacity to ensure that they have the right incentive to invest to meet long-term needs and to decrease the probability of failure in the whole system. Since short-run and long-run marginal costs differ, an extra incentive is needed.

Pricing of distribution and transmission, both natural monopolies, is regulated. Tariffs are set in U.S. dollars, and the regulation is a version of the standard price capping formula. In other words, the regulation sets maximum prices with a total pass-through of the costs of energy and indexation to the U.S. price index. In practice, transmission charges cover three components: a connection charge, a fixed charge differentiated according to voltage; a capacity charge also fixed to cover all operation and maintenance of the existing equipment; and an energy charge, a transmission loss charge reflecting the difference between the value of the energy received at a receiving node and the value of energy at a sending node. The first two components are fixed for the first five years only and can be reduced yearly, by no more than 1 percent and with a cumulative maximum of 5 percent over each management period. For distribution, the main elements are an energy charge based on seasonal electricity costs, a loss charge corresponding to losses and equivalent to about 11 percent of the distributor's purchases, connection and transmission costs, the cost of capacity in the wholesale market, and a fixed distribution charge differentiated for small and large users.

The explicit definition of penalties is one key ingredient of the success of this reform that ensures that companies do not trade off quality in providing service at given prices. Penalties are clearly spelled out in the concession contracts; revenue from the penalties (limited to 10 percent of the companies' annual income) is rediscounted to the users.

Argentina's reform is not fully complete, with many provincial distribution companies still for sale. However, even at this early stage, there is evidence of improvement. Labor productivity, measured as GWh per employee, has increased by more than 23 percent; efficiency gains measured through cuts in input requirements have increased about 20 percent; and service quality has improved significantly. However, the most noticeable achievement in Argentina has been the drop in energy prices.

With respect to prices, such results are more clear cut in cases where the private sector is responsible for distribution (nine provinces and Buenos Aires). A sharp reduction in prices, which in most cases flows directly to final consumers except when contracts are transferred, is the most obvious outcome of the reforms. For a typical residential consumer, wholesale prices represent 50 percent of the total electricity bill. In the case of the privatization of the federal distribution companies (Edenor, Edesur, and Edelap), 50 percent of their load was bought through an eight-year, fixed-price contract signed prior to privatization. The impact in the reduction of wholesale prices was approximately 25 percent. This means that a drop of 56 percent in wholesale prices, from an average of US$32 per MWh in 1993 to US$20 per MWh in 1996, implies a reduction of around 16 percent in residential tariffs. For a large industrial user, for whom wholesale prices account for up to 95 percent of electricity bills, the impact has been in the region of 25 percent.

Table 3.
Spot Prices (US$ per MWh)

	Average	Maximum	Minimum
1992	41.85	80.59	20.47
1993	32.11	58.75	20.51
1994	24.99	78.15	18.41
1995	22.06	80.13	14.58
1996	20.57	68.83	12.85
1997	17.01	70.00	12.54

Table 3 suggests that the drop in average prices is in great part explained by the drop in the minimum price. This reflects entry and availability improvements achieved by the system's new rules. Maximum observed prices are still high because in most cases they represent transmission constraints, which result in dispatch out of merit priority.

An additional trend worth noting is in prices paid for the concessions. In Buenos Aires (with service by companies shown in bold in Table 4), there is an observable trend of improved sale prices for the electricity distribution companies over time. The results are less transparent for the provincial distribution companies, since the levels and types of risks faced by investors are much more diverse than those in greater Buenos Aires. The price trend over time in greater Buenos Aires suggests that as the regulatory framework is better established, investors are more willing to reduce the risk premium, and, as a result, concessions command higher prices.

Table 4. Privatization of Distribution Companies

Distribution Company	Privatization Date	$/client	$/kWh
Edenor	**Sept 92**	**520.5**	**115.2**
Edesur	**Sept 92**	**633.3**	**142.4**
Edelap	**Dec 92**	**1,362.7**	**261.1**
San Luis	Mar 93	238.6	37.8
S. del Estero	Jan 95	165.5	75.1
Formosa	Feb 95	141.5	62.5
La Rioja	June 95	290.9	83.9
Tucumán	June 95	416.6	111.8
Catamarca	Jan 96	220.1	84.7
San Juan	Jan 96	551.0	150.7
Entre Rios	May 96	856.8	309.5
Salta	July 96	N/A	N/A
Rio Negro	Aug 96	N/A	N/A
Jujuy	Nov 96	N/A	N/A
ESEBA	**Jul 97**	**1484.4**	**282.8**

Note: Boldface indicates companies in Buenos Aires.

POST-PRIVATIZATION REGULATORY ISSUES

Although deregulation is entrenched in both Argentina and Chile, there remain areas in which its effectiveness is still questionable, in which some fine-tuning must be undertaken for the market, especially for end users to benefit fully from the regulator's oversight.

Chile

While the Chilean consumer has generally benefited from increased coverage and improvements in service quality as a result of privatization, the efficiency gains have not necessarily been translated into lower end-user charges, even after two rate reviews. Price reductions have occurred only in cases where competition has emerged. Electricity distribution prices have not come down to match the significant reduction in distribution losses since privatization. The price of electricity for residential customers has risen from US$0.0805 per kWh to US$0.1183 per kWh between 1988 and 1997. The main beneficiaries of deregulation have been the regulated electricity companies. This presents a paradox: regulated natural monopolies report higher rates of return on equity (ROE) than the competitive unregulated sectors do. In fact, the average ROE among regulated distribution companies was 30 percent in 1995, whereas for mostly unregulated generating companies the figure was 15 percent.

The regulatory framework is such that there is competition in generation and supply to large users. Nevertheless, Endesa has a dominant position; together with its affiliates it owns the transmission grid, which it manages through a subsidiary, as well as 60 percent of Chile's installed capacity (Bitrán, Estache, Guasch, and Serra 1999). Endesa also has indirect ownership of 40 percent of the distribution sector through Enersis, an investment company that recently took control of Endesa. The concentration problem is even more widespread. The second-largest and third-largest generating companies, Chilgener and Colbún, own 22 and 11 percent of installed capacity, respectively, giving a Herfindahl Index of concentration for the three largest generators of 0.43.

This current industry structure, compounded by the ambiguous regulatory framework, increases the risk of new entrants in generation. For instance, the law is not sufficiently explicit in determining how transmission grid development costs are allocated between generating companies. Criticisms of Chile's transmission pricing policies are widespread and present a major threat to competition. Charges are negotiated between the owner of the grid and generators; if agreement is not reached, then a compulsory arbitration process is triggered. Without a Chinese Wall between the grid and generation, Endesa can favor its own generation business. An illustration of this problem is the recent failure to privatize Colbún. Despite the government's efforts to sell the company, retaining Dresdner Kleinwort Benson as adviser, only one potential bidder on the short list of six presented an offer. Unofficially, the other bidders complained about the ownership structure within the sector.

More important, Endesa also owns the water rights for the most attractive potential hydroelectric generating projects. By postponing the development of these projects, it can increase the profits on its existing capacity. In fact, of the total nonconsuming water rights that have already been appropriated, only 13 percent are being used (Bitrán, Estache, Guasch, and Serra 1999). Endesa holds 60 percent of allocated nonconsuming water rights. Most of these rights belonged to Endesa prior to its privatization, when it was the only major hydroelectric generator, and it is safe to assume that Endesa's 60 percent represents the most profitable investment opportunities. Moreover, Endesa also applied for additional nonconsuming water rights that would have given it 80 percent of all water rights. A commission in charge of the rights denied the application.

The import of natural gas from Argentina, which began recently, has already lowered entry barriers in generation. Although gas transportation has natural monopoly characteristics, competition between two consortia willing to build a pipeline from Argentina and anti-price-discrimination regulation have brought transport prices down to a competitive level (Bitrán, Estache, Guasch, and Serra 1999). In fact, to obtain financing, the consortia required contracts with large customers, and this led to open competition for these customers. Combined-cycle, gas-fired power plants likely to be built close to demand centers, in conjunction with Colbún's decision to build a transmission line between its generating units and the main demand node, will diminish the impact of the transmission monopoly. Nevertheless, existing hydroelectric power plants are likely to remain the lowest priced generation option.

Some problems have arisen in supplying unregulated customers located in the franchise areas of distribution companies, which represented 23 percent of all sales to unregulated customers in 1995. If a generator wishes to sell to an unregulated customer, it must negotiate a tolling contract with a distributor. The lack of tariff uniformity in transmission and distribution gives rise to difficulties for generators bidding to supply potential customers. To make matters worse, distributors are also the main customers of generators. The lack of competition in supplying unregulated customers is also relevant for regulated customers, as the regulated node price has to be adjusted within a 10-percent band of the average unregulated price.

Finally, there are also significant problems in establishing electricity distribution costs. A benchmark is established for an efficient company, based on the weighted average distribution cost, determined in studies carried out by the NEC and by reported distribution costs. This provides companies with an incentive to provide high estimates. In 1992, the discrepancies in estimating such distribution costs varied by as much as 50 percent. An alternative solution could be to appoint an arbitrator and assess which study best reflects the costs of an efficient company.

The Antitrust Commission has ruled in favor of maintaining Enersis's vertically integrated structure. Nevertheless, the Commission acknowledged certain market imperfections. First, it recommended that amendments be made to make the mechanisms for determining transmission and distribution charges more explicit. Second, it instructed distributors to tender their energy requirements to generating companies. This avoids suspicions that distribution companies would be favoring related generators and reduces costs to end consumers. Finally, the Antitrust Commission recommended the creation of a separate joint-stock transmission subsidiary within Endesa, to be called Transelec, within a "prudent" period of time, thereby allowing part or all of the company to be sold off in the future.

Argentina

The major issues emerging from an analysis of the Argentine model suggest ways to ensure that the gains achieved in a relatively short period are sustainable. Argentina's experience emphasizes the importance of creating an overarching regulatory framework for determining tariffs. This becomes useful, for example, when inconsistencies arise in the interpretation of a concession contract, either due to inherent defects, as is the case for transmission, or due to subsequent changes in the market.

Consider the importance of adopting price caps and revenue caps in the sector. It avoids the perverse signals associated with setting tariffs equal to marginal costs of the network, since the income is fixed, and at the same time signals information regarding the location of consumers. However, for these signals to be effective, revenues and prices must be reassessed regularly. The transport concession contract illustrates this problem. Energy revenues are recalculated every five years, based on an estimate of the average losses forecast for the subsequent five-year period. The income of the transporter in the second five-year period is based on the expected average losses and expected value of energy. Since both variables are out of the transporters' control and are independent of the transport costs, this recalculation violates two efficiency conditions. First, tariffs do not reflect the costs of providing the service, and, second, the fluctuation of energy prices may result in revenues insufficient to enable a transporter to recover his invested capital.

The next lesson that can be drawn from this experience relates to the standardization of contracts. Distribution contracts in Argentina were standardized for reasons of simplicity and efficiency. Nevertheless, standardization has not been problem free. More specifically, adopting a uniform concession contract and tariff regime for the federal companies (Edenor, Edesur, and Edelap) appears to have been sensible, because these companies were the result of the splitting of a single entity in a relatively uniform market. When this approach was implemented in some of the predominantly agricultural provinces, problems emerged with the tariff structure. The two-part tariff structure used in Buenos Aires, which allows a large user to pay for capacity based on the annual maximum demand, does not work when demand is seasonal and is mainly for irrigation. Agricultural users had to pay a large capacity charge throughout the year to use pumping equipment for very short periods of time, and the availability of water is severely restricted in the agricultural region of the country. This caused social turmoil when rural producers could not afford the tariffs.

Although the two-part tariff system makes sense, based exclusively on economic efficiency, other considerations must be taken into account particularly during a transition period. The fact that the irrigation systems in these provinces were developed under a different regulatory regime, with no capacity payments, should have been taken into account in designing the concession contract.

The final issue stems from the linkages between tariffs, property rights, and investment needs in transmission. The owner of a concession is not responsible for decisions about building and financing new lines. This is based on the notion that as a natural monopoly the concessionaire would have a dominant position with respect to all other players upstream and downstream. In addition, the concessionaire earns a fixed remuneration such that no distortion is created in the spot prices of electricity or in contract prices. Expansion rules for transmission are based on decentralized decisions taken by beneficiaries of the expansion. Such beneficiaries are identified based on use of the expansion rather than on the profits derived from its use. The outcome is that under the current system, investments in transmission are very difficult to approve. Of the three major investments proposed to date, one was undertaken directly by the state, bypassing the process described above. The others were vetoed in a public hearing by a number of potential "beneficiaries" and only approved two years later, after the Secretary of Energy changed dispatch rules, and of those only one was approved at the first request.

A COMPARISON OF ARGENTINA AND CHILE

Overall, Argentina has been much more successful in ensuring that consumers benefit from the introduction of competition. In Argentina, there are 35 generating firms belonging to eight independent groups. The Herfindahl Index for the three largest firms is 0.15, which represents a highly competitive market, and large customers pay up to 30 percent less for electricity than their Chilean counterparts do (Bitrán, Estache, Guasch, and Serra 1999). The price difference is partly attributable to Argentina's wealth of primary resources, such as gas, but this benefit should decline over time, as the pipeline bringing gas from Argentina comes on stream. It may also be explained by the facts that the distribution franchises, as well as the transmission concession, have very clear third-party access rules and that vertical disaggregation has minimized monopolistic behavior. Additionally, Argentina has an independent organization responsible for administering the sector, Cammesa, and an independent regulator, ENRE. In contrast, Chile's institutional arrangements are less independent (Bitrán, Estache, Guasch, and Serra 1999). Moreover, Argentina has only one sector-specific regulator for transmission and distribution, and it is managed by a commission of experts under federal jurisdiction. This entails fewer coordination problems and increases the accountability for decisions taken or not taken. The method of self-funding and the staffing of the agency also provide some guarantees of its independence — factors that may be of some relevance in the next wave of regulatory reforms in Chile.

Lessons Learned

The first lesson to be drawn from the Argentine and Chilean experiences is that competition rather than privatization is the key ingredient for a successful transformation of the sector. Within the electricity sector, when competition was introduced, those areas performed best in terms of prices, investment levels, and service quality. By separating transmission from the wholesale market, Argentina improved upon Chile's experience, and by further fragmenting generation to reduce market power, Argentina improved upon the experiences of England and Wales.

For competition to take place, several conditions must be met. First, the primary energy source must be competitive if the wholesale market is to work competitively. No matter how many generators there are, if there is monopoly control over the primary source, for instance, gas or water, there is little or no chance of competition, as the monopolist can extract all the rents from the downstream activity. In this context, the allocation of most of the water rights to the largest generator in Chile seriously undermines efficiency of the electricity sector as a whole.

Second, natural monopolies must be distinct, with clear rules for third-party access. For transmission, the lack of clear regulation threatens to undermine the ability of market efficiency. In this respect, Argentina's model is more effective than Chile's.

Third, the ultimate test for competition is new entrants into the system. The major gains from competition in generation come from decentralizing decisions regarding when, how much, and what type of generation is brought on stream.

A further lesson is that competition should not be confined to head-to-head competition. Competition for the market and yardstick competition are also important instruments for regulators. Competitive tendering for monopoly concessions can improve the efficiency of the process. Periodic re-tendering of the concession, as proposed in Argentina, seems to be an interesting approach, although high transaction costs and the asymmetry of information between the incumbent and other participants might prove to be a serious limitation.

Yardstick competition is also a powerful instrument to help regulators extract information from the regulated companies. By comparing different companies, the regulator can increase incentives for efficiency. This requires comparable, homogeneous, and timely information on the different companies, something that is clearly lacking in the Argentine case.

Chile provides another lesson that underlies the need to ensure that competition is defined rather precisely. To enhance competition, the definition of an unregulated customer should be reduced to 100 kW, allowing supply firms to compete for clients. A solution like this would considerably diminish the role of the state because, while the authority would still retain responsibility for setting transmission and distribution rates, it would play more of an intermediary role between trading firms and transmission and distribution companies. Such increased competition would also provide better opportunities to overlap concessions in electricity distribution.[6]

Competition cannot be introduced throughout the electricity industry; clearly, distribution and transmission will remain natural monopolies and, as such, will be in need of tight regulation. In this context, further regulatory reforms should take into greater account the interests of consumers. The regulators should be granted jurisdiction to set tariffs and to ensure that the efficiency gains are passed on to consumers. This would require basing transmission and distribution tariffs on a more transparent, incentive-based formula. The issues of pricing and terms of access and interconnection remain. The current structure favors the incumbent integrated firm and, thus, does not facilitate competition. These approaches and the provision for equal access — the agenda for the next wave of privatization — would, in turn, further promote competition.

As for transmission, in Argentina, the restructuring led to a separation of transmission from generation and distribution. Nevertheless, the pricing rules are not sufficiently efficient and fail to achieve dynamic efficiency. The main challenge for Chile is to decide whether it is worth going the next step or to maintain dispatch and transmission as a joint activity. The strengthening of the institutional capability to monitor the behavior of firms is good first step, but it would be preferable — although politically difficult — to undertake the wholesale restructuring of Endesa.

Overall, separating the electricity sector vertically and horizontally tends to increase the burden and complexity of regulation. In addition to the traditional monopoly regulation issues, such as fair rate of return, asset base, and tariff structure to final consumers, other issues emerge, such as third-party access, promotion of competition, interconnection pricing, and consistency of regulation across sectors, all of which require strong technical skills and additional commitment by regulators. In this sense, the experiences of Chile and Argentina suggest that although much has been achieved, many tasks remain to be resolved in terms of fine-tuning the system and providing long-run sustainability to the reforms.

Notes

1. This section builds on Bitrán, Estache, Guasch, and Serra (1999).

2. Privatization was also conducted though a very specific approach, giving shares in return for the financial deposits users had to make per kW of connected power.

3. Entry is not free because there are water use rights; in fact, what is really consumed is the use of these water rights.

4. Node price is the price at which distributors buy energy from generating companies. It is designed to approximate long-run marginal costs and is calculated by the Ministry of Economics and the NEC.

5. The firm capacity of each producer is the maximum power that its generating units can contribute in the peak period of the system with a reliability exceeding 95 percent.

6. A more analytical assessment of the welfare gains of utilities deregulation and privatization is provided by Galal et al. (1994) and Hachette and Lüders (1993) and summarized in a critical survey by Paredes (1995).

7. The growth rate was almost 9 percent between 1990 and 1996.

References

Bitrán, Eduardo, Antonio Estache, José Luis Guasch, and Pablo Serra. 1999. "Privatizing and Regulating Chile's Utilities, 1974-2000: Successes, Failures, and Outstanding Challenges." In *Chile: Recent Policy Lessons and Emerging Challenges*, eds. Guillermo Perry and Danny Leipziger. Washington, D.C.: World Bank. 327-392.

Estache, Antonio, José Luis Guasch, and Pablo Serra. 1999. In *Chile: Recent Policy Lessons and Emerging, Challenges*, eds. Guillermo Perry and Danny Leipziger. Washington, D.C.: World Bank.

Galal, Ahmed, Leroy Jones, Pankaj Tandon, and Ingo Vogelsang. 1994. *Welfare Consequences of Selling Public Enterprises: An Empirical Analysis*. New York: Oxford University Press.

Hachette, Dominique, and Rolf Lüders. 1993. *Privatization in Chile: An Economic Appraisal*. San Francisco: International Center for Economic Growth.

Paredes, Ricardo. 1995. "Privatización y regulación: lecciones de la experiencia chilena." In *Despues de las privatizaciones: hacia el estado regulador*, ed. Oscar Muñoz. Santiago: CIEPLAN.

CHAPTER 8

Regulating the Telecommunications Sector: The Experience of Latin America

BJÖRN WELLENIUS

SUMMARY

This chapter discusses empirical material from the Latin American experience in regulating telecommunications following privatization of the state enterprises. It focuses on sector-specific legislative bases of regulation, major objectives and tradeoffs in regulatory policy, regulatory instruments, regulatory institutions, and regulatory issues. The chapter also outlines some of the challenges and opportunities for improving regulation in the near future.

During the last 12 years, Latin America has moved decisively from stagnant state telecommunications monopolies to vibrant, private-led, increasingly competitive business sectors. Competition and regulation, however, have lagged behind privatization.

Most Latin American telecommunications privatization arrangements granted five to ten years' exclusivity in core services and networks; compared with markets that were open to competition earlier, this resulted in slower growth, slower innovation, and higher prices. The trend toward open, competitive markets, however, is now accelerating. Most of the remaining exclusivity periods will expire by 2001 or earlier, recent privatizations have offered no exclusivity, other utilities are emerging as powerful providers of alternative infrastructures, technological innovation continues to reduce the minimum size of viable operations, and the countries are actively participating in regional and global trade agreements that commit them to competition.

Traditional views that a slow transition to competition is necessary to attract investment, ensure sustainable development, and reduce the imbalance between

Björn Wellenius is the Telecommunications Advisor at the World Bank in Washington, D.C. This chapter, however, has been prepared in a personal capacity and does not necessarily reflect the views of the World Bank Group, its management or staff, or its member countries. The author thanks Claude Bessé, Geoffrey Cannock, Rinaldo Colomé, Andrew Dymond, José Ricardo Melo, Fernando Navajas, Gustavo Peña, Peter Smith, Peter Stern, Eloy Vidal, Rafael del Villar, and Ricardo Yomal for valuable information and comments.

cities and rural areas are not supported by the Latin American experience. In particular, progress in rural service is more sustainable under fully commercial conditions, supplemented by small subsidies allocated using market mechanisms, than when it is imposed in license obligations.

Regulation developed most effectively where regulatory institutions were started well before privatization, where they were established with a firm foundation in telecommunications law, and where competition arrived early. Regulatory institutions have tended to be very closely tied to government; this has favored a good fit between regulation and policy but has made regulation vulnerable to government intervention. Within this scheme, when regulatory issues become political, regulatory authorities who report to a nation's president or prime minister fare better than those who report to line ministers. A sharing of regulatory functions between regulator and government has accentuated the already excessive links between both. Formal separation between regulation and operation has not prevented the operators from influencing or delaying regulatory decisions beyond what results from normal participation in the formal regulatory process. Information asymmetry is a major factor, but use of sheer political and economic power also figures prominently.

Competition has tended to make sector-specific regulation more complex but also more manageable. Antitrust law and enforcement, where available, has played a growing role supplementing the regulator in promoting and safeguarding competition. The beginnings of a shift from sector-specific to general competition regulation within countries can be seen, as well as from national to an international common denominator of regulatory practice through trade agreements.

Some of the regulatory challenges in the near future include developing institutional solutions that better match the life cycle of regulatory demand, avoiding the cost accounting bottleneck, enhancing regulatory capacity through regional cooperation and global networking, and strengthening consumer organizations. It is also timely to revisit policy and regulation, including the legal framework, in the light of increasing convergence among telecommunications, computers, media, publishing, and other traditionally separate information activities.

TWELVE YEARS OF SECTOR REFORMS — OVERVIEW

Information has become an essential factor of competitiveness, growth, and participation in the local and global economies. Telecommunications is the foundation or base on which information infrastructures are built.[1] Telecommunications comprises an integrated worldwide network to which more than 500 million users are connected. It generates about US$700 billion in annual revenues, which are growing by more than 10 percent annually or about three times the pace of the global product. Over US$1 trillion in financial transactions are carried out every day by international telecommunications networks. Telecommunications growth has been driven by technological innovation coupled with expanding market demand. In particular, the cost of processing, transmitting, and storing one unit of information has declined by a factor of 10,000 in the last 20 years. This rate of cost reduction has no precedent in history, has led to major changes in market structure, and shows no signs of abating. In most emerging economies, however, the supply of telecommunications networks and services has lagged far behind demand for decades; services are of poor quality, unreliable, and antiquated; productivity is low; and prices are generally too high and exhibit major distortions with respect to costs. This state of affairs, which had already become a widely recognized impediment to economic development, now threatens to exclude emerging economies from reaping the benefits of the rapidly expanding global information economy.[2]

Since 1987, Latin America has responded to this challenge with a veritable revolution.[3] Stagnant state telecommunications monopolies have been giving way to vibrant,' private-led, increasingly competitive telecommunications business sectors. Privatization of state enterprises began in Chile (1987), then followed in quick succession in Argentina (1990), Mexico (1990), and Venezuela (1991).[4] A second wave comprised Peru (1994), Bolivia (1995), and Panama (1997). In 1998, three more privatizations were concluded in El Salvador, Brazil, and Guatemala. Honduras and Nicaragua are preparing for privatization in 1999. Privatization in Ecuador was planned for 1998 but was postponed. As of early 1999, there were no firm plans to privatize the remaining Latin American state telecommunications companies, namely, those in Colombia, Costa Rica, Paraguay, and Uruguay. Privatization strategies have been essentially similar in all countries. A controlling interest in the state enterprise was transferred to a private owner, usually a strategic investor comprising a consortium of local and foreign investors, including an experienced foreign telecommunications company. In most cases, this was combined with the sale of state shares to other investors, employees, or the public at large, usually once the company's market value had appreciated following privatization.

The approach to competition policy, in contrast, has varied considerably among countries. Some competition in mobile cellular telephony was allowed in most countries before or at the time of privatization. Data, paging, trunking, private networks, cable television, and very small aperture terminal systems (VSAT) were also opened early. In the core telephony business, however, typically accounting for over 80 percent of investments and revenues, all the state companies privatized up through 1997 were given monopoly rights of 5 to 10 years, except in Chile, where exclusivity was never granted. Brazil, El Salvador, and Guatemala were privatized in 1998 without exclusivity, but Ecuador, Honduras, and Nicaragua are considering granting several years' exclusivity after privatization. In general, competition came after privatization. In Colombia, nonetheless, privatization of the largest telecommunications company, Empresa Nacional de Telecomunicaciones (TELECOM) was postponed while an aggressive program of competition was begun throughout the country, involving 40 (excluding private) federal, provincial, and municipal companies, as well as private companies established after 1991 and 1994 legal changes.[5]

So far, reforms in the countries that have privatized telecommunications generally have been very successful. Faster growth, better and new services, lower costs, and eventually lower prices have followed (Wellenius and Stern 1994, 111-194). For example, the early privatizations (Chile, Argentina, Mexico, and Venezuela) resulted in an acceleration in annual growth rates for main telephone lines in service, from an average 5 percent growth before privatization to 13 percent following privatization. Time waiting to get a new telephone line dropped from six years to one year. Labor productivity more than doubled, and the use of digital technology tripled. (See Table 1.)

Table 1.
Impact of Privatization on Sector Performance
— Argentina, Chile, Mexico, and Venezuela

Selected Indicators	Before	After
Service growth, percent per year[1]	5	13
Outstanding demand, years[2]	6	1
Productivity, lines/employee[3]	71	165
Technology, percent digital[4]	24	75

[1]Percent annual growth of main telephone lines in service during the five-year periods preceding and following privatization.

[2]Outstanding applications for telephone service at the end of the year preceding privatization and five years after privatization, divided by the average number of net main lines added during the previous three years.

[3]Number of main telephone lines in service divided by the number of full-time employees of the telephone company, same dates.

[4]Percent main telephone lines in service connected to digital local exchanges, same dates.

Sources: All figures in this table are calculated from *Yearbook of Statistics, Telecommunication Services, Chronological Time Series 1986-1995*, International Telecommunication Union, Geneva, 1997; and *World Telecommunications Development Report*, International Telecommunication Union, Geneva, 1998.

Not all reform attempts, however, have been equally successful. Best results were achieved where conflicting objectives were sorted out early, where clear policies and procedures were put in place, where markets were opened early to new entry and competition, and where measures were taken to enhance credibility and stability of the regulatory regime. Moreover, seven countries, or almost one-half of the 16 countries that attempted to privatize their state telecommunications enterprises, failed the first time around.[6] Of these, two succeeded on the second try (Panama and Guatemala), two are slated for another attempt in 1999 (Ecuador and Nicaragua), and three are not scheduled (Colombia, Costa Rica, and Uruguay).

This chapter collects and organizes empirical material from the Latin American experience of regulating telecommunications following privatization of the state enterprises. In discussing and drawing some practical lessons from this material, the chapter focuses, in turn, on sector-specific legislative bases for regulation, objectives and tradeoffs in regulatory policy, regulatory instruments, regulatory institutions, and regulatory issues. It also outlines some of the challenges and opportunities for improving regulation in the near future. This chapter is based on information available from publications, governments, and specialized institutions — and on information and comments obtained directly from several regulatory agencies and other sources. It also draws on discussions with several participants during and after the conference where this chapter was first presented.

By design, there are three things this chapter does *not* do. First, although the viewpoint adopted is that of prevailing international best practices, and, thus, the chapter is set in the broader context of world experience, explicit comparisons between Latin America and other regions have been excluded (except for occasional endnotes). Second, the empirical findings in this chapter may suggest research hypotheses for further investigation in terms of institutional economics or other analytical frameworks in economics or political science. That, however, would be a very different paper, calling for different expertise, and, therefore, is it left for others to undertake. Third, this chapter does discuss how regulatory decisions made at the time of privatization affected subsequent sector performance and regulation, but it does not deal with privatization strategy itself.

THE LEGAL FRAMEWORK FOR REGULATION

I deally, as sector reforms are initiated, the rules of the game are clearly spelled out in laws, decrees, and regulations; the businesses offered to investors are well defined in licenses, tender documents, and contracts of sale; and an effective regulatory capacity is in place. Latin America is moving in these directions, but in the beginning it was much less tidy. Table 2 lists the main telecommunications laws and decrees that set the context for restructuring the telecommunications sector in 15 Latin American countries.

The Precursors

Of the four first privatizations, only Chile's was carried out within the framework of a modern telecommunications law that established broad principles and rules governing the sector.[7] The other three did not attempt (or failed) to pass new legislation.

Argentina. Privatization of Empresa Nacional de Telecomunicaciones (ENTel), the state telecommunications monopoly, took place in 1990 in the context of an outdated telecommunications law enacted in 1972 by a military government. Amid fears that congressional debate would delay and potentially derail privatization, which was planned to be completed in 12 months as the flagship of President Carlos Menem's state reform program, no attempt was made to change the law. Rather, a broad state reform law passed by Congress in 1989 authorized the president to privatize ENTel, and a decree of the same year defined the new sector policies and set forth the terms and conditions for the sale. ENTel was privatized in 1990, barely two months behind schedule (Mairal 1994, 161-176).

The National Telecommunications Commission (Comisión Nacional de Telecomunicaciones — CNT), a semi-autonomous telecommunications regulatory agency, was created by a 1989 decree that was subsequently modified several times.

Table 2.
Main Legislation for Telecommunications Reform

Argentina

- Telecommunications law of 1972.
- State reform law No. 23696 of 1989 and decree No. 1105 of 1989 authorize the president to privatize ENTel.
- Decree 731 of 1989 implements privatization.
- Decree of 1989 creates Comisión Nacional de Telecomunicaciones (CNT) as regulatory authority.
- Decrees No. 660 of 1996 and No. 80 of 1997 merge CNT with broadcasting and postal authorities to create Comisión Nacional de Comunicaciones (CNC) as regulator for the broader communications sector.

Bolivia

- Law No. 1544 of 1994 establishes the basis for private capitalization of state enterprises.
- Telecommunications law No. 1600 of 1994 creates Sistema de Regulación Sectorial (SIRESE).
- Law No. 1632 of 1995 establishes the basis for competition and privatization of ENTEL.

Brazil

- Telecommunications law No. 9472 of 1997 establishes the basis for competitive sector development, creates Agência Nacional de Telecomunicações (ANATEL) as the regulatory authority, authorizes the government to privatize Telecomunicações Brasileiras (TELEBRAS) and its 24 operating subsidiaries, and removes foreign ownership restrictions.

Chile

- Decree of 1977 establishes Subsecretaría de Telecomunicaciones (SUBTEL) as regulatory authority.
- Decree of 1978 sets basic principles for privatization and competition.
- Telecommunications law of 1982 clears the way for privatization and tariff regulation and strengthens role of SUBTEL.
- Telecommunications law No. 3A of 1994 accelerates competition in all market segments and creates rural development fund.

Colombia

- Constitution of 1991 allows private provision of public telecommunications services.
- Law No. 142 of 1994 on residential public services (including telecommunications), modified by Law No. 286 of 1996, creates Superintendencia de Servicios Públicos Domiciliarios and Comisión de Regulación de Telecomunicaciones (CRT) as regulatory authority.

Table 2.—*continued*

Colombia

• CRT resolutions No. 86, 87, and 88 of 1997 open local and long-distance services to competition.

Costa Rica

• Autoridad Reguladora de Servicios Públicos established in 1996.

Ecuador

• Telecommunications laws No. 184 of 1992, No. 94 of 1995, and No. 15 of 1997 restructure Empresa Ecuatoriana de Telecomunicaciones (EMETEL), authorize its privatization, and create three regulatory agencies: Consejo Nacional de Telecomunicaciones (CONATEL), Secretaría Nacional de Telecomunicaciones (SENATEL), and Superintendencia de Telecomunicaciones.

El Salvador

• Telecommunications law of 1996 establishes the basis for private-led, competitive sector development.

• Law of 1996 creates Superintendencia General de Servicios Eléctricos y Telecomunicaciones (SIGET) as the regulatory authority for electricity and telecommunications.

Guatemala

• Telecommunications law of 1996 establishes the basis for competition and for private ownership of telecommunications, and it creates Superintendencia de Telecomunicaciones (SIT) as regulatory authority.

Honduras

• Telecommunications law of 1995 establishes Comisión Nacional de Telecomunicaciones as regulatory authority.

Mexico

• Transport and telegraphs law of 1936.

• Shareholders' meeting in 1989 approves capital restructuring of Teléfonos de México (TELMEX) and plan to sell government shares.

• New concession issued to TELMEX by ministerial decree of 1990.

• Modification in 1995 of the Constitution allows private participation in the provision of satellite services.

• Telecommunications law of 1995 opens the market widely to competition and establishes deadline to set up regulatory agency.

• Presidential decree of 1996 creates Comisión Federal de Telecomunicaciones (COFETEL) as the telecommunications regulatory authority.

Table 2.—*continued*

Nicaragua

• Telecommunications and postal law of 1995 restructures Instituto Nicaragüense de Telecomunicaciones y Correos (TELCOR) to become the regulatory authority.

Panama

• Law No. 3 of 1995 restructures the operating enterprise Instituto Nacional de Telecomunicaciones (INTEL).

• Law No. 26 of 1996 creates Ente Regulador de los Servicios Públicos as regulatory authority for telecommunications and other services.

• Law No. 31 of 1996 establishes the basic norms for regulation.

Peru

• Decree No. 702 of 1991 sets out the rules for private investment in telecommunications and creates Organismo Supervisor de Inversión Privada en Telecomunicaciones (OSIPTEL) as regulator. Modified by decrees Nos. 766 (1991), 26095, and 26096 (1992).

• Telecommunications law of 1993 and implementing regulations consolidate earlier legislation and establish the framework for competition and regulation.

• Law No. 26285 of 1994 establishes a timetable to open local and long-distance telecommunication services to competition.

Venezuela

• Telecommunications law of 1940.

• Decree of 1991 issues new concession to Compañía Nacional Autónoma de Teléfonos de Venezuela (CANTV) allowing for its privatization.

• Decree No. 1826 of 1991 created Consejo Nacional de Telecomunicaciones (CONATEL) as regulatory authority.

Source: Author's compilation.

In 1997, CNT was merged with the National Broadcasting Commission and the Posts and Telegraphs Commission into a single National Communications Commission (Comisión Nacional de Comunicaciones — CNC).

Chile. A ministerial decree of 1978 set the basic principles that guided subsequent liberalization and privatization. A law passed in 1982 enabled enforcement of specific actions to implement this policy and abrogated pre-existing, conflicting statutes. An amendment to the law in 1987 established specific means to implement privatization, including mechanisms for investment financing and a system for regulating tariffs of dominant operators. In this context, controlling interests in Compañía de Teléfonos de Chile (CTC) and Empresa Nacional de Telecomunicaciones (ENTEL), the dominant local and long-distance state-owned telecommunications companies, were privatized in 1987. By 1990, all remaining state ownership in telecommunications operating companies had been divested to employees, investors, and the public at large (Melo 1994, 145-159). The law was amended again in 1994 to accelerate competition, especially in long-distance telephony, and to create a financing mechanism to extend access to rural and low-income urban areas.

Subsecretaría de Telecomunicaciones (SUBTEL) was created by decree in 1977 as the branch of government responsible for policy and regulation, becoming extensively involved in formulating and implementing telecommunications reforms. SUBTEL's sector-specific regulatory powers were strengthened by the telecommunications law of 1982, a full five years before privatization of the state enterprises. Competition law enforcement has been the responsibility of the Comisión Antimonopolios.

Mexico. The new government's program published in 1989 opened the way for privatizing Teléfonos de México (TELMEX, the 51 percent state-owned telecommunications monopoly), which was completed in 1990. The transport and communication law of 1936, which dealt with telecommunications mainly in terms of wire and radio telegraphs, did not provide a useful framework for reform but was deemed to pose no obstacle to the privatization of TELMEX. A modern telecommunications law passed in 1995 established the basis for competition in all market segments at the end of TELMEX's exclusivity in 1996 and also clarified and strengthened the regulatory regime (Wellenius and Staple 1996). Modification of the Mexican Constitution in 1995 allowed private participation in the domestic satellite business.

The Undersecretary of Communications and Technological Development (Subsecretaría de Comunicaciones y Desarrollo Tecnológico — SCT), a branch of the Ministry of Transport and Communication, was responsible for sector policy and regulation as well as for operating the state-owned domestic satellite system, a national microwave network, the telex and telegraph service, and other facilities. In preparation for the privatization of TELMEX, as well as the later privatization of the domestic satellite system, in 1990 all operating functions of SCT were transferred to Telecomunicaciones de México (TELECOMM), a new state enterprise. SCT retained only policy and regulatory functions. A new decentralized regulatory agency, the Federal Telecommunications Commission (Comisión Federal de Telecomunicaciones — COFETEL), was mandated by the law of 1995 and established by decree in 1996 with improved powers and resources.

Venezuela. The telecommunications law of 1946 gave the state exclusive responsibility to establish and exploit telecommunications facilities but empowered the government to grant concessions and permits to private entities to provide these services. In 1965, a law for reorganizing telecommunications services granted Compañía Anónima Nacional de Telecomunicaciones de Venezuela (CANTV) a concession for 25 years. Although this law left open the possibility of granting other concessions, none were ever granted. A modern telecommunications bill that sought to open the sector gradually to competition, rein in dominant operators, and create a regulatory agency was introduced in Congress in 1990 but did not pass. The existing laws, although antiquated, did not impede the issuing of new concessions or selling of state interests in CANTV. In 1991, a decree issued a new concession to CANTV, replacing the 1965 concession, which had recently expired. The decree also established the process for selling state shares. CANTV was privatized the same year (Pisciotta 1994, 185-194).

Having failed to pass a telecommunications law that, *inter alia*, established a regulatory authority, the government in 1991 resorted to a decree to create the Comisión Nacional de Telecomunicaciones (CONATEL) for this purpose.

The Second Wave

New telecommunications laws preceded privatization of state enterprises in Bolivia, Panama, and Peru. They also provided the basis for sector regulation.

Bolivia. The telecommunications law of 1995 established the framework for privatizing ENTEL, the state enterprise providing mainly international and long-distance but also some rural services. The law also provided for developing local service in 15 existing municipal or cooperative operating companies and for eventually opening the market to new entry and competition. ENTEL was privatized the same year. A multi-sectoral regulatory authority, Sectoral Regulation System (Sistema de Regulación Sectorial — SIRESE) and, within it, the specialized Telecommunications Superintendency (Superintendencia de Telecomunicaciones) were established by law in 1994 and 1995, respectively.

Panama. An attempt in 1992 to privatize the National Telecommunications Institute (Instituto Nacional de Telecomunicaciones — INTEL), the state operator, was frustrated by opposition from organized labor. A law authorizing the sale failed to pass in Congress. In 1995 and 1996, however, three laws were passed to restructure and privatize INTEL, which was done in 1997, as well as to establish the basis for sectoral regulation. Two laws in 1996 created a regulatory authority, the Public Services Regulator (Ente Regulador de los Servicios Públicos) and established basic norms for regulation.

Peru. A 1991decree set out the rules for private investment in telecommunications. The telecommunications law of 1993 consolidated earlier piecemeal legislation, establishing the framework for competition and regulation. A law passed in 1994 provided for progressive opening of the market to competition. Compañía Peruana de Telecomunicaciones (CPT), the nominally subscriber-owned but state-controlled telephone monopoly in metropolitan Lima and Callao, and Empresa Nacional de Telecomunicaciones (ENTEL), the state monopoly elsewhere, were privatized in 1994. They subsequently merged into a single company (Telefónica del Perú). The telecommunications regulatory agency, Supervisory Organization for Private Investment in Telecommunications (Organismo Supervisor de la Inversión Privada en Telecomunicaciones — OSIPTEL), was established by law in 1993 before privatization.

The Late 1990s

New telecommunications legislation was in place before all privatizations were completed or planned for 1998 and 1999.

Brazil. After several failed attempts to build political support for restructuring, a general telecommunications law was passed by Congress in 1997, setting the rules for privatizing Telecomunicações Brasileiras (TELEBRAS), the federal holding of one long-distance and 24 regional monopolies, and removing foreign ownership restrictions. The law also established Agência Nacional de Telecomunicações (ANATEL) as a decentralized regulatory authority. TELEBRAS was privatized in 1998.

Ecuador. Three telecommunications laws of 1992, 1995, and 1997 restructured Empresa Ecuatoriana de Telecomunicaciones (EMETEL), the state operating enterprise, into two regional companies and allowed for their privatization. These laws also created three entities responsible for sector policy and regulation.

El Salvador. A telecommunications law of 1996 established the basis for opening up the sector to unrestricted entry and competition as well as for dividing the Administración Nacional de Telecomunicaciones (ANTEL), the state operator, into two fully overlapping, competing companies to be privatized. Another law, also of 1996, created a regulatory authority for telecommunications and electricity, the General Superintendency for Electrical and Telecommunication Services (Superintendencia General de Servicios Eléctricos y Telecomunicaciones — SIGET), focused mostly on access to bottleneck capacities, mainly interconnection and spectrum. Following national elections, the law was modified in 1997 and left the incumbent as a single undivided company. ANTEL was privatized in 1998.

Guatemala. The 1996 telecommunications law paved the way for privatizing Empresa Guatemalteca de Telecomunicaciones (GUATEL), the state monopoly (subsequently renamed TELGUA), simultaneously opening the sector to competition and establishing the basis for regulation by the Telecommunications Superintendency (Superintendencia de Telecomunicaciones — SIT). TELGUA was privatized in 1998.

Honduras. The telecommunications law of 1995 separated regulatory and operational responsibilities, created the National Telecommunications Commission (Comisión Nacional de Telecomunicaciones — CONATEL) as the regulatory authority, and restructured the state operator Empresa Hondureña de Telecomunicaciones (HONDUTEL) to allow for privatization.

Nicaragua. Separate telecommunications and postal enterprises were spun off in 1994 from Telephone and Posts (Teléfonos y Correos — TELCOR), the state posts and telecommunications monopoly. The telecommunications law of 1995 allows for the privatization of the state telecommunications enterprise and redefines the role of TELCOR as regulator.

Beyond 1999

Elements of legislation are in place also in countries that are not yet planning to privatize the state enterprises. Colombia, where privatization has been postponed and the market is instead being opened up to competition in all segments, has in place some elements of a legal framework for sector reform. The Constitution of 1991 allows private provision of public telecommunications services. A 1994 law on residential public services, explicitly including telecommunications, consoli-

dated provisions introduced piecemeal since 1989 and provides the main framework for current sector developments. The Regulatory Commission for Telecommunications (Comisión de Regulación de Telecomunicaciones — CRT) was
created in 1992 as the sector regulatory authority; in 1994, it became independent
from the Ministry of Communications as well as from TELECOM, which traditionally had exercised regulatory powers. In Costa Rica, the Regulatory Public Services
Authority (Autoridad Reguladora de Servicios Públicos — ARESEP) was created
in 1996.

REGULATORY POLICY

The story of telecommunications development in Latin America to a large extent
revolves around the pace at which new players can enter the market, complementing and competing with the incumbents. Until recently, competition was
deemed generally desirable but viable only in non-core services, for example,
mobile. Financial advisers for privatization argued successfully that exclusive
rights in basic telephone services and networks were needed to attract investors.
With hindsight, however, exclusivity appears to have been neither necessary nor
beneficial. Ensuring some equity of sector development was a related concern. It
was thought that private companies would concentrate their investment in the
highly profitable business and high-income residential urban areas, while rural and
low-income urban population groups would continue to be excluded. Universal
service objectives were addressed mainly by establishing specific build-out obligations under the licenses. The results suggest, however, that competitive markets did
better at meeting these objectives than monopolies and can be more readily
sustained in an increasingly liberal environment.

Competition

The pace at which competition (or, more precisely, new entry and competition) in core telephone services has been allowed has varied considerably from
country to country. Alone among the precursors, Chile never granted exclusive
rights, and, although regulatory barriers to entry in basic voice services were not
fully dismantled until 1994, the privatized companies were always under the threat
of competition. At the other extreme, Venezuela granted nine years' exclusive
rights for telephony, and Argentina granted seven years with possible extension to
10 years. The trend since then has been toward shorter or no market protection. The
second wave of privatizations granted five to six years' exclusivity of basic services,
and the three privatizations completed in 1998 gave no exclusive rights. (See Table 3.)

Table 3.
Exclusivity Granted at Privatization

Country	Year privatized	Exclusivity* years
Precursors		
Chile	1987	0
Argentina	1990	7-10
Mexico	1990	6
Venezuela	1991	9
Second wave		
Peru	1994	5
Bolivia	1995	6
Panama	1997	5
Late 1990s		
El Salvador	1998	0
Brazil	1998	0
Guatemala	1998	0

*Refers to exclusivity in the provision of local, long-distance, and international telephone networks and services.

Source: Author's compilation.

In contrast, competition in other services was introduced before or around the time of privatization, and in 1996 the first of the exclusivity periods expired (Mexico's). Table 4 summarizes the extent to which regulatory barriers to entry and competition had already been dismantled by 1997. Chile's telecommunications market had become one of the most open and competitive in the world. Competition was introduced in the late 1980s in cellular, data, value-added, and cable TV services as well as in private networks and introduced since 1994 in domestic and international long-distance telephony services (with about 10 carriers, of which three had built substantial country-wide and international networks). Chile's competition resulted in rapid network modernization, new services, and prices among the world's lowest. Competition in local services was intensifying, mainly from long-distance carriers starting wireline and wireless local service, from combined voice and cable TV service, as well as from other utilities (for example, a gas distribution company) developing local fiber networks. Mexico's market was opened widely in 1996 and a year later competition was developing effectively, especially in long-distance and international service. All other countries had in place by 1997 fairly competitive cellular, cable television, and non-basic (for example, paging) services. However, the pattern of leased lines and data was mixed, and the core telephone services were still run as monopolies.

It is now increasingly recognized in Latin America that granting exclusive rights to the privatized companies has resulted in slower growth, slower service innovation, and higher prices than could have been obtained under competition. That was, for example, the view held by the Mexican authorities in 1995 when they explored competitive alternatives to TELMEX's monopoly, which was due to expire in 1996. The authorities decided to go for a very pro-competitive new sector law and policy, lifting restrictions on the number of operating licenses and ending traditional distinctions by types of service and technology (Wellenius and Staple 1996).

The impact of competition, where allowed, has been felt in many ways. For example, competition has driven prices down, leading to higher demand and faster network growth, in turn creating opportunities for technological innovations that improve performance and reduce costs, thus allowing further price reductions. The threat of competition has driven incumbents to pre-empt demand by accelerating supply and focusing on customer service. More, better, and less expensive service has encouraged new uses, notably the Internet, which in turn has further increased demand.

Table 4.
Competition in the Telecommunications Markets in 1997

Country	Local telephone	Mobile cellular	Long -distance telephone	Interna-tional tele-phone	Leased lines	Data	Paging	Cable tele-vision
Argentina	M	PC	M	M	C	M	C	C
Bolivia	M	PC	M	M	C	C		
Brazil	M	PC	M	M ·	C	C	C	C
Chile	C	PC	C	C	C	C	C	C
Colombia	C	PC	M	M	C	C	C	C
Costa Rica	M	M	M	M	M	M	PC	PC
Ecuador	M	PC	M	M	M	M	C	
El Salvador	M	M	M	M	M			
Guatemala	M	M	M	M	M	M	C	C
Honduras	PC	C	PC	M	M	C	C	C
Mexico	C	C	C	C	C	C		
Nicaragua	M	C	M	M	M	C	C	C
Panama	M	C	M	M	M	M	C	M
Paraguay	M	M	M	M	M	M	C	C
Peru	M	C	M	M	C	PC	C	C
Uruguay	M	PC	M	M	M	M	C	PC
Venezuela	M	C	M	M	C	C	C	C

Key: M = monopoly   PC = limited competition   C = competition

Source: International Telecommunication Union, 1998a. *General Trends in Telecommunications Reform.* Vol. 1. Geneva, Switzerland.

Competitive markets grow faster. During 1984-1994, the number of main telephone lines in Brazil, Colombia, Ecuador, Peru, and Uruguay that remained state monopolies throughout the period grew as a group at 7 to 8 percent per year. Argentina, Mexico, and Venezuela grew at the same rate while they remained state owned, but, following privatization as monopolies, their annual growth accelerated to 11 percent. Growth in Chile, which privatized the state companies but granted them no exclusive rights, accelerated to 21 percent a year (Wellenius 1997b).[8] Privatization and competition in Brazil are expected to increase the number of fixed telephone lines threefold to more than 40 million between 1998 and 2003 and to increase the number of cellular phones sixfold to more than 20 million. Empirical evidence in other market segments, for example, cellular, points in the same direction.

Competition results in faster alignment of prices with costs. Table 5 illustrates that, as of mid-1996, telephone tariffs in Chile were comparable to those in competitive markets in the developed world. The Latin American privatized monopolies, in contrast, were charging much higher prices for long-distance and international calls, while prices for rentals and local calls remained too low to recover costs. For example, in mid-1995 the price of calling the United States from Argentina and Brazil was four to seven times higher than from Chile. The price of calling from Argentina, Brazil, and Mexico to Chile was two to three times the price in the opposite direction (Petrazzini and Clark 1996). Long-distance call charges within Argentina were, in 1996, around six times their cost in Chile, and 64 Kb/s leased circuits for Internet access providers reportedly cost in excess of US$20,000 per month compared with US$700 in the United States for similar distances (*Wall Street Journal* 1996, A11). This imbalance continued to result in a competitive disadvantage to business users in exchange for cross-subsidizing consumption mainly by middle-income and high-income households. It also created arbitrage opportunities. For example, in 1997 it was less expensive to call from Buenos Aires to Mendoza (also in Argentina) via call-back through Chile than directly.

Table 5. Telecommunications Tariffs in Selected Competitive Markets in 1996, US$

Country	Average	US	UK	Sweden	New Zealand	Chile
Rental/month						
Business	22	21	21	20	37	11
Residential	14	9	13	13	23	11
Local call/min	0.03	0.02	0.05	0.03	0.03	0.03
LD call/min	0.14	0.16	0.12	0.10	0.14	0.16
Int'l call/min						
Near	0.38	0.09	0.48	0.33	0.60	
Far	0.71	0.30	0.39	0.76	1.00	0.60

Figures reflect the best prices available to good residential and business customers. Standard published rates may be higher. Call charges are for peak hours. Long-distance call charges are for distances of about 150 km.

Source: Author's compilation.

Competition accelerates service innovation. As a larger proportion of the gains in productive efficiency are passed on to the users rather than wholly appropriated by the owners, the operators continuously seek to create new business opportunities with initially higher profit margins.[9] At the same time, more, better, and less expensive basic services encourage new uses. The Internet provides a good example. Use of personal computers (PCs) on the Internet depends on access to good, reliable, and relatively inexpensive telecommunications services. Among the four precursor Latin American privatizations, Chile, in 1996, had 20 Internet users per 100 PCs, similar to levels in the United States, the United Kingdom, and the Netherlands, also highly competitive telecommunications markets. Mexico and Argentina, with private telecommunications monopolies, had less than half as many users per PC as Chile did, roughly the same as in Italy. And Venezuela, like France, had about one-fourth as many users per PC (International Telecommunication Union, 1998b).[10]

Competition finds its way to some extent into markets even where it has been formally ruled out. In Argentina, for example, despite the exclusive rights of the incumbent to provide basic services, by mid-1998 there were more than 50 call-back operators, reportedly accounting together for about 25 percent of international and domestic long-distance services. This led to accelerated rebalancing of tariffs as well as to incumbents' offering promotional packages to large users.[11] Likewise, the differences between voice service (monopoly) and data service (competitive) have become blurred, as voice can be processed as data packets and carried by channels — for example, frame relay switching protocol — that cannot distinguish the nature of the original signals.

Competition is likely to accelerate. The exclusive rights granted with privatization in Mexico expired in 1996, and those in Argentina, Venezuela, and Bolivia are to end by 2001. Peru negotiated advancing the end of exclusivity by one year, to 1998 (*El Cronista* 1998a). The single largest telecommunications privatization in the region, Brazil's, took place in July 1998, accompanied within a few months by the licensing of second operators for fixed and mobile services in all regions as well as for long-distance and international services. El Salvador also privatized in mid-1998, and Guatemala privatized a few months later, both in the context of very open licensing regimes. Continued technological changes are enabling new service modalities as well as further reducing the minimum viable size of operations. In 1999, there were more than 100 competing operators in El Salvador. In Argentina, licensing for Personal Communications Systems (PCS) tendered in 1998 was expected to result in the growth of wireless services by 25 to 30 percent, as new operators compete with four established cellular companies. Including paging, the number of wireless services users in Latin America is likely to increase from about six million to 30 million by 2001.[12]

Alternative providers of telecommunications infrastructure are emerging as a powerful competitive force. For example, Transportadora de Gas del Sur, Argentina's biggest gas pipeline operator, is considering leasing excess capacity in its 5,000-km wireless digital network to telecommunications service providers, in competition with the dominant regional telecommunications company (Mercosur Telecommunications Update 1998c).[13] Metrored, a company with a fiber optical network in Buenos Aires providing corporate services, is also seeking a license to offer basic telephone service to the public (*El Cronista* 1998b). Eletrobras, the national electric power holding company of Brazil, plans to offer to telecommunications companies the use of its 1,300-km optical fiber network (representing 3 to 5 percent of the cost of national power grid interconnection) to participate in the data communications business valued in excess of $2 billion annually (*Jornal do Brasil*, July 14, 1998).

Latin America is increasingly committed to regional and world trade agreements that foster telecommunications competition. Eleven Latin American countries signed the World Trade Organization's agreement on basic telecommunications of February 1997, each committing to opening up their markets by a specific date. (See Table 6.) Initial steps toward establishing a single telecommunications market among MERCOSUR member countries were announced by Brazil and Argentina in 1998, focusing on cellular network compatibility, trunking, paging, and equipment standardization (Mercosur Telecommunications Update 1998b). Liberalization under the North American Free Trade Agreement (NAFTA) has facilitated alliances between Mexican and international operating companies, development of leased private networks and value-added services, and trade in telecommunications equipment (Ibarra-Yunez 1996). Latin American countries are also actively involved in multilateral and bilateral initiatives to replace the system for sharing revenues from international communication, which was designed decades ago for monopoly environments, by cost-oriented interconnection or termination charges that will lead to lower prices and more effective competition (Tyler and Joy 1997).

Competition and Policy Tradeoffs

The traditional view in the early years in most countries was that a gradual transition to competition over several years was necessary to attract investment, rebalance tariffs, ensure sustainable development, and reduce the imbalance between cities and rural areas. The experience of Latin America does not support any of these traditional views.

The operating companies, incumbents and new entrants alike, have been quite successful in attracting investment irrespective of monopoly privileges. The basic service companies in Chile, where exclusivity was never granted, have repeatedly placed substantial volumes of equity and debt in domestic and international markets. The privatization of the Brazilian sector attracted bid prices averaging almost 70 percent above the minimum set by the government despite the more or less simultaneous sale of competing fixed and mobile licenses in all regions. Privatization in El Salvador, a very small, middle-income market with the most liberal regulatory environment in Latin America, attracted first-tier foreign operators and was successfully privatized in early 1998. As elsewhere in the world, the conclusion seems to be that investors do not shy away from competition when the overall terms of business, including a predictable regulatory regime, offer a reasonable chance of making a fair return on investment.

One argument often made in the past for granting temporary exclusivity at the time of privatization was that the companies would need time to rebalance tariffs.

Table 6. Commitments to WTO on Basic Telecommunications

Country	Ref. paper adopted?	Maximum foreign ownership	Commitments on market access
Argentina	Yes	100%	Phase-in voice telephony competition in November 2000. Full competition without phase-in for other basic services. MFN exemption on fixed geostationary satellite service.
Bolivia	Partially	100% by 2001	Phase-in long-distance and international competition in November 2001. Local telephony provided by 15 exclusive local operators. Full competition without phase-in for private networks and mobile services.
Brazil	No	49%	End all monopolies in one year. Open markets for paging and private networks without phase-in. Cellular duopolies and phase out foreign ownership restrictions on mobile (cellular and satellite) from July 1999. MFN exemption for direct-to-home satellite broadcasting.
Chile	Yes	100%	Full competition in long-distance and international markets for all basic services. No commitment made on local services.
Colombia	Yes	100%	License two new long-distance and international operators in 1997 with exclusive rights for seven years. Regional duopolies for cellular to be liberalized after June 1999. No commitment on non-geostationary satellite services.
Ecuador	No	100% for some services.	Open market access for cellular mobile services.
El Salvador	Yes	100%	Full competition in most basic services.
Guatemala	Yes	100%	Full competition in most basic services subject to licensing restrictions on radio frequencies.
Mexico	Yes	49%, more for cellular	Competition in local voice services, also data and private networks.
Peru	Yes	100%	Competition in local, long-distance, and international telephony in 1999. Scarce spectrum to be allocated through competitive bidding.
Venezuela	No	100%	Open all telephone market segments from October 2000. Full competition, without phase-in, in cellular, data, paging, other.

In practice, however, reforms have progressed better when the governments have mustered the political will to rebalance before privatization. Leaving rebalancing to the privatized companies to carry out during years of monopoly has resulted in slow implementation, major regulatory disputes, and, eventually, attempts to delay the end of exclusivity. This is further discussed in a later section.

It is sometimes argued that the rapid opening of markets is disruptive and inherently unstable. Some observers, for example, note that the removal of the last obstacles to full competition in-long distance and international service in Chile in late 1994 led to price wars, operating losses, and an excessive proliferation of carriers. The worst excesses of the price war, however, lasted only about two months and ended in relatively stable prices well below the starting levels and far below those in countries with a monopoly in basic services. Moreover, the initial flurry of advertising and promotional offerings increased public awareness of the availability, ease, and affordability of long-distance and international calling, led to a shift from premium to mass consumption usage patterns, and accelerated traffic growth. These operations did lose money initially for one or two quarters but then turned around and remained generally profitable. Of about 10 carriers, three developed modern, country-wide domestic and international networks of their own, and the rest range from resellers to budding network-based carriers. Four years after the price wars, there are few signs of market consolidation; mainly, the smallest of the three large carriers is having financial difficulty and is likely to be bought out or liquidated. New ventures and international partnerships continue to join the fray.

As much as in other emerging and mature economies, Latin American policymakers have also been concerned that privatization and competition may lead to operators' concentrating on the most profitable market segments, leaving the government to shoulder the burden of extending service to rural and low-income areas. This is discussed further below.

Universal Service

One way to ensure a measure of equity in the development of the telecommunications sector has been to include certain service obligations under the concessions granted at the time of privatization. For example, in Mexico, TELMEX's 1990 concession required providing by 1994 switched telephone service to all localities of 5,000 inhabitants or more and to all localities with more than 2,500 inhabitants and at least 100 applicants. It also required providing at least payphones in all localities with 500 or more inhabitants. This resulted in about 22,000 small towns and villages being connected, but it left some 100,000 villages with populations between 100 and 500 inhabitants without access to the network. One of the independent cellular operators committed in 1996 to extend service to some 2,400 small locales, although by 1998 it had not done so. In one Central American country, the license of the private cellular mobile company requires it to provide the state telephone monopoly, at no cost, up to 5 percent of the mobile's capacity, including fixed wireless equipment and unlimited airtime, for developing rural payphone service. The telephone company, however, has been unable to mobilize resources to utilize this capacity. The mobile company is not allowed to provide rural fixed service directly nor to charge prices that would render it commercially viable. Consequently, the communities remain without service.

There is growing evidence that in a private-led, competitive market, the commercial drive alone results in services being extended to population groups that the state monopolies were unable to reach. In Chile, for example, in the 10 years following privatization, the number of telephone lines quadrupled to more than 2 million in 1997, the proportion of households with telephone increased from 15 percent to more than 50 percent, and payphones came within walking distance of 90 percent of the population.

It is also increasingly clear, however, that some form of government intervention, and perhaps government financing, may be needed to close remaining gaps between what the market will do by itself and what the governments want to achieve in terms of service availability throughout the population. It is also clear that in a competitive market there are limits to how much an operator can be obligated to do when service is not by itself commercially viable.

The trend is toward establishing specialized financing mechanisms to catalyze additional private investment to close the access gap. The earliest example comes, again, from Chile. Despite the remarkable success of reforms, in 1994, about 10 percent of the population, or 1.5 million people, lived in localities without even one payphone. Some 500,000 households were unlikely to be able to afford individual telephones in the foreseeable future. To increase access to public telephones in rural areas and low-income urban areas, legislation was passed in 1994 at the government's initiative to set up the Fondo de Desarrollo de las Telecomunicaciones, a telecommunications development fund, with financing from the government budget. The objective of the fund is to provide a first payphone in each rural locality, at prescribed price and quality, by offering a one-time subsidy to attract private investment in these facilities. The amount of subsidy as well as the selection of the provider is determined through competitive tender, with the licenses awarded to the bidders that require the lowest subsidy. The first round, completed in March 1996, committed US$2.1 million of public money to attract 20 times as much private money. About one-half of the private funds was used to install payphones in some 1,200 localities throughout Chile by 1998, and the other half to develop additional facilities included in the bids and licenses but not subsidized. On average, only US$1,600 of public money was thus committed per payphone. In contrast, in the late 1980s, the government had paid the incumbent operators the full cost of installing rural payphones, averaging about US$20,000 per payphone (Wellenius 1997a). Several more rounds of the fund by now have been completed, with roughly comparable results. By the year 2000, some 4,500 localities with a total of 1.8 million inhabitants will have been equipped with payphones at a total one-time cost to government of about $11 million, the equivalent of only six U.S. cents per inhabitant (*El Diario* 1998b). By then, more than 98 percent of the Chilean population will have basic access to telephone service.

Related financing initiatives are in place or being established in Colombia, Guatemala, Mexico, Peru, and Venezuela, among other Latin American countries. For example, in Guatemala a fund was created in 1996 to promote telecommunications development in rural and low-income urban areas. The fund is endowed with

70 percent of the proceeds from auctions of the radio spectrum and will be used to grant subsidies through open competitive bidding, starting with six rural areas in the first quarter of 1998. Peru has established the Fund for Investment in Telecommunications (Fondo de Inversión en Telecomunicaciones — FITEL) to extend service to 3,700 villages with fewer than 500 inhabitants.[14] A first project, providing service in 193 villages with a total of about 150,000 inhabitants in four Northwestern provinces was awarded in 1998 (Bonifaz 1998). FITEL is funded by a 1-percent levy on telecommunications revenues[15] and administered by OSIPTEL, the telecommunications regulatory agency. In Venezuela, legislation that would create a fund managed by CONATEL, the regulatory commission, to support a program of universal service throughout the country is being considered (*El Nacional*, 1998).

REGULATORY INSTRUMENTS

The main instruments available to Latin American regulators to implement sector policies are licensing, price controls, interconnection contracts, and allocation of scarce technical resources. Among scarce resources, the radio spectrum and the numbering system are the most critical.

Licensing

In countries where a modern telecommunications legal framework and an established regulatory capacity were lacking at the time of privatization, as in Argentina, Mexico, and Venezuela, the burden of defining the terms of business and rules of the game fell mainly on contracts and licenses. This was essential for reducing investor risk by limiting the opportunity for discretionary government or regulatory intervention, especially in the years immediately following privatization. The contracts and licenses spelled out in considerable detail the rights and obligations of the operators, including growth and coverage targets, pricing rules, and relationships among companies and between companies and the government. In Argentina, for example, the key binding instruments were the tender documents setting out the terms and conditions for the sale of controlling interests in each of the two regional monopolies that succeeded ENTel; contracts for sale of those companies; and the operating licenses granted to each company as well as to the monopoly international services operator and a competitive value-added services operator, both jointly owned by the two regional companies. Whereas the government's sector policy could be changed at any time, these binding instruments gave legal force to the principles of sector reform.

In Latin America, the most common instrument to license private telecommunications operators has been the concession contract between the state and the operating company. Concessions specify rights granted by the state to a company for a given number of years in return for the company's undertaking specific obligations on behalf of the state. When the concession expires, the obligations return to the state.[16] Concessions have been used for the privatization of basic telephone operations as well as for other public services, such as cellular mobile. Concessions are often privately negotiated, they may be confidential, and they typically contain important regulatory provisions. In Venezuela, for example, the concession contract governed the newly privatized CANTV for an initial duration of 30 years, including exclusive provision of basic telephone services and networks for nine years; it established a system of price-cap tariff regulation to encourage and reward efficiency; and it set forth specific requirements for service quality improvement, including dial tone, call completion, operator response time, fault repair time, waiting time for customers to obtain new telephone connections, and customer satisfaction (Pisciotta 1994).

In a competitive environment, however, entering individual concession contracts with each and every operating company places an excessive burden on the authorities and also implies the authority's discretion to grant concessions case by case. A simplified licensing regime designed so that most activities do not need individual authorization is increasingly preferred.[17] In Mexico, for example, the telecommunications law of 1995 established three types of authorizations: 1) concessions for public telecommunications networks and for use of the radio spectrum, awarded through competitive tenders and auctions respectively; 2) permits (mainly for private networks), granted as the applicant meets certain predetermined objective criteria; and 3) simple registration without prior approval for value-added services. Nicaragua's telecommunications law of 1995 established two types of authorizations, and Colombia's 1994 law of public residential services sought to remove technical distinctions between concessions and licenses (Pisciotta 1996). The simplest and most liberal licensing regime in place in Latin America is El Salvador's, where operators only need to notify the regulator for recording in a public register and use of radio frequencies is granted through auctions when demand exceeds supply or by simple authorization otherwise.

Tariffs

Prices are the single most important determinant of the commercial viability of a telecommunications business. Historically, tariffs have been controlled by Latin American authorities for all telecommunications services, using rate-of-return, price-cap, or benchmarking mechanisms.

Before privatization, rate-of-return price regulation was customary in Latin America. Under monopoly conditions, price regulation looked mainly at the aggregate revenues from all services and aimed at ensuring a reasonable return on investment. The price structure, or the relationships among prices for individual services or classes of customers, followed such political objectives as keeping low fixed charges for residential customers and avoiding increases in tariff elements that were included in the retail price index used to adjust public-sector salaries. This resulted in tariffs that bore no resemblance to the cost structure, typically very low monthly rental and local call charges but excessive long-distance and international call charges. Most countries faced privatization in this condition.

Price-cap regulation has been the dominant mode of price control of the privatized monopolies, such as those in Argentina and Mexico. Increases in the price of a weighted basket of services are limited to the increase in general price levels (measured, for example, by the consumer price index) minus a productivity gain factor. Although this mechanism in principle is easier to implement and monitor than rate-of-return regulation, in practice, determining compliance with the rules agreed upon has led to considerable disagreement between regulators and operators.

Benchmark price regulation has been used in a few instances. In Chile, the telecommunications law specified how the operators would determine tariffs with reference to a hypothetical efficient company using the best available combination of technologies and management practices. The law prescribes that these prices should be revised only every five years by the operators and that revisions must be proposed to SUBTEL for approval in consultation with the Ministry of Economy.

Although currently most Latin American countries have some form of price control in place, as countries move toward more competitive market structures, some (for example, Chile, Colombia, El Salvador, and Panama) are tending to let the operators establish prices freely except where they have dominant market power. While in all cases the regulatory authority and line ministry tend to share the responsibility for determining the regulated prices, who decides on the existence of market power varies among countries. For example, in Chile it is the antitrust authority, but in Peru and Colombia it is the telecommunications regulator.

Interconnection

Interconnection is the main constraint on developing effective competition. Interconnection comprises the commercial and technical arrangements under which one operator connects its equipment, networks, services, or customers to those of another operator. It is through interconnection that new entrants reach and are reached by the incumbent's customers. Also, the terms of interconnection largely determine the incentives for new entrants as well as incumbents to develop their networks and make them available in commercial terms to each other, thereby influencing the capital requirements of new entrants as well as the economic efficiency of the country's telecommunications system overall (Tyler 1995).[18]

The main issue of interconnection is pricing, mainly traffic-related payments but also one-time network interconnect costs. A key factor in applying interconnect pricing methods is whether the regulator imposes accounting rules, accounting separation among services provided by each company, or structural separation such as requiring dominant companies to establish separate subsidiaries for competitive services (for example, cellular) to make the internal transfer prices easier to monitor and to compare with prices for similar interconnection to competitors. Structural separation was, for example, the solution in Chile when CTC, the dominant local telephone company, after protracted regulatory proceedings that reached the Supreme Court, was allowed to build and operate its own long-distance and international facilities but only as a separate subsidiary. An alternative approach is to use benchmarks or best-practice prices from other markets, which will be discussed later in this chapter.

A related problem is recovering the cost of universal service obligations — that is, the cost of meeting service objectives required by the government that the companies by themselves would not provide. In a competitive environment, most or all operators are expected to contribute toward these costs. In Peru, for example, the telecommunications development fund FITEL is financed by a levy on the revenues of all operators. In the transition from monopoly to competition, some countries have achieved this by keeping the obligation with the incumbent but requiring competitors to make payments added to the interconnection charges. This has been the case in Mexico.

Interconnection also raises technical issues, in terms of the number and location of network points where interconnection is provided by the incumbent; the capacity and quality of circuits made available; how promptly interconnection is completed following application; and processes to be followed to apply, agree, record, and, if necessary, complain to the regulator.

Increasingly, interconnection agreements are contracts between the interconnecting parties, negotiated freely among them, with the regulator intervening only if agreement is not reached in a reasonable time. In practice, however, it has been found that the regulator needs to issue guidelines for interconnection and, thus, provide indications of how the issues would be dealt with if they were to come to him. This became necessary in Mexico soon after the market for long-distance services was opened in 1996. There is also a trend toward requiring the incumbent to publish a standard interconnection offering that applies unless the parties agree differently, requiring all interconnection contracts to be published or disclosed to the regulator and allowing the regulator to repeal an interconnection contract if it is not in compliance with regulations or guidelines.

Spectrum, Numbering, and Rights of Way

The radio spectrum is a natural resource that is available in limited supply but is not depleted by use. The rules for allocating this scarce resource among competing demands has profound economic implications. Increasingly, radio technologies are the basis for new service offerings (for example, cellular mobile) and for cost-effective alternatives to construction of conventional networks (for example, wireless local loop instead of copper cable distribution).

In Latin America, radio frequencies traditionally have been broadly allocated to classes of service and then within these classes allocated to individual applicants on a first-come, first-served basis subject to detailed technical requirements — for example, those related to the need to avoid interference among users. This method of allocation, coupled with low or no license or user fees, resulted in generally inefficient use of the spectrum.

As demand has increased, and especially as competition is increasingly based on radio technologies, ways are being tried to improve spectrum utilization. One approach has been to use market mechanisms to allocate radio frequencies to individual operators. Following the U.S. experience, Mexico has been implementing a program of spectrum auctions for a wide range of fixed and mobile applications in private and public networks since 1997. Guatemala plans to auction parts of the spectrum and use 70 percent of the proceeds to finance rural service development. In El Salvador, there are essentially no regulatory barriers to entry, but access to scarce resources, such as the radio spectrum, will be auctioned.

Auctions, however, are not permitted under some countries' laws and, furthermore, have drawbacks of their own.[19] In Chile, the PCS licenses were awarded to the bidders who committed to roll out service the fastest.

Another technical resource constraint on emerging competition is access to numbering blocks. The numbering plan traditionally was an internal decision of the monopolist, but as more operators came into play and required numbers for their customers and services, the responsibility for allocating numbering blocks and developing the numbering system to meet growing demands has moved to the regulatory authority. In practice, one way to achieve this has been by asking the dominant operator to propose a numbering plan, subject it to public review and comment by all interested parties, and finally have it approved by the regulator.

Rights of way is also becoming an important resource with economic value as competition develops. The trend is to require the incumbent to share existing rights of way with new operators on the basis of reasonable compensation for the incremental costs incurred. More interestingly, rights of way obtained for other activities are being used to develop telecommunications networks. For example, Metrogas, a company in Chile that is building a large network in metropolitan Santiago to distribute natural gas, recently available from Argentina through a new trans-Andean pipeline, is considering options for laying fiber-optic cables along the gas lines in partnership with foreign or local telecommunications companies to compete in local telephone, television, data, and multimedia services. The distinction between exploiting a right of way, as in the case of Metrogas, and becoming an alternative infrastructure provider, as in the cases of Argentina's gas and Brazil's power companies, discussed earlier, is tenuous but may result in different licensing requirements.

DEVELOPMENT OF REGULATORY INSTITUTIONS

The transition from a state monopoly to a private-led competitive market structure cannot be achieved without regulation. In part, this reflects the fact that even if all regulatory barriers to entry are abolished, competition will not ensue overnight. It is also necessary to provide a counterbalance to the dominant operator in order to protect the interests of new entrants and of customers.

Latin American countries faced privatization with little or no regulatory experience or institutional capacity. The governments had major stakes in successful and timely privatization but would get little mileage out of reorganizing or creating yet another public sector agency. The financial advisors sought to keep the transactions simple, complete them promptly, and maximize the sale price to which their remuneration was geared. The new owners sought stability mainly by writing initial regulatory decisions into the licenses and contracts of sale rather than having issues related to those decisions left to the discretion of a new agency without a track record. And the users, for whose benefit the reforms were being undertaken, were not organized and had no effective means for being heard. So, despite the intellectual appeal of early development of regulatory institutions, the initial privatizations generally moved ahead much faster than regulatory capacity.

Since then, progress has been accelerating but unevenly. As the number of players has increased and dominant operators have come under public scrutiny, a constituency for regulation has developed, and the governments have taken initiatives to improve and strengthen regulatory institutions.

Table 7 summarizes the main features of the telecommunications regulatory arrangements in all Latin American countries that have restructured the telecommunications sector or plan to do so soon. In the remainder of this section, we review how development and performance of the institutions described earlier have been affected by the institutions' legal bases; the timing of regulation relative to the initiation of privatization and the introduction of competition; basic setup, in terms of constitution, composition, and financing of regulation; distance between the regulators and the operators and the government; the main functions of regulation; and the relationship between telecommunications regulation and the competition authority.

Specific Legislative Basis

Regulatory institutions founded in telecommunications law did better than those established only on the basis of government decrees. Argentina illustrates how wrong things can go and for how long when the regulator lacks a firm legal foundation. CNT's chairman and directors, appointed by the executive power, took office at about the time privatization was completed, but government decisions on organization, staffing, salaries, budget, and accounting were delayed.[20] Urgent regulatory matters, such as establishing guidelines for interconnection pricing, specifying the information that CNT would require to monitor compliance with the licenses, and establishing regulations for competitive services stood unattended for a long time. The inability of CNT to discharge its functions effectively became clear when the government's new economic stabilization plan violated the terms of the concessions regarding tariff indexing. The problem was eventually sorted out between the operating companies and the government, not through CNT. Thereafter, CNT became "...the most unstable and politically dependent regulatory agency of Argentina; it was neither captured by dominant firms nor remained an independent body, and was in fact taken as a direct branch of the executive power" (Artana, Navajas, and Ubizondo 1998). Following periods of alternating good and poor performance and successive government interventions that replaced the authorities and changed the administrative status of CNT, the agency was merged in 1997 with the National Broadcasting Commission and the Posts and Telegraphs Commission into a single Comisión Nacional de Comunicaciones (CNC). It is too soon to assess whether CNC will do any better than its predecessor, but none of the deficiencies underlying the institutional setup in Argentina have been resolved.

In Venezuela, lack of a foundation in law, combined with economic and political problems that afflicted the country soon after privatization, resulted in CONATEL's having only limited influence on sector development. The situation has not improved much to this day.

Table 7.
Basic Features of Regulatory Institutions

ARGENTINA

Agency name
Comisión Nacional de Comunicaciones (CNC).
Also covers posts, broadcasting.

Created by Decrees (1990, 1996).

Constitution and composition Decentralized agency of Ministry of Communications. Authority vested in Board of Directors with 8 members, one of which is its President.

Financing Levy of 0.5% on billings by all operators.
Also fees for use of radio spectrum.

Agency head is
Appointed by the Minister of Communications.
Removed by the Minister of Communications.
Reports to the Minister of Communications.

Regulatory decisions can be overturned by the Minister of Communications.

Main functions of the regulatory agency
Assists Ministry in preparing technical plans, regulations; monitors compliance with laws, regulations, licenses, Ministry decisions; enforces competition rules.

Main related regulatory functions of other agencies
Ministry proposes policies to Cabinet, issues regulations, technical plans; grants operating, radio licenses; approves tariffs; establishes numbering plan, national frequencies table; supervises CNC.

Website: www.cnc.gov.ar

BOLIVIA

Agency name
Superintendencia de Telecomunicaciones. A branch of Sistema de Regulación Sectorial (SIRESE), which also regulates electricity, transport, water, and hydrocarbons.

Created by Law (1994).

Constitution and composition
SIRESE is a government agency under Minister of Economic Development with technical, administrative, and financial autonomy. General Superintendent heads SIRESE. Superintendents for each sector.

Financing Fees paid by licensees, up to 1% of gross operating revenues or market value of equipment.

Agency head is
Appointed by President of the Republic, from shortlist proposed by Senate with 2/3 vote.
Removed by judiciary or incompatibility specified in law.
Reports to Minister of Economic Development, General Controller.

Regulatory decisions can be overturned by
Telecommunications Superintendent, General Superintendent, Supreme Court.

Table 7.—*continued*

Main functions of the regulatory agency
Grants concessions, licenses, registrations; manages radio spectrum and numbering system; promotes competition, enforces rules; sets maximum tariffs for dominant operators; resolves conflicts, complaints.

Main related regulatory functions of other agencies
Ministry decides what services have unrestricted entry, establishes national frequencies plan.
Fondo Nacional de Desarrollo finances rural telecommunications.

Website: supertel@ceibo.entelnet.bo

BRAZIL

Agency name
Agência Nacional de Telecomunicações (ANATEL).

Created by Law (1997).

Constitution and composition
Public-sector agency with administrative and financial autonomy. Board of Directors with 5 members, one of which is Chairman and Executive President. Also Consultative Council of 12 members.

Financing
Fees paid to Fundo de Fiscalização das Telecomunicações (FISTEL).

Agency head is
Appointed by President of the Republic subject to Senate ratification.
Removed by Judiciary or disciplinary administrative process.
Reports to Government and Congress through Minister of Communication.

Regulatory decisions can be overturned by Courts of justice.
Main functions of the regulatory agency
Grants operating and radio concessions and licenses.
Manages radio spectrum and numbering plan.
Determines tariffs of public services.
Resolves conflicts among operators. Acts in defense of users.

Main related regulatory functions of other agencies
Minister approves licensing and universal service plans.
FISTEL also contributes to universal service, Treasury.

Website: www.anatel.gov.br

CHILE

Agency name Subsecretaría de Telecomunicaciones (SUBTEL).

Created by Decree (1978), Law (1982).

Constitution and composition Branch of the Ministry of Transport and Communication.
Regulatory authority is the Undersecretary for Telecommunications.

Financing Government budget.

Agency head is
Appointed by and removed by the President of the Republic.
Reports to the Minister and to Congress on specific matters.

Regulatory decisions can be overturned by the Minister, Antimonopolies Commission, courts of justice.

Table 7.—*continued*

Main functions of the regulatory agency
Regulates tariffs of dominant operators.
Issues licenses for private networks.
Manages and licenses radio spectrum.
Establishes, monitors technical standards.
Applies sanctions.

Main related regulatory functions of other agencies
President of the Republic issues concessions for public telecommunications operators, radio, and TV broadcasting.
Ministry of Economy plays role in setting tariffs.
Antimonopolies Commission determines who has market power and other matters of competition law.

Website: www.mtt.cl

COLOMBIA

Agency name Comisión de Regulación de Telecomunicaciones (CRT).

Created by Law (1994).

Constitution and composition Special unit with administrative and financial autonomy, under Ministry of Communications. Commission of six members: Minister (Chair), Director of Planning Dept., and three sector experts.

Financing Fees paid by regulated companies.

Agency head is
Appointed by the President of the Republic, who also appoints members.
Removed by the President of the Republic.
Reports to the Minister and to Congress and Controller on certain matters.

Regulatory decisions can be overturned by
No one, but CRT regulates on behalf of the President who can take over.

Main functions of the regulatory agency
Promotes competition.
Determines who has market power, then regulates tariffs and interconnection charges.
Establishes rules for issuing licenses for long distance and international.
Establishes quality standards.
Resolves disputes.

Main related regulatory functions of other agencies
Minister of Communications grants licenses for long-distance services and radio licenses.
Superintendent of Residential Public Services monitors service quality, investigates complaints, and imposes sanctions.

Website: www.crt.gov.co

ECUADOR

Agency name Consejo Nacional de Telecomunicaciones (CONATEL).

Created by Law (1995).

Constitution and composition Council representing President of the Republic (chair), armed forces, development agency, business associations, sector workers, Secretaría Nacional de Comunicaciones, and Superintendencia de Telecomunicaciones.

Table 7.—*continued*

Financing Fees for use of radio spectrum.

Agency head is
> Appointed by the President of the Republic, who also appoints head of Secretaría.
> Congress appoints head of Superintendencia.
> Removed by no explicit provisions.
> Reports to the Secretaría reports to CONATEL. No other explicit provisions.

Regulatory decisions can be overturned by no explicit provisions.

Main functions of the regulatory agency
> Establishes sector policies, regulations, competition rules.
> Approves plans for sector development and spectrum use.
> Establishes licensing terms, issues competitive tenders, approves major licenses before their issue.
> Approves tariffs and terms of interconnection.
> Approves budgets of Secretaría and Superintendencia.

Main related regulatory functions of other agencies
> Secretaría Nacional de Telecomunicaciones implements CONATEL decisions, e.g., issues licenses, approves interconnection contracts. Also is CONATEL's technical secretariat.
> Superintendencia de Telecomunicaciones monitors spectrum, compliance with licenses, tariffs, competition rules, technical standards. Resolves conflicts among operators and with users.

EL SALVADOR

Agency name Superintendencia General de Electricidad y Telecomunicaciones (SIGET).

Created by Law (1996, modified 1997).

Constitution and composition Public-sector agency with legal and financial autonomy.
> Board of three members and two alternates. One member is Chairman of the Board and Superintendent. One member and one alternate, each selected by unions and Supreme Court.

Financing Public sector budget approved by Congress. Fees for spectrum use.
> Other fees.

Agency head is
> Appointed by the President of the Republic, who also appoints members and alternates.
> Removed by the President of the Republic but only for reasons defined in law.
> Reports to Congress, through Minister of Economy. Supervised by Tribunal de Cuentas.

Regulatory decisions can be overturned by
> Appealing Superintendent's rulings to Board regarding legality and process.

Main functions of the regulatory agency
> Grants concessions and authorizations.
> Approves maximum tariffs in absence of competition.
> Manages radio spectrum and numbering plan.
> Issues and monitors compliance with technical standards, norms.
> Enforces competition.

Main related regulatory functions of other agencies
> SIGET liaises with Government through Minister of Economy.
> Competition authority, once in place, deals with anticompetitive behavior.

Website: www.siget.gob.sv

Table 7.—*continued*

GUATEMALA

Agency name Superintendencia de Telecomunicaciones (SIT).

Created by Law (1996).

Constitution and composition Specialized agency of the Ministry of Communications, Transport, and Public Works, with functional and financial autonomy. Head is Superintendent.

Financing Income from investing 30% of proceeds from radio spectrum auctions up to US$40m. Fees.

Agency head is
Appointed by, removed by, and reports to the Minister of Communications, Transport, and Public Works.

Regulatory decisions can be overturned by the Minister, courts of justice.

Main functions of the regulatory agency
Enforces compliance with laws, regulations, and open entry regime.
Resolves conflicts on access to bottleneck facilities.
Manages radio spectrum, numbering system, register.
Approves international accounting rates.

Website: www.sit.gob.gt

HONDURAS

Agency name Comisión Nacional de Telecomunicaciones (CONATEL).

Created by Law (1995).

Constitution and composition Decentralized agency of the Ministry of Communications, Public Works, and Transport, with technical and administrative independence. Three members (one of which is President) and two alternates.

Financing Government budget. Regulatory fees paid by operators (0.5% of revenues) go to Treasury.

Agency head is
Appointed by the President of the Republic, who also appoints members.
Removed by the President of the Republic.
Reports to the Minister on medium-term plans. Budget submitted to Congress through Minister.

Main functions of the regulatory agency
Grants concessions, licenses, and authorizations.
Regulates tariffs in the absence of competition.
Ensures interconnection and resolves disputes.
Manages radio spectrum and numbering plan.
Establishes technical standards.

Main related regulatory functions of other agencies
Government decides annual budget.
Constitution requires Congress's approval of concessions lasting beyond current government.

Website: www.conatel.hn

Table 7.—*continued*

MEXICO

Agency name Comisión Federal de Telecomunicaciones (COFETEL).

Created by Law (1995), decree (1996).

Constitution and composition Decentralized public sector agency under the Ministry of Transport and Communications. Commission of three members and a President.

Financing Fees and government budget.

Agency head is
Appointed by the President of the Republic, who also appoints members.
Removed by and reports to the President of the Republic.

Regulatory decisions can be overturned by the Minister.

Main functions of the regulatory agency
Promotes competition.
Issues opinions on granting, modifying, and terminating licenses.
Processes tenders for satellite orbital positions.
Manages the radio spectrum.
Records tariffs and monitors interconnection.

Main related regulatory functions of other agencies
Ministry of Transport and Communications grants, modifies, revokes licenses; publishes plan for the use of radio spectrum; imposes penalties.

Website: www.cft.gob.mx

NICARAGUA

Agency name Instituto Nicaragüense de Telecomunicaciones y Correos (TELCOR).
Also regulates posts, technical aspects of radio and TV.

Created by Law (1995).

Constitution and composition Decentralized public sector agency with administrative and financial autonomy. Head is Director with rank of Minister.

Financing Concession and radio spectrum user fees. Penalties.

Agency head is
Appointed by, removed by, and reports to the President of the Republic.

Regulatory decisions can be overturned by the Contraloría General de la República or courts of justice on matters specified in law.

Main functions of the regulatory agency
Issues concessions and other operator and radio licenses.
Decides on regulated tariffs.
Manages radio spectrum.
Sets interconnection norms and decides when parties cannot agree.
Sets technical standards, including for radio and TV.

PANAMA

Agency name Ente Regulador de los Servicios Públicos. Also regulates electricity, water and sewers.

Created by Law (1966).

Table 7.—*continued*

Constitution and composition Public sector agency with legal, administrative, and financial autonomy. Authority is Board of 3 directors, one of which is elected chairman.

Financing Regulatory fee paid by licensees, up to 1% of turnover. Fees for inspection and other services.

Agency head is
Appointed by the Executive branch of Government.
Removed by the Supreme Court.
Reports to the Contraloría General de la República, President of the Republic, Congress.

Regulatory decisions can be overturned by the Supreme Court.

Main functions of the regulatory agency
Grants licenses not subject to exclusivity or entry restrictions.
Sets tariffs in situations of cross-subsidies or limited competition.
Manages the radio spectrum and numbering plan.
Establishes technical and interconnection standards.
Resolves disagreements among operators, user complaints.

Main related regulatory functions of other agencies
Cabinet issues concessions with exclusivity or entry restrictions.
Ministry of Planning and Economy participates in decisions on universal service.
Ministry of Government and Justice manages spectrum for other uses.

Website: www.sinfo.net/ente_reg

PERU

Agency name Organismo Supervisor de la Inversión Privada en Telecomunicaciones (OSIPTEL). Multisectoral.

Created by Law (1993).

Constitution and compostion Public sector agency with legal, administrative, and financial autonomy, ascribed to the Cabinet. Council of 6 directors, of which 2 represent the operators.

Financing Fees paid by the regulated companies, not more than 0.5% of revenues.

Agency head is
Appointed and removed by the Cabinet, which also appoints members.
Reports to the Cabinet and to Congress, Controller, others on certain matters.

Regulatory decisions can be overturned by the Courts of justice, within the limits prescribed in the Telecommunications Law.

Main functions of the regulatory agency
Establishes competition rules and assesses market power.
Sets tariffs and interconnection charges when needed, approves interconnection contracts.
Sets rules for processing customer complaints, resolves in second instance.
Resolves disputes.

Main related regulatory functions of other agencies
Ministry of Transport issues regulations and concessions for public telecommunications services, manages radio spectrum.

Website: www.osiptel.gob.pe

Table 7.—continued

VENEZUELA

Agency name Comisión Nacional de Telecomunicaciones (CONATEL).

Created by Decree (1991).

Constitution and composition Agency within Ministry of Transport and Communications. Head is Director General.

Financing Fees, penalties, and government budget.

Agency head is
Appointed by, removed by, and reports to the Minister of Transport and Communications.

Regulatory decisions can be overturned by the Minister of Transport and Communications and courts of justice.

Main functions of the regulatory agency
Grants concessions, licenses, and authorizations.
Establishes pricing rules.
Manages the radio spectrum.
Safeguards interest of users.
Applies sanctions.

Main related regulatory functions of other agencies
Minister of Transport and Communications approves tariffs. Also approves radio broadcasting concessions before CONATEL can issue them.

Website: www.conatel.gov.ve

Source: Author's compilation.

Timing Relative to Privatization and Competition

Regulation developed more effectively when the institutions were started well before privatization. While this should not be used as an excuse to delay reforms, the lesson is that establishing and nourishing regulatory institutions should be slated as early as possible within the reform agenda. The fact that Chile had reorganized the line ministry to focus on policy and regulatory matters five years before privatization explains why the government should receive some of the credit for the success and sustainability of reforms (Melo 1997). In particular, during the last years of state ownership of the operating companies, SUBTEL developed experience in dealing with information asymmetry, as discussed further below, a major impediment for effective regulation of private companies. In Mexico, SCT was reorganized before privatization to deal only with policy and regulation. SCT played a key role in preparing for privatization, including writing up the new TELMEX concession. Subsequently, SCT was largely responsible for drafting the 1995 law and related regulations. From 1996, COFETEL, the more autonomous successor to SCT, played a major role in issuing implementing regulations and guidelines to open the market to competition as envisaged in the 1995 law, process license applications, carry out radio spectrum auctions, and resolve conflicts between new entrants and the incumbent, especially regarding interconnection. In Peru, OSIPTEL was started up on time to participate in the last months of the privatization process. It reviewed and commented on the draft concession contracts and, at the request of the bidders, was a party to these contracts, thereby adding some comfort regarding stability of the regulatory rules. Following privatization, implementing regulations that deal with OSIPTEL's operation and procedures, supervision of the operating companies, interconnection, conflict resolution, and other matters were issued.

Competition has enhanced initial development of regulatory capacity. In Mexico, for example, the regulatory authority intervened in the late 1980s in a dispute about interconnection charges levied by TELMEX (then still a parastatal company) on independent cellular operators. The authority was able to leverage its own limited regulatory experience and information by drawing on the independent cellular companies and foreign partners as well as by attracting academic and professional attention to the subject. More recently, in 1996, the regulator played off major new entrants against TELMEX in examining interconnection costs for long-distance services and was able to rule in favor of charges supporting new entry. [21]

Basic Setup

The regulatory agencies vary considerably in terms of constitution, composition, and financing. There is, however, no consensus, in Latin America or elsewhere, on whether any one configuration is clearly superior. Moreover, the preferred arrangements are closely tied to the prevailing institutional situation in each country, including how government administration is organized and managed. [22]

Constitution. Brazil's ANATEL is an agency with administrative and financial autonomy; it is headed by a chairman appointed by the President of the Republic, subject to ratification by the Senate. ANATEL is part of the public sector, yet not part of the government. At the other end of the range, Chile's SUBTEL is a branch of the line ministry, and the regulatory authority is an undersecretary. Currently, the government is considering reorganizing the supervisory functions of SUBTEL as a more autonomous Superintendencia, along the lines of the well-established regulator of banks and corporations or creating a multi-sectoral public service regulatory authority. Bolivia is somewhere in between. SIRESE is a government agency under the Ministry of Economic Development but has technical, financial, and administrative autonomy. The superintendent general is appointed by the president of the republic from a short list proposed by the Senate with two-thirds of the vote.

Composition. In several countries, the regulatory authority is an individual, but the trend is to vest it in some form of commission or council. In Bolivia, Chile, Guatemala, Mexico, Nicaragua, and Venezuela, regulatory authority rests with the head of the agency alone. In Brazil, it is vested in a Board of Directors with five members assisted by a Consultative Council of 12 members. In Peru, the authority lies in a Council of six members, and in El Salvador there is a board of three members and two alternates. Variants of commissions are also found in Argentina, Honduras, and Panama.

Financial and Administrative Autonomy. The trend is for the cost of regulation to be met from revenues generated by the regulated activities, but some agencies are still dependent on government budgets. The regulatory agencies in

Argentina, Bolivia, Panama, and Peru, for example, get up to 1.0 percent of the companies' turnover directly from the operating companies and charge fees for inspection and other regulatory services. Most agencies collect some fees for use of the radio spectrum. This is the main source of financing for the regulator in Ecuador. The regulatory agency in Guatemala is financed mainly by the income from investing 30 percent of the proceeds from radio spectrum auctions, up to a total investment of about US$40 million. In some countries, the regulator is financed by a combination of government budget and self-generated revenues. For example, in Mexico and Venezuela the regulatory agency gets revenue from the budget as well as from fees and penalties it collects from the operating companies. In Honduras, 0.5 percent of revenues paid by the operating companies are collected by the regulator but passed on to the Treasury and partly returned to the regulator through the government budget. In addition, the regulator collects and keeps radio spectrum fees as well as charges for regulatory services. In Chile, the regulatory agency's expenses are met entirely from the government budget.

The effectiveness of a regulator in carrying out its functions is affected by the extent to which it has financial and administrative autonomy. Peru's OSIPTEL, for example, outsources complex technical tasks, especially when it needs the backing of a reputable name and when there are large volumes of legal work. Also, a call center is being set up to outsource the handling of customer inquiries and complaints.[23] In contrast, like other parts of Chile's government administration, SUBTEL is unable to pay market-based remunerations to specialists and lacks flexibility to hire consultants and other services.[24]

Distance from Operators

There is widespread consensus that regulatory responsibilities must be fully separated from operational responsibilities. In Latin America, this has been formally achieved in most cases, even where the state maintains an ownership interest in operating companies. In Mexico, for example, in preparation for the privatization of TELMEX, all operating functions of the line ministry, mainly for domestic satellites and a national microwave network, were transferred to a new public-sector enterprise, with the ministry retaining only policy and regulatory functions. In Chile, at the time of privatization, regulation was exercised by the line ministry while state ownership was held by the State Development Corporation (Corporación de Fomento de la Producción), under the Ministry of Economy. In Peru, in contrast, two of the six members of the Council that oversee the regulatory agency represent operating companies.

Operators, of course, participate in the regulatory process on all matters that affect them. The rights of operators and other parties to access information, to be represented in the regulatory processes, and to appeal regulatory decisions to the regulator, the courts of justice, and other authorities are explicitly prescribed in telecommunications laws and regulations or embedded in general administrative practices. Transparency of these processes, however, and access to information on ongoing processes are not always assured.

Despite formal separation of regulatory and operational responsibilities, operators use other means to influence the regulator. For example, there is a major asymmetry in the access to information required for effective regulation. Most of the data and much of the expertise reside in the regulated companies. This is only partially offset by concessions and laws that explicitly establish the operators' obligation to provide information requested by the regulator. The resources of the regulator are generally no match for those of the regulated companies.

Regulatory capture by the operators is also a permanent risk. Regulated companies seek alliances with the regulator in pursuit of their interests, and, in turn, the regulator makes use of competing operators to leverage its regulatory strength. In this delicate balance, it can be argued that even the best performing regulatory agencies in Latin America have at one time or another been too close to one side of the debate.

Operators routinely use the appeals process to block regulatory decisions. In Chile, for example, SUBTEL rulings are suspended while appeals are considered by the courts. There is a growing sense that regulation by the judiciary is going too far. Hefty deposits have recently been introduced to discourage frivolous complaints. As the courts develop jurisprudence on regulation, the process may improve. Eventually, however, a reform of the Constitution may be needed to strike a better balance among powers. In Argentina, a coalition of operating companies and interest groups used the public hearings process to delay decisions on tariff rebalancing.

The political system provides avenues for operators to exercise pressure on the regulator. In Mexico, for example, TELMEX reportedly sought to politicize the regulatory process as a means to preserve its dominant market position and delay change.[25] In Chile, high-ranking retirees from the armed forces were given management and board positions in the privatized operating companies, reportedly as a means to maintain good relations with the military government. Political party leaders and former ministers have subsequently been retained as advisors or board members under the civilian governments (Leiva and Radrigán 1998). In Argentina and Brazil, in early 1998, decisions to keep dominant companies from bidding for new wireless licenses were overturned under pressure from the incumbents, illustrating the influence of sheer political and economic power (*El Diario* 1998a).

Distance from Government

In order to be effective and credible, a regulatory authority needs to find a compromise distance with respect to government. It is frequently stated that the regulator must be "independent" from the government, but this is an oversimplification. The regulator, rather, must be a) sufficiently distant from government to be reasonably free from arbitrary intervention in regulatory decisions and from day-to-day political interference, yet b) close enough to be responsive to government policy, to contribute to the formulation of government policy, and to count on effective support for enforcing regulatory decisions.

From this viewpoint, Latin American regulatory institutions have stayed too close to the government end of the distance range. Although several of the regulators have considerable administrative and financial autonomy and have been able for some time to perform their regulatory functions quite free of government intervention, this is not assured. In Peru, for example, OSIPTEL's decisions can only be revoked by the courts of justice and even then only within the limits prescribed by the telecommunications law. This seeming strength, however, is not guaranteed because the chairman and members of the Council are appointed and removed by the President of the Council of Ministers, which is the cabinet of the executive branch of government. There are no assurances that regulatory decisions will not be overturned by the government by way of replacing the regulatory authority, nor that regulatory policy will remain stable from one government to another. While this facilitates a good fit between policy and regulation, it is unlikely to allow the regulator to disagree on major matters with the government in turn. This may have been what happened in Mexico in early 1998, when key regulatory decisions related to an escalating conflict between new entrants and the incumbent began to be announced by the Subsecretario de Telecomunicaciones (the line ministry), not the president of COFETEL (the regulatory authority). Shortly after, the latter resigned, and the undersecretary was appointed to succeed him.

When the regulatory debate becomes political, which is often the case in Latin America on major issues, the level of government to which the regulator reports matters. In Chile, for example, although SUBTEL is an integral part of the government, it tends to lose out to other government branches with more political clout, such as the Ministry of Finance. This contrasts with Peru, where OSIPTEL reports directly to the prime minister (President of the Council of Ministers) and tends to fare considerably better, sometimes prevailing over the line ministry.

Distance from government by itself, however, does not determine success. In Argentina, CNT was initially created with administrative and financial autonomy and accountable only to the president of the republic; yet, in practice it has not done well. CNT was initially ascribed to the Ministry of Public Works, which was soon merged with the Ministry of Economy, in which CNT came under the authority of a ministry undersecretary. Start-up problems were followed by successive episodes of sweeping government intervention, all of which severely undermined CNT's effectiveness and continuity (Hill and Abdala 1993). At the other extreme, in Chile, regulation is an integral part of government administration; yet, it is credited to have been a key factor of spectacularly successful reform. Only now is the government considering separating some regulatory functions to a semi-autonomous agency along the lines of the banking regulator. The examples, regarding distance from government, of Bolivia, Colombia, Mexico, and Peru fall somewhere in between and have worked reasonably well at least for some time.

Regulatory Functions

Major regulatory functions in Latin America are often divided between the regulator and the government (see Table 7), which compounds the already excessively close links between both. For example, in Colombia the rules and terms for licensing long-distance operators are established by CRT, the regulator, but the licenses are issued by the line ministry. In Chile, licenses for private networks and for the use of radio frequencies are granted by SUBTEL, which is a branch of the line ministry, but concessions for public telecommunications operators as well as for radio and television broadcasting are issued by the president of the republic. In Mexico, COFETEL designs and carries out auctions of the radio spectrum, but authority for the spectrum rests with the line ministry.

A further complication arises from the diffuse boundary between government policy and regulation, and in some countries, the conflicts of interest between them have been noted in practice. Mexico seems to be moving toward transferring the policy function to the regulator, leaving in the line ministry only responsibility for extending service to rural areas. In Chile, the supervisory functions of the regulator are being separated out to an autonomous agency, while the line ministry, currently the regulator, would remain responsible for policy and licensing.

Sometimes the legislative branch of government also shares some regulatory functions. In Honduras, the Constitution requires that all contracts between the state and private parties lasting beyond the current government must be approved by the Congress. All telecommunications concessions are subject to congressional approval.

More technical matters, in contrast, are typically left to the regulator. Responsibility for setting and monitoring compliance with technical standards (service quality or operator performance, for example) is generally with the regulator. Some standards are written into concessions and contracts, such as sale of former state enterprises, but, generally, the regulator has considerable latitude to set and change technical norms and parameters.

Role of the Competition Authority

Antitrust law and enforcement, where available, has played an important role supplementing the regulator in promoting and safeguarding competition. In Chile, for instance, responsibility for competition is with the Comisión Antimonopolios, a quasi-judicial antitrust agency. It is this commission that determines the presence of market power; the telecommunications regulator then controls prices in consultation with the Ministry of Economy. This relationship has generally worked well, with both agencies recognizing their limited expertise in the field of the other and decisions by the antitrust agency tending to stand more firmly than SUBTEL's to challenges by the operators. A migration from telecommunications-specific to generic competition regulation is beginning as SUBTEL consults with the antitrust agency on matters that may have an impact on competition and as the antitrust agency takes some initiatives in telecommunications. In early 1998, the antitrust agency took the lead to suspend the introduction of calling part pays (CPP) for cellular service by CTC, the largest local telephone operator and owner of a cellular subsidiary, while the agency determined whether CPP discriminated against other cellular operators.

Where effective antitrust law and enforcement are not in place, the responsibility for dealing with issues of competition is with the regulator. In Bolivia, El Salvador, Peru, and Colombia, for example, the telecommunications regulators have explicit mandates to promote competition, determine who has market power, and/or control tariffs and interconnection as needed to protect emerging competitors and the customers. In Argentina, the Commission for Defense of Competition (Comisión de Defensa de la Competencia) being established may have the opportunity to move quickly into the void created by the underperforming telecommunications regulatory authority.

REGULATORY ISSUES

The main issues facing Latin American regulators in the wake of privatization have related to the key constraints on new entry and effective competition: market structure, rebalancing and regulating tariffs, and interconnection.

Market Structure

Issues of market structure and ownership have loomed large in Latin American regulation after privatization. In Chile, for example, it took more than five years before SUBTEL, the antitrust agency, and the Supreme Court decided that CTC (the main local telephone company) could develop its own long-distance and international network, but only as a separate subsidiary, and that ENTEL (the main long-distance and international carrier) could develop local networks. Determining that Telefónica Internacional could not be both the main shareholder of CTC and maintain a significant minority interest in ENTEL took about as long (Melo 1997). In Peru, in contrast, a consortium led by Telefónica Internacional was the winning bidder for both CPT, the monopoly operator in the metropolitan capital area, and ENTEL, the monopoly operator for the rest of the country, and the authorities had little difficulty subsequently authorizing the merger of both companies. Arguably, consolidation into a single monopoly operator in Peru reduced the threat of competition at the end of the exclusivity period, which is what Argentina had sought by dividing ENTel into two regional companies sold to different owners; however, decisions near the end of the exclusivity may end up being more important in this regard. An open consultative process carried out in Peru in 1998 led to a Peruvian model for opening up all services to competition in 1999, when the exclusive rights of Telefónica would expire. In the process, Telefónica agreed to end its exclusive rights one year earlier, in August 1998.

In Argentina, plans were announced in March 1998 to open telecommunications to competition gradually, by issuing only one new license for basic services in each of the two regions as soon as the exclusivity of the incumbents expires. Further, reversing an earlier decision, the regulator would allow existing mobile operators to bid for new PCS licenses. Both announcements were challenged in court by prospective bidders seeking more open and competitive markets. An attempt by the regulator to circumvent one lawsuit by changing the PCS bidding rules resulted in a court decision to block the PCS auctions indefinitely (Mercosur Telecommunications Update 1998a). In contrast, in Mexico, where TELMEX was privatized as an undivided monopoly, as exclusivity approached its end in 1996, the regulator chose not to limit the number of new entrants rather than license only a few

(Wellenius and Staple 1996). Major new local and global players quickly entered all market segments.

Tariff Rebalancing

Where rebalancing tariffs toward costs has been left to the privatized companies, it has caused endless trouble. In Argentina, rebalancing was especially difficult in the wake of privatization that took place without a firm legal base, with rules set in decrees subject to constant change resulting in shifts in market power, with a weak regulatory agency largely taken over by the government, with political support mobilized by the dominant operators, and without transparency and definition of the regulatory process. A further complicating factor was the change in government economic policy shortly after privatization, which pegged the local currency to the U.S. dollar and resulted in public expectation of constant prices in nominal terms. It became increasingly difficult to overcome the pressure of an urban coalition that sought to keep in place massive cross-subsidy of fixed charges and local call charges, at the expense of long-distance charges up to 50 times cost and international call charges among the highest in the world. More than six years of unabated conflict involving regulated companies, the regulator, government, opposition political parties, consumer associations, nonbinding public hearings, and many judicial courts eventually went all the way up to the Supreme Court. The lesson was learned: privatizations in the gas and electricity sector were preceded by rate rebalancing (Artana, Navajas, and Ubizondo 1998).

In Brazil, in contrast, rate rebalancing was carried out before the 1998 privatization of the successors of the state telecommunications. This proved to be politically possible and acceptable to the public as part of the economic stabilization program of the government, which, although painful to most population groups, had succeeded in controlling the runaway inflation that had plagued the country for many years. Coupled to virtually simultaneous licensing of second operators in basic and mobile services, rebalancing before privatization is likely to result in a greatly reduced need for regulatory intervention on tariffs.

The experience of Mexico lies somewhere in between. Before privatization, large special taxes on telecommunications bills were converted to tariff elements, resulting in a major rebalancing in the direction of costs. Completing the task, however, was left to TELMEX under a timetable linked to its exclusivity period but did not progress at the scheduled pace. Toward the end of the exclusive period, TELMEX argued, unsuccessfully, that it needed more time before it could face competition.

Tariff Regulation

Price regulation has also been a most contentious subject. At one extreme, in Chile prices tend to be controlled only where there is not enough competition. For example, the antitrust agency ruled in 1998 that in the following five-year tariff revision effective in 1999, the only long-distance price that would need to be regulated was interconnection — in contrast with 24 tariff elements of local service where competition is less advanced (Estrategia 1998a). Shortly after, however, the antitrust agency set a floor under the second-largest long-distance operator's end-user tariffs in response to a complaint by the largest carrier against predatory pricing (Estrategia 1998b).

At the other end of the range, in Colombia, much of CRT's work has focused on establishing and implementing rules for determining end-user prices. The matter is complicated by the fact that in Colombia there are six levels of residential telephone rates, geared to property value as proxy for household income, with substantial cross-subsidies among them that must be maintained under increasing competition.

Underlying the tariff problems, as well as interconnection pricing, discussed below, is the question of separating accounts by types of service. Dealing with this is proving to be as protracted in Latin America as it has been elsewhere. In Peru, OSIPTEL was involved for over three years in developing and implementing cost accounting rules, for example, to determine interconnection prices and the net cost of universal service.

Interconnection

Once the major initial issues of market structure and tariff rebalancing were taken care of, interconnection became, and is likely to remain for the foreseeable future, the single largest area of regulatory action toward developing an effectively competitive telecommunications market.

Interconnection issues have been especially visible in Mexico as new operators, in partnership with large U.S. carriers, challenged TELMEX, which was itself allied with a major U.S. carrier, from late 1996. Specific issues included the number of network points where TELMEX should interconnect new entrants, how much these should pay for TELMEX to set up the interconnection, how much should be paid for new long-distance operators to access TELMEX's end customers and contribute toward universal service, and how the spoils of international traffic revenue should be divided. The dispute became very acrimonious. At one point, TELMEX disconnected for several hours some of the main commercial customers of Avantel, a unit of MCI that provides long-distance service mainly to business customers in competition with TELMEX (AP World News 1998). According to the *Wall Street Journal*, "... MCI threatened to halt a $900 million investment program in ... [Avantel], claiming regulators were allowing TELMEX to compete in a way that prevented the unit ... from attracting customers and making a reasonable return on its investment. MCI's position was echoed ... by AT&T, which also operates a long-distance company in Mexico . . . ." By mid-1998, the companies and the regulator agreed on a package that would reduce the interconnection charges paid by the new carriers, end a 58-percent surcharge on interconnection to help meet TELMEX's alleged cost of extending service to rural areas, and pay $422 million for improvements in TELMEX's networks to enable it to carry the new companies' traffic. The issue of international settlements remained pending (*Wall Street Journal*, July 16, 1998).

SOME CHALLENGES

There is ample space for improving the design and implementation of telecommunications regulation throughout Latin America. The key challenges that merit consideration include matching institutional design to regulatory life cycle, avoiding the cost-accounting bottleneck, enhancing regional cooperation and global networking, and strengthening consumer organizations.

Matching Institutional Design to Regulatory Life Cycle

Few question the need for some regulation to enable and promote the transition from state monopolies to private-led, competitive market structures. Yet, at the onset of privatization, the countries have little or no experience in regulating telecommunications or any other public service. A succession of regulatory issues arise, peak, and decline to a low simmer. In the early years of implementing telecommunications reform, the regulatory problems primarily have to do with the relationships between operators and government, particularly in licensing. Soon after, major issues arise regarding the relationships among operators, increasingly in interconnection. Eventually, regulation focuses on the relationships between operators and consumers in disputes over such issues as prices and service complaints.

In the long run, as telecommunications and the economies overall become more market driven, and as competition law and its enforcement establish track records, telecommunications regulatory issues will increasingly become generic competition issues.[26] Moreover, as a common floor of regulatory principles and practices is adopted through participation in regional and world trade agreements, telecommunications regulation to some extent is already now migrating from domestic to international arenas.

The aggregate demand for the services of a telecommunications-specific national regulatory institution is, therefore, likely first to rise sharply, plateau, and, over the years, decline or perhaps disappear. It is not clear how long this life cycle of regulation will take in Latin American countries. Nor is it clear whether in the end there will be a residue of narrow, highly technical regulatory problems unique to telecommunications, for example, radio spectrum management, that require continued attention, nor whether these specialized matters require a dedicated institution or can be handled, in what may be the default policy choice, by the industry itself.

The regulatory institutional designs being pursued in Latin America have a very different life cycle from the one outlined above.[27] Capacity building being a slow process, these institutions are having difficulty responding well to the initial surge of regulatory problems. Expertise will, at best, build up to full capacity over the years, by which time the related issues will have peaked and started to decline. A permanent capacity in a wide range of regulatory areas may finally be in place in the medium or long term, by which time it may no longer be really needed.

Alternative, minimalist, transitory designs could offer better matches to the regulatory life cycle. A small agency, with credible decision-making capacity and generic processing capacity, could have the means to outsource most routine tasks and all expert tasks when needed; it could be set up quickly, could deal effectively with problems as they come, and could extinguish itself unless specific action were taken to renew its lease on life.[28]

The outsourcing of regulatory functions is not unheard of. In Argentina, for example, a contractor monitors the radio spectrum on behalf of CNC; the contractor's remuneration is a designated share of the annual fees charged by CNC to the holders of radio licenses.[29] Other functions that would be suitable for outsourcing include monitoring compliance with operating licenses and interconnection, which might, for example, be contracted out to external audit firms, handling customer complaints, and resolving conflicts.

Conflicts increasingly arise between incumbent operators and new entrants, between new entrants themselves, and between operators and regulators. The regulatory, administrative, and judicial resources to deal with these disputes may be overwhelmed quickly by the complexity and rising number of cases. A broad range of dispute-avoidance and resolution methods, including negotiation, mediation, and arbitration, may be applied in the telecommunications sector. This holds some promise in terms of reducing delays and costs to all parties.[30]

Avoiding the Cost-Accounting Bottleneck

In a perfectly competitive environment, prices would be determined through the market and would tend to reflect costs. Most telecommunications markets, however, are quite imperfect; in particular, when operators with dominant market power are present, some degree of regulatory intervention is required to ensure that cost-based prices are fair, transparent, and non-discriminatory.

The problem, of course, is getting to know the costs, at a growing level of disaggregation, as markets become more complex and players seek to buy and sell to each other and to customers a wide range of networks and services configured in an almost endless variety of packages. The regulatory tool of choice for getting to know the costs is cost accounting. However, experience in mature economies with ample experience in cost accounting suggests that costs thus determined are critically dependent on complex accounting rules that are specific to telecommunications and must be set by the regulator. The process can also be exceedingly costly and time consuming both to regulators and regulated companies.

Price regulation, moreover, has a life cycle akin to that of regulation in general, as discussed above. In the beginning, it is necessary; as time passes, it need only focus on selected elements; and eventually all that may be required is investigating complaints of anticompetitive behavior. So the same concern arises: Should a newly established Latin American regulator aim at setting up a system of cost accounting specifically for purposes of regulation, at considerable cost to the regulator and the operators alike, which will take at least several years before it is in working order yet be of value for purposes of regulation that will decline as competition builds up?

A more expedient and lower-cost alternative approach may be to use as reference the prices, for end users as well as interconnection, observed in other markets where it is believed that competition, cost-based regulation, or a combination of both result in prices that are reasonably close to costs. Although reference prices vary among markets, they tend to cluster fairly tightly around averages (see, for example, Table 5), which then can be used as starting points for price setting. Use of benchmark or best-practice prices may be regarded as a temporary solution to guide price regulation while satisfactory cost-accounting systems are being put in place.[31] They also may be regarded as a sufficient solution while effective competition develops, thereby reducing the need for price regulation and moving the pricing issue from the domain of sector-specific regulation to generic competition law enforcement.

Some observers argue that costs are quite different in an emerging economy from those in a mature market and that international benchmarks are not, therefore, relevant. The counter-argument is that the main elements of cost, namely, equipment price and cost of capital, are determined in global markets, not locally. Also, it may be possible to adjust the benchmarks, for example, to reflect lower salaries and wages, which would be partly offset, however, by lower labor productivity. Another reservation is that reference prices from competitive markets signal where regulated prices are likely to end, but imposing those prices from the start may seriously impair the financial viability of ongoing operations. Perhaps a timetable to get from here to there could ease the transition yet focus immediate attention on costs. Benchmarks also may need revisiting from time to time, as the reference markets themselves change.

Enhancing Regional Cooperation and Global Networking

Several initiatives are underway to facilitate informal cooperation among Latin American regulators. Latin American Regulators of Telecommunications (Reguladores Latinoamericanos de Telecomunicaciones — REGULATEL), for example, is an informal association being developed by regulators from Argentina, Brazil, Colombia, Costa Rica, Guatemala, and Mexico, with participation also by Bolivia, El Salvador, Nicaragua, Paraguay, and Venezuela. This type of association is quite sensible, given that countries have much in common regarding the nature of the regulatory issues; the options to deal with them; and their legal, administrative, and cultural environments. Sharing experiences and best practices is likely to increase regulatory efficiency overall. Moreover, a more homogeneous regulatory environment may develop in the region, which should facilitate cross-border services and investment.

The best practice envelope, however, is being pushed at a global rather than a regional level. The 'Chilean model' for funding rural telecommunications access, using market mechanisms to determine and allocate subsidies, is being considered, for example, in Mexico, Latvia, and Zimbabwe. The regulatory debate and norms emerging in the European Union on universal service and interconnection are of direct interest to Latin America.[32]

A case may be made, therefore, for complementing regional initiatives with broader global consultative networks through which individual regulators may seek occasional advice and comment. One resource for coordination is a website and on-line service (www.regulate.org) established in late 1998 by the Regulatory Colloquium under the auspices of the International Telecommunication Union (ITU) and financed by the World Bank's *info*Dev fund. The website has become a global medium for informal exchange among regulators, professionals, and academics, as well as a system for mentoring and referral to assist with specific consultations.

Strengthening Consumer Organizations

The primary objective of sector reforms is service — more, better, new, and less expensive services. Yet, users, the intended beneficiaries, have minimal participation in the design and implementation of sector reforms. Large users, such as banks, multinationals, and government departments, have political clout and are sometimes consulted, but consumers, mostly small businesses and households, are seldom organized and have neither the opportunity nor the resources to be heard.

Elements of a consumer organization movement are now in place that may pick up speed. For example, in 1998, in Santiago, Chile, Consumers International, an umbrella organization based in the United Kingdom for national consumer organizations worldwide, held a conference on restructuring and regulating electricity, telecommunications, and water supply services in Latin America. Individual country studies from Chile, Brazil, Colombia, Mexico, and Peru provided the analytic foundation for the discussions.[33]

Consumer organizations can augment their influence through flexible alliances — for example, with regulators or competing operators — and make their voices heard through regulatory processes, the media, and political channels, among other means. Regulatory authorities often have an explicit mandate to protect the interest of consumers. (See Table 7 for a list of the main functions of the regulators.) In practice, handling customer complaints can become the most resource-consuming task. Some Latin American regulators have already made progress in dealing with consumer affairs.

CONCLUDING REMARKS

This chapter has examined the Latin American experience with telecommunications regulation following privatization. The general conclusion is that although regulation has been rather imperfect, in general, ways have been found around the shortfalls, so that there is significant sector progress, including a considerable flow of capital to the sector from domestic and international sources. There is, however, ample scope for improvement, especially as the initial gains from reform have been achieved and further progress poses more stringent demands on regulation. Also, countries now beginning to institute reform in Latin America and other regions might learn from the experience in this region as much as from best practices in other parts of the world.

As one looks forward, however, the future looks quite different from the past. Traditionally distinct activities, among them, telecommunications, media, computing, publishing, and libraries, are increasingly overlapping. This is partly a matter of technological convergence; for example, digital signal processing and storage, once mainly the domain of computers, have now become the basic technology of telecommunications. It is also a matter of market convergence. Cable television companies are starting to provide residential telephone service and telephone companies get into the cable television business. Power and gas companies are providing alternative telecommunications infrastructures. Government services, education, and health support are increasingly accessed through the Internet. Electronic commerce is starting to change in fundamental ways how people participate in the economy.[34] For example, the whole *Encyclopaedia Britannica*, that bastion of quality reference books, is now available on two CD ROMs for US$100 and can run on a computer costing less than US$1,500, together less expensive than the encyclopedia volumes alone five years ago; a frequently updated version, with links to thousands of other on-line reference sources, is available for $20 per month through the Internet, which can be accessed today through telephone lines and tomorrow through television cables.[35]

Are the regulatory frameworks designed for telecommunications as a stand-alone industry suitable to handle the increasing challenges and opportunities arising from convergence? Probably not. Can countries that have largely completed sector reforms just keep doing business as usual? That would probably be unwise. Should countries only now approaching telecommunications reforms do it differently? Almost certainly yes, but how is not at all clear.

Part of the problem comes from the continued fast pace of change and the utter impossibility of predicting the future. Perhaps, then, telecommunications regulatory policy and institutions should get smaller, more flexible, and nimbler. Set a few broad rules to guide decisions rather than prescribe in detail. End traditional distinctions by types of technology and lines of business. Move faster from sector-specific to general competition law and enforcement. Increase reliance on consumer advocacy groups. And empower end users to take effective control of content and privacy.

Notes

1. Besides telecommunications, an information infrastructure comprises strategic information systems (typically about a dozen) that underpin the economy of a country at large; the policy and regulatory framework conditioning the use of information; and human resources to run these systems and, even more, to generate and use information for productive purposes. (See Talero and Gaudet 1996.)

2. See James Bond, 1997.

3. In this chapter, Latin America means South America (except Guyana, Suriname, and French Guiana), Panama, Central America (except Belize), and Mexico.

4. Here, the date of privatization indicates when a controlling interest was transferred to private owners. Reforms in Latin America followed quickly after major structural changes in mature economies — for example, the privatization of British Telecom and the breakup of ATT, both in 1984. Several Latin American markets were opened to new entry and competition well before most of those in Europe were.

5. Empresa Nacional de Telecomunicaciones (TELECOM), the state company, operates all international and most domestic long-distance service, about 15 relatively small local telephone companies, and rural services.

6. In Ecuador, the tender was suspended in late 1997, when only one investor remained interested. Attempts to restart the process in 1998 were unsuccessful. In Guatemala, the sole bid received in 1997 was deemed too low. In Nicaragua, the tender was suspended in 1994 in the face of legislative uncertainty and investor loss of interest as elections drew near. In Colombia, an initiative to privatize TELECOM, the largest state operator, was brought to a standstill by organized labor. An initiative in 1996 to corporatize the telecommunications arm of Instituto Costarricense de Electricidad and open it up to joint ventures with the private sector ran into political opposition and was abandoned. It had been preceded a few years earlier by a failed attempt at privatization without public debate. In Uruguay, an initiative to restructure the sector, including privatizing the Administración Nacional de Telecomunicaciones (ANTEL) was put to national referendum in 1992 and defeated.

7. A good telecommunications law provides the skeleton of the regulatory framework for reform. Investors, operators, and customers will be reassured by such legal structures. The benefits of amending or replacing an existing law, however, must be weighed against the political cost of controversial legislation and the potential for delays. A law with a narrower objective, for example, establishing a regulatory authority, sometimes may suffice. The broader legal framework for business in general, such as dealing with private property rights, foreign investment, and taxation, is an essential component of the environment for telecommunications reform but is not covered in this chapter.

8. Björn Wellenius, 1997b. Several factors other than competition, including broader economic reform variables, may explain at least some of the differences in telecommunications growth. A more rigorous analysis, however, is not available.

9. While maturing telephone service continues to give access to customers, overall returns on investment are increasingly dependent on new services.

10. Calculated by the author from 1996 data. The number of Internet users per PC is likely to have grown very fast in more recent years.

11. Nonetheless, by mid-1998, telephone tariffs in Argentina were still way off those in competitive markets. For example, full-rate domestic calls over about 150 km cost US$0.47 per minute. International calls to the United States, Europe, and Japan cost US$0.94, $1.59, and $3.89 per minute, respectively. Compare these rates with figures in Table 5 for competitive markets two years earlier.

12. See *La Nación*, 1998.

13. This is a free subscription service (www.export99.base.org) provided by the Kenan Institute of Private Enterprise, the University of North Carolina, and the U.S. and North Carolina Departments of Commerce.

14. This is in addition to about 1,500 villages with more than 500 inhabitants that the main operating company has committed to connect as part of its service obligations.

15. FITEL revenues from this source in 1998 are about $450,000 per month.

16. Concessions originate in continental European administrative law and reflect the concept that telecommunications services were regarded as a public service — that is, services the state had an obligation and right to provide.

17. In this arrangement, licenses are viewed as grants by the government to private companies authorizing them to provide services that have some elements of public interest. There is no general expectation that at the end of the license period the state takes over these activities.

18. The executive summary is available in the ITU's website (www.itu.int). The full report is available at the Regulatory Colloquium's website (www.regulated.org) as well as in hard copy from the ITU.

19. As illustrated, for example, by the inability of successful bidders for class C licenses in the United States to pay the large fees bid and raise capital for the necessary investments, resulting in pressures on the FCC to waive fees or attempt to repossess and reallocate the unused spectrum. A similar problem occurred in India following high bids for second fixed telephone licenses.

20. For example, fees paid by the regulated companies started to accumulate in CNT's bank account, but CNT lacked authority to draw on these funds.

21. In the first case, TELMEX demanded that the independent cellular operators pay US$0.17 per minute to terminate local calls, whereas the independents argued for $0.03. The ruling was $0.05 per minute. In the second case, TELMEX wanted the new long-distance carriers to pay $0.16 per minute for local termination, whereas the carriers wanted to pay $0.01 per minute. The ruling was $0.05 per minute, closer to international benchmarks than either party had argued.

22. Reflecting this, the World Trade Organization (WTO) reference paper on regulation, although specific on other aspects of regulation, leaves it to individual countries to decide on these features of the regulatory agency. The same is true in the case of the European Union directives, a good example of a regional framework that has considered the relative merits of a wide range of options exhaustively. (See World Trade Organization 1996.)

23. Some tasks, however, are difficult to outsource because specialist contractors are unwilling to come into conflict with the dominant operating company.

24. Outsourcing of expertise is further complicated by the fact that most local consultants do business with the operating companies. Shortage of internal and local consultant expertise becomes critical, for example, every five years, when regulated tariffs are revised.

25. Observations by a conference participant.

26. Superficial observation of the regulatory authorities of Chile, Mexico, United Kingdom, Australia, and New Zealand appears to validate this model, but closer analysis would help. The Mexican experience illustrates vividly the shift from first to second types of regulatory issues and how second-stage issues can escalate, in fact, to international attention. In Chile, decisions by the telecommunications regulator on priority issues are increasingly drawing on opinions or rulings solicited from the antimonopoly commission. An earlier undersecretary considered moving on to focus mostly on consumer protection. In the United Kingdom, the possibility of closing down OFTEL has been mooted. In Australia, the bulk of telecommunications regulatory responsibilities has been transferred to the competition authority. In New Zealand, a specialized telecommunications regulatory agency has not been established, leaving it all to the government authorities responsible for commerce in general.

27. For a traditional view of what a regulatory agency in an emerging economy could be, see Nulty and Schneidewinde 1989. A minimal solution is shown to have a professional staff of about 50.

28. Such a minimalist solution would not be very different from those in use and contemplated for such other sectors as power, water, and air transport. Accordingly, a minimalist solution may appeal to analysts who advocate multi-sectoral regulatory agencies.

29. The CNC charges annual radio license fees. A private contractor monitors radio spectrum use. The contractor keeps about one-third of the fees during the first three years and about one-half thereafter, the balance going to CNC to help finance other regulatory expenses.

30. An example of work in progress in this field is the draft white paper and memorandum of understanding prepared for the International Forum on Dispute Resolution in Telecommunications by Richard Hill (rhill@batnet.com) and John Watkins.

31. That is being done to some extent in the European Union.

32. Note, however, major differences among countries within the common European framework. In learning from this experience, Latin American regulators may wish to focus on countries that are simplifying regulatory arrangements (for example, ending access deficit charges in the United Kingdom) or keeping the regulatory apparatus and market intervention at a bare minimum (as is the case in Sweden).

33. The country volumes, as well as a summary paper, can be obtained from the Consumer and Public Service Program in Latin America (Programa Consumidores y Servicios Públicos en America Latina — CONSUPAL). Consumers International, Regional Office for Latin America, Las Hortensias 2371, Providencia, Santiago de Chile.

34. For a particularly illuminating view of electronic commerce, the ways it may affect universal service objectives and the means to achieve them, and other issues of telecommunications regulation, see Townsend 1998.

35. The figures are typical for residential use in the United States. Prices in Latin America may be higher.

References

AP World News. 1998. "Mexico's TELMEX flexes muscle, disconnects Avantel." July 16 (via NewsEdge Corporation).

Artana, Daniel, Fernando Navajas, and Santiago Ubizondo. 1998. "Contractual Adaptation in Regulated Utilities: A Few Observations From Argentina." Fundación de Investigaciones Económicas Latinoamericanas, Buenos Aires, Argentina (April).

Bond, James. 1997. *The Drivers of the Information Revolution – Cost of Computing, Power, and Convergence.* Viewpoint Note No. 118 (July). Washington, D.C.: The World Bank. (Later published as an article in *Public Policy for the Private Sector.* No. 11, September 1997. Washington, D.C.: The World Bank.)

Bonifaz, Luis. 1998. "Aporte al Desarrollo Rural: El Rol de FITEL." May 19 (mimeo).

El Cronista. 1998a. June 8.

El Cronista. 1998b. "Metrored Wants to Offer Basic Telephone Services." SABI (via NewsEdge Corporation, July 16). July 13.

El Diario. 1998a. "Argentina mantiene plazos en licitación del PCS." Santiago, Chile. April 14.

El Diario. 1998b. "CTC to Develop Rural Highway." Santiago, Chile. SABI (via NewsEdge Corporation). June 25: 17.

Estrategia. 1998a. "Cerca de 24 servicios de telefonía básica estarán sujetos a fijación." Santiago, Chile. April 24.

Estrategia. 1998b. "Resolutiva puso un límite a CTC Mundo para bajar tarifas de larga distancia." Santiago, Chile. August 24.

Hill, Alice, and Manuel Angel Abdala. 1993. *Regulations, Institutions, and Commitment: Privatization and Regulation in the Argentine Telecommunications Sector.* Policy Research Paper No. 1216. Washington, D.C.: The World Bank (November).

Ibarra-Yunez, Alejandro. 1996. "Telecommunications Trends in Mexico and Latin America." Conference on Liberalizing Telecommunications Services, Institute for International Economics, Washington, D.C. January 29.

International Telecommunication Union. 1997. *Yearbook of Statistics. Telecommunications Services. Chronological Time Series 1986-1005.* Geneva.

International Telecommunication Union. 1998a. *General Trends in Telecommunications Reform.* Vol. 1. Geneva.

International Telecommunication Union. 1998b. *World Telecommunications Development Report.* Geneva.

Jornal do Brasil. 1998. "Eletrobras offers optical fiber network." July 14.

Leiva, Fernando, and Juan Radrigán. 1998. *Chile: Los consumidores y los servicios públicos domiciliarios: ¿entre la espada y la pared?* Santiago, Chile: Consumers International.

Mairal, Héctor A. 1994. "The Argentine Telephone Privatization." In *Implementing Reforms in the Telecommunications Sector: Lessons from Experience.* Björn Wellenius and Peter A. Stern. Washington, D.C.: The World Bank. 161-176.

Melo, José Ricardo. 1994. "Liberalization and Privatization in Chile." In *Implementing Reforms in the Telecommunications Sector: Lessons from Experience*. Björn Wellenius and Peter A. Stern. Washington, D.C.: The World Bank. 145-159.

Melo, José Ricardo. 1997. "Regulación de Telecomunicaciones en Chile, Perú, y Venezuela." Instituto Latinoamericano y del Caribe de Planificación Económica y Social (January 9). Santiago, Chile.

Mercosur Telecommunications Update. 1998a. September1. www.export99.base.org.

Mercosur Telecommunications Update. 1998b. "In Pursuit of an Integrated Telecommunications Market: Brazil and Argentina Begin Discussions." October 1. www.export99.base.org.

Mercosur Telecommunications Update. 1998c. "Argentina's TGS May Lease Excess Telecommunications Capacity." October 2. www.export99.base.org.

La Nación. 1998. "Trends in the PCS Market in Latin America." SABI (via NewsEdge Corporation). October 3. Buenos Aires, Argentina.

El Nacional. 1998. "Government Secures Universal Telecoms Access." SABI (via NewsEdge Corporation). August 27.

Nulty, Timothy E., and Eric Schneidewinde. 1989. "Regulatory Policy for Telecommunications." In *Restructuring and Managing the Telecommunications Sector*. Björn Wellenius, Peter A. Stern, Timothy E. Nulty, and Richard D. Stern. Washington, D.C.: World Bank.

Petrazzini, Ben A., and Theodore H. Clark. 1996. "Costs and Benefits of Telecommunications Liberalization in Developing Countries." Institute for International Economics Conference on Liberalizing Telecommunications Services: Washington, D.C. January 29.

Pisciotta, Aileen A. 1994. "Privatization of Telecommunications: The Case of Venezuela." In *Implementing Reforms in the Telecommunications Sector: Lessons from Experience*. Björn Wellenius and Peter A. Stern. Washington, D.C.: The World Bank. 185-194.

Pisciotta, Aileen A.. 1996. "The Development of Telecom Regulatory Structures and Procedures in Latin America." World Bank Workshop on Infrastructure Regulation in Latin America, Washington, D.C. April.

Talero, Eduardo, and Philippe Gaudet. 1996. *Harnessing Information for Development — A Proposal for a World Bank Group Strategy*. World Bank Discussion Paper (March). Washington, D.C.

Townsend, David N. 1998. *Regulatory Issues for Electronic Commerce*. Briefing report for the Eighth ITU Regulatory Colloquium (December), available on the Regulatory Colloquium Website (www.regulate.org) and in hard copy from the International Telecommunication Union, Geneva.

Tyler, Michael. 1995. *Interconnection: Regulatory Issues*. Briefing report of the Fourth Regulatory Colloquium, (April). International Telecommunication Union, Geneva.

Tyler, Michael, and Carol Joy. 1997. *Telecommunications in the New Era: Competing in the Single Market*. London, England: Multiplex Press.

Wall Street Journal. 1996. "Calling Someone in Argentina? Dial M for Monopoly." August 16. A11.

Wall Street Journal. 1998. "U.S., Mexico Closing In on a Telephone Deal." July 16.

Wellenius, Björn. 1997a. *Extending Telecommunications to Rural Areas — The Chilean Experience*. Viewpoint Note No. 105 (February). Washington, D.C: The World Bank.

Wellenius, Björn. 1997b. *Telecommunications Reform — How to Succeed*. Viewpoint Note No. 130 (October). Washington, D.C.: The World Bank.

Wellenius, Björn, and Gregory Staple. 1996. *Beyond Privatization: The Second Wave of Telecommunications Reforms in Mexico*. World Bank Discussion Paper No 341. Washington, D.C.: The World Bank.

Björn Wellenius, Peter A. Stern, Timothy E. Nulty, and Richard D. Stern. 1989. *Restructuring and Managing the Telecommunications Sector*. Washington, D.C.: World Bank.

Wellenius, Björn, and Peter A. Stern. 1994. *Implementing Reforms in the Telecommunications Sector: Lessons from Experience*. Washington, D.C.: The World Bank.

World Trade Organization. 1996. *Agreement on Basic Telecommunications*. Reference Paper. Informal Doc. No. 2104. April 24.

CHAPTER 9

Banking Structures, Market Forces, and Economic Freedom: Lessons from Argentina and Mexico

WILLIAM C. GRUBEN

INTRODUCTION

The successes or failures of monetary reforms in Latin America have depended on the financial liberalizations that accompanied them and on the peculiarities of attendant financial regulations and provisions. The absence of guarantees to make bank depositors whole in a financial crisis, for example, signifies a far different distribution of likely patterns of monetary growth and exchange-rate pressures than a more conciliatory treatment of depositors would have, even if a government is otherwise committed to tight money and a strong currency. More generally, the economic literature on monetary arrangements has shown increased appreciation of the links between official protections for financial institutions in newly liberalized environments, subsequent banking crises, and exchange-rate volatility (McKinnon and Pill 1996; Kaminsky and Reinhart 1996; Krugman 1998). Of particular concern in this context are how problems of moral hazard metastasize under financial liberalization when government guarantees abridge market discipline.

This chapter presents evidence of the linkages between market discipline, government guarantees, bank performance, and exchange-rate stability in Argentina and Mexico. Mexico's encompassing deposit guarantee program, detailed later in the chapter, was associated with risky lending behavior beginning during the 1991-1992 bank privatizations. The resulting bank crisis offered irresolvable tensions in the goals of monetary policy — preserving the banks versus preserving the exchange rate — and motivated a policy trajectory that had much to do with the subsequent exchange-rate crisis.

In contrast, Argentina offered little succor for risky banks or their depositors and weathered the exchange-rate crises in the middle 1990s and again in the late 1990s.[1] Argentina's limitations on deposit guarantees and its restrictions of bank

---

William C. Gruben is Director of the Center for Latin American Economics at the Federal Reserve Bank of Dallas. Opinions expressed in this document do not necessarily reflect the opinions of the Federal Reserve Bank of Dallas or the Federal Reserve System.

bailouts were followed by a wave of bank privatizations in which, in contrast to the Mexican experience, the typical bank did not engage in behavior that would be measurable as risky ex ante. When the Asian financial crises of fall 1997 stampeded investors out of even non-Asian emerging markets, including Argentina's, a governmental conflict between supporting the banks and supporting the currency did not materialize.

While no single empirical model yields all of the foregoing narrative, the results of various researchers' econometric models of the Argentine and Mexican financial systems offer varieties of evidence that have not until now found their way into the literature. The consideration of these several models together allows them to yield conclusions collectively that their constructors could not and did not draw piecewise.

Of particular interest in this context is that, in the wake of Argentina's success in weathering the "tequila crisis," Latin American banking policymakers moved further toward facilitating market-based regulation and discipline — not only in Mexico and in Brazil but even in Argentina. The move is important not only because of Argentina's positive outcomes but also because of the increasing evidence to suggest that many indicators typically used by regulators to assess bank health and to identify bank problems have been shown to be misleading. That is, more than in industrial countries, banking crises in Latin America can surprise regulators rather than be anticipated and, therefore, planned for. Moving to policies that offer market-based signals so as to create market-based discipline may be considered particularly crucial in societies in which indicators that are not market based do not function well.

TWO CONTRASTING EPISODES IN THE TEQUILA CRISIS

Even though this chapter will address bank regulation events leading up to the tequila crisis of 1994-1995, it is useful to begin by recounting some econometric results of a study of the crisis itself. The Mexican exchange-rate and financial crisis triggered a rush of capital out of other Latin American countries, as well as out of the Philippines and Poland. Those problems, known as the "tequila effect," contributed to banking problems that developed beyond Mexico, including in Argentina. However, the impact of the tequila effect on bank depositor behavior differed by country. These differences in depositor behavior are not only important in and of themselves; they also tell us much about what precipitated the tequila crisis.

In an econometric model of the relation between deposit inflows or outflows and bank asset quality, Robert Moore (1997) found that depositor behavior in Argentina during the tequila crisis was consistent with what policymakers had hoped minimal deposit insurance would do for market discipline. That is, during the crisis of 1995, deposit flows were significantly and inversely related to bank asset quality. The worse a bank was, the more likely depositors were to pull their money out of it. Bankers who had anticipated such disciplining behavior may be seen as less likely to take risks with depositor money.

In the Mexican case, in which depositor losses were covered by a very generous deposit insurance program, Moore (1997) found that depositors were indifferent to the asset quality of a bank. Specifically, during the 1995 crisis, deposit flows were not significantly related either positively or negatively to bank asset quality.

1991: ARGENTINA'S CURRENCY BOARD MEANS FEW OR NO DEPOSIT GUARANTEES

Having addressed a peculiarity of bank depositor behavior during the tequila crisis, I now turn to earlier events in Argentina and Mexico. These events help to explain not only the foundation of differences in Argentine and Mexican depositor behavior but also the tequila crisis itself. They also help to explain bank behavior during Argentina's recent bank privatizations. In April 1991, when Argentina adopted the Convertibility Plan, which included a monetary regime based on a fixed exchange rate with full convertibility of the peso into U.S. dollars and bimonetarism, the point was to put control of the money supply out of reach of political pressures. Any attempt to issue currency above this endogenous amount would result in a loss of reserves and a threat to the convertibility of the peso.

This monetary straitjacket, which effectively meant that Argentina's monetary policy remained in lock step with the United States' policy, was in large part fitted to avert certain political intrusions by the nation's banks (Fernandez and Schumacher 1998).[2] In the past, during economic crises, the banking system had been behind political pressures that led to inflationary behavior by the government. A combination of deposit insurance and central bank intervention had effectively guaranteed that all of a commercial bank's liabilities, however small or large, would be made whole. Banking system bailouts had in the past resulted in fiscal deficits. Since attendant economic difficulties had typically abridged the government's revenue-generating abilities, expectations were that deficits would be monetized.[3]

Starting with the onset of the Convertibility Plan, government deposit insurance was gradually eliminated. In 1991, the government of Argentina curtailed coverage of the existing insurance to $1,000, and a year later even that was removed. In 1995, a new deposit insurance program appeared. The program, which was funded in total by the banks and without government fiscal commitments, offered coverage of $10,000 to $20,000 depending on the maturity and the interest rate paid. Econometric evidence suggests that from the early stages of the program depositors tended to treat the insurance as if it did not exist (Schumacher 1997). By the time the full effect of the tequila crisis was felt, the banks had made such small contributions to the insurance fund that for practical purposes it did not exist (Schumacher 1997; Fernandez and Schumacher 1998).

The explicit purpose of the policy that removed deposit insurance in 1991 and an attendant policy that established only minimal bailout prospects was to make depositors and other bank debt holders exercise market discipline to discourage banks from risky behavior.[4] Other measures to reduce the political pressure for bailouts included high reserve requirements. The assumption was that if banks were forced to remain highly liquid, capital market volatility and large declines in asset values would less likely trigger systemic problems in banking. In another effort to impose a cushion against these same problems, Argentine regulations imposed heavier capitalization for what were perceived as riskier assets or banks.[5] Higher capitalization requirements overall were imposed to discourage risky behavior. Policymakers reasoned that by increasing the amount of shareholder wealth placed at risk, they would increase the likelihood of shareholder monitoring of bank behavior, particularly of risky behavior.

MEXICO TAKES A DIFFERENT APPROACH TO FINANCIAL LIBERALIZATION

At the same time that Argentina was liberalizing its financial system, so was Mexico. Prior to moving toward the market, Mexico suffered a classic case of financial repression.[6] In 1989, however, Mexico introduced reforms to eliminate controls on interest rates generally and to eliminate prohibitions on paying interest for traditional bank deposits and restrictions over terms upon which deposits and credit were made available; it eliminated forced loans to the public sector at below-market interest rates and eliminated governmental edicts on the industry-by-industry allocation of funds. Mexico had nationalized all but two commercial banks in 1982. During the period from June 1991 until July 1992, Mexico auctioned off to the private sector all 18 government-owned commercial banks. Despite these strong efforts to allow markets to operate, Mexico continued to provide full insurance coverage for almost all depositors under a program known as Banking Fund for Savings Protection (Fondo Bancario de Protección al Ahorro — FOBAPROA). For practical purposes, the Mexican government provided an insurance program whose protection of depositors was virtually complete.

While such coverage may have been comforting to depositors, it can weaken the competitive advantage that financially strong banks would otherwise gain from doing what made them strong. When government safety nets prevail, bank liability holders, including deposit holders, are less responsive to changes in bank risk — that is, depositors do not punish riskily managed banks by fleeing them (Moore 1997). It may be expected that banks under a system of government guarantees for depositors would be motivated, under some circumstances, to make riskier loans than banks without such supports. Some of these circumstances materialized in the early 1990s, with the privatization of the Mexican banks.

In addition to depositor guarantees, another motivation toward expansive and perhaps risky lending behavior was that Mexican banks in the wake of the financial liberalizations initiated in 1989 were awash with new liabilities. Financial liberalization in a financially repressed system like Mexico's can motivate massive shifts of assets (from other sectors or from financial institutions abroad) into the domestic financial system. This is exactly what took place in Mexico. The ratio of M2 to gross domestic product rose from 7.1 percent to 30 percent between 1988 and 1994.[7]

Accordingly, when Mexico's banks were privatized into a far freer financial market environment than the country had seen in decades, the banks did indeed commence risky behavior. Immediately after privatization, the typical Mexican commercial bank produced loans and other financial services to a point at which marginal cost exceeded marginal revenue (Gruben and McComb 1997). While such behavior could not be pursued in the long run, it is consistent in the short run with a struggle for market share — a struggle in which the Mexican banks had great motivation to engage.

Indeed, despite the obvious possibilities for bad outcomes from such market-share struggles, there is much to recommend them if an institution can survive their early stages, at least in the context of retail banking, because of the tendency toward brand loyalty in consumer finance. For example, a survey of U.S. credit card users found that consumers are prone to use — for a particularly long time or to a particularly high degree — the first card they received (*Wall Street Journal* 1996).[8] The problem under a system of deposit insurance like Mexico's is that when the risks do not pay off for the bankers they are paid for by the taxpayers. The Mexican banks' risky behavior soon had results that could be expected. Delinquent loans as a percentage of total loans moved from 3.9 percent at the end of 1991 to 5.5 percent a year later to 8.3 percent in September 1994.

Although risky bank behavior was an important factor in precipitating the tequila crisis, it was not the only one. Mexico intervened strongly in foreign exchange markets in an effort to peg its currency to the U.S. dollar, but several factors made those efforts more difficult as the decade of the 1990s ensued. Among the most important factors were highly volatile capital inflows to and outflows from Mexico and the tightening of U.S. monetary policy.

During the early 1990s, high rates of capital inflow characterized the emerging markets of Latin America in general, owing to a combination of optimistic outlooks for the region's newly liberalized economies and low U.S. interest rates. Through this mechanism, Mexico accumulated large stocks of foreign currency reserves that it could use to defend the peso in times of weakness. The capital inflows represented such a large increase in the demand for pesos that Mexico's exchange-rate pegging problem at the time involved holding the exchange rate down, not up.

During the first quarter of 1994, however, U.S. monetary policy began to tighten, raising U.S. interest rates and attracting capital back to the United States. If Mexico had not raised interest rates or pursued other efforts to make Mexico a more attractive place for investment, the result would have been diminished demand for the peso and increased pressure for devaluation. At this time in Mexico, preparations were being made for the presidential elections later that year. In March 1994, ruling Institutional Revolutionary Party (Partido Revolucionario Institucional —PRI) presidential candidate Luis Donaldo Colosio was assassinated. Foreign currency reserves fell profoundly just after the March assassination but stabilized in April. To hold foreign capital in the country and reduce pressure on the peso, Mexico raised interest rates significantly, signaling that exchange-rate preservation remained important. But U.S. interest rates were also rising, and they continued to rise throughout the year.

In the third quarter and into the early fourth quarter, Mexico relaxed its interest rate intervention somewhat, even though U.S. rates continued to move up. Moreover, during the second half of 1994, real central bank domestic credit outstanding to Mexican commercial banks remained relatively high. Mexico was compensating for declines in international reserves by increasing domestic credit, a step 180 degrees in opposition to Argentina's approach.

A nation cannot peg or fix its currency, permit international capital to come and go freely, and pursue a monetary policy independent of the nation to whom it has pegged its currency. So why would Mexico try? In a 1995 article in the *Wall Street Journal*, the governor of Mexico's central bank explained his country's divergence from the U.S. monetary policy, of continued increases in interest rates throughout the year, saying that "had domestic credit expanded less, interest rates would have soared to levels that would have caused severe economic disruptions" (Mancera 1995). The central bank governor's statement may be seen as an acknowledgment both of the difficulties in 1994 in the Mexican banking system and of the tension between avoiding such difficulties and tightening Mexican monetary policy to discourage the capital outflows that had begun to characterize the nation's international financial accounts.

A central bank can always preserve a pegged exchange rate, as Mexico's was at this time, through a sustained high interest rate or a contraction in the monetary base.[9] Interest rates insufficient to prevent declining reserves suggest that other policies — such as preserving the solvency of Mexico's banking system — were dominating the central bank's commitment to a pegged exchange rate (Garber and Svensson 1994, 29).

In late November 1994, Mexico began to suffer massive capital outflows that culminated in an official announcement on December 20 that the peso would be officially devalued from 3.47 pesos per dollar to 3.99. The announcement triggered massive capital flight and a devaluation far more profound than what the government had announced. By January 27, 1995, the exchange rate had moved to 5.75 pesos per dollar. The Mexican devaluation and financial crisis triggered a rush of capital out of other Latin American countries, as well as out of the Philippines and Poland.

ARGENTINA'S BANK PRIVATIZATION

Argentina's major efforts at bank privatization did not occur until after the tequila crisis. Despite Argentina's policy rationalizations of 1989-1992, the government's role in the banking sector was still strong. It is true that in Argentina, unlike in Mexico, financial repression is said not to have characterized financial policy; a financial liberalization effort had begun during the late 1970s (Rozenwurcel and Bleger 1998), although credit allocation was not made completely market driven at that time. By the time of the tequila crisis, interest rates had long since been largely market determined.

Despite this perceived relative liberality, the role of financial institutions was relatively small in the years preceding the Convertibility Plan, although it had increased markedly by the end of 1994. An important reason was that high inflation during the late 1980s and very early 1990s discouraged Argentines from holding Argentine money. Without much money in deposits, there was not much money to lend. An additional problem for the Argentine financial system was that, prior to the tequila crisis, publicly owned banks held almost 39 percent of total deposits and granted almost 42 percent of total loans. The politicized nature of public financial intermediation meant that these institutions were virtual storehouses for past-due loans.

In addition, despite increasing requirements for bank capitalization, scores of privately owned banks found themselves inadequately capitalized when the crisis came. If any of them doubted that the central bank would fail to rescue them, their doubts were soon allayed. As of November 1994, there were 137 private-sector banks, which accounted for 57 percent of all bank assets. In addition, there were 32 banks owned by federal, provincial, or municipal governments. By December 1995, out of the earlier total of 137 private banks, 9 had failed and more than 30 had been either acquired or merged into a single bank. Privatization had not begun until one occurred in 1993, followed by three in 1994. A new intense period of privatization did not take place until 1995 (5 privatizations) and 1996 (15 privatizations).

When the privatizations did occur in Argentina, the greater market orientation of the regulatory system was expressed in substantially different post-privatization bank behavior than had been seen earlier in the decade in Mexico. To identify such differences, Jahyeong Koo and I constructed an econometric model of the market contestability of the Argentine commercial banking system and designed it to test for structural breaks in performance at various times (Gruben and Koo 1997). We tested for breaks during the period of most intense privatization, 1995.I-1997.I, during which three-fourths of the privatization that took place in the decade occurred. We also tested for behavioral breaks during other periods in the decade and examined whether there were any periods during which a typical bank operated where marginal cost exceeded marginal revenue or operated at levels suggestive of collusive behavior. In contrast to the Mexican case, Argentina did not show any period in which the typical bank operated where marginal cost exceeded marginal revenue. This result is particularly striking not only because of the difference from the Mexican outcome, but also because it diverges from a study of the Canadian liberalization of the early 1980s.

In a study of the Canadian liberalization of the early 1980s, Sherrill Shaffer (1993) found a structural break point at the liberalization. After the liberalization, the typical bank began to operate at a point at which marginal cost exceeded marginal revenue, again suggesting a risky market-share struggle like Mexico's. With reference to Shaffer's findings in the context of the role of deposit guarantees and risky bank behavior, it should be noted that Canada maintained a policy of no deposit insurance through 1966 but introduced significant guarantees in 1967. Moreover, in 1983, the maximum size of a deposit that could be insured in Canada was increased to $60,000 Canadian. The Canadian system charges its participating banks less than its costs and, therefore, typically runs large deficits. Underpricing of this type follows a model routinely noted as being conducive to the very sort of moral hazard that would trigger risky bank behavior, certainly during periods when motivations to fight for market share exist.

WHAT COMES NEXT?

There is increasing evidence to suggest that if developed countries need market discipline in their financial systems, developing countries need even more. Liliana Rojas-Suárez offers palpable statistical evidence to show that in Latin American countries, for example, it is common for banks defined as in crisis to still have capital-to-risk-weighted asset ratios well within international standards. She also shows that, contrary to the predictions of traditional early warning systems for banks, it is typical for liquidity ratios of problem banks in Latin America actually to be higher than banks that turned out not to be in crisis. In sum, financial ratios traditionally used by financial regulators are useless as supervisory tools when accounting standards and reporting systems are inappropriate (Rojas-Suárez 1998, 6).

In the wake of banking problems associated with the tequila crisis, financial regulators have become increasingly sensitive to the importance of the market mechanism. They are accordingly turning to the market. Recognizing the effectiveness of Argentina's approach to discouraging risky bank behavior, Mexican policymakers are moving to reduce deposit insurance to a program designed to protect small depositors but not those with deposits sufficiently large to suggest some skills at monitoring the behavior of the banks where they keep their money. Meanwhile, the Argentines have moved even further in their programs to make the banks abide by market discipline. Under a late 1996 set of rules, Argentine banks must issue subordinated debt equivalent to 2 percent of total bank assets. Since the debt is subordinated, signifying that its holders are at the end of the queue of creditors in the event of a bank closure, the debt holders are expected to monitor bank behavior with particular care. Accordingly, the prices of such debt are suspected to be a particularly strong signal of bank health and clearly stronger, as Rojas-Suárez's results suggest, than capitalization and liquidity ratios might be.

CONCLUSION

A consideration of differences between the Argentine and Mexican banking systems, even though both faced financial crisis during the tequila crisis of 1994-1995, is that the market-discipline-oriented policies of Argentina were more fully disposed to preserving prudent bank performance and to discouraging high risk behavior than the more traditional protections offered depositors by generous insurance programs in Mexico. The problem with those programs is that despite the virtues they may have for depositors, they loosen market discipline on bankers, since bankers are less surely punished by the government than they are by a market in which government does not intrude.

These problems may be seen in considering Moore's (1997) results on depositor behavior toward bad banks in the two countries during the tequila crisis. Argentine depositors fled unhealthy banks, while Mexican depositors — protected by a generous deposit insurance — did not exercise that discipline. The lack of such market discipline in Mexico and its presence in Argentina could be seen in differences in post-privatization bank performance in the two countries. William C. Gruben and Robert P. McComb (1997) showed that, supported by depositor guarantees and other bank supports, typical newly privatized bankers operated their institutions to a point where marginal costs exceeded marginal revenues. This was not a completely irrational stratagem, since those who followed it and did not go bankrupt were likely to finish the effort with greater market share than otherwise. Unfortunately, the cost of failure in the exercise was borne by the taxpayers. In contrast, Gruben and Jahyeong Koo (1997) showed that in the Argentine case, where market discipline was surer, the typical bank did not operate where marginal cost exceeded marginal revenue. That is, the typical bank did not take inordinate risks in efforts to gain market share.

As it has become more widely recognized that market discipline offers a more stable banking system than purely government discipline does, Latin American banking regulations have been moving in the direction of market discipline. Mexico is moving toward an Argentine approach, while Argentina is moving even more completely toward market signaling and market discipline as the keystones of national financial stability.

Notes

1. It can be argued that Mexico's exchange-rate crisis of 1994-1995 was triggered by a banking crisis, while Argentina's banking crisis of the same period was triggered by an exchange-rate crisis — or certainly by capital outflows associated with an attack on the currency. (See Santiprabhob 1997.)

2. It is important to understand that the Convertibility Plan and attendant legislation, liberalization, and reforms were part of a so-called big-bang in which notions of optimal sequence of policy measures were disregarded. (See Rozenwurcel and Bleger 1998, 1.) The establishment of a currency board monetary regime with full convertibility was accompanied by a tax reform in the same year. Equity markets were deregulated the following year.

3. Roque Fernández and Liliana Schumacher (1998) note that, as of December 1989, the total loss incurred by the Central Bank for deposit insurance and different forms of bank bailouts was US$14.6 billion. This sum was roughly the amount of all the nation's private bank assets when the 1991 Convertibility Plan, which established Argentina's currency board, was initiated.

4. Carlos Zarazaga (1995, 16) notes that, despite the textbook conventions respecting currency boards, the Argentine monetary base and Argentina's foreign reserves did not maintain exactly the same value or move exactly the same way. The difference occurred because "unlike the orthodox currency board, Argentina's convertibility law gives the central bank some flexibility to act as a lender of last resort."

5. As will be discussed, the functionality of such capitalization requirements in a Latin American context may be seen as considerably less than in the financial systems of industrialized nations.

6. The phenomenon of financial repression, typical of developing countries in the postwar period, involves a considerably stronger governmental role in financial markets than typically appears in developed countries. In an effort to subsidize certain economic sectors or industries, governments in financially repressive markets may impose deposit interest rate ceilings and also dictate loan rates and the industries that will receive the loans. Government may also force the banking system to lend to it and to make the loans at below-market interest rates. High reserve requirements may be imposed, not, as in developed countries, to restrict monetary expansion, but to allow the government to capture the resources of the financial system. Some of these measures may be reminiscent of what Asian countries did prior to the financial crises of 1997. Because the public has many options when it wants to purchase assets, high financial repression typically means that the banking system manages to capture only a small portion of public assets. The social cost can be investment levels far below what a free market would permit.

7. Argentina's financial system saw major increases as well, although the reason has perhaps more to do with the reduction in inflation and somewhat less to do with financial liberalization than in Mexico's case. The same ratio, M2 to GDP for Argentina, went from 0.3 percent in 1988 to 31.4 percent in 1994.

M2 is the component of the money supply that consists of M1 plus savings deposits, small-denomination time deposits, and money market mutual fund shares, along with some esoteric relatively liquid assets. M1 is the component of the money supply that consists of cash in the hands of the public and checking account balances.

8. A very important part of the overall expansion of credit by the newly privatized banks was, in fact, credit card debt. During the ensuing Mexican banking crisis, the delinquency rate for Mexican credit card debt was among the highest of all types of loan delinquency rates at Mexican banks. Credit records of consumer borrowers were often very sketchy, as at that time there were no generalized consumer debt reporting agencies in Mexico.

9. In fact, the rule to apply this option is what made Argentina's Convertibility Plan rules during capital outflows exactly the opposite of Mexico's sterilization or offset policy. When Mexican reserves flowed out, they were offset with increases in central bank credit to the domestic banking system. When Argentine reserves flowed out, the Argentine monetary base was allowed to fall.

References

Fernández, Roque B., and Liliana Schumacher. 1998. "The Argentine Banking Panic after the 'Tequila' Shock: Did 'Convertibility' Help or Hurt?" In S.S. Rehman, ed. *Financial Crisis Management and Regional Blocks*. Boston: Kluwer.

Garber, Peter. M., and Lars E.O. Svensson. 1994. *Operation and Collapse of Fixed Exchange Rate Regimes*. National Bureau of Economic Research Working Paper No. 4971 (December).

Gruben, William C., and Jahyeong Koo. 1997. "Contestability and Capital Flows in Argentina's Banking System." Federal Reserve Bank of Dallas. Paper presented at the Second Annual Meeting of the Network of Central Bank Researchers of the Americas, Bogotá.

Gruben, William C., and Robert P. McComb. 1997. "Privatization, Competition and Supercompetition in the Mexican Commercial Banking System." Federal Reserve Bank of Dallas. Paper presented at the 1997 meeting of the Latin American and Caribbean Economics Association, Bogotá.

Kaminksy, Graciela, and Carmen Reinhart. 1996. *The Twin Crises: The Causes of Banking and Balance of Payments Problems*. Federal Reserve Board of Governors International Finance Discussion Paper No. 544. Washington, D.C.: Federal Reserve Board.

Krugman, Paul. 1998. "Bubble, Boom, Crash: Theoretical Notes on Asia's Crisis." Mimeo. Massachusetts Institute of Technology.

Mancera, Miguel. 1995. "Don't Blame Monetary Policy." *Wall Street Journal*, January 31, A18.

McKinnon, Ronald I., and Huw Pill. 1996. "Credible Liberalizations and International Capital Flows: The 'Over-Borrowing Syndrome.'" Memorandum No. 314. Center for Research in Economic Growth, Stanford University.

Moore, Robert E. 1997. *Government Guarantees and Banking: Evidence from the Mexican Peso Crisis*. Federal Reserve Bank of Dallas Financial Industry Studies (December) 13-21.

Rojas-Suárez, Liliana. 1998. "Early Warning Indicators of Banking Crises: What Works for Emerging Markets?" Paper presented at the January 1998 Meeting of the Allied Social Sciences Association in Chicago. Washington D.C.: Inter-American Development Bank.

Rozenwurcel, Guillermo, and Leonardo Bleger. 1998. "Argentina's Banking System in the Nineties: From Financial Deepening to Systemic Crisis." Mimeo. University of Buenos Aires.

Santiprabhob, Veerathai. 1997. *Bank Soundness and Currency Board Arrangements: Issues and Experience*. International Monetary Fund Paper on Policy Analysis and Assessment PPAA-97-11.

Schumacher, Liliana. 1997. "Information and Currency Run in a System Without a Safety Net: Argentina and the Tequila Shocks." Mimeo. George Washington University.

Shaffer, Sherrill. 1993. "A Test of Competition in Canadian Banking." *Journal of Money, Credit, and Banking* 25: 49-60.

Wall Street Journal. 1996. "Business Bulletin." July 25, A1.

Zarazaga, Carlos. M. 1995. "Argentina, Mexico and Currency Boards: Another Case of Rules Versus Discretion." *Federal Reserve Bank of Dallas Economic Review* (Fourth Quarter) 14-24.

CHAPTER 10

Regulatory Policy in an Unstable Legal Environment: The Case of Argentina

ROBERTO PABLO SABA

INTRODUCTION

The goal of this chapter is to analyze some of Peter Schuck's main theoretical and normative propositions set forth in Chapter 2 in this volume and compare them with the Argentine privatization experience during the Carlos Menem administration (1989-1999). This comparison is significant for two reasons. First, Argentina in the 1990s became a leader in the privatization of public utilities in Latin America. Second, its constitutional law was originally patterned after that of the United States. However, over time Argentine law evolved differently, which can help us understand why similar legal frameworks may produce different results, which significantly affect the role of the state as a regulator.

This chapter is organized in several sections. In the first, in order to understand the privatization process in Argentina and the post-privatization environment it created, I briefly examine the political and economic context within which market reforms developed. Moreover, I focus on two key axioms that are at the heart of Argentina's divestiture process. Such axioms are important because they were the foundation upon which government market reforms were based and are responsible for many of the regulatory problems that we are facing today in Argentina. In the second section, I analyze the Menem administration's approach to market reforms when compared to Schuck's model. I contend that unlike the long-lasting *presumption in favor of market solutions* to socioeconomic problems that Schuck finds in the United States, in Argentina the presumption has taken a negative pattern. It was *against the market* from the 1940s until the 1980s, and then turned *against the state* under Menem. Based upon this discussion, in the third section, I outline the debate between deregulation vis-à-vis regulation in Argentina and the logic behind the Menem administration's deregulation bias and its flaws. In the fourth section, I compare what Schuck identifies as the different roles of public law in a post-privatization environment when applied to Argentina's present situation. In the fifth and concluding section, I sum up the argument and put forward some suggestions.

POLITICAL AND ECONOMIC CONTEXT

For decades, Argentines endured the performance of a huge and inefficient state. For a broad range of reasons — spanning from economic nationalism, to support from labor, the military, and domestic industry, to import substitution industrialization (ISI) policies — the state role and its prerogatives in socioeconomic development expanded tremendously. Most of the activities in which the state took a leadership role were associated with the production of goods and services through state owned enterprises (SOEs). In addition, the state began to intrude into the marketplace by issuing an ever-increasing number of rules and regulations that constrained the private sector. President Juan Perón (1946-1955) was the architect of this state-led development model, and many of his initial policies were expanded by a series of civilian and military administrations that followed until the late 1980s, when Argentina's fiscal crisis made these policies no longer feasible.

Following the end of the last military regime, President Raúl Alfonsín (1982-1989) of the Radical Civic Union (Unión Cívica Radical — UCR) attempted some reforms but in a piecemeal fashion. On the one hand, disagreements within the UCR over the necessity to reform the economy remained strong, and the president himself did little toward promoting reforms until late in his term. On the other hand, President Alfonsín's attempts to restructure the economy were frustrated by the largest opposition bloc in Congress, the Peronist Party (Partido Justicialista — PJ), labor unions, and many business groups.

By mid-1989, the economic crisis — punctuated by record levels of foreign debt, negative growth, capital flight, and runaway inflation — reached a point of no return, causing a major shift in the political scenario. In May 1989, UCR candidate Eduardo César Angeloz (at that time, the Argentine Constitution prevented an incumbent president from serving for a second consecutive term) lost to Carlos Menem of the PJ. Shortly thereafter, hyperinflation followed, reaching 100 percent per month. Looting became widespread, forcing Alfonsín to resign in the midst of Argentina's worst economic crisis of the twentieth century. President-elect Menem agreed to succeed Alfonsín in July, six months ahead of schedule. Although in the May elections the Peronists had also won a majority in both houses of Congress, their representatives were not scheduled to take office until December. Menem's condition, in order to take charge during such chaos, was that Alfonsín and his UCR would not oppose an emergency legislative package that he planned to introduce in the Congress.

The flagship of Menem's market reforms was privatization. SOEs, especially those providing public services, were virtually bankrupt, losing incredible amounts of money and providing very poor service or no service at all. Having inherited an insolvent state, Menem had little choice but to cut losses wherever he could, and SOEs became a prime target of his fiscal adjustment effort. However, this was easier said than done because since Perón's times, Argentines had come to regard the sell-off of SOEs as tantamount to surrendering the national sovereignty. This had been a major obstacle for all the previous administrations that had tried to privatize.[1] Yet, Menem was capable of overcoming entrenched opposition. The hyperinflation bouts of 1989 symbolized, in the eyes of many people, the collapse of the state-driven development model, and it created a fertile ground for the acceptance of radical market reforms aimed at the dismantling of the "entrepreneurial state" that only a year earlier would have been unthinkable (Palermo and Novaro 1996). The financial insolvency, mismanagement, and corruption plaguing many SOEs made them the source of all evil. This change of heart was confirmed by public opinion polls conducted in urban areas between 1989 and 1991 that showed an overwhelming support for privatization and market deregulation (Mora y Araujo 1991).

Capitalizing on this general malaise, Menem created a pro-reform coalition that included, besides his own party, Argentina's leading business conglomerates, television networks and print media, think-tanks, small conservative parties, unions, and the most important industrial interest groups in the private sector (Gibson 1997). In contrast with privatization in Eastern European countries, privatization in Argentina did not encounter much ideological opposition. Nationalism, usually a major obstacle for deregulation and privatization, found few supporters in Argentina when Menem launched his reform program. By the late 1980s, ISI arguments had definitely failed in Latin America as much as the rationale behind the command economies in Eastern Europe and the Soviet Union. This situation left only one alternative to the crisis, the adoption of orthodox economic policies that had long been advocated by the so-called "Washington consensus." Caught in dire straits, a very pragmatic Menem wasted no time in adopting the International Monetary Fund-styled economic recipe that, during his election campaign in 1989, he had openly rejected. Like most new converts, Menem embraced the new creed enthusiastically, hoping that if economic stability ensued, his administration would then be rewarded at the ballot box.

In addition, Menem was able to draw the financial and political support of foreign governments and multilateral lending agencies (IMF, World Bank, and Inter-American Development Bank). What followed was a decade of radical market reforms that produced the most profound transformation of Argentina's administrative state since the nineteenth century. Yet, Menem advocated the reforms without questioning the long-term consequences of hastily arranged transactions.

Two pieces of legislation were fundamental in producing the economic turnaround that occurred in the 1990s: the State Reform Act[2] (SRA) and the Economic Emergency Act (EEA).[3] The SRA authorized the president to place trustees in charge of all state companies for 180 days, renewable for an additional 180 days. This statute gave the executive branch full authority to privatize 32 SOEs immediately. The law listed the industries and public utilities that were subject to privatization: airlines, travel agencies, highways, shipping lines, catering companies, coal mines, oil and gas companies, steel mills, postal services, insurance companies, telecommunication companies, radio and television stations, power companies, grain elevators, ports, printing companies, sugar refineries, pipelines, and chemical and petrochemical companies (Manzetti 1999).

The EEA also allowed the executive branch to change the internal organization of these companies, break them apart, merge, or dissolve them. The trustees, accountable only to the executive branch, had broad discretion in choosing the methods for privatizing these firms (public auctions, international public offerings, direct sales, and others). The statute also established a system of workers' participation in the companies to be privatized known as the Shared Ownership Program

(Propiedad Pública Participada). The EEA, among other measures, sheltered the state from pending lawsuits and contractual obligations with government contractors.

Privatization was part of a broader market reform effort that sought to open Argentina's economy to foreign investments. The following are some of the most important measures of the EEA: 1) suspension of state subsidies (art.2) and schemes of industrial and mining promotion, mostly through elimination of tax incentives (arts. 4-14); 2) elimination of the requirement of state permission to make foreign investments (arts. 15-19); 3) suspension of the "Buy Argentine" preference (art. 23); 4) empowering the president to introduce federal budgetary changes (arts. 24-27); 5) modification of special funds and changing of the destination of incomes (arts. 28-29); 6) modification of the system for the payment of the domestic public debt (arts. 36-38); 7) modification of the Stock Exchange operations (arts. 39-41); 8) suspension of the appointment of new personnel and revision of the daily operations of the state and its agencies (arts. 42-47); 9) reorganization of the social security system (arts. 52-57); 10) reorganization of state institutions (arts. 56-58); 11) introduction of important changes in tax collection procedures (art. 59); and 12) selling of unnecessary state-owned property (arts. 60-62).

In 1991, after a period of trial and error, President Menem appointed Domingo Cavallo as the economy minister. Cavallo's first move was to send a bill to Congress known as the Convertibility Law. This law 1) established that the Central Bank could no longer finance the government's fiscal deficit and forced the Central Bank to back 100 percent of the monetary base with foreign exchange and gold reserves; 2) set up a new foreign exchange system fixing the parity of the U.S. dollar at $1 to the Argentine peso; and 3) prescribed that any devaluation first was to receive congressional approval. In addition, all indexation mechanisms were eliminated from contracts. All these measures created a favorable environment for privatization. In turn, state divestiture became a key element to generate the foreign exchange reserves necessary to maintain a fixed parity with the U.S. dollar (Starr 1997).

By the end of 1991, on the economic front, Menem's technocrats had succeeded in bringing inflation under control and luring foreign investments back into the country. On the political front, President Menem successfully isolated and thoroughly defeated opposition to his policies, which primarily came from disgruntled unions in the public sector and left-wing parties in Congress.

It must be underscored that many of the reforms just described ran counter to Perón's welfare policies of the 1940s. Yet, the pragmatic Menem rebuked the critics within his own party by arguing that had Perón been in his situation, he would have done the same. Thus, to fix Argentina's economic problems he turned to conservative-minded economists who had traditionally opposed Peronism and the state interventionist policies associated with it. From the start, Menem made his own two axioms the following, which until his 1989 election had been the core of the argument of conservative economists such as Alvaro Alsogaray:

1. The state is incapable of solving socioeconomic problems; therefore, the economic and legal institutions created to sustain ISI and welfare policies have to be dismantled.

2. The private sector is the only sector that can promote development and should be allowed to pursue its goal in the freest fashion possible.

These two axioms constituted the ideological grounds that guided Menem's market reforms and shaped the public debate from 1989 onward. The axioms were embraced by the administration's officials, the Peronist majority in Congress, and the judiciary.[4] This "ideological cohesion" across the different branches of government can be seen in numerous official statements. A typical example comes from the Supreme Court that, as discussed later, Menem "packed" with sympathetic judges only months after taking office. The Supreme Court provided the legal grounds to justify the government's agenda, using a rationale clearly based on the two axioms (Verbitsky 1993). This can be seen from one of the Court's most important rulings in the *Cocchia* case.[5] The Court's decision espoused the first axiom about the intrinsic inefficiency of the state by quoting, among other arguments, excerpts from the debate in the Argentine Congress regarding the legal framework that introduced the privatization process:

> If we examine the laws passed by Congress on the reform of the state — 23.696, 23.697, and 23.928 — there is no room for doubt about the philosophy that inspired the policies later enacted by the legislative or by the executive branch, aiming at protecting and fostering the indispensable freedom to make the market economy work, within which the state has only exclusively a subsidiary role.[6]

Supreme Court Justice Antonio Boggiano was even more explicit in his support of this assumption when he referred to the legislators' understanding of the "goals of privatization." He stated:

> The majority opinion concluded that the public administration had contributed to build up the critical situation we have described. The [legislators'] statements are explicit in referring to the 'exaggerated dimension of the state structures,' especially its public enterprises that were a 'heavy burden' on society, due to the fact that they spend much more money than they make . . . feeding the inflationary process. The idea of a 'giant,' 'oversized,' 'monumental' . . . state responsible for making the [country's] productive structure . . . 'underdeveloped,' with sectors unjustly privileged or monopolistic, appears along the whole debate.[7]

The second axiom was instrumental in justifying the transfer of hundreds of SOEs, including those in public utilities, to private companies. In order to attract domestic and foreign investors, most of the regulations that worked as obstacles to businesses were removed. However, it is important to note that this did not necessarily mean that competition ensued. In fact, often it did not, but given the ideological approach taken by the administration, it did not matter. What did matter was to create the right incentives for investors to perceive Argentina as a country of opportunity. In fact, foreign investments through privatization were essential for servicing the international debt, financing current expenditures, and sustaining the fixed exchange rate parity with the U.S. dollar established by the Convertibility Law. Given these premises, government officials considered concerns over the type of market structures in key public utilities that resulted from state divestiture as superfluous. The priority, as Menem reiterated on several occasions, was to sell and sell quickly.

What is also worth noting is that while the administration focused on designing economic policies that could have immediate positive effects, it also paid lip service to the design of a comprehensive model that would redefine the role of the administrative state as endorsed by many scholars who advocated market solutions to public problems. In reality, the reform agenda proceeded in a piece-meal, ad hoc, and often contradictory fashion, as elucidated in the next section.

THE PRESUMPTION AGAINST THE STATE

In the previous section, Argentina's socioeconomic background before privatization and the ideological axioms behind the main policy instruments that Menem adopted to solve the 1989 crisis were discussed. Let us now turn to Schuck's idea regarding the pro-market presumption and how such a presumption (or its absence) applies to the changes that occurred in Argentina. Schuck states that, a priori, there is no reason for preferring markets to regulation in order to solve public policy problems. He says that, fortunately, we do not live in complete normative, historical, and empirical ignorance but are deeply affected by values, history, and knowledge of empirical consequences. This is what has convinced or forced many countries to transform their way of doing business. Schuck then refers to the U.S. experience within this framework and points out that the U.S. Constitution implic-itly privileges market approaches in at least three ways. First, it protects property and contract rights against government infringement. Second, under the Supreme Court's interpretation of the Due Process Clause, liberty of contract is a constitu-tional right protected from political majorities. Third, the way the government is designed in the Constitution and its level of fragmentation contribute to fortify the status quo, which is market friendly. Political coalitions in favor of regulation, therefore, are difficult but not impossible to build, as demonstrated by the market-constraining regulatory activity during the New Deal and the 1960-1980 period.

My contention is that, unlike the United States' more or less linear develop-ment of a regulatory policy that fosters a greater role for market solution to public problems, Argentina went through a pendulum-like process: from a presumption against the market toward a presumption against the state.[8] Taking Schuck's framework as a model, we can critically analyze Argentina's situation in terms of what the presumption in favor of market-driven solutions is. The Argentine Constitution, at least the original one written in 1853 (which was amended in 1994), has followed the U.S. Constitution in many of its provisions. Argentina's Constitu-tion protects, as does its U.S. counterpart, private property and contract rights. However, important differences exist in the way the three branches of government have interpreted the spirit of the Argentine Constitution on key questions. The initial presumption in favor of small government and the protection of the private sphere of individuals in Argentina was changed in the 1940s through legislation passed in Congress and was later upheld by a series of Supreme Court decisions that argued in support of state interventionism in contract rights.

Beginning with Perón in the 1940s, a presumption in favor of the state and against the market came to be shared among politicians of different creeds, bureaucrats, business groups that flourished under economic protectionism, and a large stratum of public opinion. In turn, this translated into strong support for government interference in the private sector. From 1946 through the early 1980s, Peronist, Radical, and military governments expanded the state bureaucracy, special state agencies, and SOEs. By the 1980s, there were some 400 state enterprises in Argentina (Manzetti 1999). About half of the country's top 20 firms (by sales), including the petroleum company (Yacimientos Petroliferos Fiscales — YPF), the railroads (Ferrocarriles Argentinos), the electricity distributor for greater Buenos Aires (SEGBA), the telephone company (ENTEL), the state steel mill (SOMISA), the gas company (Gas del Estado), the water company (Agua y Energía), and the national air flag carrier (Aerolíneas Argentinas), were government owned. Twelve SOEs in the utility, transportation, and energy sectors accounted for about three-quarters of all state enterprise sales, employment, and investment in Argentina (Baer and Birch 1994).

As the idea of enhancing the role of the state became progressively entrenched in the minds of politicians, military officers, and bureaucrats, the Supreme Court followed suit. In this sense, the Court itself developed a constitutional interpretation of property and contract rights by which the police power of the state expanded to include the regulation of the most elementary economic transactions. This trend was nurtured under democratically elected governments as well as under the military ones that ousted popularly elected presidents (1930, 1943, 1955, 1962, 1965, and 1976). The Supreme Court issued several decisions upholding state intervention, which can be illustrated through the *Cine Callao* case.

The *Cine Callao*, usually studied in Argentine law schools as the leading case for police power, is a very good example of the kind of constitutional interpretation that eroded the supposedly original pro-market presumption inherited from the U.S. Constitution.[9] The case refers to a statute challenged by the owners of a movie theater who had been forced to hire local actors to perform small sketches before a movie. The rationale behind the statute was that local artists had little opportunity to show their skills and that their lack of employment would have a negative impact on the national cultural life. Thus, in order to protect the Argentine cultural tradition, the government decided to provide jobs for unemployed actors and a place for them to perform. Accordingly, the government decided that theater owners had to build special new stages and add, if they wished, the additional costs of this new entertainment to the ticket price for watching the movie. The owners of the Callao theater argued that this statute was an infringement of their property and contract rights guaranteed by the Constitution, because they were being forced, against their will, to hire the actors and make changes to their buildings that they did not need for showing movies. The Supreme Court upheld the decision made by the Appeals Court, which argued that in order for the government to fight unemployment, some restrictions to property and contract rights ought to be tolerated. The justification behind the decision was that rights are not extended without restrictions and that such a limitation on the exercise of these rights was justified. In its written opinion, the Supreme Court stated:

> Under that [broad] conception of police power, it should be considered legitimately included within it the power of issuing legal regulations for preventing, avoiding, diminishing or coping with, permanently or transitorily, the very serious economic and social consequences of unemployment in medium or large scale.[10]

Cine Callao was not the only decision related to this restriction on contract rights. Many others followed, espousing the same rationale, especially under

Perón's first two administrations (1945-1955), as well as under subsequent governments.

Let us now turn to what Schuck identifies as the third way in which the U.S. Constitution contributed to the building and institutionalization of the pro-market presumption: the highly fragmented, decentralized, and internally competitive system of governmental authority. If it is true that this feature of the U.S. Constitution is so important in making it difficult, though not impossible, for market-constraining regulatory programs to develop, Argentina is among those countries for which governmental authority, since its independence, has remained highly concentrated within the executive branch. Like many other Latin American countries, Argentina adopted the U.S. constitutional model; however, it ascribed much greater decision-making prerogatives to the presidency than given to the U.S. president. Juan B. Alberdi, the most influential person in the drafting of the Argentine Constitution, was the person who was highly responsible for adopting most of what was taken from the U.S. Constitution.[11] However, Alberdi also stressed at the time that, due to its internal conflicts, Argentina could not survive as a country without strong presidential leadership. Indeed, the Argentine founding fathers consulted the Chilean Constitution, which had been written a few years earlier, in order to find a model that would strengthen the executive at the expense of the other two branches of government (Nino 1992, 523-531). In the end, Argentina developed such a strong presidential system that some authors (Nino 1992; Linz and Valenzuela 1994) dubbed it "hyperpresidentialism."

As a result, the great powers that the 1853 Constitution ascribed to the president vis-à-vis the legislative and judicial branches created the seeds of an executive-dominated political system. Equally important is the fact that, in the decades that followed, this trend strengthened as Congress and the courts delegated to the executive some of their own prerogatives. Understandably, this situation had a significant effect on the decisions affecting the structure and performance of the administrative state. This enormous concentration of power in the presidency is responsible for a situation that is the exact opposite of the one described by Schuck when he refers to the United States' case. The lack of fragmentation, decentralization, and an internally competitive system of governmental authority make it very easy for the Argentine president to enact or block reforms independently from the other branches of government. This partially explains why the Menem administration could make so many radical changes so quickly with little opposition. In fact, it is no coincidence that the process of transferring power from the legislative to the executive branch accelerated under Menem (Ferreira Rubio and Goretti 1998). As noted earlier, the Supreme Court played a crucial role in providing a constitutional justification for this process through two benchmark decisions: *Peralta*[12] and *Cocchia.*[13]

The *Peralta* case exemplifies the point. The Supreme Court had to decide about the constitutionality of a decree issued by the executive on matters that traditionally had been within the realm of the Congress. The Supreme Court found the decree constitutional on the following grounds:

> Immersed in today's reality, not only Argentina's but the universal reality, we
> have to admit that some kinds of problems and the solutions that they demand can

hardly be dealt with or solved efficiently and expeditiously by [a] multipersonal [legislative] body. Confrontation of interests that delay. . .the process of making decisions; special interest pressure on those decisions, which is also the norm, since the [legislature] represents the provinces and the people; the lack of homogeneity [of the legislature] as the individuals and groups that it represents are moved most of the time by divergent interests — make it necessary that the President, whose role demands the maintenance of peace and social order, which [is] seriously threatened in this case, has to make the decision to select the measures that are unavoidable and that this reality urgently demands with no delay.[14]

This opinion, which sanctions the transference of power from the legislative to the executive branch, was further reasserted in the *Cocchia* case. In *Cocchia*, the Supreme Court went further than ever before in terms of justifying concentration (as opposed to what Schuck calls "fragmentation") of power to benefit the executive. In that decision, Justice Boggiano stated:

... there exists a modern and strong doctrine that admits, within certain reasonable limits, the delegation of legislative powers as a claim for good government in the modern State. 'Delegation of legislative powers from the assembly to the government has become a universal manifestation of the technological age,' as argued by Loewestein, without distinguishing between parliamentarian and presidential systems, and indeed he pointed out the universal character of the trend.[15]

He also added:

... in current times, the implementation of an economic policy does not seem to be possible without a close cooperation between the legislative and executive branches, even in a presidential system like the one established in the Argentine Constitution. [Louis L.] Jaffe affirms — with reference to the constitutional system of his country [United States], which is substantially similar to ours — that: 'we have to admit that the legislative and administrative are complementary rather than opposing processes, and that delegation [of powers] represents the formal method for their mutual cooperation' (see "An Essay on Delegation of Legislative Power," *Columbia Law Review*, April, 1947, vol. XLVII, Number 3, p. 360). The mentioned cooperation would find an unjustified and inconvenient limitation if the only thing that Congress could be allowed to do were to require the executive to regulate the details and minor aspects of the statutes. . . . On the contrary, agreeing on a broad delegation [of powers] brings more efficiency to the governmental apparatus as a whole, benefiting the entire society without weakening the protection of the rights of the people.[16]

Finally, after redefining the relative powers of Congress and the executive, beyond what the Constitution prescribes, Boggiano completed his interpretation of the "new" administrative state, under the aegis of market reforms, by pointing out what the role of the courts is in this new system, quoting *American Power and Light Commission v. Securities and Exchange Commission:*

After all, the protection of those individual rights eventually affected by the exercise of the delegated powers is guaranteed adequately by the judicial review of the policy under the legislator's argument behind the delegation.

The picture I have described here attempts to highlight the differences between U.S. and Argentine institutional behaviors and how they have contributed so differently to the shaping of the presumptions that are behind the adoption of regulatory approaches to solving public policy problems. Unlike the fragmentation of institutional power that weighs heavily in Schuck's model, Argentina's tradition has evolved in the opposite direction, toward concentration of authority. This trend became even more accentuated under Menem, who increased the executive's prerogatives at the expense of Congress with the blessing of a docile Supreme Court. The unprecedented powers so accrued allowed Menem to establish a new presumption: a presumption against the state. This point will be clarified later.

Menem's presumption against the state should *not* be confused with the presumption in favor of the market, as defined in Schuck's paper. The presumption in favor of the market recognizes a role for the state mainly as the institution in charge of promoting competition among economic agents, protecting property/ individual rights, and safeguarding the interests of consumers against unscrupulous business practices. Consistent with the axioms discussed in the previous section, the presumption against the state instead assumes that the market by its very nature corrects all kinds of distortions and that any regulation is an artificial means to allocate rents. Thus, the presumption against the state sees regulation as always bad and deregulation as always good. This ideological approach has pervaded the most important economic reforms sponsored by Menem in the 1990s. The retrenchment of the state came not only in terms of abandoning its entrepreneurial role as a provider of goods and services. Equally important, the state withdrew from its more basic task of refereeing the market game. Indeed, following this rather crude approach to market reforms, Menem was completely uninterested in whether true competition would ensue from privatization and deregulation. As a matter of fact, many scholarly works point to the fact that privatization was pursued with an eye to rewarding domestic groups by granting them monopolies or oligopolies in the most lucrative public utility markets (Schvarzer 1992; Schamis 1999; Vispo 1999).

REGULATORY POLICY IN ARGENTINA AND ITS IMPACT IN SHAPING THE ADMINISTRATIVE STATE

As noted earlier, the presumption against the state responds to the following logic: let the market forces interact among themselves and, no matter what, we will be better off compared with the situation prior to privatization. Even if we were to accept this controversial approach to problem solving, the complete withdrawal of the state from the regulatory realm produces other kinds of issues that have been at the center of economic analyses of the law in advanced industrial societies.

Before discussing how such issues fit the Argentine case, it is important to understand what regulation means and with what it is associated in such a country. "Regulation" in Argentina today is a negative, value-loaded word. Since colonial times, regulation was a means for the government to act unilaterally and extract rents. As a result, it came to be perceived as a very negative concept, usually associated with arbitrary decisionmaking, abuse, and the main cause of corruption. Starting in the 1940s, when the first Peronist government nationalized most of the private companies in public utilities, regulation became a synonym for state interventionism and ISI (McGuire 1997). It was understood as the opposite of competitiveness and capitalism. Of course, around the same period, similar policies took place across most of Latin America and met with substantial popular support, particularly from the urban working class, the emerging industrial bourgeoisie, the military, and nationalist intellectuals.

Yet, regulation had its own detractors. Cass Sunstein's description of the anti-regulatory attitude in the United States captures similar feelings in Argentina, which became particularly pronounced among the middle and upper classes by the late 1980s:

> The critics have claimed that regulation amounts in practice to unjustified interference with freedom of choice and is frequently an usurpation of private decisions in violation of government's first obligation, which is neutrality among competing conceptions of the good. Only purportedly in the public interest, regulation turns out on inspection to be interest-groups' transfers designed to protect well organized private groups — such as business interests or unions — at the expense of the rest of the citizenry. Government controls impose partial, narrowly held views of what is right and just, views held by elite or parochial interests. . . . Many of the most powerful attacks on regulation are empirical; they include a range of complaints. Regulation has imposed huge costs on the economy. The result has been decreased productivity, unemployment and infla-tion, and threats to international competitiveness (Sunstein 1990, 32).

In Argentina, the most popular economic analysts and media commentators, particularly in the second half of the 1980s, presented arguments similar to the above quotation from Sunstein and found in regulation one of the main causes of the country's economic decline. Their attacks targeted specific aspects of regulatory policy, such as price controls. Conservative critics, who accused the Alfonsín administration of being excessively "interventionist," unexpectedly found in the pragmatic Menem, whose Peronist party had symbolized the rise of indiscriminate regulation in Argentina, a golden opportunity to put their ideas to work after decades of frustration. In fact, Menem launched his dramatic transformation of Argentina's administrative state under the attractive label of "deregulation." Thus, if regulation had been the major reason for all the failures that Argentina had experienced, deregulation under his administration was going to be the main reason behind the country's renaissance.

Argentina is a nation in which extreme remedies have often been considered to be the only feasible alternatives, thus leaving little room for compromise (Shumway 1991). As noted, for decades, most of the country's politicians, large numbers of entrepreneurs, and average citizens supported all kinds of state interven-tionism. The reason behind this behavior was that they usually found this state of affairs beneficial to their own narrow interests. As long as the state could count on extensive economic resources, it dispensed special privileges to the major socioeco-nomic players through regulation. On the one hand, most of Argentina's business conglomerates grew thanks to economic protectionism and lucrative government contracts. On the other, regulatory statutes granted unionized workers job security, generous pensions, subsidized health services, and long vacations. As a result of this long-term practice, the state became an enormous and expensive machinery built through different layers of regulation, resulting from the unending demands of a large array of contradicting interests whose main aim was to extract rents. In order to get protection from the state, each of these groups put pressure on democratically elected and authoritarian governments alike. Usually, the groups succeeded, depending of course upon which among them had special access to governmental favors at the time they raised their claims. New regulations, departments, special agencies, and bureaucratic units mushroomed. An increasing number of civil servants were hired to handle this process, in which everybody received something without caring about the disastrous consequences for the country and the economy as a whole. Consequently, Argentina's administrative state grew larger than life and ultimately became unable to set the basic rules for an orderly economic development based upon supply and demand. Moreover, corruption increasingly became one of the most important negative externalities due to the lack of government accountability. The problem of corruption, in connection with over-regulation and interventionism, gave ammunition to those pundits and scholars who advocated radical reforms, as by eliminating regulation, the logic went, much corruption associated with it would be eradicated as well.

Between 1989 and 1999, the Menem administration made repeated efforts to link the accomplishment of its economic goals to the need for deregulating to the greatest possible extent all sorts of activities. In this sense, Menem was very successful in making people believe that once regulation disappeared, the economy would grow without obstacles. Within this context, privatization played a double role. It meant the end of government intervention in productive activities and the elimination of a host of regulatory barriers that discouraged private investments. Paradoxically, in just one decade, Argentina went from extreme government interventionism to extreme laissez faire, allowing economic groups with close political ties to acquire rents in key areas of the economy, particularly in public utilities (Schamis 1999). As a result, at the end of the twentieth century, we observe in Argentina two confusing, yet widely held assumptions with reference to the concepts of regulation and deregulation: first, any regulation is bad, and deregulation is always good. In fact, until recently, it has been difficult to find any academic debate, let alone any media or public debate, regarding what kind of regulatory policy is best suited to address the distortions created by markets that after privatization showed both poor quality service and strong features of collusive practices within the private sector. Under the dominant perspective, since "regulation is always bad," it makes no sense to think about the impact of regulation on the functioning of the market. This is not at all surprising, given the fact that in Argentina there does not exist a tradition of public policy analysis and planning that could allow public officials to anticipate the impact of their decisions. Adding to the problem is the fact that, traditionally, key decisions have been made under conditions of duress, which explains the piecemeal and often contradictory approach to problem solving.

The second misleading assumption relates privatization directly to deregulation. It suggests that privatization is, by definition, a way of "deregulating" the economy because the state pulls out from productive activities. According to this rather crude way of thinking, whether the market being privatized retains a monopolistic or oligopolistic nature is not even a matter of concern because, the reasoning goes, the private sector will always perform better than the market would have if it had remained under state ownership. This approach can be seen clearly in the early privatizations (for example, airlines and telecommunications) in Argentina, when the government purposely left the regulatory framework ill defined, based on the rationale that doing otherwise would have discouraged potential buyers. Due to unclear rules, private companies from the beginning were allowed to take advantage of loopholes in the transfer contracts, as the companies were left undisturbed in setting price and business policies under monopolistic conditions (Vispo 1999).

From the outset of his administration, Menem set the tone of the policy debate that centered on how fast his administration could privatize and deregulate. Current policy debates on "overregulation" and "underregulation," which assume the existence of an optimum level of regulation to be necessary for the state to set the rules so that economic actors must interact in a civilized way, were completely ignored (Mendeloff 1988). No room was left for "subtle" discussions about different kinds of regulations (economic or social). In sum, regulation became a sort of *taboo* topic. This situation has gone to such an extreme that few politicians aspiring to public office today would make regulation a campaign issue. On the contrary, those politicians wishing to garner support from the media and voters alike feel under pressure to show a strong commitment to deepen or at least not to alter the model that Menem ushered in. Despite current dogma on the matter, it seems clear that there are types of economic and social regulation — not government interventionism — that are necessary for creating truly competitive, efficient markets and achieving goals for the collective good (Sunstein 1990; Rose-Ackerman 1992).

Some may take issue with what I have said in the previous section about the presumption against the state and its effects on the government's withdrawal from its regulatory role. It may be contended that the role of the state is now performed by a number of new regulatory agencies created specifically to monitor the way in which private companies, mainly public utilities, perform in the market. Price controls, consumer protection, and other "regulatory" matters are the responsibility of such agencies. However, such agencies are plagued by two problems. First, the decision to create sector-specific regulatory agencies has produced a tremendous confusion in terms of regulatory policy as well as lack of institutional effectiveness. This is because such agencies have been left in charge of their own sector without general policy guidance from the government, with regard to what the general goals of regulation after privatization should be like. Moreover, the lack of coordination among such agencies has produced contradictory decisions and feuds over jurisdictional domain.

Second, the way such agencies were designed, especially their governing bodies, allows the executive ample room for political manipulation. In fact, for each agency, the majority of the governing body is appointed by the president, and, in several cases, the most important qualification of those appointed seem to have been their party affiliation rather than their technical expertise. It is also important to underscore that these are not agencies like those in the United States. The president appoints the executive board, which is *not* accountable to Congress. There are also almost no provisions for conflicts of interest, as some members have gone on to work for the regulated companies after leaving their agencies.

Referring to such problems, Roldolfo Terragno has pointed out that this multiplicity of regulatory agencies produces a dispersion of responsibility and accountability. The proliferation of regulatory agencies (based upon the assumption that they are more efficient and flexible than a centralized entity overseeing many sectors) at times creates more confusion, as their powers vis-à-vis those of Congress are not quite clear (Terragno 1999). Moreover, Juan Bautista Cincunegui (1998) has pointed out that regulatory agencies suffer additional problems: 1) lack of financial autonomy from the executive in many cases and 2) secretive decision-making processes in making administrative decisions.

ABOUT REGULATION IN POST-PRIVATIZATION ENVIRONMENTS

A recent study by the World Bank stated, "An effective state is vital for the provision of the goods and services — and the rules and institutions — that allow markets to nourish and people to lead healthier and happier lives. Without it, sustainable development, both economic and social, is impossible" (World Bank 1997, 1). This does not mean that development should be provided by the state, as the pro-state presumption would say. It means that the state in a post-privatization environment is a "partner, catalyst, and facilitator" of activities initiated by the private sector (World Bank 1997, 1).

However, this kind of reasoning, as discussed above, was rejected from the start by the Menem administration. Accordingly, the guiding principle of Menem's administration seems to have been rooted in the idea that the best regulation is the one that does not exist at all. In sum, instead of pursuing the goal of improving the effectiveness of imperfect market competition via a newly styled regulatory framework (that is, one compatible with the pro-market tenets), the Menem administration pursued a policy aimed at reducing regulation as much as possible, which is consistent with the "presumption against the state" guiding principle.

Schuck identifies three "paradigmatic roles" that public law can play in the kind of reformist, post-privatization environment in which emerging democracies are now situated. They are 1) the institutionalization of a strong presumption in favor of market solutions to social problems, 2) the maximization of the effectiveness of regulation where it is used, and 3) the establishment of extra-regulatory institutions and processes that can help to monitor and discipline the resulting hybrid system of markets and regulations.

Not surprisingly, though, these roles run against the "presumption against the state," which assumes that all kinds of regulation will have negative effects on the functioning of the economy. However, the against-the-state presumption is empirically flawed because, as we have witnessed in Argentina, indiscriminate deregulation has led to a number of market distortions. First, the lack of clear rules in many markets and weak anti-trust law in Argentina (the one adopted in 1980 is rudimental and very limited in scope, let alone hardly enforced) have allowed collusion practices among private companies. Second, in public utility sectors that were transferred under monopolistic conditions, private companies have often abused their market power at the expense of consumers. Third, from a constitutional standpoint, indiscriminate deregulation has affected the individual rights of citizens to have access to alternative provisions of services. More specifically, what I am stressing here is the fact that the role of the state as guardian — not only of a well-functioning, competitive market but also of the individual's freedom against the decisions made by the majority — has not been fulfilled. State non-interventionism in the economy does not mean that the state should relinquish its role as the guardian of the people's constitutional rights. Although we are well aware of the dangers of state interference with private activities, especially in the economic realm, the state may be the only effective way to safeguard the freedom of the people (Fiss 1996).

Let us now pay special attention to the third role that Schuck mentions, which is the establishment of extra-regulatory institutions and processes that can help to monitor, increase, and discipline the resulting hybrid system of markets and regulations (Gordillo 1998). Within the discussion about this specific role, the focus will be on the mechanisms for protection of consumers' rights.

The rationale behind Argentine regulation prior to 1989 and deregulation thereafter, as described in this chapter, have contributed to the building of a different kind of administrative law from that of other Western countries, including the United States. Schuck, for instance, says that U.S. administrative law has three structural features: 1) public process precedes the issuance of regulations, 2) independent courts impose controls over regulatory decision-making bodies, and 3) citizens can participate at every stage of the regulatory process (Schuck and Litan 1986). These features are combined with others that he associates with what he calls extra-regulatory institutions (legislative oversight, an independent judiciary, and some fundamental elements that we can find in U.S. administrative law related to rule-making and citizen participation in the decision-making process). Unfortunately, almost none of these characteristics can be found to any extent, depth, or strength in Argentine administrative law, nor in the laws of most other countries in Latin America.

For the sake of comparison, let us see how the institutions that Schuck identifies as crucial for public law to fulfill its role fared in the case of Argentina. My contentions will be, once again, that the adoption of a presumption against the state, coupled with the collusion between the Menem administration and powerful economic interests, produced in Argentina a very weak set of extra-regulatory institutions.

Administrative Law

The possibility of having a public process preceding the issuance of regulations as envisioned by Schuck is extremely difficult, if not impossible, since the Argentine legal framework does not require it and the government, especially at the federal level, has little interest in introducing changes in this sense. The lack of initiatives for opening the process to citizens' scrutiny is consistent with the concentration of most of the regulatory decisionmaking in the hands of technocrats, particularly those in the Ministry of Economy (Palermo and Novaro 1996; Vispo 1999). The technocrats of this ministry regard the existence of a public process before the issuance of regulations as dangerous, because it could jeopardize their economic reforms and freedom of action. In fact, the economic technocrats of the Menem administration have consistently done their best to insulate the policy process from the people as much as possible, arguing that doing otherwise would have allowed special interests to destroy the coherence of their reforms. Thus, government officials minimized all interference coming from the Congress as well as the public at large, as exemplified in the earlier discussion of the *Peralta* case.

In addition to these limitations, Argentina's administrative law model is not the most permeable one to the inclusion of those elements that make them so effective in the United States — in terms of avoiding market distortions and the violation of consumers' and citizens' rights. In Argentina, the lack of any kind of informal rule-making processes in the legal framework, coupled with the government's broad discretionary powers, make its administrative law quite different from the model that Schuck proposes. Moreover, Argentina lacks overseeing legal instruments, so helpful in the U.S. context, such as a Freedom of Information Act or a Sunshine Act.

To be fair, the situation in Argentina changed a bit with the Constitutional Reform of 1994, through which there was a small expansion of the standing regulation (article 43) and some recognition of the right to access information (article 43). However, most of the legal tools provided by the Constitution are still not working. This has to do, in part, with the lack of a culture of civil society that makes citizens aware of their rights in monitoring the performance of the public administration (Vispo 1999). In addition, both Congress and the government have delayed the necessary regulation of those rights and procedures provided by the Constitution (Cincunegui 1998).

Legal Tools

Even if we accept the view that Schuck has about democracy as an arena set for the competition of different groups, it is important to note that powerful lobbies' ability to capture different sectors of the public administration endangers the pursuit of the public interest and undermines the rights of the majority of the citizenry. Proposals related to the inclusion of consumer organizations into regulatory agencies may not be the panacea that some think because it is difficult to achieve a correct representation of the organizations that have a stake in the matter. A possible solution is to create institutional mechanisms and legal procedures that allow consumers to appeal at the judicial or administrative level each time players in the market break the law and go beyond their constitutional rights. This grass-roots approach may provide a good monitoring device for both the public administration and the market. Legal instruments like the *amparo colectivo*, for instance, the right of associations to bring lawsuits as a means of representation of the public interest (particularly considering that Argentina lacks a class action procedure) could be very effective. It would also be very interesting to see future effects of the expansion of the practice called public interest litigation. This is a device used by lawyers interested in bringing lawsuits not in pursuit of defending a private interest but rather with the goal of ensuring that the law is enforced. An interesting leading case in this respect was the lawsuit brought by a consumer of a telecommunications company (public phones), demanding the respect of the price cap requirement imposed by the regulatory agency. The judge ordered the company to comply with the regulation. The consumer, by herself, had no way to initiate the process, but the public interest lawyer filed the appropriate legal documents and was able to monitor the company's and the administration's performance (Böhmer 1998).

Independent Judiciary

Let us now examine the role of the judiciary. In Schuck's perspective, an independent judiciary is a fundamental element upon which the extra-regulatory institutions rely, and the judiciary's presence is a precondition for an effectively functioning market. Unfortunately, the credibility of Argentina's judiciary is seriously flawed, as it is vulnerable to political pressure, particularly when such pressure comes from the executive. In fact, whereas Schuck's model postulates the control imposed by independent courts over regulatory decisionmaking, the Menem administration has worked actively against it. President Menem's great political influence on the courts is well documented. As soon as he took office, using the argument that the five-member Supreme Court was not able to cope with its huge caseload, Menem sent a bill to Congress that allowed him to appoint four new members to the highest court. With his party's majority controlling the Congress, Menem's bill passed, which was tantamount to "packing" the Court with sympathetic justices (Verbitsky 1993). The Senate appointed the four new pro-government members after a very short discussion, which gave the president the assurance that the Supreme Court of the nation would not defy his decisions on crucial administrative matters. To complete his strategy of co-optation of the judiciary, Menem appointed a score of new judges. Since then, opinion polls have shown that people regard the judicial system as politically manipulated and untrustworthy. The issuing of many controversial decisions favoring the administration in an overtly biased way has been denounced by domestic and foreign observers as having created a situation of "judicial insecurity" (Verbitsky 1993).

Legislative and Administrative Oversight

According to Schuck, one of the most important extra-regulatory institutions is the one embodied in Congress in its role as controller of the executive and the public administration that supports it. He stresses the need for a powerful legislature that not only approves legislation but also "[exerts its power] through the energetic exercise of its power to investigate, monitor, oversee, and influence the views of the key officials in the agencies and other executive branch organs" (Schuck, Chapter 2, this volume).

Unfortunately, the power of the Argentine Congress does not match that of the U.S. Congress. In theory, the Argentine Congress performs two major tasks: setting the political agenda (and the approval of the necessary legislation to implement it) and controlling the executive power. However, Carlos Nino (1992) has shown that the Argentine Congress does not fulfill either. As noted, Argentine institutional and constitutional practices have contributed to a gradual and sustained weakening of the legislative branch. The post-1989 decisions made by the Supreme Court sanctioned this trend (see the *Peralta* and *Cocchia* cases) and tilted the balance in favor of the executive. Indeed, if we examine the institutions and agencies responding to Congress that possess some level of effectiveness, only the Auditoría General de la Nación (an institution comparable to the U.S. General Accounting Office), revamped by the 1994 constitutional amendments, fits Schuck's standards.

If citizen participation can be characterized as very weak in the different stages of the Argentine regulatory process, it became almost non-existent during the Menem administration. The executive has made most of the administrative decisions ascribed to Congress through emergency decrees of "necessity and urgency." This way of making decisions prevents citizens' participation through their representatives in Congress. Many of the emergency decrees that Menem has used during his presidency have been considered to be unconstitutional by many of Argentina's major legal scholars (Sabsay and Onaindia 1994). Before 1989, such decrees were used fewer than 30 times, whereas Menem adopted them over 400 times (Ferreira Rubio and Goretti 1998).

In sum, the Menem administration has shown no concern for the participation, as Schuck would expect, of all affected interests and institutions in the formulation and implementation processes of regulatory policy. Instead, due to political and economic considerations, the president allowed only a restricted number of privileged sectors to exercise some influence behind the scenes on the regulatory decision-making process. Indeed, the so-called dangers of "factional tyranny" turned out to be real (Sunstein 1994). Most public officials linked to the regulatory decision-making process happened to be connected in some way or another with the companies that were competing to acquire SOEs. In some instances, those who were about to be regulated drew up the rules under which they were going to be working (such as highways, water, railways cargo).

SOME FINAL THOUGHTS

The unparalleled economic crisis of 1989 was instrumental in creating the conditions for a deep transformation of the state in Argentina that occurred under the Menem administration. However, the operating principle of the presumption against the state of the 1990s replaced the widespread presumption against the market that ran between the 1940s and the 1980s. This new presumption was different from the presumption in favor of the market prevalent in the United States, as it was against regulation as whole. Since state interventionism was viewed as equal to regulation, Argentina moved in the opposite direction, based on the assumption that indiscriminate deregulation was the magic solution for all the country's problems.

This strategy relied strongly on the power of the executive and the expertise of its technocrats, who managed to overhaul the administrative state, thanks to the support of Congress and the Supreme Court. Menem's indiscriminate issuance of urgency decrees was also extremely helpful toward the accomplishment of his policy goals. Government backers have consistently argued that this high concentration of power in the hands of the executive, enhanced by Congress's delegation of its law-making power, was indispensable in tackling the crisis. The same people have contended that executive domination over the whole political system was compensated for or balanced by the role of judges as guarantors of the protection of those citizen rights occasionally affected by the government's decisions. Unfortunately, the judiciary itself lacked credibility, and people, in turn, lacked trust in its members due to obvious reasons based upon fairness and transparency. Justice Boggiano's argument in the *Cocchia* case, discussed earlier in this chapter, illustrates the type of questionable justifications — used to save face for the government — that people have come to distrust.

The executive had its way, and Congress and the Courts, by their actions or omissions, followed suit. The three paradigmatic roles at the beginning of Schuck's chapter in this volume (the ones that "public law can play in the kind of reformist, post-privatization political and policy environment in which emerging liberal democratic states are now situated") are alien to the Argentine context. In fact, the structural transformations of the state and the consistency of economic policies could not be decided in the Argentine Congress nor threatened by judges deciding on individual cases, as the Supreme Court would have overruled them. In so doing, these transformations have resulted in an administrative state in which the lack of transparency, lack of access to information, lack of real citizen participation opportunities, and lack of controls all undermine the rule of law. This situation came about because some of the most crucial components of Menem's agenda were enforced through decrees and laws whose constitutionality appears dubious; indeed, many of them could be easily overturned in the future by an administration that is unfriendly to a market economy.

Of course, it is true that Argentina has experienced a spectacular transformation of its economy and public administration without resorting to the extreme authoritarian means of the past. There is no doubt about this. The old interventionist-state model is behind the times, but for a true market economy to emerge, substantial changes have to take place. Legal instruments such as anti-monopolistic legislation, rule-making processes, a freedom of information act, and a sunshine act would be first steps in this direction. It is also crucial to produce a shift in Argentina's political culture that makes citizens aware of their rights, especially but not only as consumers. Some attitudinal changes have occurred since the country returned to democracy in the early 1980s, thanks to the efforts of civil society organizations and public interest-minded professionals who have worked hard to this end.

However, in developing countries such as Argentina, the road toward the establishment of competitive markets and true democratic processes, as is the norm in North America and Europe, is still a long one. In this chapter, I have tried to show how economic policies that, in theory, are supposed to spur the emergence of a market economy instead have produced processes that are far from being democratic and markets prone to rent-seeking. In the 1990s, policymakers in Argentina and other Latin American countries enforced dramatic economic changes but forgot that such changes respond to a vision of socioeconomic relations based upon democratic principles. This is why the kinds of regulatory reforms fostering competition and transparency not only failed to materialize in Argentina but actually were hampered. This points to the fact that in assessing the impact of market reforms in developing countries, the attention should go beyond the fiscal achievements of macroeconomic adjustment. To assess correctly whether market reforms are indeed producing the expected results, we have to take into account not only economic factors but also institutional, legal, and political issues as well.

Notes

1. In an interview in 1990, the former president [Alfonsín] said, "We worked to get the whole reform passed, but no one would give us support. . . . If I had taken the steps Menem has, I would have been hanged." Cited from Armijo (1994:15).

2. *Anales de Legislación* [A.D.L.A.]. 1989. Law 23.696. This law was originally intended to be in effect for one year. Congress later expanded that period to three years. A.D.L.A. Law 23.990.

3. *Anales de Legislación* [A.D.L.A.]. 1989. Law 26.697.

4. "En la visión de la gente el mercado va ganando." 1999. *La Nación,* March 14; and Diego Saralegui, 1999, "Argentinos en busca de madurez," in "El Espejo de las Américas" (Special Issue), *La Nación*, March 17.

5. *La Ley*, 1994-B, 643-669.

6. The translation is mine. The original text says, "Que si se examinan las leyes que sancionó el Congreso sobre la reforma del Estado — 23.696, 23.697 y 23.928 — no existen dudas acerca de la filosofía que inspiró a las políticas después implementadas por el mismo legislador o, en su caso, por el Ejecutivo, tendientes a proteger y estimular el marco de libertad indispensable para el funcionamiento de una economía de mercado en la cual el Estado asume un papel exclusivamente subsidiario" (*Cocchia Case*, Cons. [paragraph] 11).

7. The original text says, ". . .fue mayoritaria la opinión que consideraba que la Administración Pública del Estado había contribuído a generar la crítica situación descripta. Son elocuentes las referencias a la 'exagerada dimensión de las estructuras estatales', especialmente de sus empresas públicas que constituirían una 'pesada carga' sobre la sociedad, pues gastan mucho más de lo que recaudan . . . realimentando en gran medida el proceso inflacionario'. La idea del Estado 'gigante', 'sobredimensionado', 'monumental' e 'hipertrofiado', culpable de una estructura productiva 'empequeñecida y atrasada' con sectores injustamente privilegiados o monopólicos, aparece en todo el curso del debate" (Cons. [paragraph] 9, quoting *Diario de Sesiones del Senado de la Nación*, pages 1310, 1317, 1338, 1339, 1344, 1348 a 1350, 1358, 1393, 1397, and 1398; and *Diario de la Cámara de Diputados*, pages 1854, 1873, 1886, 1893, 2112, 2119, 2120, 2123, and 2147, among others).

8. A similar move could be found in the U.S. experience under the Reagan administration, although some authors would say this sort of moving away from state activism was only in discourse but not in reality. See Rose-Ackerman 1992.

9. *Fallos*, 1960, vol. 247:121.

10. The original text says, "Que dentro de esa especie [amplia] del poder de policía, ha de considerarse legítimamente incluída la facultad de sancionar disposiciones legales encaminadas a prevenir, impedir, morigerar o contrarrestar, en forma permanente o transitoria, los graves daños económicos y sociales susceptibles de ser originados por la desocupación en mediana o gran escala" (Cons. [paragraph] 9).

11. Juan Bautista Alberdi, *Bases*, Chapter XXV. See also Nino 1992, 523-526.

12. *Peralta, Luis A.* y *otro c/ Estado Nacional (Ministerio de Economía y Banco Nacional de la República Argentina) s/amparo*, decided in Argentina's Supreme Court on December 27, 1990; published in *Fallos*, vol. 3113: 1513; reported in *El Derecho*, April 22, 1991.

13. *La Ley*, 1994-B, 643-669.

14. In the original text, "Que inmersos en la realidad no sólo argentina, sino universal, debe reconocerse que por la índole de los problemas y el tipo de solución que cabe para ellos, difícilmente pueden ser tratados y resueltos con eficacia y rapidez por cuerpos pluripersonales. La confrontación de intereses que dilatan — y normalmente con razón dentro del sistema — la toma de decisiones, las presiones sectoriales que gravitan sobre ellas, lo que es también norma, en tanto en su seno están representados los estados provinciales y el pueblo — que no es una entidad homogénea sino que los individuos y grupos en él integrados están animados por intereses muchas veces divergentes — coadyuvan a que el Presidente, cuyas funciones le impone el concreto aseguramiento de la paz y el orden social, seriamente amenazados en el caso, deba adoptar la decisión de elegir las medidas que indispensablemente aquella realidad reclama con urgencia impostergable" (Cons.[paragraph] 29).

15. The translation is mine. The original text says, ". . .existe una moderna y fuerte corriente doctrinaria que admite, dentro de ciertos límites de razonabilidad, la delegación de facultades legislativas como una exigencia de buen gobierno del Estado moderno. 'La delegación de Facultades legislativas de la asamblea en el gobierno se ha convertido en una manifestación universal de la época tecnológica, sostiene Loewenstein, sin distinguir entre sistemas parlamentarios y presidencialistas; antes bien señala el carácter universal de la tendencia" (*Fallos*, 1994, Cons. [paragraph] 24, Justice Antonio Boggiano's opinion and *La Ley*, 1994-B, 633).

16. The original text says, "Que en la actualidad no parece posible la implementación e una política económica gubernamental sin una estrecha colaboración entre las ramas legislativa y ejecutiva, aun en sistemas de corte presidencialista como el establecido por la Constitución Nacional. [Louis L.] Jaffe afirma — con referencia inmediata al sistema constitucional de su país, que guarda una sustancial analogía con el nuestro — que: 'Debemos reconocer que la legislación y la administración constituyen procesos complementarios más bien que procesos opuestos, y que la delegación representa el término y el método formales para su mutua cooperación' (confr. "An Essay on Delegation of Legislative Power," 1947, *Columbia Law Review* XLVII (3, April): 360). La colaboración referida encontraría una injustificada e inconveniente limitación si sólo se permitiera al Congreso encomendar al Ejecutivo la reglamentación de detalles y pormenores. . . . Por el contrario, la aceptación de una delegación amplia dota de una eficacia mayor al aparato gubernamental en su conjunto, con beneficio para toda la sociedad y sin que a causa de ello se vean necesariamente menoscabados los derechos de los habitantes de la Nación" (vote of Justice Antonio Boggiano, *La Ley*, 1994-B, Cons. [paragraph] 28, 633).

References

Alberdi, Juan Bautista. 1964. *Bases*. Buenos Aires: De Palma.

*Anales de Legislación de Argentina (A.D.L.A.).*1989. Law 23.990; Law 23.696; Law 26.697. [The *Annals of Legislation of Argentina* documents all laws passed in Argentina and is published annually in Buenos Aires by the government.]

Armijo, Leslie Elliott. 1994. "Menem's Mania?: The Timing of Privatization in Argentina." *Southwestern Journal of Law & Trade in the Americas* 1(1): 1-28.

Baer, Werner, and Melissa Birch, eds. 1994. *Privatization in Latin America: New Roles for Public and Private Sectors*. Praeger: New York.

Boggiano, Antonio. Various opinions of Argentine Supreme Court Justice Boggiano are cited from *Fallos*.

Böhmer, Martin. 1998. "El derecho de interés público en la Argentina." In *Acciones de Interés Público en el Cono Sur*. Santiago de Chile: Forja.

Cincunegui, Juan Bautista. 1998. "La participación de los usuarios en los servicios públicos." *Revista Argentina del Régimen de la Administración Pública* 237 (June): 103-119.

"Cocchia, Jorge Daniel c/ Estado Nacional y otros/ acción de amparo." 1993. *Fallos* 316: 2624; decided on December 2, 1993.

Cocchia, Jorge Daniel. 1994. Cited in *La Ley*, 1994-B. Cons. [paragraph] 11: 633.

Cueto Rua, Julio. 1994. "Privatization in Argentina." *Southwestern Journal of Law & Trade in the Americas* 1(1): 61-75.

El Derecho. 1991. April 22.

"En la visión de la gente el mercado va ganando." 1999. *La Nación*, March 14.

"An Essay on Delegation of Legislative Power." 1947. *Columbia Law Review* XLVII (3).

Fallos. 1960. 247: 121. [*Fallos* is the official collection of the Supreme Court's decisions, published by the Supreme Court itself. "Cons." (as used in the endnotes) is the abbreviation for paragraph.]

Ferreira Rubio, Delia, and Matteo Goretti. 1998. "When the President Governs Alone: The Decretazo in Argentina." In *Executive Decree Authority*, eds. John Carey and Matthew Shugart. New York: Cambridge University Press.

Fiss, Owen. 1996. *Liberalism Divided*. Boulder, Colo.: Westview Press.

Gibson, Edward. 1997. "The Populist Road to Market Reform: Policy and Electoral Coalitions in Mexico and Argentina." *World Politics* 49 (3): 339-370.

Gordillo, Augustín. 1998. *Tratado de Derecho Administrativo*. Tomo 2. Buenos Aires: Macchi.

Jaffe, Louis L. 1947. "An Essay on Delegation of Legislative Power." *Columbia Law Review* 47 (3:April).

La Ley. 1994-B. Buenos Aires: La Ley. [This compendium of all published laws is issued on a trimester basis.]

Linz, Juan, and Arturo Valenzuela, eds. 1994. *The Failure of Presidential Democracy*. Baltimore: The Johns Hopkins University Press.

Manzetti, Luigi. 1999. *Privatization South American Style*. New York: Oxford University Press.

McGuire, James. 1997. *Peronism without Perón*. Stanford, Calif.: Stanford University Press.

Mendeloff, John. 1988. *The Dilemma of Toxic Substance Regulation: How Overregulation Causes Underregulation*. Cambridge, Mass.: MIT Press.

Mora y Araujo, Manuel. 1991. *Ensayo y Error*. Buenos Aires: Planeta.

Nino, Carlos. 1992. *Fundamentos de derecho constitucional*. Buenos Aires: Astrea.

Palermo, Vincente, and Marco Novaro. 1996. *Política y poder en el gobierno de Menem*. Buenos Aires: FLACSO.

Peralta, Luis Arcemio y otro c/Estado Nacional (Ministerio de Economía y Banco Nacional de la República Argentina) s/amparo. 1990. *Fallos* 313: 1513; decided on December 27, 1990.

Rose-Ackerman, Susan. 1992. *Rethinking the Progressive Agenda: The Reform of the American Regulatory State*. New York: Free Press.

Saralegui, Diego. 1999. "Argentinos en busca de madurez." In "El Espejo de las Américas." *La Nación*, March 17 (Special Issue).

Schamis, Hector. 1999. "Distributional Coalitions and the Politics of Economic Reform in Latin America." *World Politics* 51 (January): 236-268.

Sabsay, Daniel, and José Onaindia. 1994. *La constitución de los Argentinos*. Buenos Aires: Errepar.

Schvarzer, Jorge. 1992. "La restructuración de la economía argentina en nuevas condiciones políticas." Working Paper. Buenos Aires: Cisea.

Schuck, Peter, and Robert Litan. 1986. "Regulatory Reform in the Third World: The Case of Peru." *Yale Journal of Regulation* 51.

Schuck, Peter, ed. 1994. *The Foundations of Administrative Law*. New York: Oxford University Press.

Shumway, Nicolas. 1991. *The Invention of Argentina*. Berkeley: University of California Press.

Starr, Pamela. 1997. "Government Coalitions and the Viability of Currency Boards: Argentina under the Cavallo Plan." *Journal of Interamerican Studies and World Affairs* 39 (2, Summer): 83-133.

Sunstein, Cass. 1990. *After the Rights Revolution: Reconceiving the Regulatory State*. Cambridge, Mass.: Harvard University Press.

Sunstein, Cass. 1994. "Factions, Self-Interest, and the APA: Four Lessons Since 1946." In *The Foundations of Administrative Law*, ed. Peter Schuck. New York: Oxford University Press.

Terragno, Rodolfo. 1999. "La proliferación de los entes reguladores." *La Nación*, March 26, 9.

Verbitsky, Horacio. 1993. *Hacer la corte: La construcción de un poder absoluto sin justicia ni control*. Buenos Aires: Planeta.

Vispo, Adolfo. 1999. *Los entes de regulación, problemas de diseño y contexto: Aportes para un urgente debate en la Argentina*. Buenos Aires: Norma.

World Bank. 1997. *World Development Report 1997*. New York: Oxford University Press.

Conclusion

Luigi Manzetti and Marco dell'Aquila

Summary

As Arnold C. Harberger notes in Chapter 1, privatizations in Latin America were often driven by fiscal considerations and, as result, were executed rapidly in order to generate much needed income for governments. Unfortunately, because of the hastiness that characterized many transfers, scant attention was paid to the form and structure of the industry after privatization. In the rapid sell-off process, Latin American governments usually disposed of assets with the criterion of maximizing profits. The result was often the creation of monopolistic or oligopolistic markets under private ownership at the expense of economic efficiency considerations and, in some cases, transparency of the process itself.

Regulatory functions were generally created after transfers had occurred. Invariably, this gave the incumbent a significant advantage over the newly created regulator. Once the rules were set, the regulator could only introduce modest changes. In order to enact major changes, the government, under pressure from customers and/or industry players, could merely step in and follow the processes laid down by law. The Chilean government tried to address some of the problems of outdated and poorly designed regulatory frameworks using antitrust law, but this strategy has been the exception to the rule since such legislation is rather poor and scarcely used in the region. In other cases, governments under political pressure acted unilaterally, in open violation of transfer contracts, by altering their tariff regimes, possibly the hottest issue in utility regulation. Examples of this kind can be found in the electricity sector in Peru and the water sector in the Argentine province of Tucumán.

Much debate is centered on the appropriate way to lay out the regulatory legislation and its enforcing institutions. On the one hand, Argentina exemplifies the complexities that affect multiple regulatory agencies at the national and provincial levels, which have given rise to inefficiencies and lack of decisionmaking. On the other, Chile shows that if establishing clear regulatory laws in advance has positive consequences down the road in terms of property rights and the predictability of institutions, it also demonstrates that regulatory policy must be flexible enough to adapt to changing circumstances in market structure and technology.

THE MAIN FINDINGS

Many of the chapters presented in this volume share several conclusions. Among them, the most important ones are the following:

1. It is essential to have a regulatory framework in place prior to privatization in the form of a law rather than ad hoc executive decrees, as the latter allow governments a considerable amount of discretion in interpreting contracts and can be easily amended.

2. In markets where there are no natural monopolies, it is important to create a competitive environment prior to privatization.

3. In large countries, it may be more effective to have a single, market-specific agency to act as a regulator. In small countries with few economic and human capital resources, a "super-agency" overseeing several sectors may be the best solution.

4. The presence of stable institutions increases the chances that the regulator will be effective.

5. Regulators should not be allowed to join the industry they supervised after their term in office expires at least for several years to avoid conflict of interest problems.

6. A regulator needs as much independence from government as possible.

7. If a regulator inherits a poorly deregulated industry, the extent to which it can be improved is limited.

8. The regulator is a referee who applies rules; the government and the legislature set those rules.

9. Government and the regulators must assess the progress of the market on a regular basis and make changes as appropriate.

10. Telecommunications is a more problematic sector to regulate than others due to the rapid changes in technology, as opposed to power and water. Water is the sector where the possibility of competition is least possible and, therefore, is more prone to government regulation than other sectors.

SOME POSSIBLE SOLUTIONS

The chapters in this volume propose a variety of solutions to some of the problems mentioned above. There is much consensus that the field of regulation in Latin America and, for that matter, in advanced industrial societies is in a continuous evolutionary process. More research will be needed as more data are acquired and new technology advancements make early regulatory policy outmoded. Nonetheless, there is substantial agreement among the contributors to this volume that the best way to regulate is actually to push for market competition whenever possible (Arnold C. Harberger, Antonio Estache and David Martimort, George G. Kaufman, William C. Gruben, and Björn Wellenius). Indeed, the best mechanism to achieve efficient markets and to provide quality and affordable services for consumers is to foster market competition, which is likely to induce self-regulation. In this way, the regulator's role is facilitated and confined to fewer fundamental tasks.

As Estache and Martimort emphasize, diminishing the impact of transaction costs is essential for efficient regulatory policy to emerge. This means identifying structures and processes that influence regulatory policy and designing institutions that can lower costs at both levels. For example, problems often arise from the incompleteness of contracts, but there are a variety of possible solutions to obviate this problem. What matters is to recognize these problems ahead of time and to build institutions flexible enough to solve them.

Latin American countries will also need to devise and enforce an effective antitrust policy that can complement regulatory institutions. This is another major task ahead of us since antitrust law is only now developing in the region. First, Chile and, more recently, Brazil and Mexico have made some progress in this direction, but in the rest of Latin America much remains to be done. In point of fact, regulatory institutions cannot do it all, and antitrust law can reach where regulatory law cannot. Moreover, there are a number of extra-regulatory institutions, as discussed in Peter Schuck's chapter, that can help regulators in their task. Regrettably, the problem is that in most of Latin America, such extra-regulatory institutions are either too weak or simply nonexistent. As the countries of the region solidify their democratic processes, it is vital that legislative oversight, the judiciary, interest groups, the media, and administrative law play a more active role in scrutinizing government regulators and firms.

This point brings us to Roberto Pablo Saba's comments in Chapter 10. It is clear that despite the many drawbacks of the privatization process, a significant shift has occurred in the role of government, from that of owner and employer of hundred of thousands of employees to that of regulator, or overseer, of the private sector. As most authors in this volume agree, within this new scenario, the government's primary task is to ensure that a level playing field is established to foster competition, the rules of the game are observed, the property rights of the private investors are guaranteed, and consumers are ultimately protected. In this respect, neither public utilities nor financial services can any longer be viewed as a source of influence by politicians. Fiscal pressures and the imposition of more austere fiscal policies mean that governments are no longer willing or able to open their purse strings and continue to finance loss-making public corporations indefinitely. The private sector has now taken a firm hold in the public utilities and finance sector.

However, Saba notes that what is worrisome is the fact that in Argentina (and similar patterns can be observed else where in the region), governments have been willing to dismantle the old rather than building the new. In other words, many administrations took a rather reductionistic view of market reforms that singled out government intervention as the culprit of all evil and thus proceeded to dismantle it. Yet, in many instances, this ushered a kind of savage capitalism that would be unthinkable in an advanced industrial society because, Saba argues, the results of market reforms in Argentina have been based upon an against-the-state presumption rather than upon the pro-market presumption dominant in the United States and other industrialized democracies. What, therefore, is striking is that, compared with the monumental effort to reform the region's economies, there have not been equal efforts toward revamping political and judicial institutions. Once caught in dire straits, populist and left-wing politicians, from Carlos Saúl Menem to Fernando

Henrique Cardoso, adopted the new credo. Yet, in order to function, markets do need states that enforce the law and put limits on the discretion of politicians. An example of the role of the state in a modern society can be seen in the Clinton administration's "Reinventing Government" agenda. As Saba underscores, until Argentina and the rest of Latin America adopt a positive conception of the state based upon the rule of law — so that the state is not interventionist but rather works to protect property and individual rights — the potential benefits of market reforms will be limited. In fact, almost invariably, strong economies coincide with strong rather than weak states. It is encouraging, though, that recently multilateral lending institutions such as the World Bank and the Inter-American Development Bank are advocating greater attention to issues of state capacity-building as the best safeguard toward the consolidation of the market reforms ushered in earlier. Not surprisingly, such agencies see the creation of modern regulatory institutions as a top priority.

Lastly, on the political dimension of regulation, it should not be forgotten that, as much as theorists talk about insulating regulatory policy from politicians' interference, it is almost impossible to make regulators completely independent because their appointment depends upon the executive and, in some cases, the legislative branches of government. There is still much debate on how to decrease political interference but no readily available solutions that can work everywhere irrespective of the setting have been forthcoming. Yet, if regulatory institutions are to play a meaningful role and establish themselves as the guarantors of the fair functioning of a market economy, politicians' temptation to manipulate them must be reduced as much as possible. As long as the executive branch can staff regulatory institutions with docile political appointees or undercut their authority when they refuse to go along with governmental wishes rather than markets, Latin America will have camouflaged monopolies and shady deals, neither of which coincide with neoliberal economic principles and democratic governance. The people of Latin America must decide whether they wish to support governments that advocate fully functioning regulatory institutions as guarantors of market economies or to acquiesce to governments that pretend to do so.

Contributors

Marco dell'Aquila is the Co-founder and Editor of *Infrastructure Journal* and Managing Director of Power Capital Limited, an advisory company providing commercial, economic, and financial advice to energy companies and utilities entering deregulating European energy markets. He was a Director with GE Capital with regional responsibilities for the Mediterranean and certain emerging markets. He has worked as a regulatory economist with Putnam, Hayes and Bartlett on the privatization of the United Kingdom's electricity industry. Mr. dell'Aquila holds a BSc in Civil and Structural Engineering from the University of Manchester's Institute of Science and Technology (UK) and an MA in International Economics and International Relations from Johns Hopkins University's School of Advanced International Studies.

Antonio Estache holds a Ph.D. in Economics from the Université Libre de Bruxelles. For the last 15 years, he has been with the World Bank, where he has contributed to reforms of the public sector, including tax reforms, infrastructure concessions design, and the setting up of regulatory regimes, mainly in Africa and Latin America. He is currently Lead Economist, responsible for the design and implementation of training and research programs on economic regulation in developing countries, and also serves as Lead Advisor for Latin America, responsible for policy aspects of the reform of infrastructure services. Dr. Estache's main research areas are specialized aspects of public economics and of the theory of regulation applied to network industries. Among his recent publications are articles in the *Journal of Public Economics, World Bank Economic Review*, and *Utilities Policy*.

William C. Gruben is the Director of the Center for Latin American Economics at the Federal Reserve Bank of Dallas. He received a Ph.D. in economics from the University of Texas at Austin and served as a research associate at the University's Institute for Latin American Studies. He has published extensively on Latin American finance, financial liberalization, and privatization.

Arnold C. Harberger, Professor of Economics at the University of California, Los Angeles, has studied the economies of Latin America for more than 40 years. His former students, including more than 12 Central Bank presidents and more than 20 cabinet ministers, have played major roles in the processes of economic liberalization and modernization in the region, particularly in Chile, Mexico, and Argentina. Dr. Harberger is Professor Emeritus at the University of Chicago, where he taught for 38 years, including 12 years as Chairman of the Department of Economics. He is a member of the National Academy of Sciences of the United States, a fellow of the Econometric Society and of the American Academy of Arts and Sciences, and a past president of the American Economic Association. Dr. Harberger's research contributions have been mainly in the fields of public finance, cost-benefit analysis, international economics, the economics of inflation, and economic policy for developing countries.

George G. Kaufman is the John F. Smith Professor of Finance and Economics and Director of the Center for Financial and Policy Studies at the School of Business Administration, Loyola University Chicago. He has published extensively in the *American Economic Review, Journal of Finance, Journal of Financial and Quantitative Analysis,* and other professional journals and is the author or editor of numerous books, including *The U.S. Financial System: Money, Markets, and Institutions* (sixth edition, Prentice-Hall, 1995). He is co-editor of the *Journal of Financial Services Research.* Professor Kaufman has served as a consultant to many government agencies and private firms, is executive director of the Financial Economists Roundtable, and is co-chair of the Shadow Financial Regulatory Committee, a group of independent banking experts who analyze and comment on economic, legislative, and regulatory factors affecting the financial services industry.

Luigi Manzetti, Associate Professor of Political Science at Southern Methodist University, is currently a Visiting Associate Professor at Duke University. His latest works include *Privatization South American Style* (Oxford University Press, 1999) and several articles on corruption and market reforms in Latin America.

David Martimort is Professor of Economics at the Université de Toulouse and has been a visiting scholar at Harvard University. Professor Martimort specializes in utility regulation and has published several articles on this subject.

Martín Rodríguez-Pardina holds a Ph.D. from Cambridge University. He teaches and does research at the Instituto de Economía of the Universidad Argentina de la Empresa in Buenos Aires. Dr. Rodríguez-Pardina has published several articles on electricity privatization in Latin America and has been a consultant for the World Bank and several Latin American governments.

Roberto Pablo Saba holds a J.D. from the University of Buenos Aires Law School and is a J.S.D. candidate at Yale Law School. He is the Director of the Center for Postgraduate Studies at the University of Palermo Law School in Buenos Aires and teaches constitutional law at the University of Palermo and the University of Buenos Aires.

Peter H. Schuck is the Simeon E. Baldwin Professor of Law at Yale Law School. His major fields of teaching and research are torts, immigration and refugee law, and administrative law. His most recent books include *The Limits of Law: Essays on Democratic Governance* (February 2000); *Citizens, Strangers, and In-Betweens: Essays on Immigration and Citizenship* (1998); and *Paths to Inclusion: The Integration of Migrants in the United States and Germany* (co-editor, 1998). He is a member of the American Law Institute's advisory committee for the Restatement of Torts (Third) General Principles, is a contributing editor to *The American Lawyer,* and has served as an arbitrator and an expert witness in a variety of disputes.

Mary M. Shirley is Research Manager, Competition Policy and Regulation, in the Development Research Group of the World Bank. She is the author of books on privatization, regulation, and government, including *Privatization: The Lessons of Experience* (with John Nellis and Sunita Kikeri); *Bureaucrats in Business: The Economics and Politics of Government Ownership* (with a large team); and numerous journal articles. Dr. Shirley is co-founder and board member of the International Society for New Institutional Economics.

Björn Wellenius is the Telecommunications Adviser at the World Bank. The main focus of his work is developing policy and regulatory environments that enable private investment and competition in telecommunications in emerging economies. He has experience in approximately 40 countries in Europe, Latin America, Asia, and Africa. Dr. Wellenius has published five books on telecommunications restructuring, telecommunications and economic development, and developing the electronics industry. He has a Ph.D. in Telecommunications from the University of Essex, England, and an electrical engineering degree from the University of Chile, where he was Professor of Telecommunications Systems before joining the World Bank.

Index